M & E HANDBOOKS

M & E Handbooks are recommended reading for examination syllabuses all over the world. Because each Handbook covers its subject clearly and concisely books in the series form a vital part of many college, university, school and home study courses.

Handbooks contain detailed information stripped of unnecessary padding, making each title a comprehensive self-tuition course. They are amplified with numerous self-testing questions in the form of Progress Tests at the end of each chapter, each text-referenced for easy checking. Every Handbook closes with an appendix which advises on examination technique. For all these reasons, Handbooks are ideal for pre-examination revision.

The handy pocket-book size and competitive price make Handbooks the perfect choice for anyone who wants to grasp the essentials of a subject quickly and easily.

DATA PROCESSING

Society of Company and Commercial Accountants
Annual Textbook Award
1974

THE M & E HANDBOOK SERIES

Data Processing
and Management
Information Systems

R. G. ANDERSON

FCMA, M Inst AM(Dip), FMS
Senior Lecturer in Data Processing,
West Bromwich College of Commerce and Technology
Management Services Division

THIRD EDITION

MACDONALD AND EVANS

Macdonald & Evans Ltd
Estover, Plymouth PL6 7PZ

First published 1974
Reprinted 1975 (twice)
Reprinted 1976
Second edition 1978
Third edition 1979
Reprinted 1981

© Macdonald & Evans Limited
1979

ISBN 7121 0417 8

Filmset in Great Britain by
Northumberland Press Ltd, Gateshead, Tyne and Wear
printed by Richard Clay (The Chaucer Press) Ltd,
Bungay, Suffolk

Preface

The third edition of this HANDBOOK has been prepared not very long after the second edition was published to take account of the speed with which events are occurring in the field of data processing. This new edition therefore is a valiant attempt to bring to the student the current state of technological developments in this age of the microcomputer. In addition, this third edition has been updated to provide for the requirements of recent examination papers set by The Institute of Cost and Management Accountants, and The Association of Certified Accountants and The Institute of Accounting Staff, and is designed to reflect the current requirements of other examining bodies as detailed below.

This HANDBOOK now includes a chapter on minicomputers and microcomputers, outlining the features of current models. In addition, a chapter has been devoted to interactive processing applications, a technique now widely applied in businesses using smaller computers. This edition has also been restructured to facilitate a greater appreciation of the subject and to ease the burden of the student by helping him or her to grasp essential aspects of the various topics more easily. Details relating to general systems concepts and management information systems (M.I.S.) have been greatly enlarged and structured separately in the book. The number of diagrams has also been increased to enable the reader to obtain a greater understanding of specific topics by outlining them pictorially. The number of decision table and flow-charting problems has been increased to enable the student to obtain a greater appreciation of logical problems, which are a feature of business systems and which must be fully provided for when designing systems.

Developments in computer memory and backing storage media have also received attention, along with current methods of data capture. This edition also includes details of visible record computers, data transmission, systems analysis, computer programming, financial aspects and methods of financing the acquisition of a computer, database, business models and simulation. Details of cybernetic control including feedback are also outlined as well as an appreciation of communication theory, the nature of systems relationships, and the characteristics of various types of system including probabilistic, deterministic, and adaptive, etc. The nature of centralised and distributed processing systems is also included.

This HANDBOOK is designed to provide a comprehensive course of study, and to act as a work of reference, concerning the field of data processing, general systems concepts and management information systems. Its contents should prove invaluable for administrative managers, accountants, and anyone requiring a basic knowledge of data processing methods, concepts and principles together with an appreciation of the importance of management information in the every day running of a business.

In particular, the HANDBOOK should be invaluable for students preparing for professional examinations where a knowledge of data processing, systems concepts, types of systems, systems behaviour and systems analysis and design is required. The syllabuses of the following bodies have been catered for:

The Institute of Cost and Management Accountants (I.C.M.A.).
The Institute of Administrative Management (I.A.M.).
The Institute of Management Services (I.M.S.).
The Association of Certified Assountants (A.C.A.).
The Institute of Chartered Accountants (I.C.A.).
The Society of Company and Commercial Accountants (S.C.C.A.).
The Institute of Accounting Staff (I.A.S.).

The HANDBOOK is also suitable for the requirements of the Business Education Council (BEC).

1979   R.G.A.

Acknowledgments

I gratefully acknowledge permission to quote from the past examination papers of The Institute of Cost and Management Accountants, The Association of Certified Accountants and The Institute of Accounting Staff. The co-operation and assistance of the following organisations and persons, without whose help this book would not have been possible, is also gratefully acknowledged.

Accountancy Age, Haymarket Publishing Ltd: provision of material on various matters from published articles.

Mr K. J. Atkin (author of *Basic Computer Science*): provision of information relating to bubble and holographic memory.

Mr A. Baker (one of my former I.C.M.A. students): provision of information on the structure of Cobol and the preparation of a Cobol application program for use in this book.

Charles Richards Fasteners Limited: provision of information forming the basis of a number of computer run charts for use in this book.

Computer Power—National Coal Board: provision of O.C.R. goods issue note for illustration in this book.

Mr P. Dowell (one of my former I.C.M.A. students): preparation of Assembly code source program and print out for use in this book.

International Business Machines Corporation: permission to use information from various publications and literature with regard to computer concepts and hardware.

International Computers Limited: permission to use information from various publications and literature with regard to computer concepts, hardware and systems analysis documentation.

Litton Business Systems Ltd: provision of information in respect of Kimball tag applications.

Lloyds Bank Limited: permission to reproduce cheque specimens encoded with magnetic ink characters.

Midlands Electricity Board: provision of optical mark meter reading sheets, consumer bill and procedure chart for inclusion in this book.

The National Computing Centre: for standard flowchart symbols.

NCR Limited (*Messrs D. Tennant, B. Jervis and V. Davies*): provision of information for inclusion in this book in respect of the 8130 microcomputer; 8250 minicomputer; 8450 medium scale mainframe computer and the 280 Retail Terminal System, and material and diagrams for Chapter IX.

Philips Data Systems: provision of information in respect of the P410 Small business computer.

Post Office Telecommunications: provision of information relating to Datel services and other aspects of telecommunications.

J. Sainsbury Ltd: provision of information on Supermarket ordering systems.

Contents

Preface   v
Acknowledgments   vii

Part One: PROFILE OF DATA PROCESSING

I   *Concepts of Data Processing*   1
Data processing—a specialist activity; Types of documents, records and files; General processing terms; Historical outline of data processing in the organisation; Centralised data processing; Distributed processing

II *Comparison of Data Processing Methods*   22
Outline of data processing methods; Comparison of data processing methods—basic elements

Part Two: PROFILE OF COMPUTERS

III *The Electronic Computer and its Development*   31
Definitions of a computer; The development of computer technology; Mainframe computer configurations; NCR N–8450 General purpose medium-scale mainframe computer; Real-time computer configuration; Defining the central processing unit; The control unit; The arithmetic/logic unit; Internal storage; Advantages and disadvantages of a computer

IV *Minicomputers*   55
General considerations; NCR 8250 General purpose minicomputer: general outline; Additional hardware; Software

V   *Microcomputers*   62
Development of micro technology; Operator-oriented microcomputer information processing system—NCR 8130; Hardware; Software

ix

VI   *Visible Record Computers*   70
      General outline; Accounting computers; Magnetic
      ledger computers; Integrated system application using
      a magnetic ledger computer; General aspects of
      electronic accounting machines; Philips Data Systems
      P410 Small Business Computer; Advantages and dis-
      advantages of electronic accounting machines

VII   *Processing Techniques (1)—Batch Processing*   80
      General outline of technique; File security; Data
      control; Data validation; Check digit verification;
      Auditing and the computer; Organisation of a
      medium-sized batch processing installation

VIII *Processing Techniques (2)—On-line, Real-time,*
      Multiprogramming and Time Sharing   109
      On-line processing; Real-time processing; Multipro-
      gramming; Time sharing

IX   *Processing Techniques (3)—Interactive processing*
      Applications   126
      Basic considerations; Interactive distribution control
      system (I.D.C.S.); Interactive payroll accounting
      system; Interactive general ledger system

X   *Computer Bureaux*   153
      General considerations; Data processing by computer
      bureau

XI   *Data Transmission*   160
      Basic concepts; Communication equipment; Com-
      munication terminals; Post office Datel services;
      Terms used in data transmission

PART THREE: INPUT, OUTPUT AND BACKING STORAGE

XII   *Computer Input and Output*   171
      Input—general considerations; Optical characters
      and marks; Magnetic ink characters: The 80-column
      punched card; Paper tape: general considerations;
      Recording data on paper tape; Advantages and dis-
      advantages of paper tape; Output

XIII   *Data Preparation and Data Capture*   192
        Card punching and verification; Paper tape punching
        and verification; Magnetic tape encoding and verifica-
        tion; Encoding of other magnetic media; Optical
        character encoding and verification; Optical mark
        encoding and verification; Magnetic ink character
        encoding and verification; Data collection systems;
        Kimball tags; Data collection and transmission
        system

XIV   *Backing Storage*   218
        Introduction; Magnetic tape (reels); Parity checking
        of magnetic tape characters; Recording data on mag-
        netic tape; Advantages and disadvantages of magnetic
        tape; Magnetic tape (cassette); Exchangeable mag-
        netic discs (hard discs); File organisation—magnetic
        discs: serial; File organisation—magnetic discs; in-
        dexed sequential; File organisation—magnetic discs:
        other methods; Virtual storage; Diskettes; Integrated
        discs and data modules; Advantages and disadvant-
        ages of direct access storage; Developments in
        backing storage

PART FOUR: IMPLEMENTING A COMPUTER

XV   *Analysis and Development of Computer Systems*   237
        Essential factors for successful implementation of a
        computer; Systems analysis; Stages of systems
        analysis; Recording techniques used in systems analy-
        sis; Systems design; Systems specification; Decision
        tables; Flowcharting computer applications; Bench-
        mark tests; Data processing standards; Coding
        systems

XVI   *Computer Programs*   294
        Elements of computer programming; Development of
        programming languages; Principles of programming;
        Program switches; Flowchart exercises; Elements of
        COBOL (Common Business Oriented Language);
        Emulation

XVII   *Software*   331
        General characteristics of software; Sub-routines;
        Utility programs; Executive and operating systems;
        Diagnostic routines; Assembler; Compiler; Applica-
        tion packages

XVIII *Financial and Economic Aspects of Computers*
    Initial costs of implementing a computer; Annual
    operating cost; Accounting treatment of initial costs;
    Criteria for assessing the economic viability of a
    computer

XIX *Methods of Financing the Acquisition of a Computer*   350
    General considerations; Purchasing a computer;
    Renting a computer; Leasing a computer

PART FIVE: GENERAL SYSTEMS CONCEPTS AND MANAGEMENT INFORMATION SYSTEMS

XX *Systems Theory and Concepts*   359
    Definition of systems theory and systems; System
    relationships; Classification of systems

XXI *Goals and Objectives of Systems*   374
    Over-all objectives, unity of direction and corporate
    objectives; System and sub-system objectives; Moti-
    vational influences and conflict of system goals

XXII *Control Theory*   380
    Basic elements of control; Cybernetic control; Feed-
    back; Open-loop system; Closed-loop system; Delay
    factor; Communication theory

XXIII *Concepts of Management Information Systems* 401
    Management Information Systems (M.I.S.) defined;
    Data relating to business operations; Information
    relating to business operations; Planning information;
    Control information; Functional and total informa-
    tion systems

XXIV *Development of Management Information Systems* 414
    Establishing the information needs of management;
    The approach to the development of M.I.S.; Corpor-
    ate information adviser; The approach to improving
    the flow of information in a business; The costs and
    benefits of producing information; Information and
    the level of management; Information related to the
    type of business

XXV *Database and Management Information Systems* 427
Database defined; Structure and problems of setting-up a database; Database management system (D.B.M.S.); Structural data relationships; The data-base administrator

XXVI *Use of Computers in Management Information Systems* 436
Data processing and management reports; Management planning and decisions; Business models and simulation

Appendixes 445
I Examination technique; II Data representation in the computer; III Word processing

Index 459

PART ONE

PROFILE OF DATA PROCESSING

CHAPTER I

Concepts of Data Processing

DATA PROCESSING—A SPECIALIST ACTIVITY

1. Processing activities. Data processing is a specialist activity performed by the administrative organisation for the business as a whole and is concerned with the systematic recording, arranging, filing, processing and dissemination of facts relating to the physical events occurring in the business.

Whereas the factory processes raw materials and produces goods for sale, the administrative organisation processes basic data and produces basic business documents and control information for management to keep them informed of events within the business; this enables them to take whatever corrective action is necessary to achieve the objectives of the particular business.

Before production can be commenced in the factory, raw materials and parts have to be procured, which involves the data processing system in the preparation of purchase orders. When supplies are received they have to be recorded on appropriate stock or job records, which again involves data processing. The accounts of suppliers have to be updated to show the value of the goods purchased from them and the remittances made to them.

When production is due to commence, materials and parts have to be issued to the production centres and suitably recorded on issue notes which are subsequently recorded on stock and job records. The issues are often priced and extended, which are also data processing operations.

Factory operatives are remunerated either for their attendance time, piecework or bonus earnings, and here the data processing system is concerned with wages calculation, preparation of payslips and payrolls and the collection and summarisation of data with regard to production orders or jobs.

On completion of production, the goods are despatched to customers, which involves the data processing system in the

1

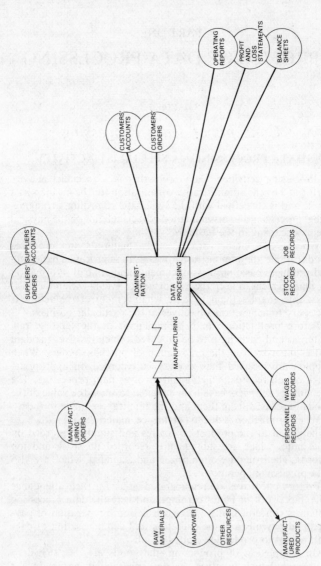

FIG. 1 *Outline of manufacturing and related data processing activities*

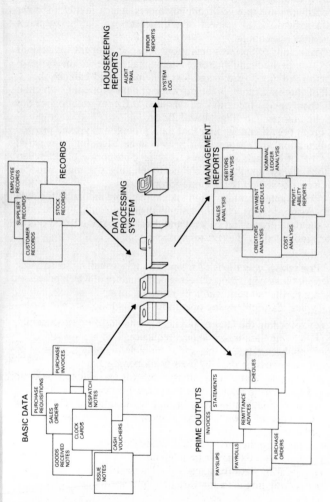

FIG. 2   *The nature of data processing*

preparation of despatch documentation, invoices, sales ledger up-dating and the preparation of statements of account. Eventually, remittances are received from customers, which involves further data processing in respect of adjustments to the balances on customers' accounts.

The results of business operations for specific operating periods are summarised and presented to management in the form of operating reports, profit and loss statements and balance sheets. All of this, and more, is the province of data processing which, if effectively performed, may be classified as the information service of the business (*see* Figs. 1 and 2).

From this, it can be seen that data processing systems provide information and information provides the basis for managerial control of business operations to achieve corporate objectives as effectively as possible, which means making the most suitable decisions based on the information provided.

A management information system therefore embraces the data processing systems, control systems (using information provided by the data processing system) and decision-making based on the facts indicated by the control systems.

2. Processing operations. An operation is usually the smallest identifiable step in a procedure, the performance of which processes data a further stage towards its required form.

Typical data processing operations are as follows:

(*a*) recording the facts of physical events on source documents;
(*b*) sorting data into a logical sequence;
(*c*) analysing data by classification code;
(*d*) summarising data by classification code;
(*e*) merging related data—master records and transaction data;
(*f*) calculating related data factors, e.g. quantity × price;
(*g*) comparing data—actual results with anticipated results or the existence of specific circumstances such as stocks reaching re-order level;
(*h*) verifying the accuracy and validity of data;
(*i*) filing records for future reference;
(*j*) updating data (balances + / − transactions);
(*k*) rearranging data for various requirements;
(*l*) communicating facts;
(*m*) posting transactions by hand or machine;
(*n*) embossing metal plates for addressing machine operations;
(*o*) marking data on mark-sensed cards for automatic punching;

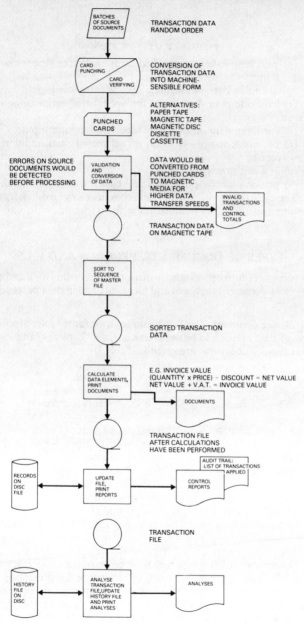

FIG. 3 *Cycle of activities in a typical computer-oriented batch processing application*

(*p*) punching data into punched cards and paper tape for computer input;

(*q*) encoding data in magnetic ink for computer input;

(*r*) bar coding on documents for optical reading of computer input;

(*s*) encoding data on magnetic tape for computer input;

(*t*) file maintenance—deletion of old records and addition of new records;

(*u*) revising prices and rates;

(*v*) printing schedules, reports and basic business documents.

The cycle of activities in a typical computer-oriented batch processing application are outlined in Fig. 3; for specific details *see* VII.

TYPES OF DOCUMENTS, RECORDS AND FILES

It is important to appreciate the reason for recording data and the types of documents, records and files contained in data processing systems.

3. Source document. This is a document used for the initial recording of data relating to business transactions. Typical examples of this type of document are given in Table I.

TABLE I   SOURCE DOCUMENTS

Type of document	Data recorded
Despatch note	items despatched to customers
Time sheet	time spent on jobs
Clock card	attendance time
Piecework ticket	data relating to "payment by results" schemes
Issue note	issue from store
Goods received note	receipts into store
Purchase requisition	requesting items to be purchased

Source data of this type needs to be converted into machine-sensible form, e.g. punched cards or paper tape for processing by computer installations. Dual-purpose punched cards or mark-sensed punched cards may sometimes be used as source documents as initial data is recorded on them which is subsequently punched into the same card, thereby providing both a visible record which can be interpreted easily by clerical staff and a punched record for interpretation by data processing equipment. Data should be captured at the earliest possible time, as near to the source of the transaction as possible and in such a way that unnecessary transfers of data from one document to another are avoided (*see* XV, **30**).

4. Record. Records such as ledger cards are required for recording transactions from source documents relating to sales, stocks, suppliers and wages, etc., in order to obtain an historical record of transactions and the current status of each record.

There are several types of record, and which type is used is largely dependent upon the processing method employed. Examples are shown in Table II.

TABLE II   TYPES OF RECORD

Loose leaf ledger sheet	manual recording method
Ledger card	mechanical or electronic accounting machine application
A segment of magnetic tape or disc (*see* XV, **31**)	electronic computer installation

5. Master file. A master file is a group of related records, e.g. stock file, customer file, employee file, supplier file. This type of file is periodically updated with current transaction data, in order to show the current status of each record in the file. Other types of master file contain reference information such as product prices, names and addresses and wage rates, etc. Such files may be used for general reference, or can form an integral part of data processing activities. Each record in a file is allocated an identification number or reference key and filed in ascending number order to facilitate ease of access or reference (*see* XV, **31**).

There are also several types of master file, and which type is used is also dependent upon the processing method employed.

(*a*) Loose leaf ledger or binder (*see* Table II above).
(*b*) Container of ledger cards (*see* Table II above).
(*c*) Reel of magnetic tape or exchangeable disc packs (*see* Table II above).

6. Intermediate document. This type of document provides a link between source documents and records. Examples of intermediate documents are as follows.

(*a*) *List of transactions and proof total* to provide a check on the accuracy of posting to ledger cards, etc.

(*b*) *Summary of transactions* to provide totals for posting to a general ledger and other requirements (*see* (*a*)).

    (*i*) Summary of expenses incurred by cost centre.

    (*ii*) Summary of issues from stores.

    (*iii*) Summary of purchases and sales.

    (*iv*) Summary of earnings of employees on different tasks.

(*c*) *Analysis of transaction totals* for control purposes.

    (*i*) Analysis of labour cost by job number.

    (*ii*) Analysis of manpower in each function.

    (*iii*) Analysis of purchases by expense code.

7. Report. A report may be defined as the final usable output (in printed form) from the data processing system. The output may be as follows (*see* XV, **29**).

(*a*) *Basic business documents:*

    (*i*) invoices;

    (*ii*) statements of accounts;

    (*iii*) payslips and payroll;

    (*iv*) purchase orders.

(*b*) *Control reports:*

    (*i*) aged analysis of account balances;

    (*ii*) operating reports.

In a manual processing system a report may be prepared in manuscript form initially, followed by typewritten copies for circulation.

In respect of electro-mechanical and electronic accounting machines the report would be produced by the machine's print unit.

With regard to an electronic computer installation, printed reports are produced by a printer.

GENERAL PROCESSING TERMS

8. Data. Data is the term used to define facts which do not serve any useful purpose until they have been converted into a more meaningful form by data processing operations. Data is both a singular and plural term which describes a single unit or a collection of facts. For example, facts regarding hours worked in respect of each employee in a department is simply a collection of data but when the hours have been analysed into hours spent on individual jobs then the data is more meaningful and in fact becomes information (*see* **9**). Data is the input element of a data processing system (*see* XXIII, **3, 4**).

9. Information. Information is derived from processed data as indicated in **8** above. To be classified as information it must serve a useful purpose by informing the recipient of something with which he wishes to be informed. This applies to situation reports to management as they are able to implement control action if necessary or be used as a basis for making decisions. Information is the output element of a data processing system (*see* XXIII, **7**).

10. File updating. The process of recording data on a record in a master file from a transaction file in order to ensure that the record indicates the latest information in respect of outstanding balances, etc. Updating is carried out systematically at pre-defined times and frequencies.

A payroll, for instance, may be produced either weekly or monthly, depending upon the frequency of the pay period. The master file is updated concurrently with preparation of the payroll, to show the cumulative position for the year to date in respect of gross and net earnings, P.A.Y.E. deductions and deductions in respect of superannuation and national insurance, etc.

11. File amendment. File amendments include the addition of new records or the deletion of obsolete records from a master file. For example, the addition of new starters and the deletion of terminations from the payroll or employee master file. Reference files may require amendment occasionally in respect of changes of names and addresses, product selling prices and wage rates, etc. (*see* Fig. 4).

12. Transaction data. Data relating to business transactions which is recorded on source documents. Data of this type relates to items sold to customers, items purchased from suppliers, items issued from stores, remittances received from customers and remittances made to suppliers, etc. The data comprises a transaction or movement file.

13. Transaction processing. The modern "buzz" word is "transaction-driven" processing whereby individual business transactions are processed interactively as they take place. This is in

CUSTOMER MASTERFILE AMENDMENTS

Completion notes:

1) Always complete AMEND-code and ACCOUNT-no. on first card.
   For AMEND-code 1 = Insert new account
   2 = Amend account details
   3 = Delete account no.

2) For insertion of new account. complete all of first card and complete other cards as necessary.

3) For amending of an account record complete details on cards 1–9 as required (if it is needed to delete one line of say delivery instructions, write the word DELETE in the relevant box - this must start at the beginning of the field and applies only to cards 2–9).

4) For deletion of an account record, no details (other than those in note 1 above) are required.

Card code	Batch No.	Amend code	ACCOUNT	On pre Card	Area	SYMBOL	Insured limit	Credit limit	pre pad On	POINTER	MAP REF.	MILEAGE
E O				1								

1ST LINE OF INVOICE NAME & ADDRESS | 2ND LINE OF INVOICE NAME & ADDRESS (card 2)
3RD LINE OF INVOICE NAME & ADDRESS | 4TH LINE OF INVOICE NAME & ADDRESS (card 3)
5TH LINE OF INVOICE NAME & ADDRESS (card 4)
1ST LINE OF DELIVERY NAME & ADDRESS | 2ND LINE OF DELIVERY NAME & ADDRESS (card 5)
3RD LINE OF DELIVERY NAME & ADDRESS | 4TH LINE OF DELIVERY NAME & ADDRESS (card 6)
5TH LINE OF DELIVERY NAME & ADDRESS (card 7)
1ST LINE OF DELIVERY INSTRUCTIONS (card 8)
2ND LINE OF DELIVERY INSTRUCTIONS (card 9)

SALES DEPT.	DATE
Issued by:	/ /
Credit Limit £	/ /
Approved:	/ /
ACCOUNTS DEPT.	
Approved:	

FIG. 4. Customer masterfile amendment form

distinction to batch processing whereby batches of transactions are processed together at pre-defined periods of time (*see* VII). Instead of inputting transactions by automatic input devices such as card readers or paper tape readers, transactions are input by an operator-activated keyboard which may be an integral part of a visual display unit (V.D.U.). By this means it is possible to update a record stored in a computer's backing storage or retrieve information from backing storage, perhaps after making an enquiry regarding the status of a stock item or the credit rating of a customer. When transaction processing is effected by remote locations using terminals then communication lines and equipment are required (*see* IX).

14. File reference. Accessing or referring to a record on a master file, for example:

(*a*) referring to a customer name and address file when preparing an invoice;

(*b*) referring to a product or commodity file to obtain a price for each item despatched when preparing an invoice;

(*c*) referring to a wage rate file when calculating gross wages.

15. File activity or "hit" rate. The proportion of records updated or referenced in relation to the total number of records on a master file. This is very important in an electronic computer installation in respect of master records stored on magnetic tape. This is because each record throughout the file must be read until the one required for processing is accessible. Each record also has to be written to a new tape even though it is not affected by current transaction data.

In this case, a file with a low "hit" rate can be wasteful of processing time and the use of discs would create a large improvement in the time required for file updating (*see* VII, **9**) and (XIV, **17**).

16. Data preparation. Before data can be processed it must be converted, in most instances, from "human-sensible" form as recorded on source documents to "machine-sensible" form. This is achieved by data preparation operations which traditionally include punching of data into cards or paper tape or encoding data on magnetic tape in respect of computer input. The modern methods of input are designed to eliminate the need for data preparation by direct input methods (*see* XIII).

17. File security. Computer systems store information on magnetic media which can be accidentally erased or overwritten. It would be drastic if this occurred without adequate file security precautions as all of the business records on a specific file would be lost. The purpose of file security is to provide the means of reconstituting information on master files when they have been corrupted by equipment malfunctions or erased or overwritten in error. This is a fail safe procedure (*see* VII, **13–17**).

18. Computer run. A run may be defined as a unit of processing consisting of a number of operations or processing steps performed by a computer under the control of a specific program. Each run is shown on a computer run chart (*see* Fig. 3).

19. Computer program. A program is a set of instructions which informs a computer of the steps required for achieving a defined task. Each instruction defines a basic operation to be performed, identifies the address of the data to be processed, the peripheral device (input or output device) to be used (*see* XVI).

HISTORICAL OUTLINE OF DATA PROCESSING IN THE ORGANISATION

The incidence of data processing in an organisation depends upon a number of factors, amongst which are the size of the business, the volume of data to be processed, the dispersion of operating units and the information needs of the various functions and departments of the business.

In general, as volumes of data for processing increased, it became necessary to consider the use of mechanised or computerised methods. It was then necessary to consider whether data processing should be centralised for the business as a whole in order to concentrate resources to achieve economy in data processing operations. Some of these factors, with regard to businesses of varying size, will now be considered.

20. The smaller business. The smaller type of business usually had a general office controlled by an office manager responsible for all the data processing requirements of the business. The method of data processing used would perhaps consist of manual clerical operations, with auxiliary aids such as adding/listing machines and desk-top calculators. In this situation, the volumes of data of various types would not be very great and the use of sophisticated machines for processing the data would not be economically viable.

In this case, all data processing would be centralised in the general office.

21. The medium-sized business. This type of business would be structured on a functional basis and each function would be self-contained with regard to its data processing requirements. This particularly applies to the accounting function which, traditionally, processed data in respect of business operations and produced reports, statistics and business accounts.

Adding/listing machines were often used for pre-listing trans-actions to provide control totals to enable the accuracy of postings to be checked. Desk-top calculators would be used to perform calculations relating to wages, costs, stores issue valuations and checking purchase invoice extensions, etc. Keyboard accounting machines (mechanical or electronic) would be used for posting ledgers (stores ledger, purchase ledger, sales ledger, general ledger and cost ledger, for example) and the preparation of the payroll, payslips and tax and earnings record cards, etc. If a visible record computer was used, calculations would also be performed, enabling invoices and other similar documents to be prepared without the need for other machines such as desk-top calculators.

Typewriters may be widely used for typing reports and sum-maries of transactions. Addressing machines may be used for head-ing clock cards, ledger cards and statements of account and printing fixed payroll data, in addition to the basic task of addressing envelopes.

Other functions such as purchasing and sales would also be suit-ably equipped to perform their specific data processing require-ments.

22. The larger business. The larger type of business often found it necessary to implement a greater degree of mechanisation or computerisation. Before the era of computers, keyboard account-ing machines were often replaced by electro-mechanical punched card equipment which was used for processing data relating to functions other than the accounting function, as shown in Table III.

When such an installation was used for a wide variety of tasks relating to numerous functions it was often used as a centralised data processing service on an inter-functional basis. Such a course of action rationalised data processing activities and generally resulted in a reduction of operating costs and the provision of a much improved information flow.

The accountant often controlled the installation as, in many instances, the punched card installation replaced the previous machines used for processing accounting data. However, the inter-functional use of such equipment which materialised caused difficulties of control, since the accountant had divided responsibility as he was also responsible for processing the data of other functions. This situation often required the management of the installation to become the responsibility of a specialist data processing manager who was able to concentrate on data processing problems, systems development and servicing the needs of functional managers. Inter-functional friction was at the same time eliminated.

TABLE III   FUNCTIONAL DATA

Stock control	production of stock schedules and balance cards
Sales	preparation of invoices, statements of account, balance cards and sales analysis
Costs	production of cost and wages analysis schedules
Production control	processing of incoming orders, job tickets and parts requirements
Wages	preparation of payroll, payslips and tax and earnings records

In addition to a punched card installation, the larger business often had a centralised comptometer section, providing a calculating service to all functions of the business. Many firms also had a number of keyboard accounting machines for specific tasks, either of a specialised nature or of a low volume, which were not considered suitable, or at least were not required, to be processed by punched card equipment.

From the foregoing outline it is perhaps clear that the larger firm employed a variety of data processing methods for particular needs. Computers are now widely used by businesses of all sizes and the need for a variety of processing methods has largely disappeared as many applications have been transferred to a computer. Even so, firms having computers may still use electromechanical accounting machines for small-volume ledger posting operations, even though they are technologically obsolete.

CENTRALISED DATA PROCESSING

23. The computer as a centralised service in a single operating unit.
When a business comprises only one factory or office as opposed
to a group of factories or other business units, and a computer
is implemented in the organisation the way in which it is used
requires careful consideration. Sometimes the computer, under
such circumstances, may only be used for processing routine
accounting applications such as payroll, sales ledger, stock control
and purchase ledger, etc.

To obtain the maximum benefit however, the computer should
be used to aid management in problem-solving and decision-
making by the use of quantitative application packages for linear
programming, statistical stock control, production planning, network analysis and discounted cash flow, etc. When a computer is
used for all the functions within the business it is a centralised
facility in the form of a data processing and information system.

**24. The computer as a centralised service in a group of operating
units.** When a business organisation is a widely dispersed con-
glomeration of various types of operating unit, including factories,
warehouses and sales offices and a computer is in use, it is usually
located at the head office of the group. In these circumstances the
objective would be to provide the best possible service for the
data processing and information needs of all functions and operating units in the group.

The benefits to be derived from a centralised service may be
summarised as follows.

(*a*) Economy of capital expenditure due to the high cost of
computers (in the 1960s and early 1970s) through having only one
computer for use by the group instead of several located in the
various units.

(*b*) If one large powerful computer is implemented, the resultant
advantages are: increased speed of operation, storage capacity and
processing capability.

(*c*) Economy in computer operating costs due to the centralisation of systems analysts, programmers, computer operators and
other data processing staff as compared with the level of costs that
would be incurred if each unit in the group had its own computer on a decentralised basis, i.e. avoiding the duplication of
resources.

(*d*) Centralisation would also facilitate the standardisation of applications but this would depend upon the extent of diversity in the dispersed operations regarding payroll and invoicing structures, etc.

If the computer is also communications oriented, whereby all operating units are equipped with transmission terminals connected to the central computer, then basic data may be speedily transmitted for processing by remote job entry (*see* VIII, **3**) and the results transmitted back and printed on a local printer. This would reduce any time delay in receiving computer output through the post or messenger service. The possibility of an integrated management information system then becomes feasible, as data from dispersed units is speedily processed for local use and information becomes available at head office by means of the computer files for corporate planning (*see* Fig. 5).

Such a centralised computing service should be structured in the organisation at a level which enables the data processing manager to report to a higher level of management than the departmental level or functional level for which he is providing a service. This enables policy matters to be established at Board level, rather than at functional level, which establishes the use of the computer on a corporate strategic basis in order to optimise its use. If the data processing manager reports to the managing director, he is free from direct inter-functional conflict as problems are resolved at a higher level.

DISTRIBUTED PROCESSING

25. Systems architecture. Distributed processing must not be confused with decentralised processing, even though decentralisation is a feature of distributed processing. Prior to the advent of the computer, different companies in a group may well have used their own data processing installation, i.e. a decentralised facility. The centralisation of data processing, as outlined in **23** and **24** above, was the trend of the 1960s, but the tendency of the late 1970s has been a reversal of this situation, largely due to the development of mini- and microcomputers (*see* IV and V). These computers cost much less than mainframes, which makes it a viable proposition to install them in departments and branches on a distributed processing basis. This is the philosophy of providing computer power where it is most needed, instead of concentrating all processing in a single centralised computer system. Systems architecture is a design philosophy whereby small computers in dispersed operating units

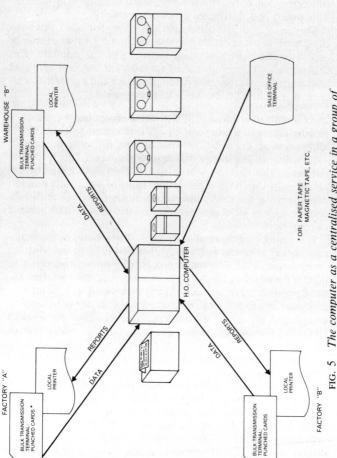

FIG. 5 *The computer as a centralised service in a group of operating units: communications-oriented—remote job entry*

WAREHOUSE "B"

BULK TRANSMISSION TERMINAL: PUNCHED CARDS

LOCAL PRINTER

REPORTS

DATA

H.O. COMPUTER

SALES OFFICE TERMINAL

* OR: PAPER TAPE MAGNETIC TAPE, ETC.

FACTORY "A"

BULK TRANSMISSION TERMINAL: PUNCHED CARDS *

LOCAL PRINTER

REPORTS

DATA

FACTORY "B"

BULK TRANSMISSION TERMINAL: PUNCHED CARDS

LOCAL PRINTER

DATA

REPORTS

may be connected by a communications network to each other and also to a large, centrally-located mainframe. The mainframe may support a large database, which would allow information of a strategic nature to be retrieved on demand for corporate planning. This would be a distributed processing network.

The mini- and microcomputers may be dedicated machines being used for a single main purpose and, in some instances, may be used as stand-alone processing systems when appropriate. This situation allows a high degree of autonomy at the local operating level which encourages motivation, flexibility and a greater acceptance of responsibility by the local management.

26. Co-ordinating influence of distributed processing. Simplicity of gaining access to a computer by relevant operating personnel at all levels of an organisation is not an easy matter to accomplish even within a single unit business organisation equipped with terminals. This problem is accentuated when there are many dispersed units within the organisation, many of which may be interdependent, e.g. marketing and manufacturing functions, as all units must be fully aware of the operational status of each other's sphere of operations.

It becomes even more of a problem when a business is a multinational organisation with widely-dispersed subsidiaries. With the implementation of distributed processing systems, this is not so much of a problem because it is of no consequence whether the small computers are located in the same building as a mainframe computer or whether they are situated the other side of the oceans. Distributed processing allows a business to select the level of processing autonomy in respect of depots, factories, warehouses or sales offices.

Distributed processing also includes the use, on a decentralised basis, of intelligent terminals, i.e. terminals with processing capabilities which may be used on a local basis for off-line operation or for on-line operations linked to a host computer. The choice of terminal may be selected according to local needs and may include badge readers and data collection terminals in factory departments, tag readers and point-of-sale terminals in retail sales outlets, visual display units (V.D.U.s), *see* VIII, **18**, for offices; V.D.U.s and/or printers for warehouses and video units in the sales department for on-line entry of order details (*see* Fig. 6).

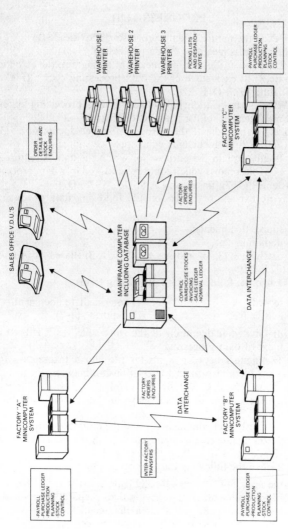

FIG. 6 Outline of characteristics of a distributed processing network

SALES OFFICE V.D.U.'S

ORDER DETAILS AND STOCK ENQUIRIES

WAREHOUSE 1 PRINTER

WAREHOUSE 2 PRINTER

WAREHOUSE 3 PRINTER

PICKING LISTS AND DESPATCH NOTES

MAINFRAME COMPUTER INCLUDING DATABASE

CONTROL
WAREHOUSE STOCKS
INVOICING
SALES LEDGER
NOMINAL LEDGER

FACTORY ORDERS ENQUIRIES

FACTORY "C" MINICOMPUTER SYSTEM

PAYROLL
PURCHASE LEDGER
PRODUCTION PLANNING
STOCK CONTROL

DATA INTERCHANGE

FACTORY "A" MINICOMPUTER SYSTEM

PAYROLL
PURCHASE LEDGER
PRODUCTION PLANNING
STOCK CONTROL

FACTORY ORDERS ENQUIRIES

DATA INTERCHANGE

INTER FACTORY TRANSFERS

FACTORY "B" MINICOMPUTER SYSTEM

PAYROLL
PURCHASE LEDGER
PRODUCTION PLANNING
STOCK CONTROL

PROGRESS TEST 1

1. Define the nature of data processing activities. **(1)**

2. (*a*) What is meant by "data processing"? **(1)**

(*b*) Describe or illustrate by means of a diagram, the activities which occur at each stage of the data processing cycle (Fig. 3) [I.A.S. June 1977, Q1]

3. What is the relationship between a data processing system and a management information system? **(1)**

4. Define and indicate the purpose of source documents. **(3)**

5. (*a*) List four documents which provide source data.

(*b*) Briefly explain the purpose for which the data is required.

(*c*) List four reports which could be produced by a data processing system. **(3, 7)** [Based on I.A.S. Dec. 1976, Q7]

6. Write explanatory notes on the following data processing terms:

(*a*) source documents;

(*b*) updating;

(*c*) batching. **(3, 10** and *see also* VII, **1, 3)** [Based on A.C.A. June 1975, Q1]

7. Define the following data processing terms:

(*a*) record;	(*c*) intermediate document;
(*b*) master file;	(*d*) report. **(4–7)**

8. (*a*) Give your definition of the word "file" as it is used in the context of data processing.

(*b*) Distinguish between a master file and a transaction (or movement) file and explain the relationship between them. **(5, 10, 12)** [Based on A.C.A. June 1977, Q6]

9. (*a*) Explain the difference between "data" and "information".

(*b*) List with brief comments, five of the desirable properties of information produced for management. **(8, 9**, *see also* XXIII, **3–19)** [Based on A.C.A. June 1976, Q1]

10. Define the following data processing terms:

(*a*) file updating;	(*f*) file activity;
(*b*) file amendment;	(*g*) data preparation;
(*c*) transaction data;	(*h*) file security;
(*d*) transaction processing;	(*i*) computer run;
(*e*) file reference;	(*j*) computer program.

(10–19)

11. Outline the historical incidence of data processing in an organisation. **(20–2)**

12. Indicate the nature of centralised data processing. **(23–4)**

13. Outline the nature and characteristics of distributed processing. **(25–6)**

14. (*a*) Describe the characteristics of centralised data processing and decentralised data processing.

(*b*) Compare the advantages for a large organisation of centralised and decentralised data processing arrangements. **(23–6)** [A.C.A. Dec. 1978, Q8]

CHAPTER II

Comparison of Data Processing Methods

OUTLINE OF DATA PROCESSING METHODS

1. Selection and review of processing methods. Although data processing can be performed without the use of sophisticated machines, it is often essential that they should be used owing to the volume of data to be processed in a specific period of time. In general, the method chosen should suit the company's processing needs and if, for instance, the volume of data for processing increases because more personnel are on the payroll or new customers require the production of more invoices, statements, sales ledger updating and sales analyses, it becomes necessary to review the methods being used.

2. Manual method. Operations performed by a clerk assisted by specific aids, such as a pocket calculator or adding/listing machine, etc. Such clerical activities may include the extension of priced despatch notes (quantity × price) and the updating of handwritten ledger records, etc. (*see* **8** and Fig. 7).

3. Keyboard accounting machine—mechanical method. Operations performed by a machine consisting of a keyboard actuated by a machine operator. The operator enters data for processing by depressing appropriate keys and the results of processing are printed on specific documents. A typical operation is posting the value of a sales invoice to the debit of a customer's ledger account while at the same time preparing a statement of account and proof sheet (*see* **9** and Fig. 8).

4. Minicomputer. A minicomputer is a small computer in comparison with a mainframe but performs similar tasks in respect of business data processing applications. Data for processing may be input by a keyboard on a C.R.T. display unit for interactive, transaction-driven processing and reports printed on a matrix printer. Backing storage may be in the form of flexible discs, integrated discs or magnetic tape stored on cassettes 600 feet (182 metres) reels (*see* IV and Figs. 17 and 18).

5. Microcomputer. This is a very small computer, consisting of a processor on a single silicon chip. They are smaller than "minis" but are capable of processing data in respect of the traditional accounting applications. A "micro" is operator-oriented, as input is achieved manually by means of a keyboard. Information from files may be displayed on a visual display unit. Information is normally stored on flexible discs or magnetic tape cassettes in a similar manner to minis. Mainframes tend to use hard discs rather than flexible discs for backing storage (*see* V and Fig. 21).

6. Visible record computer (V.R.C.)—electronic method. This class of machine is a development of the electro-mechanical keyboard accounting machine. Data is input for processing by the depression of appropriate keys on the keyboard by a machine operator. The main difference with this class of accounting machine is that it is electronic in operation, not mechanical, and has full calculating facilities which are not available on the mechanical accounting machine. Depending upon the type of V.R.C., such machines can be used for many accounting procedures including payrolls, stock schedules and ledger updating, etc.; the preparation of invoices is also possible. V.R.C.s may have optional peripheral devices attached for automatic input and output. The devices include punched cards, edge-punched cards and punched paper tape readers and punches. Some V.R.C.s have magnetic stripe ledger cards which contain master record data both in machine-sensible (magnetic) form and normal printed form (*see* VI and Fig. 22).

7. Mainframe computer installation—electronic method. A computer consists of not one machine but a series of related machines. Normally, however, the generic term "computer" is widely used to describe the central processing unit and the peripheral devices used for electronic data processing. The term will be used in this sense throughout the book (*see* **10**).

A computer may be defined as a machine which accepts data from an input device, performs arithmetical and logical operations in accordance with a pre-defined program and finally transfers the processed data to an output device either for further processing or in final printed form, such as business documents, schedules and management control reports.

Before computer processing can commence, the data must first be prepared in machine-sensible form. Data may be represented by holes punched into cards or into paper tape. In addition, data may be input in the form of optical or magnetic characters.

Whichever mode of representing data is selected, it is necessary to have a special input device for the purpose of sensing the data and transferring it into the computer's internal memory for processing. The device may be a card reader, paper tape reader, optical character reader or magnetic ink character reader, etc.

The data in punched cards is decoded by the card reader into machine code which is transferred to the processor's memory for processing. It is necessary to represent data for processing in a computer by binary coded characters which create pulse sequences (electrical flows) to allow data to flow through electronic circuits for processing. As the pulse sequences are represented by "on" and "off" electrical states this forms the basis of representing data in binary code. Binary is a two-state number system which is compatible with electrical flows which are also two-state, "on" and "off". The two numbers of the binary number system are "1" and "0" and these are represented by an electrical "pulse" and "no pulse" signal respectively. Combinations of pulses, that is sequences of "on" and "off" states, are the basis of forming binary coded characters. Each character is formed by a series of binary digits referred to as "bits", which is a contraction using the first and last letters of "binary digits".

It is important to appreciate that descriptive data elements such as customer, supplier and employee names and addresses, etc. are processed in binary coded characters (B.C.D.) but data to be used in calculations, i.e. quantities and prices, must be processed in pure binary form (*see* Appendix II).

The data is processed at electronic speed under the control of the computer's control unit and the internally stored program. All operations are performed automatically and the output is usually produced by an output device known as a line printer.

Master files are usually stored magnetically in the form of magnetic tapes or magnetic discs. Programs are stored either on magnetic tape or magnetic disc.

It is normal practice to have the input, output and storage devices attached to the central processing unit which controls their use. In this case, the devices are said to be "on-line".

A computer may be used for an infinite variety of tasks, including the preparation of payrolls, payslips, invoices, statements, purchase orders and for updating master files containing historical records relating to employees, stocks, suppliers' accounts, customers' accounts, costs and production. They are also used for planning, problem-solving and presenting information to management on which to base decisions (*see* Fig. 9 and XXVI, **1–6**).

COMPARISON OF DATA PROCESSING METHODS— BASIC ELEMENTS

All data processing methods, whether manual, mechanical or electronic, consist of five basic elements, i.e. input, processing, storage, output and control. Each will now be analysed in respect of these five elements.

8. Manual method (*see* **2**).

(*a*) *Input*. A clerk receives data relating to business transactions in the form of source documents. The type of source document received depends upon the duties of the clerk, but in general the source documents include orders from customers, clock cards indicating the attended time of employees, invoices from suppliers, invoices relating to items despatched to customers and stores issue notes, etc.

(*b*) *Processing*. The data contained in the source documents are subjected to specific operations, such as quantity × price or hours worked × hourly rate, etc. The operations are performed by the clerk either mentally or with the aid of a pocket calculator or an adding/listing machine, etc. Appropriate records are updated as necessary.

(*c*) *Storage*. Records in the form of ledger cards constitute the storage media, which contain data in respect of amounts owed to suppliers or amounts owed by customers, cost data and employee wages data, etc., which require to be updated with current transaction data. The records are stored in filing trays or cabinets to facilitate reference when necessary.

The files may also store reference data in the form of schedules relating to product prices, wage rates, stores issue prices and cost rates, etc. This type of reference data is required so that invoice values, wages earned and the cost of stores issues may be calculated (*see* I, **10, 11, 13–15**).

(*d*) *Output*. After processing data, the output is often business documents such as extended invoices for items despatched to customers, extended clock cards recording the gross wages payable to employees or extended stores issue notes recording the cost of items issued to jobs, etc. In addition, the output may consist of completed statements of account, a stores issue summary or a report of operations for management control. A further type of output is updated ledger cards, showing the amount outstanding on each customer's ledger card, the current cumulative position of an employee's earnings and tax, and the balance of stock of each item in the stores.

(*e*) *Control.* A clerk, to some extent, controls his own actions in the performance of a task based on his experience. Initially, however, a clerk's actions are governed by a procedure manual containing an outline of the steps necessary to perform a task. The activity of the clerk is subjected to over-all control by the section supervisor (*see* Fig. 7).

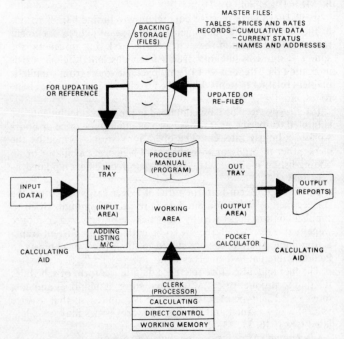

FIG. 7   *A clerical data processing system*

9. Keyboard accounting machine—mechanical method (*see* 3).

(*a*) *Input.* The machine operator receives business documents such as invoices, goods received notes, stores issue notes and extended clock cards, etc. The data to be processed is read from the documents by the operator and is input by the depression of selected keys on the keyboard. Brought forward balances are also entered by the keyboard.

(*b*) *Processing.* When the machine is set in motion, many operations are carried out on the data automatically. For instance, if the amount of an invoice is input, the machine will print the amount and the date, add the amount to be brought forward balance and accumulate the total.

(*c*) *Storage.* Records in the form of ledger cards are stored in filing trays in a similar manner to the manual method already outlined. The transient retention of data is facilitated by the machine's internal registers. The registers accumulate data which is printed out if necessary in the form of totals or outstanding balances (*see* I, **4**).

(*d*) *Output.* The result of processing is often a printed document such as a statement of account, payroll and payslips and updated ledger cards. In addition, it is customary to provide a summary of postings in the form of a day book sheet (proof sheet) for comparison with a pre-list, in order to ensure that all postings have been made and that they have been made accurately.

(*e*) *Control.* The processing steps are, to some extent, automatically controlled by means of a control bar which moves the carriage to desired column, printing positions without manual intervention.

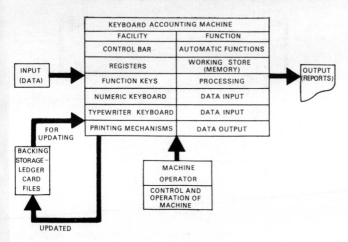

FIG. 8 *A mechanical (keyboard accounting machine) data processing system*

The operations performed by the machine operator are guided by a procedure manual. The whole of the activity is controlled by the section supervisor (*see* Fig. 8).

10. Computer installation—electronic method (*see* 7).

(*a*) *Input.* Data for processing must first be converted into a machine-sensible form before being input. Data must therefore be subjected to data preparation activities, which may consist of punching data into either cards or paper tape or encoding data on various types of magnetic media. The machine-sensible media is then input for processing by means of an appropriate input device.

(*b*) *Processing.* The operations to be performed on data are carried out by the central processing unit (C.P.U.), which has electronic circuitry for performing arithmetical and logical operations. The processing is carried out automatically by means of the internally stored program (processing instructions).

(*c*) *Storage.* Master files are normally stored on magnetic media; for serial access magnetic tape is used and for direct access magnetic discs are used. This is referred to as "backing" storage (as

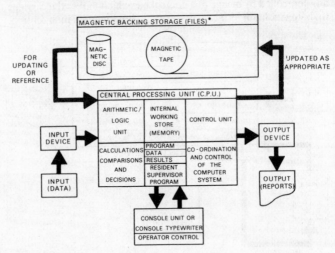

FIG. 9   *An electronic computer data processing system*

* Master files: (1) Tables: prices and rates. (2) Records: cumulative data; current status; names and addresses

distinct from "internal" storage), which may be classified as the computer's filing cabinets.

The temporary retention of data and instructions is facilitated by the computer's internal memory or working store, which may be core or semiconductor storage.

(*d*) *Output.* The result of processing is usually a series of printed documents, such as invoices, payrolls and payslips, management reports and stock schedules, etc. The printed output is produced by a printer linked to the computer.

As the documents are produced, the magnetic backing files are updated to record the current status of accounts and stock balances, etc.

(*e*) *Control.* The processing operations are automatically controlled by the internally stored program, in conjunction with both the resident supervisor program (software) and the computer's control unit (hardware), which is an integral part of the C.P.U.

The computer's operations are also controlled and monitored by the computer operator with the aid of either a console unit, V.D.U., or console typewriter which facilitates two-way communication between man and machine (*see* Fig. 9).

PROGRESS TEST 2

1. Discuss the following statement: "Data processing can be performed without the use of sophisticated machines".   (**1**)

2. Indicate the basic features of the following data processing methods:

(*a*) manual	(*d*) microcomputer
(*b*) keyboard accounting machine	(*e*) visible record computer
(*c*) minicomputer	(*f*) mainframe computer

(**2–7**)

3. Define the five main elements of any data processing system. (**8–10**)

4. A computer is sometimes described as having five basic elements. Other descriptions divide storage into two categories, internal and external, so making a total of six basic elements.

Describe briefly the two categories of storage and explain fully the purposes which they serve.   (**10**, *see also* III, **23–9**, XIV) [A.C.A. June 1976, Q2]

PART TWO

PROFILE OF COMPUTERS

CHAPTER III

The Electronic Computer and its Development

DEFINITIONS OF A COMPUTER

Although a basic definition of a computer has already been out-lined (*see* II, **7**, **10**), it is of interest to note that various terms are used to describe a computer, amongst which are automatic data processor, digital computer and electronic computer. The reasons for using such terms are now considered.

1. Automatic data processor. A computer is automatic in opera-tion, in the sense that when the program and data for processing have been input to the computer's internal memory, the required output is produced without manual intervention, as all the program instructions are executed automatically.

2. Digital computer. The term "digital", as distinct from "analog", is used to describe the type of computer used for commercial data processing. Digital computers process discrete numerical digits, while an analog computer represents physical variables such as rates of flow, temperature or oil pressure by analogy by means of variations of electrical voltage proportional to physical vari-ables. Analog computers are used in scientific and engineering work and do not achieve the degree of accuracy of digital com-puters which is essential for business processing.

3. Electronic computer. A computer consists of electronic circuits and components through which pulses of electricity flow represent-ing data to be processed or which has been processed. Electronic technology is classified in respect of computers by reference to a specific "generation", as described under **4–7** below.

THE DEVELOPMENT OF COMPUTER TECHNOLOGY

Electronic computers were first used for commercial processing during the early 1950s, and they were based on a technology now referred to as the First Generation. Technological developments occurred at a very fast rate and in the late 1950s the technology applied to the design of computers became known as the Second Generation. Eventually, in the early 1960s technological developments were such that a Third Generation of computers became available. Fourth Generation computers came into existence in 1974.

The technical characteristics of computers may be classified according to the "generation" to which they belong.

4. First generation computers. The first generation of computers were in operation during the years 1954–59, and their technological basis was circuitry consisting of wires and thermionic valves. The valves, being hollow in construction, were non-solid state as electrical pulses had to flow through the space (vacuum) in the valve in a similar manner to the pre-transistorised type of radio. Computers belonging to this generation had the following characteristics:

(*a*) comparatively *large* in size compared to present-day computers;

(*b*) generated *a lot of heat*, which was not consistent with reliability as the valves tended to fail frequently;

(*c*) *low capacity internal storage*;

(*d*) *individual* non-related models;

(*e*) processors operated in the *millisecond speed range* (one-thousandth of a second);

(*f*) internal storage consisted of a *magnetic drum* and *delay lines*.

5. Second generation computers. This generation was in operation during the years 1959–64. The advance of technological knowledge enabled the wires and thermionic valves of the first generation to be replaced with printed circuits, diodes and transistors. These components were based on "solid state" technology, as electricity did not have to flow through space as in the thermionic valve. "Solid state" is the technology applied to the design of modern domestic tape recorders and transistor radios.

Computers of this generation had the following characteristics:

(*a*) *smaller* in size compared to the first generation computers;

(*b*) generated a *lower level of heat*, as the components were much smaller;

(*c*) *greater* degree of *reliability*, as transistors and solid state components generally are not subject to such a high failure rate as thermionic valves;

(*d*) *higher capacity internal storage*;

(*e*) use of *core storage* instead of magnetic drum and delay lines;

(*f*) related series of processors—the *family concept*;

(*g*) processors operated in the *microsecond speed range* (one-millionth of a second);

(*h*) high cost *direct access storage*.

6. Third generation computers. Third generation computers came into existence in 1964, and are in current use. The technology forming the basis of their design is microminiaturisation, consisting of micro-integrated circuits very similar to the solid state technology of the second generation but much more compact. The circuits are built of a number of integrated components rather than individual components which require to be soldered together. Integrated circuits, based on silicon technology (*see* V, **1**), are much smaller than their predecessors, which enables higher processing speeds to be achieved, because with smaller circuits data pulses can flow from point A to point B much more quickly than is possible with larger circuits. The reason for this is that electricity flows at a constant speed (the speed of light) and the only way in which data pulses can be speeded up is by reducing the distance they have to travel.

Computers of this generation have the following characteristics:

(*a*) *smaller* in size compared to the second generation computers;

(*b*) *higher capacity internal storage*;

(*c*) remote *communication* facilities;

(*d*) *multi-programming* facilities;

(*e*) *reduced cost of direct access storage*;

(*f*) processors which operate in the *nanosecond speed range* (one-thousandth of a microsecond—American billionth of a second);

(*g*) ranges of computers with a common architecture whereby the models in a range are upward compatible; i.e. a program written for one model can be run without any significant change on a larger and more powerful computer in the range;

(*h*) use of high-level languages such as Cobol;

(*i*) wide range of optional peripherals.

7. Fourth generation computers. The introduction of systems network architecture in 1974 may be considered to be the inception of the fourth generation. A standard architecture was derived which provided for upgrading networks of computers without alteration of application programming. This compares with the upward compatibility of computers in a range which was a feature of the third generation (*see* **6**). This generation also includes the introduction of microtechnology and the advent of microcomputers, retail terminal systems, databases and extremely large internal and external storage capacity.

MAINFRAME COMPUTER CONFIGURATIONS

8. Definition of configuration. A computer configuration is the collection of machines (hardware) which form a complete computer system; consisting of a central processor and its peripheral devices. Peripheral devices consist of input, backing storage and output devices which are normally connected to, and controlled by, the processor. Modern computer technology is such that a wide range of peripheral devices and processors are available from which to build the computer configuration most suitable for the processing needs of a particular business. The choice of the most suitable configuration is established during the feasibility study (*see* XV, **1**).

A computer configuration is selected initially to suit both the current and the foreseeable future needs of the business with regard to the volume and type of data to be processed.

Eventually, it may be necessary to increase the processing power of the computer installation to contend with increasing volumes of data and the need for more management information. At one time, under these circumstances, it was necessary to change the existing computer for a more powerful model, but this is now unnecessary. Computer installations may now be enhanced on site on a modular basis as required, for example by:

(*a*) increasing the *capacity of core storage* (*see* **27**) by the addition of another module of 4K, for example, which increases the current capacity from say, 8K to 12K or more;

(*b*) the installation of *additional exchangeable disc storage devices* for increasing the volume of data which is immediately accessible during processing, or to obtain direct access to programs;

(*c*) increasing the *speed of input* by exchanging a 300 c.p.m. card reader with a 600 c.p.m. model;

(*d*) increasing the *speed of output* by exchanging a 300 l.p.m. line printer with a 600 l.p.m. model;

(*e*) Exchanging the *processor* for a more powerful model (*see* **6**(*g*));

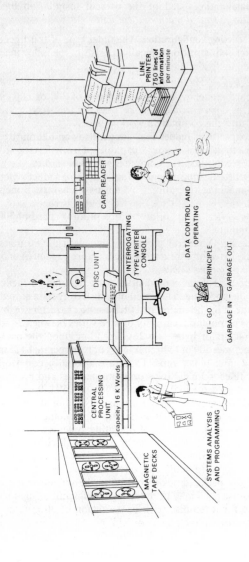

FIG. 10 Pictorial illustration of an older type of mainframe computer configuration (magnetic disc and tape-oriented)

(Courtesy of J. A. Crabtree & Co. Ltd.)

(*f*) increasing the speed of the present installation by the addition of an *extended mathematical unit*.

9. Batch processing configuration. The older type of third generation computer configuration typically consists of the following (*see* Fig. 10).

(*a*) *Input devices.*

(*i*) A card reader with a reading speed of 300 or 600 cards a minute. This device would only be used for transferring transaction data into the computer's working store.

(*ii*) A paper tape reader may be used (as an alternative, or in addition, to a card reader) capable of transferring 1,000 characters a second into the computer's working store.

Data may be captured in paper tape as a by-product of other accounting machine operations by means of a tape punching attachment.

(*b*) *Output device.* A line printer with a printing speed of 300 or 600 lines a minute.

(*c*) *Processing.* A central processing unit with 32 000 units or more (words, bytes or characters) of core store capacity.

(*d*) *Backing storage devices.*

(*i*) Four tape decks would usually be required to facilitate sorting and file updating. The speed of transferring data stored on magnetic tape is in the region of 20K to 60K characters or bytes per second. The potential capacity of tape varies between 20 to 40 million characters or bytes (*see* **26**) depending upon the packing density (sometimes 800 or 1600 characters or bytes per inch (25 mm) of tape) and inter-block gaps. Tapes are a serial access storage media and are economical for storing master files and programs. They are best used for high "hit-rate" files (*see* VII, **9**).

(*ii*) Two or three disc drives are usually required for storing master files, data to be used in multiprogramming operations required on demand, segments of operating systems and application programs until called into main memory. According to the version used, disc drives are capable of a data transfer speed in the region of 200K to 400K characters or bytes per second. The capacity of disc packs varies according to the version in use also but for a six-disc pack may be in the region of 8 million characters or bytes and for a ten-disc pack in the region of 30 million, i.e. 30 megabytes (or characters). (*See* XIV.)

(*e*) *Console typewriter.* (*See* VII, **7**.)

This configuration is illustrated in Figs. 10 and 11.

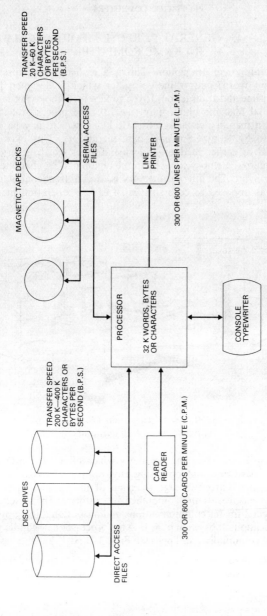

FIG. 11 *Older type of batch processing mainframe computer configuration*

NCR N–8450 GENERAL PURPOSE MEDIUM-SCALE MAINFRAME COMPUTER

10. General system description. This is a modern medium-scale (sixteen-bit word) mainframe computer which is designed for batch, on-line and transaction-driven processing, employing multiple virtual machine philosophy (*see* **13**). The processor has a basic main memory capacity of 128K bytes, which may be expanded to 512K bytes in 64K byte increments. This may be contrasted to earlier medium-scale mainframes which generally had an internal memory capacity in the region of 32K characters, words or bytes. The internal memory is M.O.S. (semiconductor) (*see* **29**) as opposed to core storage of earlier generation mainframes.

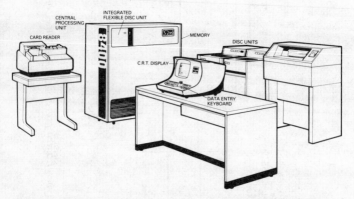

FIG. 12   *NCR N–8450 general purpose medium-scale mainframe computer: basic configuration*

The system has complete flexibility which allows the user to select the hardware and operating environment that best suits individual needs from a large selection of mainframe features, terminals, peripherals and comprehensive software. The system is also designed for telecommunications and an optional integrated communications subsystem built into the processor can handle up to twenty communication lines (*see* Figs. 12 and 13).

11. Choice of hardware. The capacities of the hardware devices and their transfer speeds may be contrasted with the older type

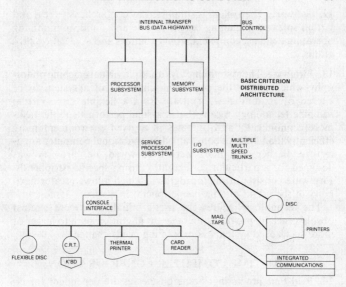

FIG. 13 *NCR N–8450 hardware architecture*

of medium-scale mainframe outlined in **9** above. This particular computer system has a choice of the following devices.

(*a*) Card readers: up to 900 c.p.m. (cards per minute).

(*b*) Card punches: up to 450 c.p.m.

(*c*) Tape readers: up to 1500 c.p.s. (characters per second).

(*d*) Tape punches: up to 200 c.p.s.

(*e*) M.I.C.R. Reader/sorters: up to 1200 d.p.m. (documents per minute).

(*f*) Matrix printers: up to 173 c.p.s.

(*g*) Line printers: up to 3000 l.p.m. (lines per minute).

(*h*) Magnetic tape units: 40 to 320K b.p.s. (bytes per second) transfer rate.

(*i*) Disc units: up to 200 million bytes per unit with a transfer speed up to 806K b.p.s.

(*j*) Data module: up to 140 million bytes per dual-spindle unit with a transfer speed up to 885K b.p.s.

(*k*) Cassette drives and freestanding flexible disc drives may also be used.

12. Software. The system is supported by comprehensive real and virtual software including batch, on-line and multiprogramming operating systems, compilers, utility routines and application programs.

13. Firmware. The system employs multiple virtual machine philosophy which allows the processing character of a system to be altered by loading new firmware from a flexible disc. Virtual machine technology means that a system performs specific tasks more economically and operates in a given environment more efficiently than systems constrained by traditional computer architecture. Earlier computers were hard wired, i.e. circuitry was designed for a particular configuration using specific peripherals. Firmware consists of microprograms, which allows greater flexibility in the use of alternative peripherals.

The technology insures the user's initial investment against obsolescence by providing an inherent migration path to larger or more specialised systems as processing needs change.

REAL-TIME COMPUTER CONFIGURATION

14. Real-time processing. Some businesses are dependent for efficient operation on up-to-date information being immediately available on request (*see* VIII, **7–12**). This is particularly the case in respect of businesses with geographically dispersed operating units, such as airlines with dispersed booking offices.

The term "real-time" refers to the technique of updating files with transaction data immediately the event to which it relates occurs. This is in distinction to "batch processing", which processes related data in batches at pre-defined periods of time (*see* VII, **1**).

A real-time computer system is communications-oriented, and provides for random enquiries from remote locations with instantaneous responses; because of this characteristic, this type of operation is referred to as on-line or "conversational" processing.

Real-time processing is suitable when it is necessary to have the latest possible information in the following types of business operations:

(*a*) wholesale suppliers and manufacturers—availability of stocks;

(*b*) airlines—flight seat availability (*see* Fig. 14);

(*c*) steel making—yield optimisation;

(*d*) manufacturing—status of production orders.

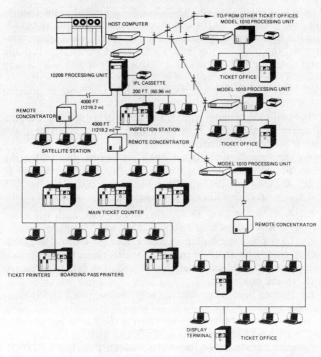

(Courtesy of Raytheon Cossor Data Systems)
FIG. 14   *Typical airline reservations and ticketing real-time system*

The main disadvantage of a real-time system relates to the cost of terminals and communication equipment if remote access facilities are required for dispersed operating units. The cost of the computer for real-time processing need not be very great as the current range of small computers are capable of processing transactions as they occur on a real-time interactive basis. A further disadvantage relates to the time and cost of developing such a system especially as they require to be supported by an integrated database, complicated database management systems and communications software.

15. Real-time configuration. The real-time configuration to be outlined is used in a steelworks to optimise Plate Mill yield. The weight of ingots varies and when an ingot is cogged in the Blooming Mill its actual length is unknown until it reaches the shear and has been topped and tailed. The previous manual system pre-planned the allocation of ingots assuming a theoretical running length and the last portion of an ingot was not allocated to any order. The length of this piece is unknown until shearing is completed and at a later stage must be matched as close as possible to an order item.

The real-time system provides a terminal at the shear so that the planning decision as to how the ingot is cut up is left until the length has been measured and input to the computer. The computer then searches the order book for orders that match the chemical analysis of the ingot and calculates the combination of order slab lengths which produces minimum scrap.

The configuration has the following features.

(*a*) A duplexed PDP II–40 computer system, each processor having 64K words of core storage with a word length of 16 bits.

(*b*) Inter-processor buffer—a communication channel to enable the watch-dog timers to interrogate the processors to determine if failure has occurred and to enable file updating data to be passed between the processors.

(*c*) Unibus link for connecting together the two PDP–II computers.

(*d*) Programmable multiplexer. Two of these units are attached to the unibus of each processor. Each unit enables sixteen asynchronous communication lines to be connected to a single PDP–II.

(*e*) Disc drive and controller. The unit consists of a disc drive controller and the first drive. Up to seven additional disc drives can be added to the controller. The disc system consists of disc cartridges of 1.2 million 16 bit word capacity mounted on each drive.

(*f*) Terminals are distributed as follows:

(*i*) a teletype in the steel plant office to output steel orders from the planning department and input details of heats made— Heats are quantities of metal in the furnace for melting and refining;

(*ii*) V.D.U. in the laboratory to input analysis details;

(*iii*) a display terminal in the soaking pit recorder's office to collect details of heat arrivals and charging;

(*iv*) eight terminals, one for each pit, along the soaking pit landing, to input which position within the pit is being discharged;

(*v*) a display terminal in the cogger's cabin, to display the cogging section required and for the cogger to indicate when cogging is completed;

(*vi*) two terminals, one either side of shear, for input of the ingot running length;

(*vii*) display terminals for the shearsman and shear operator to output shearing and for the shear operator to indicate details when each slab is sheared;

(*viii*) display terminal for the marker;

(*ix*) display terminal for piler operator;

(*x*) teletype for slab yard stocktaker to output and input stacking information;

(*xi*) teletype for the foreman to print information about occurrences that require attention, e.g. a heat being charged before the analysis has arrived;

(*xii*) two printers in the foreman's office to output security details about cogging and shearing for all ingots charged into the pits to be used in case of computer failure;

(*xiii*) a V.D.U. and teletype is provided for the production controller, who plays an important part in the systems operation, being able to deal with all extraordinary situations, e.g. making the decision about a heat arriving in the Blooming Mill for which there are no, or insufficient, orders, etc.

It is recognised that the reader will not fully appreciate the operation of this system but the primary intention is to indicate the hardware features of a real-time configuration partly for the reader to be aware of the characteristics of this type of system compared with a batch processing configuration. The configuration is outlined in Fig. 15.

DEFINING THE CENTRAL PROCESSING UNIT

16. General characteristics and compatibility of processors. The central processing unit or processor (often abbreviated to C.P.U.) is the main unit within a computer system, and consists of three components: arithmetic/logic unit, control unit and internal working memory (*see* Fig. 16).

The processor accepts data for processing from an input device, carries out instructions specified by the program and outputs the results by means of an output device. Modern computers are often designed as a related family or series, whereby each processor in the series is compatible with each other. Compatibility is a design technique which enables any peripheral device to be con-

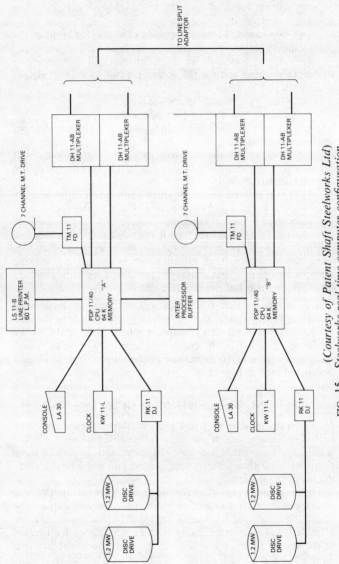

(Courtesy of Patent Shaft Steelworks Ltd)
Steelworks real-time computer configuration
FIG. 15

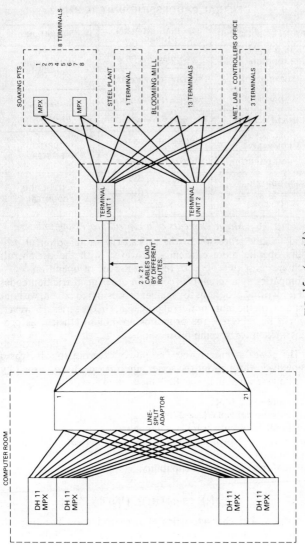

FIG. 15 (contd.)

CENTRAL PROCESSING UNIT (C.P.U.)		
ARITHMETIC/LOGIC UNIT	INTERNAL WORKING STORAGE	CONTROL UNIT
ARITHMETIC: – ADDITION	ACCUMULATORS	INSTRUCTION REGISTER
– SUBTRACTION	SUPERVISOR PROGRAM	
– DIVISION	APPLICATION PROGRAM	OPERATION DECODER
MULTIPLICATION	INPUT DATA	
LOGIC: – COMPARING	WORKING STORAGE	ADDRESS REGISTER
– MATCHING	OUTPUT INFORMATION	
– SORTING	CONSTANTS	INSTRUCTION COUNTER
DECISIONS	TABLES	

FIG. 16 *Major elements of a central processing unit*

nected to any processor in the series. The more powerful processors operate more efficiently, however, with the peripherals which are most suitable with regard to speed of operation.

Compatibility also enables common order or instruction codes used for writing programs for smaller processors to be run, without alteration, on the more powerful processors in the series. However, as might be expected, the programs are not so efficient as programs written for specific processors.

17. The power of processors. The power of processors increases progressively throughout the series, and may be distinguished by the following attributes (*see* **8**):

   (*a*) store cycle time;
   (*b*) storage capacity (*see* **27**);
   (*c*) number of data transfer channels;
   (*d*) number of programs which may be interleaved for multi-programming operations;
   (*e*) real-time processing capability.

THE CONTROL UNIT

18. Purpose and characteristics of a control unit. The over-all control of a computer system is accomplished by the control unit, which is an integral part of the central processing unit.

The control unit co-ordinates the various parts of the computer system—the arithmetic/logic unit, internal working store and the peripheral units—to form a composite, integrated data processing system. In addition, the control unit also controls the transfer of data to, from and within the working store, as required by the program. The control unit also acts as a switching device to enable data pulses to flow along the appropriate channels.

A control unit, in respect of a single-address type of computer, consists of the following components:

    (*a*) instruction register;
    (*b*) decoder;
    (*c*) address register;
    (*d*) instruction counter.

The instruction register receives instructions from the internal working store in the sequence required for processing. The function or operation part of the instruction is then transferred to a decoder for translation of the operation to be executed, which causes the appropriate circuits to be connected for carrying out the operation in the arithmetic/logic unit.

The address register makes the required circuit connections to enable the data contained in a store location to be transferred to a specified accumulator via a register.

An instruction counter is used for recording the number of instructions executed, and is incremented by 1 after completing each instruction.

19. Cycle of operations. As both instructions and data are in binary form, there must be some means of enabling the computer to distinguish between them to avoid processing instructions as data. This is achieved by two distinct operation cycles known as "instruction" and "execution" cycles. The instruction cycle is concerned with connecting store locations to the adder to allow the transfer of data for processing. The execution cycle carries out the requirements of the instruction (*see* XVI, **10, 11**).

THE ARITHMETIC/LOGIC UNIT

The arithmetic/logic unit performs arithmetic operations, data handling operations and logical functions. The unit consists of a "mill" (adder/subtractor), electronic circuits, one or more "working registers" to which operands may be transferred whilst being operated on and, in some computers, accumulators for storing the results of calculations.

20. Arithmetic operations. Although a computer performs all types of arithmetic operations—addition, subtraction, multiplication and division—it is important to appreciate that subtraction is performed by the addition of the "complement" of the number to be subtracted to the other number involved in the calculation.

Multiplication is performed by combinations of "shifts" to the left and addition. Division is performed by combinations of "shifts" to the right and subtraction.

The reader is recommended to refer to Appendix II at this point, for an outline of binary notation.

21. Definition of logic operations. Logic operations, as distinct from arithmetic operations are concerned with comparing, selecting, matching, sorting and merging of data. When comparing data factors, the logical ability of the arithmetic/logic unit differentiates between positive and negative differences between the data factors and, in accordance with the results of the comparison, the alternative sequence of instructions to be executed is determined automatically. This is known as a "conditional" transfer, and it provides the means for processing data on the "exception" basis—that is, data requiring special processing according to the circumstances disclosed by the data. Conditional transfers of this type are appropriate when it is necessary to compare the credit limit of each customer with their account balance for the purpose of indicating, by means of a special print-out, those customers whose balances exceed the credit limit for credit control. This is referred to as exception reporting. In a stock control application the program may provide for the comparison of stock balances with re-order levels to indicate those items which require replenishment. This may be done either by printing out a re-order list or a purchase order directly. This may be referred to as "automatic decision-making" (*see* Fig. 113).

Similarly, within a budgetary control application actual costs may be compared with budgeted costs and variance reports printed out, again on the basis of exception reporting. It is this important attribute of computers that makes them so useful as a tool of management (*see* XXVI, **1–4**).

22. Example of a logic operation. For example, if it is necessary to test the credit limit of each customer to decide whether the current balance is in excess of this limit, a comparison is made as follows:

Credit limit	£500
Account balance	£400
	———
Positive difference (credit limit not exceeded)	£100 ===

The credit limit is not exceeded and this is detected by the computer as a positive difference. No action is necessary.

Credit limit	£500
Account balance	£600
	———
Negative difference (credit limit exceeded)	£100 ===

In this case the credit limit is exceeded, and this is detected by the computer as a negative difference and action will be taken accordingly, most likely by printing out a special notice to be sent to the customer.

This type of problem is incorporated in the program as a series of questions—is the balance less than ($<$), or equal to or greater than ($\geqslant$), and the results determine the series of instructions to be processed.

INTERNAL STORAGE

23. General outline. Developments in electronic and related technology have affected the type of internal storage used in computers. Early computers had internal memories consisting of nickel delay lines or magnetic drums. More recent computers have core storage but this has tended to be replaced by semiconductor (M.O.S.) memory in later computers.

24. Summary of types of internal memory. The most usual types of memory in current use are:

   (*a*) core storage;
   (*b*) semiconductor memory (M.O.S.).

25. Purpose of internal memory. The internal memory of a computer is an integral element of the processing unit and may be referred to as the computer's working memory. It is used for storing software in the form of operating systems, application programs and utility routines, etc. In addition, the data input for processing is stored in the memory, as are the results of processing until they are output either to backing storage or to an output device such as a printer or V.D.U.

Data stored in the memory, as well as instructions, can be addressed and accessed very quickly and for this reason internal memory is often referred to as "immediate access storage" (I.A.S.). This attribute is ideal for having all programs and master files (consisting of business records and reference files) stored internally for immediate access when required. Unfortunately, however, internal storage, particularly core storage, has tended to be expensive and it has been necessary to use slower and less expensive types of storage for such purposes. Internal storage has to be complemented therefore by external storage, that is storage external to the processor, which is referred to as backing storage. This is used for mass storage needs whereas internal storage is used for immediate access requirements.

Backing storage is less expensive, has a higher storage capacity but a slower access time than internal storage. Programs, master files and reference files are stored in backing storage until required for processing, when they are transferred to the internal memory. All programs and data must be resident in the internal memory before processing is possible.

26. Units of storage. The units of storage in a computer system are usually expressed in bytes and/or words which indicates the number of binary digits (bits) in a unit of storage. At one time computers had units of storage expressed in terms of characters consisting of six bits but this has tended to be replaced by the byte which consists of eight bits. ICL 1900 computer series use the six-bit character as a unit of storage which is a sub-unit of a "word" which is twenty-four bits. Therefore a twenty-four-bit word can store four six-bit characters. Similarly, the IBM 360 series of computers use a thirty-two-bit word capable of storing four eight-bit bytes. The modern small computer tends to have a unit of storage in the form of a sixteen-bit word but an exception to this is the Radio Shack TRS–80 microcomputer which consists of an eight-bit processor.

27. Capacity of storage. Until recently medium-scale mainframe computers had internal storage capacities, typically in the region of 32 to 48K bytes or words, but even the small mini or micro now has a capacity which greatly exceeds this. Typical storage capacities may be summarised as follows:

(a) micros 4K to 64K bytes;
(b) minis 48K to 128K bytes;
(c) modern mainframes 128K to 512K; $\frac{3}{4}$ to 2 million bytes.

The abbreviation "K" is used to denote 1000 units of storage but it is actually 1024 units of storage, i.e. 2^{10} which is an expansion of base 2, the base of the binary number system. "K" should not be confused with kilo (k) which stands for 1000, i.e. 10^3 which is an expansion of base 10, the base of the decimal number system.

28. Core storage. This type of storage consists of small rings (cores) of ferro-magnetic material which are threaded on wires by hand which makes this type of storage very expensive to produce. Core storage consists of a number of adjacent core planes for storing bytes, one plane for each bit position in the byte.

The cores are magnetised to represent binary numbers—a zero is represented by negative polarity and a one by positive polarity. By means of combinations of negative and positive states in adjacent core planes it is possible to represent numeric, alphabetic and special characters each of which have their individual binary code.

29. Semiconductor memory. This type of memory has tended to supersede core storage in most computers, i.e. micros, minis and mainframes. The reason for this is attributable to four factors, *viz.* it is smaller, has a higher capacity, is less costly and is faster with regard to access time.

Semiconductor memory is produced from silicon chips and is based on Metal Oxide Semiconductor (M.O.S.) technology. It is also referred to as "Metal Oxide Semiconductor Field Effect Transistor technology", i.e. M.O.S.F.E.T. Field Effect Transistor technology is abbreviated to F.E.T.

There are two types of semiconductor memory:

(a) random access memory (RAM);
(b) read-only memory (ROM).

RAM is for normal working storage requirements and its capacity may be enhanced on site if necessary. This type of memory tends to be volatile which means that the information it contains is lost if a power failure occurs. This is overcome in some computer systems by a memory support system whereby a battery energises the memory when necessary to avoid loss of data. As the media is volatile it is not likely to be used as backing storage because this would create problems for the restoration of data in the event of a power failure.

ROM is physically fixed and cannot be altered by writing over existing memory locations. In some instances, computers have "read-only" memory chips containing the compiler for converting programming language, i.e. instructions in user format for commands, etc., into machine code. This avoids the need for special compilation runs (*see* XVII, **15**). This type of memory is non-volatile.

ADVANTAGES AND DISADVANTAGES OF A COMPUTER

30. Advantages. These are summarised as follows.

(*a*) *Speed of operation.* The central processor of a computer system operates at electronic speed, that is at the speed of light, which means that data pulses flow through the system at 2.997925×10^8 m/s (186,000 miles per second).

(*b*) *Automatic operation.* Once data has been input to the processor all data processing is automatic under the control of the internally stored program.

(*c*) *Flexibility.* The modern general purpose computer may be used for a variety of purposes, i.e. concurrent batch and on-line processing, multi-programming, real-time processing and data collection, etc.

(*d*) *Reliability.* As the main unit in a computer system, the central processor, is constructed from electronic components it is not so prone to malfunctions from wear and tear in use as are machines of a mechanical nature.

(*e*) *Choice of configuration.* A wide range of optional peripherals are available for many computer systems which allow a business to implement those which most suit its processing requirements, i.e. an optical character reader may be used instead of a card reader for computer input.

(*f*) *Management information.* Due to the characteristics of a computer it is possible to increase the level of useful information supplied to management for control and decision making.

(*g*) *Accuracy.* Due to program checks and controls applied to data before and during processing invalid data is detected and corrected. This factor ensures that the ultimate output from a computer has a high degree of accuracy and is, therefore, more reliable.

31. Disadvantages. Considering all of the advantages listed above, it would not appear that there could be any disadvantages, but unfortunately there are. They may be enumerated as follows.

(*a*) Unless the *feasibility study* is carried out satisfactorily, the resulting decision may be to go ahead and install a computer when in fact it should not be, or not to install a computer when in fact it should be (*see* XV, **1**). Either result will have repercussions on the business.

(*b*) Analysing and designing computer systems is a skilled task and the ultimate results will *reflect the skill and care* applied to this activity.

(*c*) Similarly the care and skill applied in *writing* the computer programs will affect the ultimate results.

(*d*) The whole of the business administration requires to be *investigated*, and changes effected, to obtain the best results, and this may cause drastic upheavals for both systems and staff. Of course, changes must take place to keep up to date with changing circumstances, but this is a problem that has to be overcome.

(*e*) Several man-years of investigation and preparation may have elapsed before a computer system becomes *operational*.

(*f*) It is extremely difficult to obtain *skilled systems analysts and programmers* because of the increasing demand for them.

(*g*) The *initial cost* of a large installation can be very high, but this may be offset by the rental terms and tax allowances which are available. Minis and micros cost much less than mainframes, however.

(*h*) Because of the speedy development of new technology in the field of electronics, and electronic computers in particular, a computer may be *technologically obsolete* before it is installed. However, unless the decision to go ahead is given to install the latest model of computer available, stagnation may follow, or, at the least, competitors will gain advantages.

(*i*) The need to obtain *standby facilities* in the event of breakdown of any part of the computer system.

PROGRESS TEST 3

1. Define what you understand by the term "electronic computer". (**1–3**)

2. Since computers were first used for commercial data processing, they have been subjected to great development. Computer development is often classified into generations, i.e. first, second, third and fourth generations. Outline the main features of development of these generations. (**4–7**)

3. What do you understand by the term "configuration"? (**8**)

4. Outline a typical third generation mainframe batch processing configuration. (**9**)

5. Outline the general characteristics of a modern medium-scale mainframe computer. (**10–13**)

6. Outline the nature of a real-time computer configuration. (**14**)

7. (*a*) What is meant by the term "real-time processing"?

(*b*) Explain the hardware and software facilities which are required for the operation of a real-time system. (**14, 15,** *see also* VIII, **4, 5, 7–12**) [A.C.A. June 1975, Q4]

8. "Computer installations may be enhanced on a modular basis". Discuss this statement. (**16**)

9. Define the characteristics and main sections of a central processing unit. (**16–29**)

10. What is the relevance of the logical ability of a computer to exception reporting? (**21, 22**)

11. State the two basic types and nature of internal storage. (**23–9**)

12. What do you understand by the term "units of storage"? (**26**)

13. Indicate typical storage capacities of micro-, mini- and mainframe computers. (**27**)

14. Summarise the main advantages and disadvantages of a computer. (**30, 31**)

CHAPTER IV

Minicomputers

GENERAL CONSIDERATIONS

1. Definition. A minicomputer as the name implies is a small computer, relative to a mainframe computer and may be defined as a scaled-down mainframe, as the processor and peripherals are physically smaller. Although the processor may be physically smaller, its memory capacity may in fact be greater. Medium-sized mainframes often had internal memory capacities in the region of 8K to 48K, a typical capacity being 32K. These mainframes are still in use and have core storage which is very expensive to produce because it is assembled by hand. Semiconductor memory is now being widely used in all types of computers; micros, minis and mainframes. It has a much higher capacity for its size in relation to core storage and is much cheaper.

It is interesting to note that minicomputers now have memory sizes which typically range from 48K to 128K bytes, whereas micros tend to have memory capacities in the range 4K to 64K bytes, the higher end of the range having a greater capacity than older type mainframes in some instances. However, more recent models of mainframe have greatly increased internal memory capacity, e.g. NCR 8450, 128K to 512K bytes and the ICL 2950, three-quarters to two million bytes, both using M.O.S. technology (*see* III, **23–9**).

In respect of peripherals, large disc packs (six to ten discs) are often replaced by smaller disc packs, containing two discs, and by flexible disc units. Some minis can be enhanced by small tape units using tape reels containing 600 feet (182.88 m) of magnetic tape rather than 2400 feet (731.2 m) as used on mainframes.

Minis tend to have sixteen-bit words, equivalent to two bytes, whereas mainframes have larger word lengths, e.g. ICL 1900 series have a word length of 24 bits and IBM System/360 computers have a word length of 32 bits. Although these manufacturers have later models the word lengths are mentioned for purposes of comparison.

Minicomputers have a full instruction set, arithmetic and logical ability and could replace the small- to medium-sized mainframe. Possibly within the next few years there will only exist dedicated minis or micros and super-mainframes. Minis cost much less than mainframes and almost any job that a mainframe can do can also be done by a mini.

Minis are faster in operation than micros and may have different circuitry, whereby the arithmetic/logic unit is on a single chip but has separate decoding circuits and memory boards. A micro-computer is built around a single chip microprocessor.

The term minicomputer can be misleading as they were primarily developed for testing and monitoring systems including component testing, pollution monitoring, process control and many other uses. They were complicated to program and had minimal input/output capabilities. Today, the minicomputer has grown in status in every respect except physical size. The introduction of high-level pro-gramming languages, larger memories and a wide choice of peripherals has increased its versatility and productivity.

Although technical details need not concern management, the choice between large centrally located mainframes and minis dis-persed on a distributed processing basis does need thinking about (*see* Figs. 5 and 6).

NCR 8250 GENERAL PURPOSE MINICOMPUTER: GENERAL OUTLINE

2. General system description. This minicomputer system is suit-able for the small- and medium-sized business in respect of basic data processing applications and for the larger business as a means of implementing distributed processing. The system can operate on an interactive transaction driven basis (*see* IX), as well as in local and remote batch processing mode. The system also has multi-programming capability and integrated data base processing is facilitated. In addition, the system has minimal environmental con-straints which allows it to be installed in the normal office environment.

The system is keyboard-oriented for data entry but has optional facilities for automatic input by means of a card reader. The basic system may also be enhanced by additional memory modules or increments, additional disc units, several C.R.T. display units, magnetic tape unit and communications adapter to permit remote batch communications.

3. Basic system configuration. The basic system configuration is as follows (*see* Figs. 17 and 18):

(*a*) processor with 64K bytes M.O.S. memory;

(*b*) processor control console;

(*c*) magnetic tape cassette handler;

(*d*) integrated disc unit;

(*e*) C.R.T. display unit;

(*f*) matrix printer;

(*g*) battery back-up unit to protect memory contents during power loss.

4. Processor. The general purpose processor is a powerful sixteen-bit word minicomputer, of modular design which allows system enhancements by plug-in circuit boards. The basic model has 64K bytes of M.O.S. (metal oxide semiconductor) memory expandable in 16K-byte increments to a maximum of 128K bytes (64 000 words). Solid-state M.O.S. memory was selected because of its inherently greater reliability and lower power consumption.

The processor and memory are housed in a cabinet which can also contain one or two integrated magnetic tape cassette handlers and one or two integrated disc drives capable of storing up to 9.8 megabytes (million bytes) of data each. The discs are mounted in a pull-out unit below the cassette handler. This single spindle unit holds one fixed two-surface disc and one removable two-surface disc. Each disc has a capacity of approximately 4.9 million bytes. An additional integrated pull-out disc unit may be added if required. The cabinet also contains interfacing logic for peripherals and terminals (*see* Fig. 17).

5. C.R.T. display unit (terminal). Visual display terminals provide direct man/machine interface for data entry and retrieval. Terminals have typewriter-format keyboards and a separate ten-key pad in standard calculator format for entry of all-numeric data. Data is displayed as black characters against a white background and displays twenty-four lines of eighty character positions each.

The system can accommodate multiple local or remote C.R.T. terminals, one of which is used as an operator's console. This is classed as "home" screen which can also be used as a work station. Display terminals enable file contents to be accessed for enquiry requirements and for instantaneous updating.

6. Matrix line printer. The printer is a free-standing peripheral capable of printing 180 characters per second. Each character consists of a pattern of dots in a seven by seven matrix. The characters are formed as the print element moves parallel to the platen, from left to right at a constant speed. The print element has a vertical column of seven equally-spaced wires, which are individually controlled. Activation of one or more of the solenoid-actuated print wires forces an inked ribbon against the paper and platen to form up to seven rows of horizontal dots. An entire printline is assembled and edited in a buffer set aside in the processor memory, then sent to the printer which is fully-buffered. It can be used as a remote printer, local printer, or as a slave printer to the C.R.T. display unit.

ADDITIONAL HARDWARE

7. Disc units. Additional freestanding disc units can be added to the system providing a maximum of almost 80 million bytes of randomly accessible data storage for applications requiring large files. Like the integrated units, freestanding disc drives each have one fixed and one removable double-surface platter that stores up to 4.9 megabytes. Average data transfer speed for each drive is over 312 kilobytes per second, i.e. over 312 000 bytes.

8. Magnetic tape handler. This unit provides industry standard magnetic tape files stored on seven-and-a-half inch (190.5 mm) reels containing 600 feet (182.88 m) of tape. The tape is nine-channel to accommodate an eight-bit byte plus a parity bit. The data transfer speed is either ten or twenty kilobytes (thousand bytes) per second depending upon recording density which can be either 800 b.p.i. (bytes per inch) or 1600 b.p.i.

9. Flexible disc unit. Single and dual flexible disc drives are available for data interchange. Each single-surface flexible disc stores up to 243K bytes. A dual spindle unit stores up to 486K bytes. Data transfer rate is thirty-one kilobytes (thousand bytes) per second.

10. Printers. As an alternative to the matrix printer several models of fully buffered printers are available to meet a wide range of reporting requirements. Line printers with speeds of 200 l.p.m. (lines per minute) or 300 l.p.m. can be used or a band printer operating at 600 l.p.m. The band on this type of printer is manufactured from stainless steel and contains 384 engraved characters. Printing is accomplished by a rotating hammer striking the ribbon and paper against the horizontally rotating steel band.

11. Card reader. This unit provides the system with automatic punched card input. The unit reads eighty-column cards at a rate of up to 300 cards per minute (c.p.m.). As a card is read an interface in the card reader translates each character from the twelve-bit card code to a corresponding eight-bit byte which is transmitted to the processor.

SOFTWARE

12. Operating system. The operating system for this minicomputer is IMOS III (Interactive Multiprogramming Operating System) which executes multiple programs or system processes including Cobol compilation, text editing, sorting, system commands, etc. Each job works with its assigned system resources, i.e. peripherals, disc files and memory. The multiprogramming environment is specifically designed to permit direct data entry and batch processing either locally or from remote locations. System execution time is divided among active jobs via a round-robin, interrupt-driven technique, which treats all user jobs with equal priority.

The software can be divided into three categories:

(a) memory-resident operating system;
(b) non-resident portions of the operating system;
(c) separate utility routines.

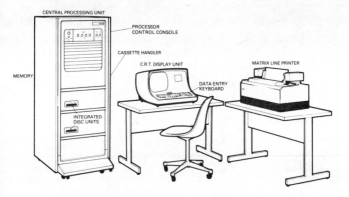

FIG. 17 *NCR 8250 general purpose minicomputer system: pictorial illustration of basic configuration*

The memory-resident portion of the operating system includes the following routines; interrupt service, C.P.U. scheduler, input/output control, physical block I/O, timer processing, logical I/O and primary system command processor and loader, error recovery, task manager, resource manager.

The majority of the non-resident portions of the operating system are brought into memory and executed as required. These modules are loaded into memory by the resident loaders.

13. Utility routines. These include the following:

(*a*) sorting utility, which sorts input data into ascending or descending alpha or numeric order on user specified keys;

(*b*) data capture utility, captures data generated to and from on-line devices; as data is captured it is stored in a runtime designated buffer; when a listing is desired, it can be output to an assigned printer;

(*c*) a log of all peripheral errors, which is maintained on the operating system disc;

(*d*) a tally of activity, which is kept relating to input messages and output messages between on-line terminals and remote printers and the processor. The tally can be printed out.

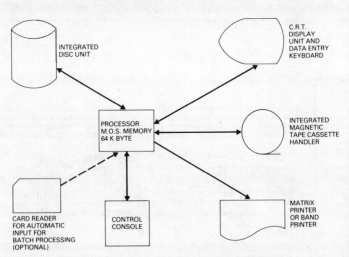

FIG. 18   *NCR 8250 general purpose minicomputer system: diagrammatic illustration of basic configuration*

14. Compiling. Available with the operating system is a one-pass memory resident compiler written to accept NCR IMOS Cobol statements. The source for Cobol compilation can be from a disc file, cassette file or punched card file. The source program will be converted into an executable object program which is output to disc and a compilation listing will be output to the printer including any errors.

PROGRESS TEST 4

1. (*a*) What features of the minicomputer distinguish it from the larger "third-generation" computer?

(*b*) For what applications is the minicomputer most suited?
(1, 2)

2. Outline the units in a typical general purpose minicomputer configuration. **(3–11)**

3. What software support would you expect a minicomputer to have? **(12–14)**

CHAPTER V

Microcomputers

DEVELOPMENT OF MICROTECHNOLOGY

1. Large scale integration. The year 1964 heralded the introduction of the third generation computers which were based on micro-integrated circuits; the technology of microminiaturisation. The circuits were built of a number of integrated components rather than individual components and were much smaller than the previous transistorised circuits (*see* III, **6**). Rapid development has since been made in producing chips only a few millimetres square containing many transistors. Currently it is possible to have about 100 000 components on a chip. This technology is referred to as L.S.I., i.e. large scale integration, which enables a complete processor to be etched on a single chip of silicon. A small computer consisting of a processor and memory based on L.S.I. technology is known as a microcomputer.

The processor chips are about 5 mm square and 0.1 mm thick. The memory of the computer also comprises silicon chips of about the same size. A complete computer also requires circuitry for the connection (interfacing) of peripherals with which to communicate with the microprocessor and a power supply (*see* Fig. 19).

Dual in-line packages (D.I.P.s) contain one chip which is an integrated circuit. Chips are mounted on a printed circuit board which is plugged into sockets on a bus for connection to other circuit boards. These boards are required for input, output and memory interfaces.

The processing power of microcomputers is increasing at a rapid rate due to advances in silicon technology. The technology is referred to as M.O.S.F.E.T. which stands for Metal Oxide Semiconductor Field Effect Transistor or sometimes Metal Oxide Silicon Field Effect Transistor. This technology is also referred to as M.O.S. (Metal Oxide Semiconductor) (*see* III, **29**).

Already microprocessors have evolved into a new generation of microcomputer with as much memory and processing power on a single chip as some minicomputers many times larger may have.

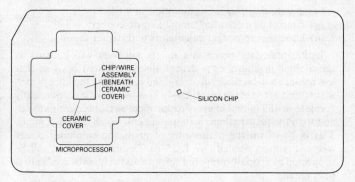

FIG. 19 *Silicon chip and microprocessor superimposed on a punched card*

These microcomputers and the more complex memory chips are so complex that they need to be designed with the aid of a computer, processed by computer-controlled machines and tested by a computer.

The first commercially available microcomputer was introduced by Intel in 1971. It is expected that by the mid-1980s that several millions of microscopic components will be placed on chips only the size of a soapflake. Semiconductor manufacturers would then be able to pack the equivalent of the largest computers onto a single chip.

A project to develop a cheap, large computer made up of dozens of microprocessors has been given Government backing. The project is called DEMOS which embraces hardware and software. DEMOS may have up to 250 micros and would be useful in real-time process control, distributed database and simulation applications.

2. Applications. Microprocessors have many potential applications including:

    (*a*) monitoring laboratory experiments;

    (*b*) controlling continuous processes such as chemicals and petrol refining;

    (*c*) word processing systems in the office;

    (*d*) banking terminals;

    (*e*) point-of-sale terminals;

(*f*) controlling petrol consumption in a motor car;
(*g*) control of a fully automatic electric cooker;
(*h*) basic unit in pocket calculators and digital watches.

In business data processing microcomputers will be used as stand-alone machines on a decentralised dedicated basis so that less reliance will be made on centralised computing facilities, which was a trend of the 1960s (*see* I, **23–4**). This will make it economically viable to install micros in every department as costs continue to fall and with the fact that microcomputers cost much less than minis. This is based on the philosophy of providing computer power where it is most needed (*see* I, **25–6**). Dedicated systems will be supported by specially prepared software in the form of application packages.

Administrative efficiency will be enhanced as the delays of processing data by a large central computer would be eliminated. On the other hand although distributed processing allows a high degree of autonomy and allows local processing of data on which to make decisions, much of the data generated in each operating unit is required centrally for corporate planning purposes (*see* I, **25**).

Because computer power is so inexpensive using microcomputers it is not necessary to operate it on a multi-shift system, unless the volume of data for processing warrants this, to justify its economic viability, as is normally the case with third generation mainframes. A few hours operation each week may amply justify the capital investment because of the cost savings which may be obtained from its use.

There is great concern, however, with regard to the effect of the micro on employment as they gradually take over the tasks formerly done by people. In some instances the concern is quite justified, but then there is always the opposite side of the coin to consider. In this case the micro is likely to stimulate the growth of new processes and new products which will create jobs—albeit of a different nature. This, of course, can be overcome by retraining—such is the way of technological advancement.

Micros will probably be used as hyper-intelligent terminals with more processing capability than current terminals. Accountants will use micros for analysing data, either by the use of personal micros or from a centralised computer databank, to produce management accounting reports.

3. Software. Users will be provided with standard package programs for specific applications which will allow the user to concentrate on the problem or task in hand rather than programming languages and computing problems. An important factor governing the use of micros particularly in accounting applications will be the cost of software which tends to be a high proportion of total system costs. In general, the cost of hardware tends to be falling while software as a percentage of total costs continues to rise.

Some micros have software compilers but others have "read-only" memory chips which contain the interpreter or compiler for converting programming language into machine code. Read-only memory is referred to as ROM and is a memory which is physically fixed and cannot be altered by writing over existing memory locations as is the case with normal memory (*see* III, **29**).

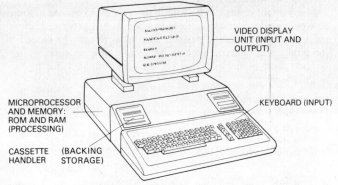

FIG. 20 *General impression of a basic microcomputer configuration*

A typical microcomputer configuration consists of a microprocessor with 4K ROM and 4K RAM (additional memory may be added optionally), a keyboard for the entry of data, a video display unit for displaying data entered into the system and the results of calculations and system messages, etc. and a cassette handler. In addition software support includes an operating system, interpreter and application programs (*see* Fig. 20).

OPERATOR-ORIENTED MICROCOMPUTER INFORMATION PROCESSING SYSTEM—NCR 8130

4. General system description. This is a larger type of microcomputer system with the option of using ledger cards, if desired, which many small companies prefer due to historical familiarity of using them in previous clerical and/or mechanical accounting machine systems. The microcomputer is a general purpose "business information processing system", which is the phrase currently in vogue for defining a data processing system.

The system allows data to be processed on a random, interactive, direct-entry basis which enables files to be updated immediately as transactions occur. As a result records show the current status which enables management to be provided with up-to-date information. If desired, the system may also be used in a batch processing mode. It may be used as a stand-alone processing system or two or more systems can be combined to form a distributed processing network for data interchange and access to a centrally located common database (*see* 1, **25**).

Many applications can be completely processed on-site in these networks while other applications can be partially processed before transmission to a central system. The network may be based on the public telephone network or on an in-house network.

The system is ideally suited for the traditional accounting applications such as:

(*a*) purchase ledger;
(*b*) sales ledger;
(*c*) payroll;
(*d*) stock control;
(*e*) general ledger.

The system can edit, format, validate and batch data, and receive data from a central system and prepare reports locally allowing decisions to be made on business situations based on the most recent information.

The system is operator-oriented and is easily learned and operated without skilled computer specialists. The operator can interrupt any program, make an enquiry to a specified record, receive the information and resume program operation. This is a distinct advantage over mainframe computers operating in batch mode as it is difficult to deal with random enquiries (*see* VII, **11**).

It must be appreciated however that this computer system can only run one program at a time so that if the payroll is being run it is not possible to implement nominal ledger or sales ledger enquiries, but instead only payroll enquiries. This is achieved under program control mainly by selecting the code for the payroll enquiry routine. The same considerations apply to any application —enquiries can only be made on the job running at the time.

HARDWARE

5. System configuration. The system consists of the following devices (*see* Fig. 21):

    (*a*) universal processing unit;
    (*b*) C.R.T. display;
    (*c*) visual record printer;
    (*d*) alphanumeric keyboard;
    (*e*) integrated flexible disc.

A freestanding matrix line printer may be substituted for the visual record printer; additional on-line data capacity may be provided by a freestanding flexible disc recorder; and a freestanding magnetic data cassette recorder may also be used for information interchange between NCR systems. Details will now be provided in respect of the basic system devices.

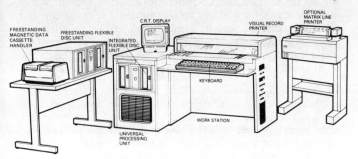

FIG. 21   *NCR 8130 operator-oriented information processing system—pictorial illustration of a microcomputer*

6. Universal processing unit. The processing unit contains a semiconductor memory (sixteen-bit word) of 64K bytes, direct memory access (D.M.A.) modules, power supply and control. The unit also contains the integrated flexible disc and interfaces with the keyboard and C.R.T. display. A memory support system energised by a battery protects the contents of internal storage during power failure, preventing a loss of data and the need to re-start processing.

7. Alphanumeric keyboard. The keyboard is used for the input of data and has the widely used alphanumeric typewriter keyboard arrangement. It also has a ten-key numeric pad, for high-speed entry of numeric data, and processing control keys. Key depressions are identified by an audible tone and errors by an alarm tone.

8. C.R.T. display. The C.R.T. display is the control centre of the system enabling the operator to read program instructions, system messages, keyboard data to be input and master file information. The display consists of white characters on a black screen. The large, dot matrix characters are easy to read and are displayed on sixteen lines with thirty-two characters a line providing a total display of 512 characters.

9. Visual record printer. The V.R.P. prepares audit journals, accounting records and reports printing at a speed of up to 180 characters per second. A bar code reader provides additional processing convenience as control information is encoded on ledger cards and other cut forms. The bar code may be encoded by the V.R.P. or included on pre-printed forms. It is used to access magnetic master file media either on magnetic disc or cassette. Bar codes can represent account identification, invoice numbers and other information. The screen displays the account number of the ledger card to be updated and the disc master file selects the appropriate ledger card to ensure use of the correct card.

10. Matrix line printer. As stated above, this printer may be substituted for the visual record printer. The printer can print invoices, cheques, accounting records and management reports in a wide variety of formats. The machine prints at fifty lines per minute. Each character is a seven by seven dot matrix.

11. Integrated flexible disc. This is the primary file device which is used for storing the operating system, application programs and master files. The two-drive recorder processes double density and single density flexible discs (floppy discs, *see* XIV, **36, 37**). It is a point of interest that all double density discs are recorded in A.S.C.I.I. format with a total capacity of 452 608 bytes. Single density discs are recorded in E.B.C.D.I.C. format to provide a total capacity of 242 944 bytes.

    (*a*) *A.S.C.I.I.*—American Standard Code for Information Interchange. A character code adopted as standard by the American National Standards Institute in 1963.

(b) *E.B.C.D.I.C*—Extended Binary Coded Decimal (B.C.D.) Interchange Code. Derived from the standard B.C.D. code (*see* Appendix II, **6**).

SOFTWARE

12. Application packages. Pre-prepared programs are available for common processing requirements. The packages are completely documented, including implementation and operation (*see* IX).

13. Operating system. The operating system is disc-based and controls operations from the work station to the magnetic file storage, printer and other peripherals. The system software communicates with and controls the application programs. This includes initiation and termination, data input and output, file management and control, on-line enquiry and general resource management. The operator is guided step-by-step through each operation.

14. Programming language. The system uses Cobol 74 with visual record extensions. Cobol is the universally accepted business language (*see* XVI, **15–19**).

15. Utility programs. A complete range of general purpose utility programs (utilities) controls day-to-day operating procedures and functions. Diagnostic routines are available for locating and correcting errors. An enquiry utility permits instant access to the on-line disc master files.

PROGRESS TEST 5

1. Outline the main characteristics of microtechnology.   (**1**)
2. Indicate potential applications for microprocessors.   (**2**)
3. Outline the uses of a microcomputer in business data processing.   (**2, 4**)
4. How may a microcomputer improve the administrative efficiency of a business?   (**2**)
5. Indicate the nature of software support for microcomputers.   (**3, 12–15**)
6. Outline the units in a typical microcomputer configuration for business use.   (**5–11**)

CHAPTER VI

Visible Record Computers

GENERAL OUTLINE

1. General features. Electronic accounting machines, in addition to producing basic documents often produce a visible record in the form of a ledger card. It is for this reason that this type of machine is called a Visible Record Computer (V.R.C.).

This type of computer updates ledger cards with current transaction data, unlike the larger computer installation which updates records held on magnetic tape or magnetic disc files, but not on ledger cards.

The V.R.C. was developed from the electro-mechanical keyboard accounting machine, incorporating the benefits of electronic technology. It provides electronic computer power on a smaller scale than the larger electronic computer installation, and is particularly suitable for the data processing needs of the medium-sized business, especially when the need to provide a more efficient method of processing arises.

The V.R.C. is often called an office computer or desk-top computer.

2. Types of electronic accounting machine (V.R.C.). There are two basic types of V.R.C., and they are distinguishable by the type of ledger card used. The first type uses a normal ledger card and is known as an *accounting computer*. The second type uses a magnetic stripe(s) ledger card for recording data and is known as a *magnetic ledger computer*.

ACCOUNTING COMPUTERS

This type of machine is operated in a similar manner to an electro-mechanical keyboard accounting machine, as the operator is required to enter brought forward balances from ledger cards by the keyboard for updating purposes. It is this operating feature which distinguishes the accounting computer from the magnetic ledger computer.

70

3. Applications. The accounting applications possible with this machine are quite wide, and include the following:

(*a*) *Sales accounting*—preparation of invoices, statements and ledger cards, etc.

(*b*) *Stock control*—posting of receipts and issues to stock record cards and the provision of stock summaries.

(*c*) *Payroll*—including pay advice slips and tax and earnings record cards.

(*d*) *Purchase ledger updating* and purchase summaries, etc.

MAGNETIC LEDGER COMPUTERS

This type of computer is very similar to the accounting computer, except that it has facilities for storing data magnetically either on a single stripe or on several stripes located either on the reverse side or front face of a ledger card. The ledger card is also printed on the front face in the normal manner, thereby providing both a visual and machine-sensible record.

The main difference in the operation of this machine centres on the magnetic stripe ledger card, which allows a greater degree of systems integration (*see below*).

4. Characteristics of the magnetic ledger computer. In general, the main features are similar to those of the accounting computer, except that facilities are provided for reading data from the magnetic stripe(s) into the internal memory for processing and writing data, after updating, to the magnetic stripe(s).

5. Magnetic stripe ledger card. When the ledger card is placed into the chute, the required data are automatically read and stored in the internal memory.

Input of variable data such as quantities despatched is by means of the keyboard, and after the data has been processed the basic document is printed (an invoice, for instance), and the ledger card is then updated both in print and magnetically.

The use of magnetic stripe ledger cards reduces the amount or data which the operator is required to enter by the keyboard. As a result, the speed of processing is increased as data is read and transferred into the memory at electronic speed instead of at the keying speed of the operator. The number of keying errors is also reduced, and the level of accuracy of the data being input increases.

The following type of information may be recorded on the magnetic stripe(s):

(a) *Sales ledger card:*
  (i) name and address of customer;
  (ii) customer account number;
  (iii) credit limit;
  (iv) balance outstanding;
  (v) analysis of balance outstanding—amount for the current period, amounts outstanding for one month, two months and three months and over;
  (vi) discount rate;
  (vii) area code.

(b) *Stock ledger card* (product record):
  (i) item code number;
  (ii) item description;
  (iii) unit of issue;
  (iv) unit selling price;
  (v) unit cost price;
  (vi) stock balance;
  (vii) re-order level;
  (viii) quantity ordered but outstanding;
  (ix) re-order quantity;
  (x) V.A.T. rate (or code depending upon whether the rate is stored in the internal memory instead of the magnetic stripe).

(c) *Payroll* (employees' personal tax and earnings record card):
  (i) employee number;
  (ii) employee name and address;
  (iii) P.A.Y.E. code number;
  (iv) N.H.I. rate;
  (v) hourly wage rate or salary;
  (vi) weekly or monthly free pay amount;
  (vii) gross earnings from previous employment;
  (viii) tax paid in previous employment;
  (ix) gross earnings year to date;
  (x) tax paid year to date;
  (xi) standard deductions.

6. Capacity of magnetic stripe. The capacity of the magnetic stripe varies between the various models of machine available, but a typical example is 384 bytes per side or 768 bytes per card.

7. Applications. The accounting applications for which this type of machine is used are similar to those of the accounting computer.

INTEGRATED SYSTEM APPLICATION USING A MAGNETIC LEDGER COMPUTER

It is possible to integrate what may otherwise be separate procedures with this type of machine, thereby eliminating unnecessary preparation and set-up time and achieving a reduction in the overall processing time.

The application to be outlined is a typical invoicing, sales ledger and stock ledger system, which should give the reader a clear understanding of the mode of operation of this type of machine.

8. Systems objective. The system is designed to achieve the following system requirements or outputs:

(a) preparation of an *invoice* for each customer's order received;

(b) updating appropriate *stock ledger cards* relating to each item invoiced and received (receipts not included for simplicity);

(c) updating appropriate sales ledger cards with the *amount of each invoice* and indicating accounts with balances which exceed credit limits;

(d) preparation of *statements of account* for each customer;

(e) preparation of a *back-order action report* to indicate stock shortages and items required to be re-ordered;

(f) preparation of an *aged analysis report*.

9. Preparation for processing. Before processing is commenced, it is necessary to carry out the following activities.

(a) *Obtain* the appropriate documents and records and report forms, e.g.:

   (i) batch of customers' orders;
   (ii) sales ledger file;
   (iii) stock ledger file;
   (iv) statements of account;
   (v) back-order action report;
   (vi) proof sheet;
   (vii) continuous stationery invoice sets;
   (viii) account balance action report.

(b) *Set up machine* (initial requirements):

   (i) load program;
   (ii) locate proof sheet round platen;
   (iii) insert continuous stationery for invoices.

10. Processing. The following activities are carried out after setting up the machine.

(*a*) Select *the first order* from the batch.

(*b*) Key in *customer's account number*.

(*c*) Select customer's *sales ledger card* and insert in machine.

(*d*) If the customer's *account number* does not agree with that keyed in, the ledger card is ejected, but if it is in agreement the customer's invoice address and delivery address (if different) is automatically read from the magnetic stripe(s) on the sales ledger card (together with other standard data) and printed on the invoice.

(*e*) Key in *stock item number*.

(*f*) Select stock ledger card for the *first item* on the customer's order selected and insert in machine.

(*i*) If the stock item number does not agree with that keyed in, the ledger card is ejected.

(*ii*) If the stock item number is in agreement with that keyed in by the operator, the operator then keys in the quantity ordered which causes the item code number, description, price and V.A.T. rate to be printed automatically on the invoice from the magnetic stripe(s) on the stock ledger card.

(*iii*) The value of the quantity ordered, discount and V.A.T. are automatically calculated and printed on the invoice.

(*iv*) If the quantity in stock is insufficient for the order, then the quantity available is printed and extended on the invoice.

(*v*) The invoice details are posted to the stock ledger card which in effect updates the ledger card in normal print and magnetically on the stripe(s).

(*vi*) The back-order action report for the item being processed is inserted in the machine in readiness for indicating if re-ordering is necessary.

(*vii*) In addition, stock shortages and back-order balances are recorded on the back-order action report and ledger card.

(*g*) The above procedure is *repeated for each item on the order* until all items have been processed. The sales ledger card is then re-inserted which causes:

(*i*) the invoice to be totalled and printed for the gross amount;

(*ii*) the net amounts to be totalled and printed;

(*iii*) the V.A.T. value to be totalled and printed and added to the net amount to produce the amount due on the invoice;

(*iv*) the sales ledger to be updated with the invoice amount, the customer's statement to be printed (after loading the appropriate stationery) and if the new account balance exceeds the customer's credit limit, it is indicated on both the customer's ledger card and an action report (having already been inserted in the machine). It is important to note that the ledger card is updated both magnetically on the stripe(s) and in print.

(*h*) The foregoing procedure is repeated for each customer's order, and at the end of the run each ledger card is inserted in the machine to produce an aged analysis report automatically.

It is possible to integrate other procedures in a similar manner, e.g. payroll and costing, expenditure analysis and budgetary control, etc.

GENERAL ASPECTS OF ELECTRONIC ACCOUNTING MACHINES

11. Processor memory. The memory of a processor is used for storing data before, during and after processing, prior to being printed in usable form.

Different machines have various types of internal memory, according to their basic design.

12. Programs. Programs are provided by the manufacturers for specific applications so it is not usual to employ programmers for this class of machine. Programs are stored either on cassettes or floppy discs.

13. Backing storage. Static reference files can be stored externally (off-line) in a similar way as for a larger computer. When processing is being carried out, the required information from backing storage is read into the memory of the processor.

Data held in backing storage may consist of files of customers' names and addresses, stock levels, wage rates and product prices, etc.

Types of backing storage in general use include:

(*a*) punched paper tape;
(*b*) punched cards;
(*c*) edge-punched cards;
(*d*) magnetic tape;
(*e*) magnetic stripe ledger cards;
(*f*) non-magnetic stripe ledger cards;
(*g*) magnetic disc;
(*h*) magnetic tape cassettes;
(*i*) floppy discs.

PHILIPS DATA SYSTEMS P410 SMALL BUSINESS COMPUTER

14. General considerations. This computer model has been classed as a V.R.C. because of its ability to use magnetic ledger cards. It is however a small business computer in its own right and this leads to the important consideration that even small machines have quite powerful computing facilities which makes it difficult to categorise specific machines into a particular class. Such is the case with this computer. This computer may be expanded from a basic model, referred to as the P410 Office computer system, by the addition of disc storage, display stations and line printers, etc.

15. Computer configuration. The larger "small business computer system" has the following configuration (*see* Fig. 22).

(*a*) *Processor.* The main memory capacity is expandable from 16 to 64K bytes of core storage in 8K or 16K increments. The basic model has a memory capacity of 24K to 32K. The control memory has a capacity of 6K (forty bits) of M.O.S. R.O.M. memory, i.e. Metal Oxide Semiconductor Read-Only Memory (*see* III, **29**).

(*b*) *Operator console.* This consists of an alphanumeric and a numeric keyboard, console line display and a console printer of the matrix type printing 100 c.p.s. There are also two front-feed devices (one for magnetic ledger cards) and two continuous-stationery feeds.

(*c*) *Magnetic tape cassette station.* The system can have up to four stations which may be used for storing data or, on the basic system, storing programs.

(*d*) *Magnetic disc unit.* There are two cartridges per drive one of which is fixed and one removable.

16. Other hardware. If required, various input and output peripherals may be added to the system including:

(*a*) card reader—300 c.p.m.;
(*b*) card punch—50 c.p.s.;
(*c*) line printer—200 l.p.m.;
(*d*) remote display or printer station;
(*e*) key-to-cassette data collection system.

17. Input. All operations are performed on a standard alphanumeric and numeric keyboard. Special equipment is available for collecting data on magnetic tape cassettes for batch processing applications.

18. Processing. Interactive processing is facilitated by a small, one-line display screen next to the keyboard. Part of the display is reserved for instructions from the machine to the operator. Another part of the display shows the data typed in by the keyboard so that it can be visually checked before being processed. Data can be processed interactively on a transaction basis or by batch processing both of which can be performed simultaneously and independently. Data for batch processing is read into the system from cassettes and processed without interference to operator input for transaction processing.

19. Storage—magnetic discs. Discs can be used for storing library programs which are called into operation as required by typing in their name on the keyboard. Fixed data such as customer addresses and product descriptions, etc. can also be stored on disc. The entry of a code number facilitates the printing of these fixed data items on relevant documents.

20. Storage—magnetic cassettes. Programs may be stored on cassettes if required. This particularly applies to the basic model.

21. Storage—magnetic ledger cards. Magnetic ledger cards may be used for storing fixed data and some variable data which are updated after each transaction. This is optional and may be used instead of magnetic discs.

22. Output. The system prints a summary of each transaction entered on ledger cards. Summaries of all transactions, daily journals and other print-outs are produced on continuous stationery. Printing is done by a matrix printer with a speed of 100 c.p.s.

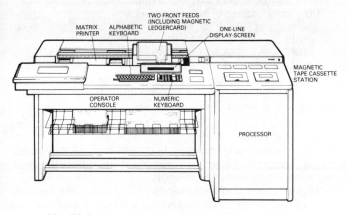

FIG. 22   *Philips Data Systems P410 small business computer: basic model*

23. Programming. Individual programs can be prepared by the user if necessary using either Cobol or Basic programming languages. This may be unnecessary however as a program library is available from the manufacturer in respect of basic applications common to many organisations.

ADVANTAGES AND DISADVANTAGES OF ELECTRONIC ACCOUNTING MACHINES

Although these machines originated from the electro-mechanical accounting machine, they are in effect computers, and in order to obtain the best results from their use the systems existing in a firm should be critically examined, so that the type of new machine most suitable for the needs of the business is installed.

In general, this class of machine provides a more efficient means of processing data than electro-mechanical accounting machines; the relative advantages and disadvantages are discussed below.

24. Advantages.

(*a*) *Electronic speed* of operation as compared with mechanical speed.

(*b*) Increased *internal storage capacity* for accounting data, totals, etc.

(*c*) Increased level of *automatic operation*, especially when using magnetic stripe ledger cards and peripheral units.

(*d*) Greater degree of *systems integration*.

(*e*) Increased *level of control* of processing by means of stored programs.

(*f*) *Electronic calculating* facilities.

(*g*) *Silent operation* (no moving parts).

(*h*) Scope easily enhanced by the addition of *peripherals*.

(*i*) Increased *reliability* through use of electronic components as opposed to mechanical moving parts.

In addition to their comparative advantages over accounting machines of the mechanical type, they also have advantages over the larger computer installation. In the first instance, they do not require a critically controlled environment, apart from the maintenance of a minimum temperature.

Highly trained staff are unnecessary, as the operator has only to learn a relatively simple sequence of keyboard operations since the processing operations are program-controlled. A competent operator is essential, however, as the output speed is determined by the speed and accuracy of the operator in the use of the keyboard.

25. Disadvantages.

(*a*) Higher *cost* of machine.

(*b*) Greater degree of *systems investigation and design* is necessary to provide for the level of systems integration required (this is, of course, offset by the benefits obtained).

(*c*) A greater degree of *disruption* may be incurred in the event of the absence of the operator or of machine malfunction.

PROGRESS TEST 6

1. Outline the general features of a visible record computer. **(1)**
2. There are two basic types of V.R.C.—those which are called accounting computers and those which are known as magnetic ledger computers. Indicate the characteristics of both types of machine. **(1–7)**
3. You have just attended a demonstration of a visible record computer. Draft a report of the findings of the demonstration under the following headings:

(*a*) definition of visible record computer;

(*b*) applications for which this type of equipment could be used;

(*c*) the main advantages and disadvantages of this type of equipment. [I.C.M.A.] **(1, 2, 8–10, 24, 25)**

CHAPTER VII

Processing Techniques (1)— Batch Processing

GENERAL OUTLINE OF TECHNIQUE

1. Definition of batch processing. The technique of batch processing is very widely applied in clerical, mechanical and electronic data processing systems. It is concerned with processing batches of related data for a defined period of time as the basis for obtaining processing efficiency. Many businesses have high volume routine data processing requirements and have installed batch processing computer configurations to obtain the benefits of high speed accurate data processing. The main features of a batch processing configuration are automatic input and output devices, which operate with a minimum of manual intervention under the control of a stored program after the devices have been loaded with transaction data and appropriate print-out stationery.

Batch processing operations relate to specific applications such as payroll, stock control, invoicing and sales ledger, purchases and purchase ledger and the nominal ledger, etc. Each application consists of a number of computer runs each of which is designed to accomplish a defined stage of processing in respect of each transaction (*see* **12**).

2. File conversion and creation. When applications are to be transferred to a computer the master files must be converted from their present form to a computer compatible form. This means the conversion of records from a visible form, on ledger cards, to an invisible form, on magnetic tapes or discs (*see* Fig. 23).

Before conversion, it is necessary to reconcile the balances and other data on existing records before punching the details of each record into a punched card. This procedure may necessitate punching data elements into a different sequence to that used at present. New code numbers may also be required in which case the existing codes must be converted to the new codes on the punched cards (*see* XV, **47–52**).

File conversion to punched cards creates a high volume punch-

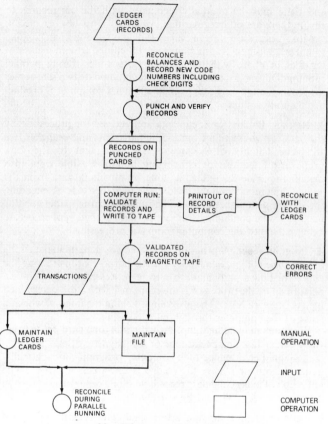

FIG. 23   *File conversion and creation*

ing operation and suitable arrangements must be made for this
commitment especially as the cards must also be verified. The
actual file conversion is not yet complete as the cards must be
further converted to magnetic media. This is accomplished by
transferring the data in cards to the processor by means of a card
reader. Card to tape, or disc conversion is then achieved by a data
validation program, already prepared in readiness for processing
the transaction data of the relevant application.

During the file conversion run the new records are printed out and these must be manually reconciled with the old records to ensure there are no irregularities. All errors must be corrected.

Most files are not static as variable data is for ever changing due to normal business transactions and difficulties arise in maintaining files in phase with the manual system files during parallel running. During this phase it is necessary to update two sets of files for reconciliation purposes to ensure that the computer is producing accurate results.

3. Batches. Batches of documents are received for processing by the data control section from user departments and branches (*see* **18**). The batches of documents are then sent to the data preparation section for converting human-sensible data into machine-sensible data. This is done by punching data from the source documents into punched cards or paper tape or encoding the data onto magnetic tape. The punched cards, paper tape or magnetic tape containing transaction data is then verified before being passed to the computer room for processing.

4. Program input. A program, prepared for a particular task, is fed into the computer memory for the purpose of instructing the processor how a particular job is to be processed. Each operation performed by the processor is in accordance with a pre-determined instruction (*see* XVI). The program is held in the internal working store of the computer throughout processing.

Programs may be held in punched cards (one card *per* instruction), paper tape, magnetic tape or on magnetic discs.

A single performance of a computer program on each transaction record or master file record is known as a "pass". The entire job of processing data records with one program is known as a "run" (*see* XV, **38**, and Figs. 100–107).

5. Data input. Current transaction data, with regard to earnings for each employee, sales to customers, purchases from suppliers and receipts and issues of stores items, etc., are input to the computer, usually by punched cards. The transaction data is punched into the cards by punch operators using a punching machine. The data is represented by holes in specific columns of each card. The holes are sensed by a card reader and the impulses transmitted into the data input area of the internal memory.

6. File amendments. The process of amending files has already been outlined (*see* I, II). However, it is considered that a practical exercise relating to file amendments will serve to clarify the procedure involved. For this purpose the following question has been selected from the June 1976 examinations of the Institute of Accounting Staff (I.A.S.). The wording of the question has been modified to some extent to serve the present purpose more specifically.

From the following, illustrate and explain the effect of file amendments on a newly created carried forward master file on magnetic tape.

OLD MASTER FILE

	Record number	Name	Credit Limit £	Balance due £
(1)	106075	Syson	5000	4275
(2)	106076	French	1000	450
(3)	106080	Bishop	2000	0000
(4)	106082	Osborne	4000	2500
(5)	106085	Corbett	8000	6350

AMENDMENT FILE

	Record number	Name	Transaction code	Credit Limit £	Balance due £
(A)	106076	French	1	7500	
(B)	106077	Green	3	4000	0000
(C)	106079	Ball	1	4250	
(D)	106080		2		
(E)	106082	Osborne	1	3000	

Transaction code: 1—Amendment
                     2—Deletion
                     3—Insertion

The solution to the question is outlined below:

The effect of applying the amendments to the file are shown as follows:

Record number	Name	Credit Limit £	Balance due £
106075	Syson	5000	4275
106076	French	7500	450
106077	Green	4000	0000
106082	Osborne	3000	2500
106085	Corbett	8000	6350

The following details provide an explanation of the amendments.

106075	Remains unchanged and is copied to the carried forward file
106076	Amendment to credit limit on carried forward file
106077	A new record to be added to the file
106079	Indicated as an amendment but does not exist on the file. The record is signalled as an error and excluded from the master file
106080	Deletion from the file
106082	Amendment to credit limit on carried forward file
106085	Remains unchanged and copied to carried forward file

Activities concerned with file amendments on magnetic tape include the reading in of a record to the processor's memory from the master file together with an amendment from the amendment file. The "key" fields are compared to establish if there is a match. Appropriate action is then taken either to write the record unchanged on the new file if it is not affected by an amendment, or if it is affected by an amendment it is adjusted in the memory before being written to the new file. If the amendment is a deletion, then the record is omitted from the new file but if it is a new record then it is added to the new file. All this must be effected before the master file is updated by transaction data. It is essential that records are amended before being used in processing.

7. Data processing. The processor, in accordance with the program, carries out the defined operation and transfers the results to the output area of internal memory. The processor performs the arithmetic operations of addition, subtraction, multiplication and division. It also performs the operations of shifting data and comparing data as well as testing for various conditions, e.g. the balance of items in stock compared with re-order levels, in accordance with the instructions contained in the program and takes appropriate action according to the results of the testing. Depending upon the type of computer installed, its operation is controlled and monitored by an operator either by means of a console unit, console typewriter or video monitor.

(*a*) *Console unit.* The console unit of a computer system provides the means for controlling and monitoring the operations of the computer by the operator. The operator, by means of push buttons, can switch the computer off and on, start or stop operations and read in programs and data as required. The contents of internal memory are also displayed on the console unit.

(*b*) *Electric typewriter* (*console typewriter*). The electric typewriter provides the means of communication between the computer system and the operator. The computer communicates by means of signals which actuate the typewriter, which prints messages indicating the end of processing, error conditions, advises that a tape unit requires to be loaded or that the line printer requires to be replenished with stationery (*see* III, **9**).

(*c*) *Video monitor. See* IV, **5** and V, **8**.

8. File updating. An important feature of batch processing is file updating and in this respect it is important to appreciate that all data and the records, to which the data relates, must be stored in the internal memory of the processor before any data processing operation or file updating is possible. In respect of data stored in punched cards this is transferred to the processor by a card reader. Records are transferred by means of the appropriate backing storage device, which is normally either a tape deck or disc drive, depending upon the media used for storing master files—magnetic tapes or discs.

Before processing commences the appropriate files are obtained from the tape and disc library by the computer operator. After updating they are returned to the library for storage until they are required for the next updating run. In the meanwhile the files are stored off-line and are not accessible by the computer until the next run and this creates problems with regard to facilitating random enquiries from user departments (*see* I, **5** and II).

File updating is performed systematically at pre-defined periods of time depending upon the circumstance. To some extent the frequency of processing data and file updating is dependent upon the volume of transactions in some instances because of the necessity of avoiding a build-up of data on the one hand and the need to achieve a smooth work throughout on the other (*see* I, **8**).

The preparation of invoices and updating the sales ledger master file may necessitate a daily run because of the relatively high volume of transactions involved. If it was performed weekly the processing time may be so long that it would preclude the processing of other important applications—the payroll for instance.

In some instances applications have natural updating and processing frequencies, a case in point being the factory payroll which has a natural weekly updating frequency. On the other hand a monthly staff payroll has a natural monthly updating frequency.

The frequency of updating is often dependent upon the information needs of management for business control. One instance of this is when the status of stocks is a key factor in running a business effectively, which necessitates daily updating because management require a daily schedule in order to be aware of shortages and excess stocks. Appropriate action is then effected in respect of purchase orders for raw materials and production orders in relation to sales orders.

9. File activity or "hit" rate. The proportion of records updated or referenced on each updating run in relation to the total number of records on a master file is referred to as the "hit" rate. This is a very important consideration in computer configuration deliberations regarding the type of storage media most suitable for specific applications, i.e. magnetic tape or magnetic disc.

In respect of magnetic tape files, it is necessary to access each record on the file serially, even though some of the records are not affected by current transactions. What is more, the whole of the file has to be rewritten on to a new tape file. In this case, a file with a low "hit" rate can increase processing time and would be better stored on magnetic disc, which has direct access capability. Direct access requires only those records affected by transactions to be accessed for updating. In addition, records stored on disc do not have to be written to a different disc after updating since records are overwritten.

As a payroll has a high "hit" rate, there is no advantage in storing it on magnetic disc, as every employee's record needs to be updated each pay period. Magnetic tape has a high storage capacity and is cheaper than magnetic discs. On the other hand, a stock file may contain records which are only affected by transactions occasionally, therefore the whole of the file does not change each time a computer run is made. In this case, processing time can be reduced by storing stock records on magnetic disc (*see* I, **15**).

10. Output. The results of processing operations are transferred from the output area of internal memory to a specified output device. In most cases, the output is produced by a printer, e.g. payslips, sales invoices, statements of account and purchase orders, etc. Transaction summaries and error reports may also be printed out.

The output may also consist of printed management control

reports, or in the form of results displayed on a remote cathode ray tube in response to an enquiry.

With modern developments, it is possible for output from one computer to be transmitted to another computer for further processing.

11. Problems of dealing with random enquiries. It has already been intimated that the off-line storage of master files creates problems in respect of random enquiries from user departments (*see* **8**). To deal with such enquiries on an individual basis is not economically viable, as it would necessitate the setting up of runs specially for each enquiry which would be very disruptive. If enquiries are sufficiently numerous, however, it may be viable to schedule a special enquiry run to deal with batches of enquiries. In this case, access to appropriate records such as customer or supplier accounts can be facilitated by an enquiry package program. When an application is run daily then the details printed out may be adequate to deal with enquiries and this avoids the necessity of arranging a special run thereby saving important processing time. A 24-hour turn-round time for dealing with enquiries may be suitable in most business instances but if this is inadequate an on-line enquiry system may be developed. In this instance, files must be stored on a direct access media such as discs, accessible by user departments by means of local enquiry terminals (*see* VIII, **1, 4**).

The main problem of dealing with enquiries on a batch processing computer configuration is the absence of human-sensible records, as these are stored on magnetic media which are only machine-sensible. In clerical (manual) and mechanised systems access to records for enquiry purposes is facilitated by loose leaf records and ledger cards. All that is necessary to deal with an enquiry is to refer to the appropriate record in the file.

12. Example of batch processing application-integrated order-entry system. Figure 24 outlines a typical batch processing application for processing incoming orders from customers. The application provides for the control of stocks, invoicing, sales ledger updating and sales analysis. This is an integrated system serving the needs of several functions and the results are accomplished by a suite of programs, as a separate program is required for each stage of processing—that is for each run. It is possible to achieve the same results by separately organised systems but this approach is not so effective as integrated systems. The various runs are organised as follows.

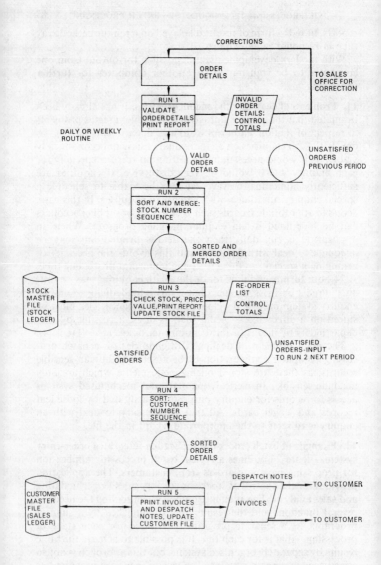

FIG. 24 *Integrated order-entry system*

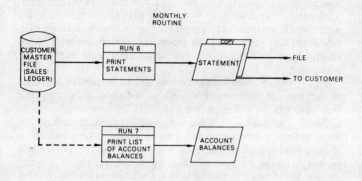

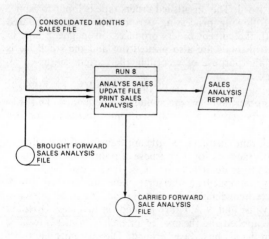

FIG. 24 (cont.)

Run 1. Order details are validated and a printed report is produced indicating order details which are invalid for various reasons, such as incorrect product details or omitted data elements. Such items are referred back to the sales office for correction. Valid order details are recorded on magnetic tape. Control totals are also calculated and printed on the report for comparison with batch control totals attached to the batches of documents received for processing.

Run 2. Valid transactions are sorted into stock number sequence to facilitate access to stock records stored on disc for checking stock availability and price, etc.

Run 3. The stock file on disc is accessed in accordance with the items ordered which are recorded on the magnetic tape from Run 2. The appropriate stock records are input to the processor's memory for the purpose of checking stock availability, pricing items ordered and calculating values. Order items for which there is sufficient stock are referred to as satisfied orders and those for which there is insufficient stock are referred to as unsatisfied orders. Each category is recorded on separate magnetic tapes.

A printed report is produced indicating those items of stock which require replenishment to satisfy order items which are at present unsatisfied. The unsatisfied orders tape is input to Run 2 during the following processing period. This is consolidated (merged) with the current orders produced on magnetic tape in Run 1. Control totals are also printed out and the stock file is updated for the purpose of recording the current status of all items in stock.

Run 4. The satisfied order items, already priced and valued, are sorted to customer number sequence on magnetic tape. This is to facilitate speedy access to relevant customer records stored on disc.

Run 5. Relevant customer records are transferred from disc to the processor's memory for the purpose of printing the customer's name and address details on invoices. Each customer's order requirements are input from the sorted tape produced in Run 4. From this tape item details in respect of product number, description, price, value and V.A.T. are printed on invoices. Discount rates are also applied and the invoice for each customer is totalled after all item details have been printed. The customer file (sales ledger file) is then updated with the value of goods supplied for recording the current balance owed by the customer. Despatch notes are also printed.

Run 6. At the end of the month customer records are accessed on the disc file for the purpose of printing statements of account. The statements are despatched to customers to inform them of their indebtedness.

Run 7. Also at the end of the month customer records are accessed on the disc file for the purpose of printing a list of account balances which may include an "age analysis" of such balances. This is for the purpose of credit control.

Run 8. At the month end, the month's consolidated sales file is input together with the brought forward sales analysis file. The sales are analysed perhaps by customer, product, area and salesman for providing information to sales management. This is facilitated by the printing of a sales analysis report. The sales analysis file is updated and a carried forward file produced.

FILE SECURITY

13. Purpose of file security. The purpose of a file security system is to provide a basis for reconstituting master files containing important business information, as it is possible to overwrite or erase a file in error.

It is essential that file security precautions be incorporated in those electronic computer data processing systems which store master files on a magnetic media, to safeguard against the consequences of loss of data, errors or corrupted data.

Without such precautions, it would be necessary to reprocess data, in the event of loss or corruption, from the last run when the file was known to be correct.

The re-processing of data for a number of previous runs is very disruptive to the work scheduled for the computer, and consequently has an adverse effect on the productivity of the electronic data processing (E.D.P.) department. It is, therefore, imperative that the reprocessing of data is kept to a minimum.

14. The generation technique of file security. In respect of master files recorded on magnetic tape, the technique of file security applied is known as the "generation" technique because files relating to two previous periods are retained transiently in addition to the current updated file and the current movement file. The two previous period files plus the current file comprise three generations, which are referred to as Grandfather—Father—Son. The technique operates as follows.

(a) The first master file produced is referred to as the "Son tape".

(b) The "Son tape" produced during the following updating run replaces the first "Son tape", which becomes the "Father tape".

(c) The next updating run produces a new "Son tape", the first "Son tape" (at present the "Father tape") becomes the "Grand-father tape". The previous "Son tape" now becomes the new "Father tape".

(d) On the next updating run, the original "Son tape" (now the "Grandfather tape") is overwritten, and can in fact be used for producing the new "Son tape" (*see* Fig. 25).

15. The dumping (copying) technique of file security. With regard to master files recorded on magnetic discs, the existing records are overwritten during updating, and consequently the previous records are destroyed.

File security in respect of disc files is often achieved by the technique of "dumping", which involves copying the updated records from one disc to another disc or to magnetic tape. In the event of loss of data on one disc, the situation is resolved by using the records for further processing from the spare disc or the magnetic tape reel on which the records were "dumped".

The records are retained in this manner until the next dump is carried out and proved to be free of errors and corrupted data.

It is also possible to apply the "generation" technique to disc files, by the retention of three generations of records either on one disc or on separate discs.

16. File safety. The records retained for re-generation purposes are filed for safety away from the computer centre, in case of damage by fire, etc. Therefore, even though the files retained in the computer centre are damaged or destroyed the records are still available in the remote filing location.

Other physical precautions which may be used to protect files from loss or damage include the following.

(a) A write-permit ring may be used to prevent overwriting of information on magnetic tape. When the ring is removed from the tape reel the file can only be read. When the ring is placed into position it depresses a plunger on the tape deck allowing the tape to be overwritten.

(b) Prevention of unauthorised access to computer room.

(c) Implement suitable security measures to prevent sabotage if this is a possibility. This may require security guards patrolling

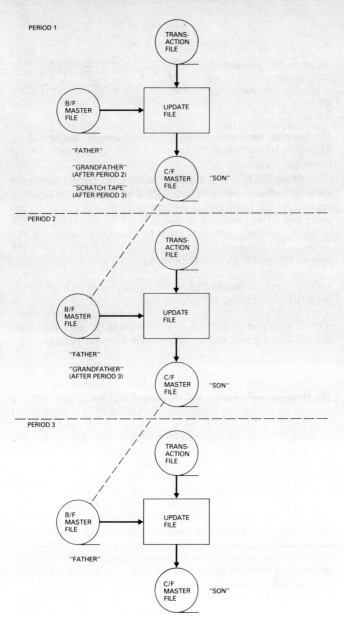

FIG. 25 *Generation technique of file security*

regularly and perhaps the installation of alarms connected to the local police station to signal a break-in.

(*d*) File labels encoded on magnetic files indicate the date when the information may be overwritten. Validation programs are used for this.

17. Ensuring the confidentiality of information on magnetic files. This is largely achieved by means of software and includes the following aspects.

(*a*) Particularly in time sharing systems it is normal practice for each authorised user to be provided with a password which is entered on the keyboard of the terminal and transmitted to the computer. The password is not printed or displayed on the terminal, however, so that it cannot be observed by anyone in the vicinity. The password allows access to specific files related to the user of the system (*see* VIII, Table V).

(*b*) Information on a file may be stored in a "scrambled" format which can only be decoded by providing the system with the decoding key to unscramble the information.

(*c*) Specific terminals may be prohibited from receiving transmitted information by lock-out procedures. In this way only designated terminals will actually receive file information.

DATA CONTROL

18. General considerations of data control. It is one thing to process data, quite another to know that all the necessary data required for processing has been received, processed, errors signalled and corrections made. In order to control the flow of data in and out of the data processing system, it is normal practice to incorporate a data control section in the data processing organisation.

The data control section receives all incoming data for processing from internal operating departments or outlying branches. The data may already be batched when received in readiness for data preparation operations, unless the data is already in a form suitable for direct input to the computer. Each batch of data has a batch control slip attached, on which is recorded batch number, department or branch number, document count (number of documents in the batch) and other control totals if relevant such as hash or meaningful totals.

Each batch is recorded in a register in the control section for maintaining a record of the date when the batch was received.

The batches may be vetted for correctness and completeness of data in general terms and then sent to the data preparation section for punching data into punched cards or paper tape or for encoding on magnetic tape. The data preparation section must also record control data such as department or branch number and batch number by writing this data on the paper tape. Data are, of course, verified to ensure the accuracy of data preparation operations before being sent for processing. After processing, the batches of documents and the printed output from the computer are sent to the data control section, where they are entered in the register as a record that all batches have been processed or otherwise. It is then necessary to check for errors discovered during processing, as outlined below.

19. Errors correction routine. When the printed documents from the computer are received by the control section, they are checked for errors, signalled by an error diagnostic code or alternatively a separate error list is printed.

One of the first tasks undertaken by the control section is to compare the control totals with those generated by the computer, as it is possible that documents may have been overlooked during data preparation and not presented for processing and it is therefore essential that the fugitive documents are identified, traced and presented for processing.

After errors have been identified, it is necessary to extract the appropriate input document from the batch for correction. Corrected errors are then re-assembled in a batch with a batch control slip attached for re-punching and processing. The new batch number is recorded on the print-out for cross-reference and control. The control of corrections is carried out in a similar manner to the control of original data.

DATA VALIDATION

20. Objectives of data validation. The objective of a data validation system is to detect errors at the earliest possible stage, before costly activities are performed on invalid data. It is therefore essential to ensure that source data is correctly recorded initially before data preparation (punching or encoding) takes place. Similarly, it is important to check the accuracy of data preparation operations before data is processed, and this is achieved by verification procedures.

When data is input for processing, it is subjected to a vetting procedure by means of an edit program which allows valid data to be written to the media to be used in subsequent processing—magnetic tape or disc.

Invalid data may either be written to another magnetic tape, or may be printed out on the line-printer as a special report, or errors may be indicated on the main report. The choice of method depends upon individual circumstances, and the manner in which the system is designed.

21. Validation checks. During the various stages of processing on the computer several types of check may be performed.

(*a*) Check to ensure that data are of the *correct type* in accordance with the program and master file.

(*b*) Check to ensure that data are for the *correct period*.

(*c*) Check to ensure that master files have the *correct generation indicator*.

(*d*) Check digit verification detects transposition errors when recording "key" fields on source documents in respect of customer account codes, stock codes or expenditure codes, etc. (*see* 22–4).

(*e*) Check to ensure that each character has the *correct number of bits*—parity check (hardware check).

(*f*) Check to ensure that records and transactions are in the *correct sequence*.

(*g*) Check to ensure that fields contain the *correct number and type of characters of the correct format*.

(*h*) Check to ensure that data *conforms to the minimum and maximum range of values*, for example, stock balances, gross wages and tax deductions, etc. As the range of specific items of data may be subject to fluctuation, the range limits may be punched into parameter cards and read in prior to a run instead of being incorporated in a program (*see* Figs. 100–6).

(*i*) In a nominal ledger computer application the validation of nominal ledger codes would be accomplished by reference to a nominal description file as an alternative to using check digits.

(*j*) In an order-entry system product codes would be validated by reference to a product file and customer account codes by reference to a customer file as an alternative to using check digits (*see* Fig. 26).

(*k*) Some errors may be detected by various types of check, e.g. a five-digit product code being used instead of a six-digit salesman code could be detected by a check on the type of transaction (*see*

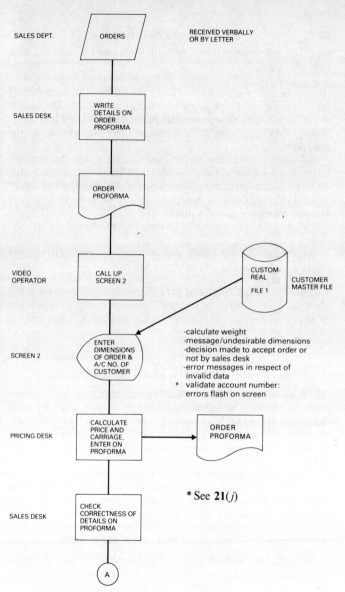

FIG. 26 *Order processing routine (illustrating validation of customer account number)*

(*a*)). The difference in the number of digits could be detected by a field check (*see* (*g*)).

(*l*) An error in the quantity of raw material being recorded in tonnes instead of kilograms could or should be detected by visual inspection rather than a computer validation program. The unit of weight is normally pre-recorded on punched cards recording transaction data and weight designations are pre-defined in the program.

(*m*) Compatibility checks are used to ensure that two or more data items are compatible with other data items. For instance, discounts to customers may be calculated on the basis of order quantity but the discount may only apply if the customers account balance is below a stated amount. This is clearly indicated by the I.C.M.A. question from the November 1976 examinations (*see* XV, **34**).

(*n*) Probability checks are used to avoid unnecessary rejection of data as data can on occasions exceed normal values in a range by purely random causes. If this arises with an acceptable frequency (probability) at a defined level of confidence (normally 95 per cent), then the data need not be rejected. This would tend to reduce the level of rejections and the time expended on investigating causes of divergences.

CHECK DIGIT VERIFICATION

22. Purpose of check digit verification. It is important to appreciate that the accuracy of output from data processing can only be as accurate as the input from which it is produced. Errors often occur in the initial recording and transcription of numerical data, such as stock numbers and account codes, frequently through transposition.

Check digit verification is a technique designed to test the accuracy (validity) of such numerical data before acceptance for processing. The data vet program performs check digit verification as part of the editing routine. Data is rejected as invalid when the check digit is any other number than the correct one. The data must then be re-punched and represented for processing.

23. Check digit. A check digit is a number which is added to a series of numbers (in the form of a code number for stock or customer identification) for the purpose of producing a "self-checking" number. Each check digit is derived arithmetically, and bears a unique mathematical relationship to the number to which it is attached. The check digit is normally added in the low-order position.

24. Modulus. Before indicating the way in which a check digit is calculated, it is necessary to understand what is meant by a "modulus". A modulus is the figure used to divide the number for which a check digit is required. Moduli in common use are 7, 10, 11 and 13.

25. Check digit calculation.

(*a*) Assume modulus 11 is selected for the purpose of calculating a check digit.

(*b*) Assume the number for which a check digit is required is 2323.

(*c*) Divide 2323 by 11 and note the remainder. Remainder is 2.

(*d*) Obtain the complement of the remainder and use this as the check digit. $11 - 2 = 9$ (complement = check digit).

(*e*) The number including its check digit now becomes 23239.

26. Calculation of a check digit using weights. A weight is the value allocated to each digit of a number according to a specified pattern, to prevent acceptance of interchanged digits. A more refined method of obtaining a check digit is achieved by the use of weights.

(*a*) Assume the same number and modulus as in the above example, i.e. 2323 and 11 respectively.

(*b*) The selected series of weights are 5, 4, 3, 2.

(*c*) Multiply each digit of the number by its corresponding weight as follows:

		Weight	*Product*
Units digit	3	2	6
Tens digit	2	3	6
Hundreds digit	3	4	12
Thousands digit	2	5	10
		Sum of products	34

(*d*) Divide sum of products by modulus 11 and note the remainder. Remainder is 1.

(*e*) Obtain the complement of the remainder and use this as the check digit: $11 - 1 = 10$ (assigned the letter **x**).

(f) The number including its check digit is 2323**x**.

A check may be applied to confirm that 10 or **x** is valid as follows:

Sum of the products   34
Add calculated check digit   <u>10</u>

                            <u><u>44</u></u>

Divide by modulus 11 and note any remainder.

As there is no remainder, the check digit is valid.

AUDITING AND THE COMPUTER

27. The approach to auditing computer applications. The work of both internal and external auditors is affected by the introduction of an electronic computer. While they need not be computer experts, they should be familiar with the mode of computer input, processing and output in order that they may conduct test checks with understanding. Auditors should also be familiar with computer programming so that they may recommend adequate controls to be built into the programs when they are being prepared. It is difficult and costly to amend programs once they have been completed, especially as they take a great deal of time to prepare initially. As we have seen, computer programs are becoming very complex with the development of integrated systems and exception reporting, which often eliminate intermediate result print-outs.

An earlier approach was known as "The Black Box" technique; the auditor extracted a sample of records and had them calculated manually. The results were then compared with the output from the computer and if there were no differences it was assumed that everything was satisfactory. In this respect, "The Black Box" was the computer and in order to audit records it was not necessary for the auditor to know anything about how the computer processed the data or about the programming techniques.

The auditor may, however, assume wider duties in the present electronic data processing era. He must as before observe the principles of *internal check*, the separation of functions to prevent collusion and fraudulent intent. This includes the separation of data origination, control of input by means of "batch totals", data preparation and processing, systems and programming.

28. Documentation of procedures. Other controls required are that procedures should be documented and routed through the internal audit department. This may consist of:

(a) procedure narrative;
(b) flowcharts (indicating processing steps);
(c) coded program together with a print-out from the computer;
(d) operating instructions for the computer operator;
(e) error routines;
(f) log sheets for recording computer operating and downtime;
(g) program modifications.

29. Checks and controls. It must be ensured that adequate control totals are kept before entry into the computer, which is usually done by the control section. Sometimes hash totals are used as a safeguard against data being lost or corrupted during processing (*see* **18** and **19**).

Validity checks are usually incorporated to test data against predetermined limits:

(a) date check—number of days in month;
(b) weekly wage level earned by employees;
(c) weekly tax level by employee.

Sequence checking is also done to ensure that records are in the correct order.

30. Testing of transactions. The testing of transactions may be achieved by means of:

(a) samples;
(b) statistical samples;
(c) spot checks;
(d) test packs (a set of punched cards holding program and data for a test run of a computer: the results are compared with precalculations);
(e) enquiry programs (Auditfind).

31. Computer time for checking purposes. Computer time must be placed at the disposal of the auditor for conducting such checks as necessary. It may also be necessary to have a print-out of static information contained in magnetic backing store, for example:

(a) material prices;
(b) product prices;
(c) wage rates;
(d) discount rates;

(*e*) credit limits;

(*f*) account details of suppliers and customers.

32. Original documents. Original documents should be held on file for further checks as necessary, i.e. clock cards, piecework tickets, despatch notes and orders, etc. There could be pressure, however, from personnel responsible for systems design to eliminate as many as possible of these original documents since the data could be prepared automatically as direct inputs by means of electronic counters, mark-sensed cards, by-product punched paper tape or magnetic tape from cash registers and time records, together with other data recorders.

ORGANISATION OF A MEDIUM-SIZED BATCH PROCESSING INSTALLATION

33. Main sections and types of staff. The sectional organisation of a batch processing installation is shown in Fig. 27 and may be summarised as follows.

(*a*) Head of department—data processing manager:

(*i*) responsible to: director of administration, managing director or company secretary according to specific requirements;

(*ii*) immediate subordinates: chief systems analyst, chief programmer and operations manager.

(*b*) Chief systems analyst responsible for activities of systems analysts.

(*c*) Chief programmer responsible for activities of programmers.

(*d*) Operations supervisor responsible for activities of chief computer operator and all operators, data preparation supervisor, tape and disc librarian and data control supervisor.

34. Principal duties of data processing manager. The duties of a D.P. manager may be summarised in the following manner:

(*a*) interpretation and execution of data processing policy as defined by the data processing steering committee or Board of directors;

(*b*) controlling immediate subordinates in the attainment of project objectives;

(*c*) participation in policy formulation;

(*d*) liaison with user departments to ensure their interests are fully provided for;

(*e*) ensuring that company policy is adhered to;

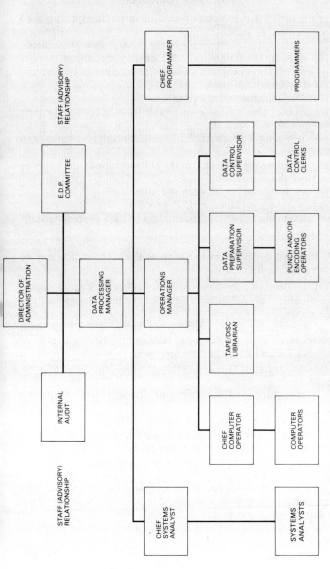

FIG. 27 *Organisation chart of batch processing computer installation*

(*f*) ensuring that computer operating instructions are updated when the need arises;

(*g*) assessing the effectiveness of file maintenance procedures;

(*h*) assessing the suitability of file security procedures;

(*i*) ensuring that program modifications are applied effectively;

(*j*) monitoring test runs;

(*k*) post implementation evaluation;

(*l*) ensuring that staff attend suitable training courses for their development;

(*m*) assessing performance of staff for salary awards and promotion;

(*n*) co-ordinating the whole of the D.P. operations and ensuring that work flows smoothly;

(*o*) resolving conflict between subordinates;

(*p*) providing guidance on D.P. problems;

(*q*) development and implementation of data processing standard (*see* XV, **5**).

35. Principal duties of chief systems analyst. The duties may be summarised as follows;

(*a*) liaison with user departments to ensure their requirements and problems are fully discussed before systems design and implementation;

(*b*) interpreting terms of reference before embarking upon systems investigations in order to establish the problem, areas of investigation and limits to the assignment;

(*c*) comparing the cost and performance of alternative processing methods and techniques;

(*d*) organising and co-ordinating the activities of systems analysts;

(*e*) reviewing performance of systems analysts;

(*f*) organising and reviewing systems documentation to ensure it complies with data processing standards;

(*g*) reviewing the progress of projects and reporting status to the D.P. manager;

(*h*) presenting recommendations to data processing and user department management with regard to possible courses of action or design philosophy to achieve defined objectives;

(*i*) co-ordinating the implementation of new or modified systems;

(*j*) reviewing performance of implemented systems and assessing the need for amendments or additional training of staff;

(*k*) discussion of proposals with chief programmer.

36. Principal duties of chief programmer. These are summarised below:

(*a*) liaison with chief systems analyst to determine philosophy of proposed systems and establish the type of programming language to use—high level or assembly code (low level);

(*b*) review of systems specification to establish the details of systems requirements before discussing these with assigned programmers;

(*c*) defining test data requirements and monitoring test runs;

(*d*) reviewing programmers' performance;

(*e*) reporting status of program development to D.P. manager.

37. Principal duties of operations manager. These are summarised as follows:

(*a*) control of all sections for which he is responsible, i.e. computer operations, data preparation and data control;

(*b*) development of operating schedules for all jobs to be run on the computer;

(*c*) ensuring that data is received on time from user departments;

(*d*) maintaining records on equipment utilisation;

(*e*) implementing standard procedures when appropriate to improve efficiency;

(*f*) controlling stocks of data processing supplies, tapes, stationery and punched cards, etc;

(*g*) maintaining a log of computer operations;

(*h*) report to D.P. manager of situations such as hardware malfunctions, staffing problems and other operational matters.

PROGRESS TEST 7

1. Define batch processing. (**1**)

2. After the formal approval of a system specification, the next stage in a computer project is to implement the newly-designed system. An essential part of implementation is file conversion whereby a master file, typically held on a magnetic medium, is created.

Explain, with the aid of a flowchart, the activity of file conversion and indicate the importance of this work. (**2** and Fig. 23) [A.C.A. June 1976, Q5]

3. Stock records, at present kept on a card index, are to be converted into a magnetic tape file. You are required to state:

(a) the main steps in the conversion; and

(b) the control procedures that would be included at each stage. (**2** and Fig. 23) [I.C.M.A. Nov. 1975, Q4]

4. Indicate the nature of batches of transaction data.   (**3**)

5. Outline the nature of batch processing activities.   (**4–8**)

6. Why is file activity or "hit" rate an important factor when considering the choice of storage media for master files?   (**9**)

7. Indicate the various methods of output from a computer system.   (**10**, *see also* XII)

8. What do you consider to be the inherent problems of dealing with random enquiries in batch processing applications?   (**11**)

9. Some computer systems are said to be based on the concept of integrated data processing. Explain, with reference to a suitable example, what is meant by the term "integrated data processing". (**12** and Fig. 24) [Part of A.C.A. Dec. 1976, Q7]

10. "The purpose of file security is to provide a basis for reconstituting master files stored on magnetic media in the event of loss or corruption of data contained in the files." Discuss this statement.   (**13**)

11. What do you understand by the term "Generation technique" of file security?   (**14**)

12. Due to a combination of an inexperienced operator and an electrical fault the main master file of 150,000 policy holders' records was destroyed.

Describe what precautions should have been taken so that the above situation could be retrieved in the case of:

(a) a tape based installation;

(b) a disc based installation.   (**14–16**) [I.C.M.A. Nov. 1978, Q7]

13. When is the "dumping" or "copying" technique of file security used?   (**15**)

14. What safeguards would you recommend for the protection of master files against fire?   (**16**)

15. A file containing highly confidential information is held on magnetic tape. Discuss in detail the procedures which should be adopted to:

(a) ensure the confidentiality of the data on file;

(b) protect the data from loss or damage.   (**16, 17**) [I.C.M.A. May 1978, Q4]

16. Outline the routine activities carried out in a data control section for controlling batches of data from receipt of basic documents to despatch of processed output.   (**18, 19**)

17. What are the objectives of validating data?   **(20)**

18. Input validation runs are designed to eliminate the processing of incorrect data. The procedure involves writing a program which contains checks to be applied to all or some of the data fields which make up a record. Briefly describe ten checks that could be performed during a validation run.   **(21–6)** [I.A.S. June 1978, Q5]

19. Explain, with relevant examples which are known to you, the following methods of ensuring the validity of data entering a computer system:

(*a*) punched card verification
(*b*) check digit verification
(*c*) range or limit tests.   **(21–6** and *see also* XIII, **2)** [A.C.A. June 1975, Q2]

20. Controls are invariably incorporated into the input, processing and output stages of a computer-based system.

(*a*) State the guidelines which should normally be followed in determining what controls should be built into a system.

(*b*) Identify and briefly describe one type of control which might be used to detect each of the following input data errors:

(*i*) error of transcription resulting in an incorrect customer account code;

(*ii*) quantity of raw material normally written in pounds weight but entered in error as tons;

(*iii*) entry on a despatch note for a product to be despatched from a warehouse which does not stock that particular product;

(*iv*) five digit product code used instead of a six digit salesman code;

(*v*) invalid expenditure code entered on an invoice.   **(20–6)** [A.C.A. June 1977, Q8]

21. (*a*) Distinguish between data verification and data validation.

(*b*) Briefly describe four of the main checks you would expect to find in a typical data validation program.   **(21–6** and *see also* XIII, **2)** [I.C.M.A. Nov. 1975, Q1]

22. (*a*) Draw a general schematic diagram of a validation routine assuming a computer configuration that has punched card input and magnetic tape storage.

(*b*) Describe FIVE types of checks that are commonly used within a validation program.   **(21** *see also* Figs. 24 and 102) [A.C.A. Dec. 1978, Q5]

23. Define what you understand by "check digit verification" and state the purpose of the technique. (**22–6**)

24. What is a check digit? (**23**)

25. What is a modulus? (**24**)

25. Indicate two methods of calculating check digits. (**25, 26**)

27. Outline what you consider are important considerations in the approach to auditing computer applications. (**27–32**)

28. Your company is considering the installation of a medium sized batch processing computer. You are required to outline:

(*a*) the organisation to be set up to manage the proposed facility, showing:

    (*i*) the main sections; and

    (*ii*) the types of staff required in each section;

(*b*) the principal duties of the data processing manager and of any two of the sectional managers. (**33–7** and Fig. 27) [I.C.M.A. May 1976, Q1]

29. Draft the organisation chart of a large computer department and outline the main duties of the sections reporting to the operations manager. To whom do you think the data processing manager should be responsible? Give your reasons. (**33–7** and Fig. 27) [A.C.A. Dec. 1975, Q3]

CHAPTER VIII

Processing Techniques (2)—On-line, Real-time, Multiprogramming and Time Sharing

ON-LINE PROCESSING

1. Definition of on-line processing. The technique of processing data by computer by means of terminals connected to, and controlled by, a central processor. In this way, various departments in a company can be connected to the processor by cables. If operating companies are a number of miles away from the processor then they are linked by means of telegraph or telephone lines (*see* Figs. 28, 55, 56).

This type of processing provides direct access to information files by terminal users and also enables them to update files with transaction data. Such systems are often used as a more efficient alternative to batch processing. In this case, instead of preparing data in a machine-sensible form for processing in batches at pre-defined periods of time, input of transaction data is effected by terminal at random time intervals (*see* XI for further aspects of data transmission).

2. On-line applications. Systems are being developed or are already in use for a wide range of applications in different types of industry including electricity and gas boards, banking, building societies, tour operators, retailing and stock exchanges, etc.

(*a*) *Electricity and gas boards.* By means of terminals situated in showrooms it is possible to inform prospective customers of the availability of appliances in response to their enquiries.

(*b*) *Banking.* It is possible to inform bank customers of the status of their account in response to an enquiry by accessing the relevant file using an on-line terminal.

(*c*) *Building societies.* The use of terminals to enter details of clients' transactions in respect of savings, investments and mortgage repayments from branches to the central computer.

(*d*) *Tour operators.* Reservation offices accept telephone enquiries from travel agents regarding the availability of holidays in respect of clients' enquiries. By means of terminals the availability of the required holiday can be checked and booked immediately.

(e) *Stock exchanges.* Terminals located in major stock exchanges throughout the country and the offices of participating brokerage firms enables the speedy processing of share dealings.

(f) *Stock control.* Terminals located in warehouses provide the means for automatic re-ordering of stocks, updating of stock records, reservations, follow-up of outstanding orders and the printing of picking lists, etc.

3. Remote job entry. "Remote job entry" or "remote batch processing" is a technique which enables batch processing to be employed by remote operating units by sharing a centrally located computer. For this purpose the remote operating units are equipped with data transmission facilities in the form of a bulk communications terminal for transmitting data in punched cards, paper tape or magnetic tape. The data is then processed at the central computer and the results may either be transmitted back to the remote operating units and printed on a local printer or they may be printed at the computer installation and despatched by post or messenger service to the remote units (*see* Figs. 5 and 56).

4. Comparison of on-line and real-time processing. Real-time systems process transactions in a time-scale that permits the effective control of business operations enabling them to optimise their performance. Computer based real-time systems are of necessity on-line systems as terminals connected to a remote processor are a basic requirement of such systems.

On-line systems are not necessarily real-time systems, however, as they are sometimes used as a more efficient alternative to batch processing. The use of on-line systems for updating files alleviates one of the problems associated with batch processing, regarding the problem of dealing with random enquiries. In this instance, files are updated continuously and the latest status of records in respect of customer accounts and stocks can be provided by direct access instant response facilities (*see* VII, **11**).

5. Communications software. On-line terminal operations are controlled by communications software, which control messages being transmitted by various terminals simultaneously. The software assembles and checks the messages before passing them to the computer, either for information retrieval requests or for file updating. For this purpose the communications software must

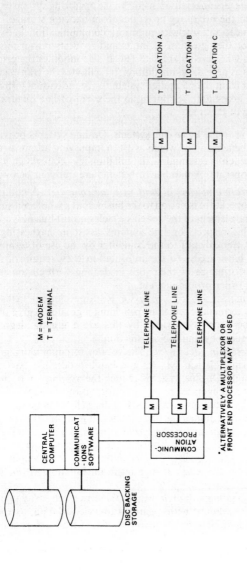

FIG. 28   On-line data transmission system

communicate terminal requirements to the operating system so that it can call in the necessary programs from backing storage.

Communications software monitors communication lines and terminals for the detection of faults and requests retransmission of messages when errors are detected. It also modifies the priority of terminals as necessary. In addition, it facilitates the transmission of messages from the computer system to the individual terminals which may necessitate re-routing in the event of line or terminal faults being discovered.

6. Benefits provided by on-line systems. On-line systems provide a number of benefits all of which assist in improving administrative efficiency which is essential in the inflationary economy in which businesses operate. A number of benefits are outlined below.

(a) *Integration of clerical staff with the computer.* A computer should not operate in isolation to the business as a whole but should be an integral element of the systems which support business operations. In this respect, on-line systems assist in harnessing the activities of clerical staff to the computer by the use of terminals. They then have access to the information they require for the efficient performance of their jobs in dealing with customer enquiries and order processing, etc.

(b) *Elimination of tedious tasks.* Routine clerical tasks are replaced by terminal operations providing a greater degree of job interest. The benefits provided by this are a greater degree of operating efficiency and job satisfaction.

(c) *Reduction in paper work.* The volume of paper work generated by normal clerical systems and batch processing systems is relatively high. On-line systems reduce the volume of printouts required for management reports as information may be displayed on terminal screens on demand. To reduce the volume of paperwork assists in stemming the tide of increasing administrative costs.

(d) *Improved accuracy.* As terminal messages are checked for accuracy before being transmitted to the computer by data validation programs the quality of information in a system will increase as input errors are reduced. As a result information will be more reliable.

(e) *File updating improved.* Master files are more easily updated by terminal keyboard with regard to transaction data, as special runs do not require to be set-up as is the case with batch processing applications.

(f) *Management information more readily available.* Management information becomes more readily available by direct access facilities, which enables managers to obtain a greater degree of control of the operations for which they are responsible.

(*g*) *Improved customer service.* Improvements in the level of customer service can be expected in those systems concerned with appliance sales, holiday bookings and account enquiries, etc.

(*h*) *Reduced data preparation costs.* On-line systems dispense with the need to convert human-sensible data into machine-sensible data thereby eliminating punching and verifying operations. This saves time and the costs associated with such operations. Data is input in a shorter time-scale as a result and processing as a whole becomes more cost effective. (*See* IX for examples of interactive processing applications.)

REAL-TIME PROCESSING

7. Real-time concept. The concept of real-time has already been outlined, *see* III, **14**, but it is important to appreciate that the use of a computer for real-time processing, although often a practical necessity, is not automatically implied. If, for instance, a perpetual inventory technique is applied to a clerical stock control system and all stock transactions recorded immediately they occur, rather than at defined periods of time then, in effect, it is a real-time system. This type of system, however, may have a slow "response time" in the provision of management information and the updating process may be slow due to the volume of transactions. Therein lie some of the reasons why a computer is necessary, particularly as some types of business have dispersed operations such as airlines with dispersed booking offices.

Some computer systems are dedicated to real-time operations and others are designed to operate in both batch and real-time mode.

8. Master files. In real-time systems, master files containing operating information are normally stored on magnetic disc and need to be permanently on-line to the processor for updating and retrieval requirements. Whereas with batch processing applications the master files are stored off-line between processing runs.

9. Output. Real-time systems display information on the screen of V.D.U. terminals in a transitory manner, which contrasts with batch processing systems which have a predominance of print-outs. Even while information is being displayed on a V.D.U. screen in response to a request for such information, its status can be seen to change as events occurring in other dispersed locations are updated on the information file.

10. Operating systems. An essential element of a real-time system is software in the form of an operating system which, in respect of a combined batch and real-time computer configuration, provides interrupt facilities to deal with real-time requirements. The interrupted batch program(s) is temporarily transferred to backing storage and the program required to deal with the real-time operation is called into the processor's memory. After the real-time operation has been dealt with the interrupted program is transferred back to internal storage from backing storage and processing is recommenced from a "re-start" point. All of which takes but a few seconds.

11. Processing steps. Real-time processing processes each transaction or message through all relevant steps, whereas batch processing processes all transactions through specific steps before proceeding with other steps. The structure of processing steps is stipulated in the run sequence.

12. Dynamic nature of real-time systems. Real-time systems are dynamic as they accept random input at random time intervals and the status of files change dynamically as a result. It is this characteristic which makes it difficult to audit or recover the system in the event of system failure. Both of these factors are provided for by means of periodic check points, say every 2 to 3 minutes, at which point all relevant restart and audit information are dumped to magnetic tape. The dumps can be used to restart the system.

MULTIPROGRAMMING

13. Definition of multiprogramming. A small computer installation may process one program at a time and find that it is quite adequate for its processing load. In such instances the running of the application programs is controlled by a basic control program such as ICL 1900 series Executive.

Eventually as more applications are transferred to the computer, it may be found that there is insufficient processing capability operating on the present basis of one program at a time. Multiprogramming may then need to be considered whereby two or more

TABLE IV COMPARISON OF BATCH AND REAL-TIME
PROCESSING SYSTEMS

Batch processing	*Real-time processing*
1. Routine high volume applications: —Invoicing —Payroll —Sales ledger updating —Stock ledger updating —Nominal ledger updating	1. Business control applications: —Steel making —Stock control —Airline operations and aircraft seat reservations
2. Data collected for a defined period of time and processed in batches	2. Random data input at random time intervals as events occur
3. No direct access to system by user departments	3. Direct access to system by user departments using terminals
4. Files only on-line during a processing run	4. Files permanently on-line
5. Magnetic tape files may be used for sequential access to records. Disc files may be used as an alternative to increase processing productivity by restricting access to records affected by current transactions— particularly useful means of storage for low hit-rate files	5. Direct access files only— usually magnetic discs
6. Information on master files only as up to date as last updating run	6. Information on master files updated dynamically as events occur
7. Detailed documents, reports and transaction lists printed	7. Information normally displayed on a V.D.U. screen as messages. As an alternative, messages may be printed on a teletype terminal

TABLE IV   COMPARISON OF BATCH AND REAL-TIME
PROCESSING SYSTEMS (*cont.*)

Batch processing	Real-time processing
8. Audit trails facilitated by printing out lists of trans-actions applied during updating and by printing out file contents using an audit package	8. Audit trails not so well provided for as control is centred around the number of messages input rather than details of transactions
9. All transactions recorded on source documents which must be converted to machine-sensible input by costly and time consuming data preparation operations	9. Transaction details input directly by terminal keyboard, sometimes from source documents, sometimes not, depending upon the system. Absence of costly and time consuming data preparation operations
10. Information from computer files only accessible during a specially set-up run	10. Information permanently accessible on demand

programs can be processed concurrently. This enables over-all processing time for all programs to be reduced even though the time required to process individual programs may be increased due to switching between programs. Such operations are still controlled by the basic control program but the computer operations staff are responsible for determining the program mix, that is the programs which are to be run together, and the order in which they are to be run. This is referred to as work scheduling and in a large installation it becomes a complex and time consuming task. (*See below.*)

14. Operating system. As the purpose of multiprogramming is to increase the utilisation of the computer system as a whole, there is a need to employ more powerful software in the form of an operating system incorporating automatic work scheduling features. A programmer may then specify scheduling factors in a "job description" which allows the operating system to perform work scheduling activities automatically. A "job description" specifies the name of the job, the peripherals (input and output devices) required, priorities, the streams of data to be input and output and the time programs take to run.

15. Mode of operation. Multiprogramming operates in the following way—when processing is interrupted on one program, perhaps to attend to an input or output transfer, the processor switches to another program. This enables all parts of the system, the processor and input and output peripherals to be operated concurrently thereby utilising the whole system more fully. When operating on one program at a time the processor or peripherals would be idle for a large proportion of the total processing time even though this would be reduced to some extent by buffering. Buffering enables the processor to execute another instruction whilst input or output is taking place rather than being idle whilst the transfer was completed. Even so, when processing one program at a time, basic peripherals are used for input and output such as card readers and line printers which, being mechanical, are slow compared to the electronic speed of the processor and this causes imbalance in the system as a whole.

16. Off-lining. Multiprogramming employs the technique of "off-lining" which requires the transfer of data from punched cards (or paper tape) to magnetic media, such as discs, before programs are run. Similarly, output from some programs would also be output to magnetic media for printing when the printer becomes available. In this way it is possible to process the payroll and prepare invoices by loading both programs into the main memory. While the line printer is printing an invoice line the processor switches to the payroll. Afterwards the processor reverts back to the invoice application. As the printer is being used for printing invoices, payroll data would be recorded on magnetic media for later conversion when the printer is available.

TIME SHARING

17. Time sharing defined. Time sharing is an on-line processing technique which enables many users to gain access to a centrally located computer by means of terminals. Each user is geographically remote from the computer and from each other. Each user is also unaware that the computer is being accessed by anyone else which creates the impression of having a computer for one's sole use. This is made possible by the computer continually switching between the various terminals at extremely high speed under the control of an operating system. These facilities may be provided either by an in-house installation or by a computer time sharing bureau.

18. Terminals. There are basically two types of terminal used in time sharing applications; one type is the well-known teletypewriter which is a machine similar to an electric typewriter but which has communication facilities like a teleprinter. The other type is a visual display unit (V.D.U.), which is a device similar in appearance to a television screen except that it also has a keyboard for entering data or instructions into the computer system.

Terminals can be connected to any office telephone extension but a modem or acoustic coupler is required for converting digital signals transmitted by terminals into analog signals required by telephone lines. As a terminal may be connected to any telephone extension this provides complete flexibility in the use of terminals within an organisation as they may be located in any executive's office. In fact the author has used a portable terminal sitting on a settee in the lounge of a friend's home which was connected to a computer in London by the domestic telephone. This facility means that executives or representatives can use a computer from a hotel room whilst on a roving commission if required.

19. Accessing the computer for time sharing operations. The stages outlined below indicate the various activities necessary for accessing and using a centrally-located time sharing computer by a remote terminal.

(*a*) Plug in terminal and acoustic coupler to power supply, perhaps using a two-way adaptor.

(*b*) Switch on mains power supply.

(*c*) Switch on acoustic coupler—a red light glows.

(*d*) Set acoustic coupler to full duplex operation.

(*e*) Set terminal (teletypewriter) to full duplex operation.

(*f*) Use telephone to dial computer direct or via a regional office multiplexor of the time sharing bureau. Gaining access to the computer, say in London, direct incurs long distance call charges, whereas going via the regional office only involves local call charges.

(*g*) When contact is established with the computer it responds by transmitting a high-pitched whistle.

(*h*) Place telephone in acoustic coupler and close lid—a green light glows.

(*i*) Log into the system (*see* **20**).

(*j*) Use the system for required purpose (*see* Fig. 29).

(*k*) Log out of the system (*see* **20**).

(*l*) Switch off power supply, remove telephone from acoustic coupler and replace.

```
TSL FILES A/B
WHICH SYSTEM ?




                B
TSL FILES B TSLB11 15:40:58 TTY141

.LOGIN
JOB 15 TSL FILES B TSLB11 TTY141
ID: 2663,10025
PASSWORD:

ACCT REF: RHODES,STAFF
1542    11-MAY-76        TUE

.XBASIC

NEW OR OLD--NEW
NEW FILE NAME--PRINT
READY
100   PRINT 23.2,23.2↑2,23.2↑3
110   END
RUN


PRINT   11-MAY-76        15:44:43


 23.2           538.24          12487.2

READY
SYSTEM

EXIT

.KJOB
CONFIRM: F
JOB 15, USER [2663,10025] LOGGED OFF TTY141    1546   11-MAY-76
CONNECT TIME 00:03:49 PRU 1
```

FIG. 29   *Logging in and out of a time sharing system*

20. Logging in and logging out procedure. Figure 29 shows a terminal record of the stages undertaken for logging in and out of a time sharing system. To assist the reader in understanding the printout Table V will serve to illustrate the various responses of the computer and system user. 1, 2, 3, etc. are steps in the procedure.

TABLE V   ANALYSIS OF RESPONSES OF THE
COMPUTER AND SYSTEM USER

Computer responses	User responses	
1. TSL FILES A/B WHICH SYSTEM?	2. B	(CR)
3. TSL FILES B TSLBII 15:40:58 TTY141	4. LOGIN	(CR)
5. ID:	6. 2663,10025	(CR)
7. PASSWORD:	8. (Password entered on keyboard but not printed for security purposes) (CR)	
9. ACCT REF:	10. RHODES,STAFF	(CR)
11. 1542 11-MAY-76 TUE	12. XBASIC	(CR)
13. NEW OR OLD—	14. NEW	(CR)
15. NEW FILE NAME—	16. PRINT	(CR)
17. READY	18. 100 PRINT 23.2,23.2↑2,23.2↑3	(CR)
	110 END	(CR)
	RUN	(CR)
19. PRINT 11-MAY-76 15:44:43 23.2 538.24 12487.2 READY	20. SYSTEM	(CR)
21. EXIT	22. KJOB	(CR)
23. CONFIRM:	24. F	
25. JOB 15, USER [2663,10025] LOGGED OFF TTY141 1546 11-MAY-76 CONNECT TIME 00:03:49 PRU 1	} Computer response	

Observations on computer and user responses:

1. WHICH SYSTEM?	This is an enquiry which system the user wishes to be connected to as the time sharing bureau has several systems.

Computer responses	User responses
2. (CR)	The user must depress the carriage return key (CR) on the terminal after entering each line as shown on the printout.
3. TSLBII	Assigned job number.
4. 15:40:58	Time of logging in.
5. TTY141	Channel number.
6.	Monitor dot which indicates that the user can go ahead.
7. ID:	Request for user's account code.
8. PASSWORD:	Request for user's password which enables the user to gain access to computer files and programs.
9. ACCT REF:	Details of job to be entered on invoice charging for the services provided by the time sharing bureau. Used for reference purposes.
10. 1542 11-MAY-76 TUE	The time, date and day the user was connected to the system.
11. XBASIC	Connects the user to the system for using BASIC programming commands and instructions. XBASIC means extended BASIC language.
12. NEW OR OLD—	The system is asking the user whether a previous program held in backing storage is to be used or whether a new one is to be developed.
13. NEW FILE NAME—	The system is asking the user to provide a name for the file to be developed.
14. READY	BASIC system awaiting commands or instructions from the user.

TABLE V   ANALYSIS OF RESPONSES OF THE
COMPUTER AND SYSTEM USER (*cont.*)

Computer responses	*User responses*
15. 1Ø0 PRINT, 11Ø END, etc.	User developed program.
16. PRINT 11-MAY-76, etc.	File heading, i.e. title of report printed out containing results of processing.
17. 23.2 538.24, etc.	Calculated results.
18. SYSTEM	Transfer to system monitor in readiness for logging out after completing job.
19. EXIT	User informed that he has left the BASIC system.
20. KJOB	Terminate connection—kill job.
21. CONFIRM:	Requires user to confirm that he wishes to leave the system.
22. F	Response to CONFIRM—achieves a fast log out from the system.
23. ØØ:Ø3:49	The time connected to the system—hours, minutes and seconds. (Basis of charging.)
24. PRU 1	Processor time used—processor units. (Basis of charging.)

21. Time sharing operations. Time sharing facilities provide direct access to a computer for obtaining instant responses to questions asked or statements made in an interactive conversational mode. This means that both the user and the computer converse by transmitting messages to each other. The user types messages or commands on a terminal keyboard which are then transmitted to the computer. The computer responds by transmitting messages to the terminal which are either printed or displayed on the screen depending upon the type of terminal used.

By this means accountants, corporate planners and managers are assisted in their activities concerned with planning and problem solving involving sensitivity analysis, network planning, linear programming, capital budgeting and trend forecasting, etc. These requirements are facilitated by library programs which may be called in for use as required. Alternatively, it is possible to develop one's own programs. In either case the computer calculates the data input by the user and provides the results in the format required—either a printed report format or, in some instances, a graphical display.

22. Programming for time sharing. As most users of time sharing systems are not computer programmers, relatively simple languages have been developed to enable users to converse with the computer at command level. One such language is known as BASIC—*B*eginners *A*ll purpose, *S*ymbolic *I*nstruction *C*ode.

A few rules of writing a Basic program are:

   (*a*) each line contains one program statement;

   (*b*) each line begins with a line number which is used to sequence the statements;

   (*c*) each program statement begins with a key word or command;

   (*d*) arithmetic operations are signified by special symbols:

       (*i*) ↑ Exponentiation (raising to a power);
       (*ii*) * Multiplication;
       (*iii*) / Division;
       (*iv*) + Addition;
       (*v*) − Subtraction;

   (*e*) variable names can be used to refer to values subject to calculation.

For example, if it was required to write a program to calculate and print the mean of five numbers it could be prepared and input for execution in the following way:

```
100 INPUT A,B,C,D,E
110 M = (A + B + C + D + E)/5
120 PRINT "MEAN" = ;M
130 END
```

As an additional example, if it was required to calculate and print 132, 132^2, 132^3 the program could be prepared as follows:

```
100 PRINT 132, 132 ↑ 2, 132 ↑ 3
110 END
```

Alternatively the program could have been written:

```
100 PRINT 132, 132*132, 132*132*132
110 END
```

A simple program to value items in stock may be compiled as follows:

```
100 PRINT "STOCK VALUATION"
200 READ C, Q, P
300 V = Q*P
400 PRINT C, Q, P, V
500 DATA 656, 200, 1.5
600 END
```

C = Code number of stock item
Q = Quantity in stock
P = Item price
V = Value of items in stock (Q × P)

The use of such variables as Q and P enables the same program to be used for similar calculations for any number of stock items with different values in respect of Q and P.

Programs may be entered through the keyboard of the terminal or may be pre-punched into paper tape and read in automatically by the paper tape reading device on the terminal.

PROGRESS TEST 8

1. Define and give examples of on-line processing applications. (1–3)

2. Distinguish between on-line and real time processing. Give an example of a commercial data processing application where real time processing would be applicable and explain what characteristics make it necessary to consider this type of processing. (4, *see also* III, 14 and Table IV) [I.C.M.A. May 1976, Q6]

3. Indicate the nature of software for the control of on-line terminals. (5)

4. Outline the benefits provided by on-line processing applications. (6)

5. (*a*) What is meant by the term "real-time" processing?

(*b*) Explain the hardware and software facilities which are required for the operation of a real-time system. (4, 5, 7–12 and *see also* III, 14, 15) [A.C.A. June 1975, Q4]

6. Compare the different characteristics of batch and real-time processing. (Table IV)

7. (*a*) What are the characteristics of a real-time processing system?

(*b*) Give the advantages and disadvantages of a real-time system together with TWO examples of such a system.   (**4, 6–12**, and *see also* III, **14, 15**) [A.C.A. Dec. 1978, Q3]

8. Define multiprogramming. Discuss the hardware and software facilities necessary to facilitate multiprogramming.   (**13–16**)
[I.C.M.A. Nov. 1978, Q6]

9. "Time sharing is an on-line interactive processing technique which enables many users to gain access to a centrally-located computer by means of terminals." Indicate the main features of time sharing operations.   (**17–22**)

CHAPTER IX

Processing Techniques (3)—Interactive Processing Applications

BASIC CONSIDERATIONS

1. Nature of interactive processing. There is a tendency at the present time for many computer applications to be processed using the interactive processing technique (*see* IV and V). The technique is interactive in the sense that the user and the computer communicate with each other in a conversational mode by means of a terminal, usually a V.D.U. with a keyboard. The technique is also referred to as "transaction-driven" processing as transactions are dealt with completely on an individual basis through all the relevant processing operations before dealing with the next transaction. This is in distinction to batch processing which processes transactions in batches through each processing stage, i.e. validation, sorting, calculating, updating and printing, etc.

Transaction data is input either by a computer operator using a terminal or, alternatively, from remote points such as sales offices, warehouses, factory departments or accounts office according to the needs of a given application. Interactive processing allows files to be updated as transactions occur and enquiries to be dealt with on an immediate response basis.

Although on-line processing has already been outlined in VIII, and interactive processing falls into this category, or may even be classified as real-time, the technique is outlined separately in this chapter to define the specific nature of on-line processing, as some on-line applications are not fully interactive. For instance, some on-line order entry systems only enter order details into the system via a terminal—the transactions are not fully dealt with as they occur but are stored on backing storage for subsequent batch processing (*see* Fig. 30).

2. Interactive processing applications. In order to demonstrate the characteristics and practical aspects of interactive processing a number of applications are to be outlined. The applications are

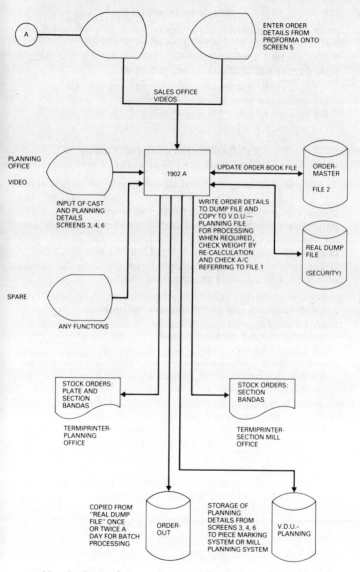

FIG. 30   *On-line order-entry routine (illustrating relationship of on-line order-entry to batch processing)*

processed by application packages the details of which are reproduced by the kind permission of NCR Limited.

The selected applications which should interest distribution management and accountants are as follows:

    (*a*) interactive distribution control system (I.D.C.S.)

    (*b*) interactive payroll accounting system

    (*c*) interactive general ledger system

INTERACTIVE DISTRIBUTION CONTROL SYSTEM (I.D.C.S.)

3. Mode of processing. A typical user of the system could be entering order details, making stock enquiries, posting receipts and producing invoices in the order office whilst picking lists or despatch notes are being printed in the warehouse and purchase invoice details, cash receipts, journal transfers and possibly price changes are being handled on a V.D.U. in the accounts office.

The system allows an order clerk to enter a customer's order details via a V.D.U. and the computer then:

    (*a*) checks credit;

    (*b*) extracts any one of 999 delivery addresses;

    (*c*) checks and reserves stock;

    (*d*) triggers stock replenishment;

    (*e*) selects and uses correct price for quantity;

    (*f*) applies a trade discount;

    (*g*) places a back-order if applicable;

    (*h*) values the order;

    (*i*) re-checks credit;

    (*j*) sorts the item lines to bin location sequence;

    (*k*) prints a warehouse picking document;

    (*l*) resorts the item lines to order sequence;

    (*m*) applies V.A.T.;

    (*n*) totals the invoice;

    (*o*) analyses the total into goods value, goods by V.A.T. code, trade discount and special charges;

    (*p*) prints the invoice;

    (*q*) enters a transaction to the sales ledger.

(*See* Fig. 31.)

The I.D.C.S. System will accept current orders for immediate supply, back orders for items not yet available in stock, and forward orders for a planned future delivery.

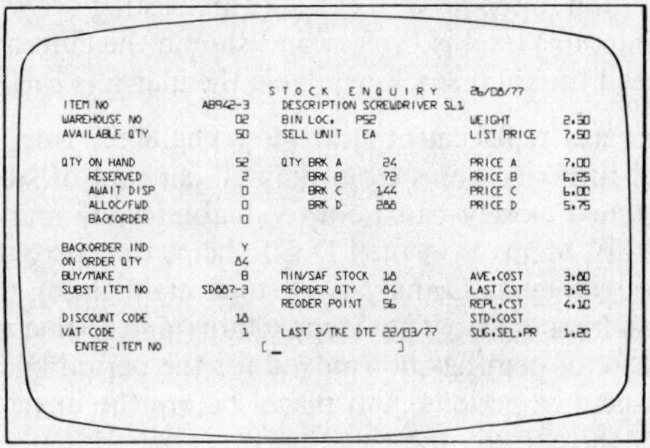

FIG. 31   *Video screen display: on-line stock enquiry*

4. Prices, discounts and costs. For those distributors offering quantity price incentives, the I.D.C.S. System allows for up to eight quantity break prices in addition to the standard list price. A flexible discounting structure allows trade discounting by customer and product groupings. Enhancements to include overriding product group and invoice total value discounts or surcharges are envisaged.

To provide the all important gross margin calculations and cost accounting functions, the system caters for up to four different cost values on each stock item: last cost, average cost, replacement cost and standard cost. Stock may be valued at any time at any one of the stored cost prices.

5. System status. The system processes all stock and cash transactions as they are entered via the V.D.U.'s so that credit status reporting is current to the minute and stock enquiries (Fig. 31), always show the very latest situation.

An important supervisory control tool is the summary of orders received, released to the warehouse, confirmed as picked and invoiced. All figures shown are correct to the last entry for today and the period to date.

6. Stock control. The system includes a comprehensive stock control module designed to operate as a free-standing system in situations where it is called for. The major control tool is the Stock Ordering and Expediting Report printed daily and reporting on those items where the current requirements and future allocations cause the re-ordering parameters to be broken. The report also draws attention to the need to expedite an existing order when the safety (minimum) level is broken and should the current requirements exceed the total stock available the alarm is raised again.

7. Stocking and replacement strategies. The 80:20 rule, where 80 per cent of turnover stems from only 20 per cent of stock items, unless watched closely can tie-up valuable assets and seriously depress return on investment. I.D.C.S. helps to control this tendency by providing ABC analysis of stock highlighting the investment in each category. The Stock Status and Demand Report reveals when an item has not moved for the period and for how many consecutive periods, and places before the buyer the sales pattern for the current and three previous periods.

8. NCR total system. The NCR total system for the wholesale manufacturing distributor brings together the modular Interactive Distribution Control System (I.D.C.S.) and the Interactive Financial System (I.F.S.).

Within I.D.C.S. both modules are complementary although the stock control module can be used as a stand alone system under the name of Interactive Stock Control. When the Sales Ledger module of I.F.S. is part of the total system the customer master file and name and address file will be shared by I.D.C.S. to avoid duplication. In I.F.S. the three systems will stand alone although the Purchase Ledger and Nominal Ledger systems are designed to work as one integrated system when required to do so.

9. Reports. Typical reports produced by the system of prime importance to distribution management include:

    (a) stock evaluation report—average cost;
    (b) open forward orders report—analysis;
    (c) credit limit excess and aged balance report.

(*See* Fig. 32.)

INTERACTIVE PAYROLL ACCOUNTING SYSTEM

10. System objectives. The system is designed to calculate gross and net earnings, produce pay advices, print cheques and bank giro credits. It also maintains cumulative information of earnings, pay-as-you-earn, National Insurance, other deductions and non-taxable allowance (O.D., N.T.A.). File additions, deletions and amendments can be made, when required, using the keyboard and visual display facility. Likewise, specific record contents can be

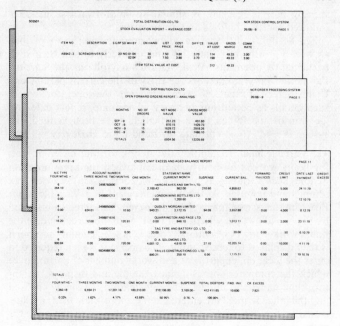

FIG. 32   *Distribution management reports*

displayed in response to enquiries. Periodic departmental analyses with coin analysis facilities and a comprehensive audit trail are included in the specification.

11. System operation. Master files are held on a magnetic medium which facilitates easy access for additions, deletions and amendments using a simple typewriter style keyboard and a visual display screen. When an operator chooses to run the Payroll Master File Maintenance Program, a screen displays the various record types which may be changed, see Fig. 33. Say a change in income tax percentages occurs. The operator enters 03 and the income tax header record is displayed to allow the appropriate tax data field to be changed, see Fig. 34. All data is displayed after entry and must be verified by a positive response on the bottom line before entry into the system takes place. Following this operation, all employees will be processed under the new tax conditions when the specified starting date is reached. A similar straightforward sequence is followed for all additions and amendments.

The flexibility of the system allows users to specify pay periods as weekly, fortnightly, monthly and quarterly to suit their own particular requirements. At the start of a payroll run, the Start-of-Pay Period Program permits the entry of the current parameters. Using screen format 60 (*see* Fig. 35) the operator enters such details as period number, pay advice date, report date and location details. When these particulars have been verified, the system is ready to accept data for build up to gross pay.

12. Variable input. In addition to catering for four different rates for hours worked by hourly paid employees, the same program handles such variables as holiday pay, commission, sick pay, tax refunds and bonuses. At the commencement of a Variable Input Program run, screen format 30 is displayed. This screen, illustrated by Fig. 36, allows the selection of the type of input required. If the hours worked are to be entered, code 32 is selected and this screen is then displayed to receive input. The operator is then required to enter the location, department and works number of an employee which the computer checks against the file and displays the appropriate name and initials. The information is visually checked and the hours worked are entered in the appropriate fields as illustrated in Fig. 37. The data is entered on file when the operator enters the appropriate confirmations in response to the DATA OK? message at the bottom of the screen and the screen clears ready for the next entry.

The system's ability to deal with the more unusual circumstances is illustrated if a request for a tax refund from an employee on sick leave is considered. The employee is not entitled to normal pay and not subject to normal deductions. Using screen format 35, illustrated in Fig. 38, the employee's location, department and works number are entered and employee's name and initials checked by the operator. A positive entry in response to the DATA OK? enquiry on the bottom line sets a record flag which will ensure that the Gross-to-Net Program processes the record, determines the refund due and enables a pay advice to be produced for the appropriate amount. The gross-to-net audit report will print details of this record and state that the employee is being processed for tax refund only.

13. Gross-to-net. When all variable input has been entered on the master files, the Gross-to-Net Program is initiated (*see* Fig. 39),

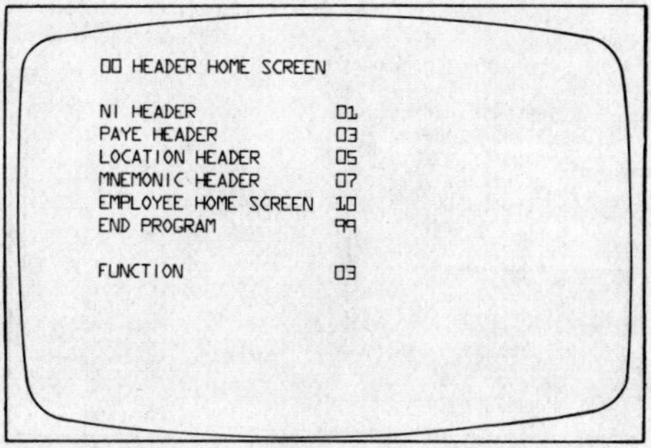

```
   00 HEADER HOME SCREEN

   NI HEADER              01
   PAYE HEADER            03
   LOCATION HEADER        05
   MNEMONIC HEADER        07
   EMPLOYEE HOME SCREEN   10
   END PROGRAM            99

   FUNCTION               03
```

FIG. 33 *Screen display: record types*

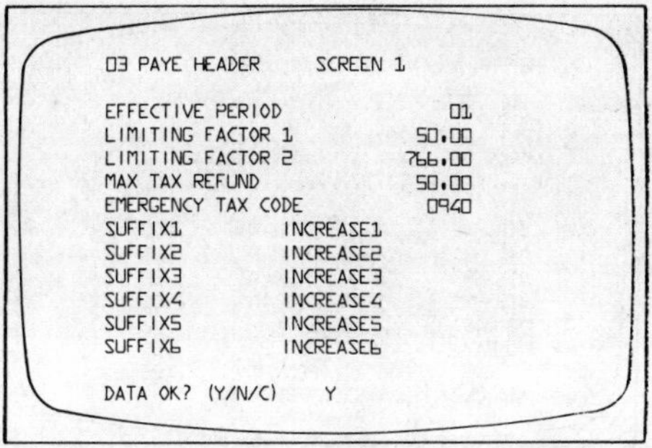

```
   03 PAYE HEADER     SCREEN 1

   EFFECTIVE PERIOD              01
   LIMITING FACTOR 1         50.00
   LIMITING FACTOR 2        766.00
   MAX TAX REFUND            50.00
   EMERGENCY TAX CODE         0940
   SUFFIX1        INCREASE1
   SUFFIX2        INCREASE2
   SUFFIX3        INCREASE3
   SUFFIX4        INCREASE4
   SUFFIX5        INCREASE5
   SUFFIX6        INCREASE6

   DATA OK? (Y/N/C)    Y
```

FIG. 34 *Screen display: income tax header record*

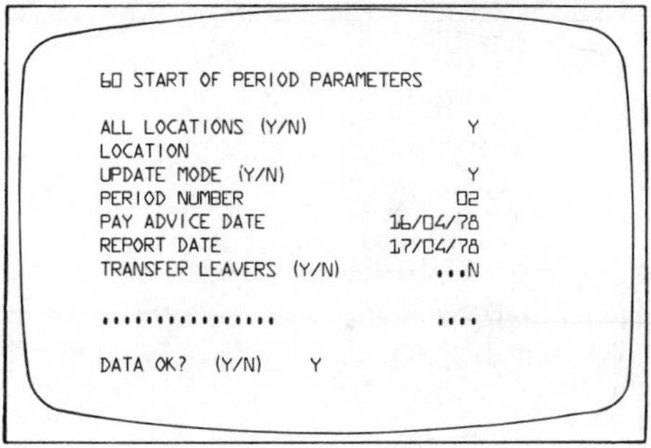

```
   60 START OF PERIOD PARAMETERS

   ALL LOCATIONS (Y/N)           Y
   LOCATION
   UPDATE MODE (Y/N)             Y
   PERIOD NUMBER                02
   PAY ADVICE DATE        16/04/78
   REPORT DATE            17/04/78
   TRANSFER LEAVERS (Y/N)     ...N

   ................           ....

   DATA OK?  (Y/N)    Y
```

FIG. 35 *Screen display: start of period parameters*

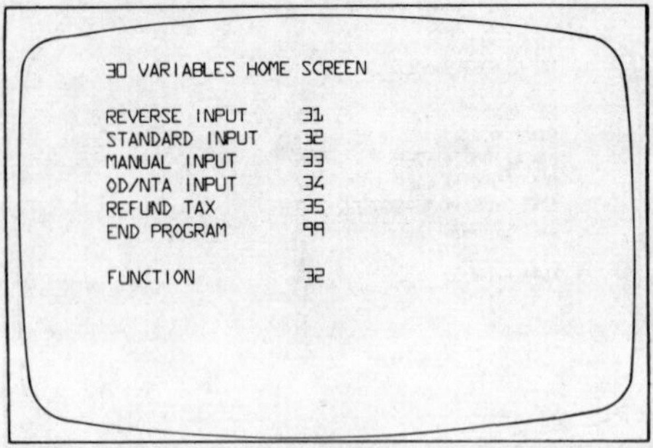

FIG. 36   Screen display: variable input

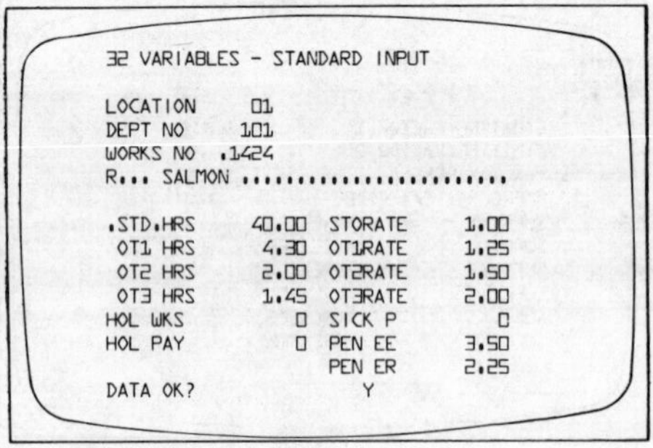

FIG. 37   Screen display: standard input

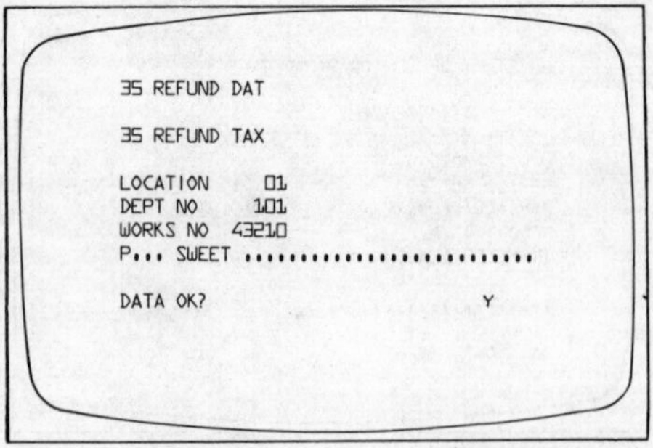

FIG. 38   Screen display: tax refund

to calculate net pay and prepare the records for pay advice production.

Separate files are held for employees paid on each different periodic basis. Users with wage and salary mode employees paid on the same periodic basis may choose to have these records on the same or separate files. On completion of Variable Input and Gross-to-Net Programs, records on the master files can be processed to produce pay advices, cheques and bank giro credits to the user's particular requirements. The visual display is used to determine the records which are to be processed. The screen illustrated in Fig. 40 allows the operator to select a full file pay advice print or to specify the details of a partial print.

When a file is being processed for the printing of cheques, the screen illustrated in Fig. 41 allows the operator to set the print parameters and advises when the cheque production is complete. Full details of pay advice, the major reports and audit features produced by the system can be seen in the following pages.

14. Interrogation of records. NCR shares the belief of modern business managers that communication between computer and operating staff should be simple and immediate. Using the interactive features of the NCR 8000 series computers the Enquiry Program is designed to meet this demand and provide users with easy access to the information stored on the payroll master files. Information on file is fully secure whilst being accessed by the enquiry program and no amendments to data can be made.

When the enquiry program is initiated the enquiry home screen, illustrated in Fig. 42, is displayed showing the screen formats which display the contents of a record in logical groups. If an enquiry regarding an employee's pension data is to be processed, the operator enters 45 and the screen illustrated in Fig. 43 is displayed, showing all the pension details on file for the specified employee.

In addition to the facility to display nine particular groups of data, a further screen displays all the current monetary values that print on the pay advice (*see* Fig. 44). The system allows the operator to work through a record sequentially with the 9 screens or to access the various data groups at random moving back and forth in the same employee record. It is also possible to keep to one screen format and move through a number of employee records.

15. Payroll Master File. The Payroll Master file is organised into five records and three levels as shown in Table VI.

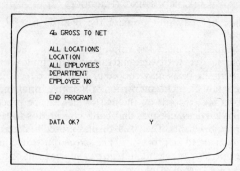

```
46 GROSS TO NET

ALL LOCATIONS
LOCATION
ALL EMPLOYEES
DEPARTMENT
EMPLOYEE NO

END PROGRAM


DATA OK?              Y
```

FIG. 39 *Screen display: gross to net*

```
50 PAY ADVICE RUN PARAMETERS

LOCATION                 01
FULL PRINT                N
DEPT START NO           .04
CLOCK START NO        14497
DEPT END NO              06
CLOCK END NO         16932
PAPER CHANGED            Y
TEST PATTERN            Y
PAPER ALIGNED        ....Y
NO. ADVICES PRINTED  .....
MORE REQUESTS           .

DATA OK?              Y    ...
```

FIG. 40 *Screen display: pay advice printing*

```
72 CHEQUES PRINT RUN

RESTART
LOC 02 DEPT 202 WKS NO

TEST PATTERN OK?      Y

END OF LOC CHNGE STNRY

CHEQUES COMPLETE

DATA OK?              Y
```

FIG. 41 *Screen display: cheque printing*

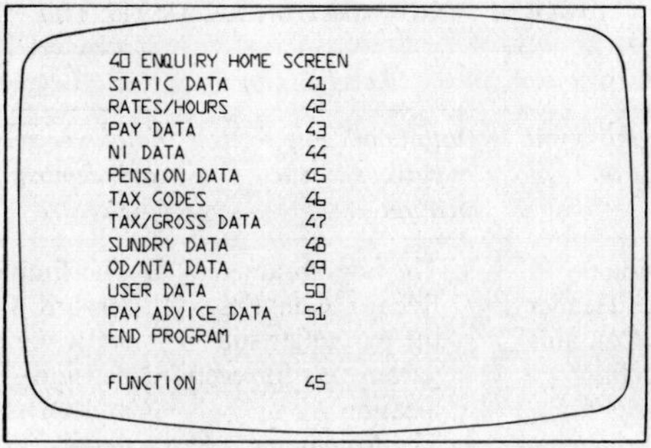

```
40 ENQUIRY HOME SCREEN
STATIC DATA        41
RATES/HOURS        42
PAY DATA           43
NI DATA            44
PENSION DATA       45
TAX CODES          46
TAX/GROSS DATA     47
SUNDRY DATA        48
OD/NTA DATA        49
USER DATA          50
PAY ADVICE DATA    51
END PROGRAM

FUNCTION           45
```

FIG. 42   *Screen display: enquiries*

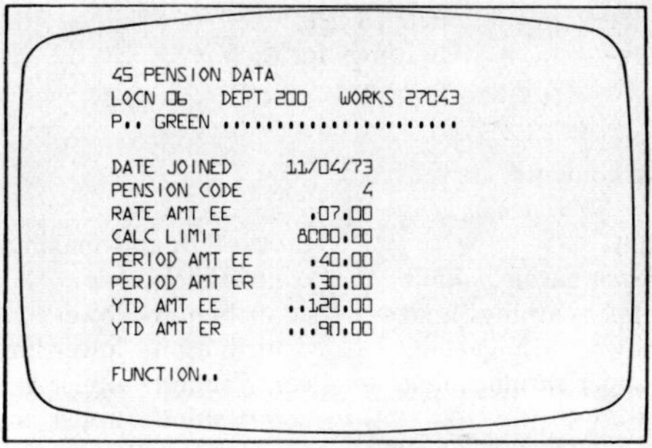

```
45 PENSION DATA
LOCN 06   DEPT 200   WORKS 27043
P.. GREEN ....................

DATE JOINED      11/04/73
PENSION CODE            4
RATE AMT EE         .07.00
CALC LIMIT        8000.00
PERIOD AMT EE       .40.00
PERIOD AMT ER       .30.00
YTD AMT EE         ..120.00
YTD AMT ER         ...90.00

FUNCTION..
```

FIG. 43   *Screen display: pension data*

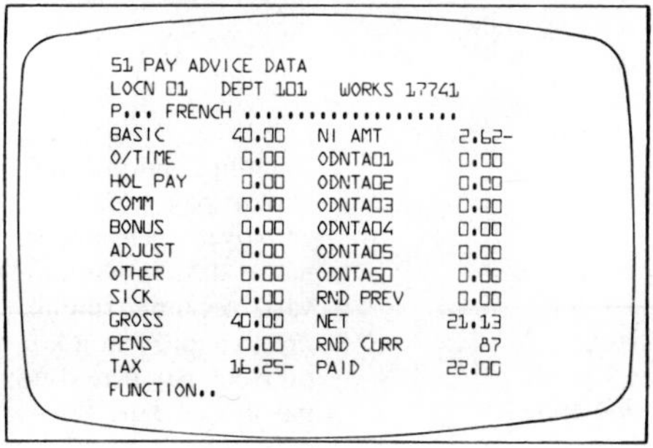

```
51 PAY ADVICE DATA
LOCN 01   DEPT 101   WORKS 17741
P... FRENCH ....................
BASIC    40.00   NI AMT      2.62-
O/TIME    0.00   ODNTA01     0.00
HOL PAY   0.00   ODNTA02     0.00
COMM      0.00   ODNTA03     0.00
BONUS     0.00   ODNTA04     0.00
ADJUST    0.00   ODNTA05     0.00
OTHER     0.00   ODNTA50     0.00
SICK      0.00   RND PREV    0.00
GROSS    40.00   NET        21.13
PENS      0.00   RND CURR      87
TAX      16.25-  PAID       22.00
FUNCTION..
```

FIG. 44   *Screen display: pay advice data*

TABLE VI   ORGANISATION OF MASTER FILE

Level 1	Level 2	Level 3
Data applicable to all employees at all locations	*Data applicable to the employees at each location*	*Employee records at each department or cost centre*
1. The National Insurance Header Record. Contains the deduction percentages for each N.I. category. 2. The Pay-As-You-Earn Tax Header Record. Contains P.A.Y.E. tax parameters.	3. The Site Parameter Record. Contains the particular site parameters for each location. 4. The Mnemonic Field Reference Record. Contains the customer defined field headings for each location.	5. The Employee Record. Contains static data, rates, pension, Tax, N.I., and OD/NTA details for each employee.

(*a*) Master-file contents—Level 1.

   (*i*) *Record 1—N.I. header:*

table stop amount;	table of 7 items maximum
contractors in lower earnings limit	contribution code
contractors in upper earnings limit	contribution—lower limit % employee
contracted out lower earnings limit	contribution—lower limit % employer
contracted out upper earnings limit	contribution—upper limit % employee
table item count	contribution—upper limit % employer

   (*ii*) *Record 2—P.A.Y.E. header:*

first effective pay period no	table of 6 items max.
limiting factor 1	suffix code for increase
limiting factor 2	table 2 item count
max. refund first pay day new employee	table of tax rates and bandwidths
emergency tax code	

(*b*) Master file contents—Level 2.

   (*i*) *Record 3—location header:*

employer's name	rounding option code
employer's address	current pay period no.
employer's tax ref.	employer's pension ref.
employer's tax district	no. of days in working week
P.A.Y.E. year start date	variables input run no.
ways of salary made	maintenance run no.
pay internal code	previous pay period no.
coin analysis option code	pay advice date
mnemonic option code	date to print on other reports
hours accumulation code	no. of records for this location

(ii) Record 4—mnemonic header:

trade code

hours worked at basic

hours worked at premium 1 rate

hours worked at premium 2 rate

hours worked at premium 3 rate

worked hours or premium hours

basic pay

overtime premium pay

holiday pay

commission

bonus

adjustment

other

sick pay/deduction

performance

basic rate (hourly, weekly, monthly)

premium 1 rate

premium 2 rate

premium 3 rate

costcode

table of 50 O.D./N.T.A. mnemonics

O.D./N.T.A

holiday credits

(c) Master file contents—Level 3

(i) Record 5—employee record

(1) Static record:

Company/location

Department

Clock/works no.

Type code

Employee surname

Employee initials

Sex (M of F)

Married/single

Date of birth

Employee no.

Date of employment

National Insurance No.

Method of payment code

Bank sort code

Bank account number

Category code (range 1–6)

Trade code

Cost code

(2) Pay rates and hours worked:

Rate of pay basic

Rate of pay premium 1

Rate of pay premium 2

Rate of pay premium 3

Hours at basic

Hours at premium 1

Hours at premium 2

Hours at premium 3

(3) Period pay for make up to gross:

Basic pay

Premium 1 pay

Premium 2 pay

Premium 3 pay

Holiday pay

Bonus

Adjustment

Other pay

Sick pay

(4) Tax and gross data:

Tax code

Calculation basis flag

Paid status flag

Refund status flag

Tax period no.

First period no. this employment

First gross this employment

Suspended tax refund

Week 53 gross

Week 53 tax

Previous employment gross

Previous employment tax

Current period gross

Current period tax

Current period net

Y.T.D. gross

Y.T.D. tax

(5) National Insurance data:

Current N.I. code	Employers
Previous N.I. code 1	Contracted in ⎫ Y.T.D. amounts
Previous N.I. code 1	Contracted out ⎭ Previous N.I. code 1
N.I. adjustment code	Employers
Contracted in ⎫ period amount	Contracted in ⎫ total amounts
Contracted out ⎭ current N.I. code	Contracted out ⎭ all N.I. codes
Employers	Employers
Contracted in ⎫ Y.T.D. amounts	
Contracted out ⎭ current N.I. code	

(6) Company pension data:

Date joined company pension schemes	Pension period amount—employee
Company pension code	Pension period amount—employer
Pension rate % or amount—employee	Pension Y.T.D. amount—employee
Pension rate % or amount—employer	Pension Y.T.D. amount—employer
Pension calculation limit	

(7) Sundry flags & data:

Date of leaving	Pay period holiday weeks
Leaver code	Current period rounding
Status flag	Previous period rounding
Manual input flag	Ledger card—line no.
Pay advice flag	Ledger card—new card flag
Holiday flag	Record amendment count

(8) OD/NTA data:

OD/NTA table items	Normal amount
OD/NTA table (12 items max.)	Actual amount
Code (range 01–50)	Total amount
Type (range 0–5)	

(9) User data:

File area allocated for users special requirements

INTERACTIVE GENERAL LEDGER SYSTEM

16. Application philosophy. The Interactive General Ledger System incorporates traditional accounting control and comprehensive financial reporting in a completely automated application. It channels all accounting transactions into an integrated information base that serves as the control module for the complete system. It can be implemented as a stand-alone system or utilised in conjunction with other general accounting applications such as payables, receivables, and payroll. It can handle any current account numbering scheme in either a single-client or multi-client environment.

Basic accounting data, including comparative budget data and previous years' history, is accumulated in a single master file that reflects both current and future needs with the ability to extract reports by department, division, and cost centre for budget and cost analysis. Complete audit control is provided by debit/credit balancing at all levels of processing, and the reports produced comply with general accounting practices.

The general ledger application is an interactive, transaction-oriented processing system. It employs double-entry bookkeeping methods, balancing each debit and credit entry with either an off-setting entry or control total, and immediately updating all related master files. A trial balance at either the detail or control total level may be taken at any time. Balances are maintained by account for each period, providing a means of creating a trial balance for any previous period. Detail debit and credit transactions may also be retained by account at the user's option.

The system is easy to install, operate, and maintain. As an interactive system, the clerical workload is significantly reduced and the possibility of transcription errors, bookkeeping errors, and the unauthorised use of the general ledger accounts is eliminated.

17. Direct data display. The screen display is the control centre for the system. At a glance, the operator can read program instructions, system messages, data to be input, and data file information. A position indicator informs the operator what information may be required to complete a posting or answer a question. The operator enters the requested information and visually checks the data before it is processed.

Account posting is completed in a matter of seconds—it is fast and easy; it is verified; it is correct; and the entry will appear on all affected reports. Correction procedures are just as easy—operator merely replaces the character and/or digits with the correct value.

The general ledger application accepts both automatic postings from other related applications and general journal entries initiated by the operator. All automatic postings and general entries include complete source document reference information for internal audit and control. New accounts can be easily added to the integrated data base, and existing accounts deleted. Changes to account information can be performed during routine maintenance operations.

18. Master menu. General ledger processing operations are concise, straight-to-the-point ... operator merely follows the instructions on the video display. From the master menu display (*see* Fig. 45), the operator selects one of five processing functions such

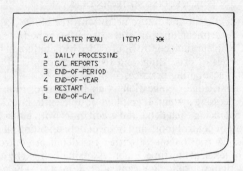

FIG. 45 *Screen display: general ledger master menu*

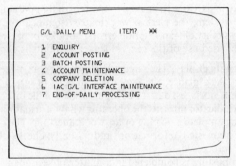

FIG. 46 *Screen display: general ledger daily menu*

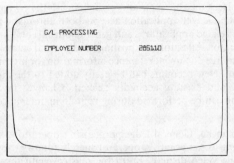

FIG. 47 *Screen display: security code/employee number*

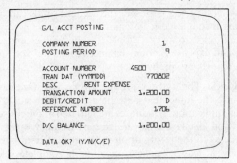

```
G/L ACCT POSTING

COMPANY NUMBER              1
POSTING PERIOD             9

ACCOUNT NUMBER        4500
TRAN DAT (YYMMDD)       770802
DESC      RENT EXPENSE
TRANSACTION AMOUNT     1,200.00
DEBIT/CREDIT              D
REFERENCE NUMBER         1706

D/C BALANCE           1,200.00

DATA OK?  (Y/N/C/E)
```

FIG. 48   *Screen display: general ledger account posting*

as Daily Processing or End-of-Period. Before continuing, the operator must enter employee number and/or security code. After security code verification by the program, the selected processing function is displayed—G/L Daily Menu.

19. Daily menu. The G/L Daily Menu schedule displays seven functions (*see* Fig. 46): Enquiry, Account Posting, Batch Posting, Account Maintenance, Company Deletion, Interface Mainten- ance and End-of-Day Processing. Again, before any entries are processed the operator's security code must be verified (*see* Fig. 47). Then, the operator can follow the position indicator and enter the data requested under the G/L Account Posting display (*see* Fig. 48). Before transferring data to memory and updating the account, the display is visually verified for accuracy.

20. Control. The general ledger system incorporates a variety of validating, auditing, and control techniques to ensure the accuracy of the financial reports. The monthly trial balance and monthly reporting transactions detail constitute the traditional accounting tools. All posting functions accumulate total of debits and credit entries and must be equal before end-of-run processing can be performed.

When trial balance is performed, any difference between debits and credits is posted to an error account. This account balance must be cleared before financial statements are prepared.

21. Period/year-end closing. During the period cycle, the current period totals are closed and transferred to history totals. A general journal is printed and details of posted entries purged from the system. After a period is closed, the account totals can be revised or updated through file maintenance.

Year-end close-out is completely automatic and transfers revenues and expense account balances to capital account before financial reports are prepared.

22. Enquiries. The system provides for instantaneous on-line enquiry into the integrated data base and the master files of the interfaced applications. Enquiries are initiated at the console by the operator and displayed on the screen. Enquiry security codes restrict access to the information in the system data base.

The general ledger application offers a complete selection of enquiries, ranging from current data and budget information to historical data, for any and all accounting periods. The operator merely selects and enters the identifying code or account number for the desired information (*see* Fig. 49).

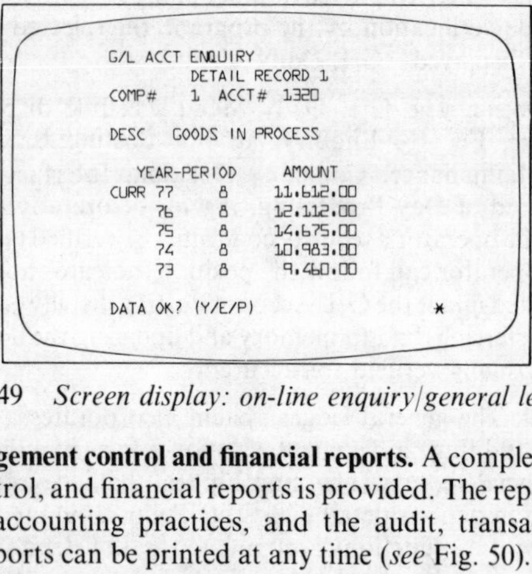

```
    G/L ACCT ENQUIRY
              DETAIL RECORD 1
    COMP#   1  ACCT#  1320

    DESC   GOODS IN PROCESS

       YEAR-PERIOD      AMOUNT
    CURR 77     8      11,612.00
         76     8      12,112.00
         75     8      14,675.00
         74     8      10,983.00
         73     8       9,460.00

    DATA OK? (Y/E/P)              *
```

FIG. 49   *Screen display: on-line enquiry/general ledger*

23. Management control and financial reports. A complete range of audit, control, and financial reports is provided. The reports follow accepted accounting practices, and the audit, transaction, and control reports can be printed at any time (*see* Fig. 50). The range can include:

    (*a*) chart of accounts listing;
    (*b*) master file listing;
    (*c*) transaction journal;
    (*d*) account activity/journal report;
    (*e*) maintenance audit trail;
    (*f*) trial balance;
    (*g*) history/budget listing;

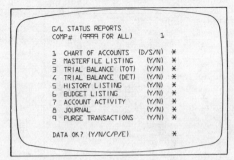

```
G/L STATUS REPORTS
COMP# (9999 FOR ALL)        1

  1  CHART OF ACCOUNTS  (D/S/N)  ✳
  2  MASTERFILE LISTING    (Y/N)  ✳
  3  TRIAL BALANCE (TOT)   (Y/N)  ✳
  4  TRIAL BALANCE (DET)   (Y/N)  ✳
  5  HISTORY LISTING       (Y/N)  ✳
  6  BUDGET LISTING        (Y/N)  ✳
  7  ACCOUNT ACTIVITY      (Y/N)  ✳
  8  JOURNAL               (Y/N)  ✳
  9  PURGE TRANSACTIONS    (Y/N)  ✳

DATA OK? (Y/N/C/P/E)               ✳
```

FIG. 50   *Screen display: general ledger status reports*

(*h*) comparative balance sheet;

(*i*) income/expense report;

(*j*) comparative income/expense report.

24. Income/expense report.

(*a*) The report is prepared automatically and summarises activity for current and year-to-date periods.

(*b*) Revenue/expense account percentages are based on gross revenue/sales (*see* Fig. 53).

25. Comparative income/expense.

(*a*) Report lists revenue and expenses for current/prior/to-date periods, budget allocations, and variance percentages.

(*b*) Current period and year-to-date section compare revenue/expense balances to either prior period balances or budget allocations and list applicable variance percentages (*see* Fig. 54).

26. Trial balance.

(*a*) Report is prepared automatically, with operator supervision, from the integrated general ledger data base.

(*b*) Beginning and ending debit or credit balance is listed for each account.

(*c*) Total debit/credit balances and net difference are summarised for the current and four previous periods (*see* Fig. 51).

27. Comparative balance sheet.

(*a*) Report is prepared in its entirety without operator intervention.

THE NATIONAL CO 1 TRIAL BALANCE 30 SEP 19—— PAGE
DIVISION 1

CURRENT PERIOD 9

CO NO.	ACCT NO.	DESCRIPTION	BEGINNING BALANCES DEBITS	BEGINNING BALANCES CREDITS	ENDING BALANCES DEBITS	ENDING BALANCES CREDITS
1	1110000000	CASH	50,750.92		49,605.92	
1	1120000000	SECURITIES, STOCKS	800.00		800.00	
1	1130000000	SECURITIES, BONDS	700.00		700.00	
1	1210000000	ACCOUNTS RECEIVABLE	32,278.00		35,287.00	
1	1220000000	ALLOW. FOR UNCOLL. A/R	820.00		787.00	
1	1310000000	FINISHED GOODS	7,491.00		7,216.00	
1	1320000000	GOODS IN PROCESS	12,112.00		11,612.00	
1	3330000000	MATERIALS	9,923.00		9,923.00	
1	1720000000	FACTORY BLDGS. AT COST	65,000.00		65,000.00	

FIG. 51 *Trial balance*

THE NATIONAL CO DIVISION 1	1 COMPARATIVE BALANCE SHEET		15 SEP 19—	PAGE 12
CURRENT PERIOD 8				
CO NO. ACCT NO. DESCRIPTION	CURRENT BALANCE	PRIOR YEAR BALANCE	DIFFERENCE	VAR %
1 1110000000 CASH	49,605.00	50,750.00	1,145.00—	2.26—
1 1120000000 SECURITIES, STOCKS	800.00	800.00	.00	.00
1 1130000000 SECURITIES, BONDS	700.00	700.00	.00	.00
1 1190000000 .CASH ASSETS	51,105.00	52,250.00	1,145.00—	2.19—
1 1210000000 ACCOUNTS RECEIVABLE	35,287.00	32,278.00	3,009.00	9.32
1 1220000000 ALLOWANCE FOR UNCOLL.A/R	787.00	820.00	33.00—	4.02—
1 1290000097 .ADJUSTED RECEIVABLES	36,074.00	33,098.00	2,976.00	8.99
1 1290000098 ..LIQUID ASSETS	87,179.00	85,348.00	1,831.00	2.15

FIG. 52 *Comparative balance sheet*

```
                    THE NATIONAL CO              1  INCOME-EXPENSE REPORT                  15 JAN 19——   PAGE 5
                    DIVISION 1

PERIOD 1                                            PERIOD                                    YEAR-TO-DATE

CO NO. ACCT NO.  DESCRIPTION                    AMOUNT              %                     AMOUNT              %

1 4000000000 SALES PRODUCT 1                    96,723.42         38.02                 531,978.70         38.02
1 4010000000 SALES PRODUCT 2                    89,559.94         35.21                 492,576.15         35.21
1 4020000000 SALES PRODUCT 3                    68,087.13         26.77                 374,479.05         26.77
1 4500000097 .TOTAL SALES                      254,369.89        100.00               1,399,033.90        100.00

1 6010000000 PURCHASES                         178,058.91         70.00                 979,323.74         70.00
1 6200000000 SALARIES – OFFICE                  10,800.00          4.25                  57,950.00          4.14
1 6210000000 SALARIES – SALES STAFF              7,500.00          2.95                  34,800.00          2.49
1 6220000000 SALARIES – PLANT                   18,414.10          7.24                 107,287.95          7.67
1 6300000000 UTILITIES                           1,129.73           .44                  11,021.97           .79
```

FIG. 53 *Income/expense report*

PERIOD 2

CO NO. ACCT NO.	DESCRIPTION	PREVIOUS	CURRENT	BUDGET	VAR%	ACTUAL	BUDGET	VAR%
						YEAR-TO-DATE		
1 4250000000	SALES – DIVISION 1	4,128.00	4,450.00	4,000.00	11.25	8,400.00	8,000.00	.05
1 4260000000	SALES – DIVISION 2	3,850.00	4,395.00	3,750.00	17.20	8,420.00	7,500.00	12.27
1 4270000000	SALES – DIVISION 3	3,975.00	4,350.00	3,900.00	11.54	8,105.00	7,800.00	3.91
1 4280000000	SALES – DIVISION 5	4,695.00	4,895.00	3,700.00	32.30	8,370.00	7,400.00	13.11
1 4500000097	.GROSS SALES	16,648.00	18,090.00	15,350.00	17.85	33,295.00	30,700.00	8.45
1 6010000000	SALARIES – DIVISION 1	925.00	1,000.00	900.00	11.11	2,000.00	1,800.00	11.11
1 6020000000	SALARIES – DIVISION 2	900.00	900.00			1,800.00		
1 6030000000	SALARIES – DIVISION 3	900.00	900.00			1,750.00		
1 6040000000	SALARIES – DIVISION 5	900.00	900.00			1,800.00		
1 6500000097	.SALESMAN'S SALARIES	3,625.00	3,700.00	900.00	311.11	7,350.00	1,800.00	308.34

FIG. 54 *Comparative income/expense report*

(*b*) Current period is compared to previous year period. Increase/decrease amount is listed with percent of variance.

(*c*) Minor/major distribution totals are computed for assets, liabilities, and capital (*see* Fig. 52).

28. General Ledger Master File

(*a*) *System Record*

Company number	Multi-company
Account	Company Consolidation
Record Type	Maximum Companies to
Automatic Year-end Closing	Consolidate
Budget Feature	Maximum Levels of Total
Number Years History	Memo Chart of Accounts Flag

(*b*) *Company Consolidation Record*

Record Key	Company/Division Number
	(up to 25 companies)

(*c*) *Company Header Record*

Record Key	Trial Balance Flag
Current Period	Error Amount
Number of Periods	Lowest Revenue Account Print
Automatic Year Close	Sequence Number
Budgets	First Balance Sheet Print
Current Year	Sequence Number
	Highest Revenue Account Print
	Sequence Number

(*d*) *Print Control Sequence Record*

Record Key	Print Sequence
Account Type	Line Slew Before
Print Flag	Line Slew After
Debit-Credit Flag	Total Level
Revenue Base Flag	Description

(*e*) *Detail Record*

Record Type	Account Description
Account Type	Tracer Number
Print Flag	Closed Period Y.T.D.
Debit-Credit Flag	Closed Period Balance
Revenue Base Flag	Current Period
Ledger Print Control Page	Current Period Plus 1
Ledger Print Control Line	Current Period Plus 2
Print Sequence	Current Period Plus 3
Prior Year Closed Y.T.D.	Current Period Plus 4

Prior Year Closed Balance
  (*f*) *History Record*

Record Type	History Amount (up to 13 periods

  (*g*) *Budget Record*

Record Type	Budget Amount (up to 13 periods)

29. Summary. The NCR Interactive General Ledger System is completely documented, including implementation and operation procedures. It can be readily installed as a stand-alone system or in conjunction with other accounting applications. It is an effective and versatile application for processing and controlling the general ledger. The system:

(*a*) maintains clearly-defined audit trails and internal control for all levels of processing;

(*b*) employs double-entry bookkeeping methods for balanced, up-to-date general ledger control;

(*c*) offers complete flexibility in single-client and multi-client processing with individual or multiple financial reports;

(*d*) produces general ledger reports completely independent of a chart of accounts;

(*e*) performs fiscal year accounting independent of the calendar year;

(*f*) provides for up to thirteen accounting periods in a year;

(*g*) maintains account summary totals as historical data for all periods in a year;

(*h*) maintains budget information on all valid accounts for comparative analysis;

(*i*) posts journal entries for the current period and to any of four open future periods;

(*j*) provides nine levels of total accumulation for reporting purposes;

(*k*) transfers account balances and control information automatically at year-end closing;

(*l*) improves financial control over all business activity without a major restructure of accounting procedures or retraining efforts.

PROGRESS TEST 9

1. Outline the nature of interactive processing. **(1)**

2. Indicate the main features of an interactive distribution control system (IDCS). **(3–9)**

3. Outline the features of an interactive payroll accounting system. **(10–15)**

4. Specify the basic philosophy and processing features of an interactive general ledger system. **(16–29)**

CHAPTER X

Computer Bureaux

GENERAL CONSIDERATIONS

1. Definition. A computer service bureau is a company which operates a computer to process work for other companies, in other words, an organisation which provides a service for clients in the specialist field of E.D.P.

2. Types of computer bureaux. There are basically three types:

(*a*) *independent companies* specially formed for the provision of computing services to clients;

(*b*) *computer manufacturers* with separately structured computer bureaux, a notable example being BARIC Computing Services Ltd., which is a joint venture between Barclays Bank Ltd. and International Computers Ltd.;

(*c*) computer users with *spare capacity* who allow other firms to use their computer system either for standby facilities or for program testing prior to the installation of a similar computer system.

3. Services available from computer bureaux. In general, the range of services provided by computer bureaux is as follows.

(*a*) *Data preparation or conversion.* This service consists of the conversion of source data into a machine-sensible form for processing by computer. Conversion may be in the form of punched cards, paper tape, magnetic tape or optical characters. A bureau may be used for the initial conversion of master files when changing procedures to E.D.P.

(*b*) *Systems investigation and design.* This consists of the analysis of existing procedures and their conversion for processing by computer.

(*c*) *Program preparation and testing.* This service provides an addition to the service indicated in (*b*) above.

(*d*) *Hiring computer time.* Here the service to the client consists of processing the client's data using the programs supplied by the client. The hire charges usually vary according to the time of day the service is provided and the length of time the bureau's facilities are used.

(*e*) *Do-it-yourself service* (*D.I.Y.*). The provision of computing facilities to allow the clients' computer operators to process data with their own programs. The service is usually available during off-peak periods.

(*f*) *Time sharing.* Access to the bureau's computer by means of communication links, which in effect provides each user with computing facilities as if he had an in-house computer.

(*g*) *Compete package* (*full service*). In this respect, the bureau provides a comprehensive service embracing all the stages of implementing a computer (except actual installation) as if a computer was to be implemented on-site. This includes systems analysis and design, program preparation and testing and the processing of data.

(*h*) *Consultation.* Provision of advice on data processing problems.

(*i*) *Package programs.* Most bureaux provide package programs which may be used either on the bureau's or on the customer's computer.

4. Reasons for using bureaux. Any particular company will of course have specific reasons for using a computer bureau, but in general the following reasons are common:

(*a*) to obtain valuable initial experience of processing by computer before deciding whether or not to install an in-house computer;

(*b*) to provide standby facilities, by arrangement, in case of breakdown of the in-house computer;

(*c*) to provide facilities for coping with peak data processing loads owing to insufficient capacity of the in-house computer;

(*d*) non-availability of finance for the installation of an in-house computer;

(*e*) space restrictions for accommodating a computer installation;

(*f*) to avoid the responsibility of operating an in-house computer;

(*g*) insufficient volume of work to justify the installation of a computer;

(*h*) to obtain the benefit of computer power at reasonable cost;

(*i*) to provide more information for management control by

using the bureau facilities to process data captured in the form of paper tape from accounting machine operations;

(*j*) to test and prove programs to be run on a similar computer, when installed, to that used by a bureau;

(*k*) to obtain the skill and experience of bureau operating staff in the processing of data;

(*l*) recognition that a bureau is likely to have powerful, up-to-date equipment, made economical by processing a wide variety of work at high volumes;

(*m*) recognition that a bureau will be using, as far as possible, the most efficient techniques and software aids;

(*n*) to process jobs that cannot be processed economically by an in-house computer.

5. Disadvantages of using bureaux. One of the main disadvantages of using a bureau is the loss of control over the time taken to process data (turn-round time) suffered by an organisation, because of the competing requirements of other clients of the bureau.

In some instances, an organisation may be better served by an in-house computer but may be reluctant to take the plunge; as a result, no experience is gained directly in operating a computer installation. This may create indirect benefits to competitors, especially in the problem-solving applications for which a computer is so valuable. This means that competitors who use computers for their problem-solving needs probably generate optimum solutions, whereas a business without a computer may lose this advantage.

6. The Computer Service and Bureaux Association (COSBA). This Association was inaugurated in January 1968 to provide a *Code of Practice for COSBA Members*. An important feature of the code of conduct is the mandatory acceptance by COSBA members that information or data passed to them by a client is absolutely confidential.

There are two classes of member of COSBA. Full members are experienced and established companies operating as computer service bureaux or software houses. Associate membership is open to smaller companies and those in associated fields of service, such as data preparation.

DATA PROCESSING BY COMPUTER BUREAU

7. Computer bureaux and the smaller business. The administrative efficiency of smaller businesses may be increased by utilising the data processing services of computer bureaux. Such services may be used for computing the payroll, wages analysis, purchase analysis and maintenance of the purchase ledger, sales analysis and maintenance of the sales ledger and the control of stocks, etc.

Smaller firms have similar data processing requirements to larger firms but they cannot justify the installation of an in-house computer due to the relatively low volumes of data involved. This situation may change with the advent of the low cost microcomputer. Nevertheless, by using a computer bureau the smaller firm can harness electronic computer power to its data processing requirements and become administratively more efficient as a result.

Computer bureau charges are based on the level of service provided, therefore the cost of processing low volumes of data will be relatively low which makes this course of action an economic proposition. The alternative would be either to increase the number of staff to process the data so as to provide management information for business control or to retain present staff levels and dispense with the provision of important information to management.

It is, of course, essential to obtain estimates of bureau charges for specific data processing requirements for comparison with existing costs but even if bureau charges are higher the additional information provided may create benefits, by being able to control the business more efficiently, in excess of the extra costs.

Bureaux often provide standard computer programs for processing clients' data which may be used to advantage providing they are compatible with the needs of the business. On occasions it may be a prudent course of action to modify existing systems to comply with the features of package programs because by doing so, outmoded systems may be completely updated, and create additional administrative efficiency.

There now follows an outline of various bureau applications indicating the type of data to be submitted and the output which can be provided.

8. Computer bureau payroll application. Initially the bureau must produce a payroll master file either on magnetic tape or disc and this is facilitated by recording relevant information on input forms provided by the bureau (*see* VI, **5** (*c*)). Other data requirements include the following.

(*a*) Standard data:
(*i*) wage rates (unless provided as initial employee data);
(*ii*) overtime premium rates;
(*iii*) piecework rates;
(*iv*) standard working hours.
(*b*) Amendment data:
(*i*) new starters;
(*ii*) leavers;
(*iii*) changes to deduction rates;
(*iv*) changes to overtime premiums;
(*v*) changes to wage rates.
(*c*) Variable transaction data—supplied weekly:
(*i*) hours worked by employees on hourly rates or, alternatively, variations from standard working hours;
(*ii*) details of units produced by employees.

The information which would be received back from the bureau would typically include: pay advices, payroll, National Insurance schedules, lists of deductions, various analyses and annual tax returns.

9. Computer bureau purchase accounting. Initially the bureau must produce a supplier master file which is facilitated by recording relevant information on input forms provided by the bureau. This information would include the name, address and current balance of each supplier. Other data requirements include the following.

(*a*) Amendment data.
This basically consists of:
(*i*) addition of new suppliers' names and addresses;
(*ii*) deletion of names and addresses of suppliers not now applicable;
(*iii*) change of address of suppliers.
(*b*) Variable transaction data:
(*i*) suppliers' invoices;
(*ii*) suppliers' statements of account;
(*iii*) details of remittances to suppliers;
(*iv*) suppliers' credit notes and other adjustments.

The information which would be supplied by the bureau would typically include a list of creditors at the end of each accounting period, purchase analysis, list of purchases to date from each supplier, purchase ledger accounts and remittance advices for each current supplier, V.A.T. analysis and an audit trail. If required the bureau could also print cheques for payment or credit transfer slips. In addition the purchase ledger would be updated.

10. Computer bureau and sales invoices. A bureau may be employed for the preparation of sales invoices and for this purpose it would be necessary to supply relevant information on input forms supplied by the bureau. This information would include the name and address of each customer and product details in respect of descriptions and code numbers, prices and V.A.T. rates. Product details may already exist at the bureau if they are processing the finished stock accounting application.

The variable transaction data in respect of sales may be supplied to the bureau in any convenient form. From the combination of customer and product details and the variable data in respect of sales, invoices are produced ready for despatch. This application could either stand alone or provide the input of invoice data to the sales accounting application.

11. Computer bureau sales accounting. Initially the bureau must produce a customer master file which is faciliated by recording relevant information on input forms provided by the bureau. This information would include the name and address of each customer and other relevant information (*see* VI, **5**(*a*)). Other data requirements include the following.

(*a*) Amendment data:
    (*i*) addition of new customers' names and addresses, credit limit, discount rate and area code, etc.;
    (*ii*) deletion of names and addresses of customers not now applicable;
    (*iii*) change of address of customers.
(*b*) Variable transaction data:
    (*i*) copy of sales invoices (or extended advice notes);
    (*ii*) details of remittances from customers;
    (*iii*) customers' credit notes and other adjustments.

The information which would be supplied by the bureau would typically include a list of debtors at the end of each accounting period, sales analysis, statements of account for each customer, credit control reports, V.A.T. analysis and an audit trail. In addition the sales ledger would be updated.

12. Computer bureau stock accounting. The bureau must first produce a stock master file unless this is already in existence for sales invoicing purposes. The master file would typically contain information as outlined in VI, **5**(*b*). Other data requirements include the following.

(*a*) Amendment data:

(*i*) addition of new product details;

(*ii*) deletion of details in respect of discontinued products;

(*iii*) changes to selling prices, unit cost price, control parameters and V.A.T. rate, etc.

(*b*) Variable transaction data:

(*i*) despatches to customers;

(*ii*) receipts into stock.

PROGRESS TEST 10

1. A computer service bureau is a company which operates a computer to process the work of other companies. What types of computer bureaux are available and what type of service would you expect to obtain from a computer bureau? **(1–3)**

2. For what reasons would you consider using a computer bureau? **(4)**

3. (*a*) Describe the services which may be offered by a large computer bureau.

(*b*) Assume that your company's hourly payroll is prepared by a bureau. List, with brief explanations:

(*i*) three examples of transaction or amendment data which would need to be despatched to the bureau weekly;

(*ii*) three examples of information which would be received back from the bureau. **(3, 8)** [A.C.A. Dec. 1975, Q6]

4. A company has considered its data processing load. It has decided that computer facilities are required and you have been asked to examine the alternatives to an in-house computer.

Draft a report outlining the alternatives available giving their advantages and disadvantages. **(1–5)** [I.C.M.A. May 1976, Q7]

5. Indicate the features of purchase accounting by computer bureau. **(9)**

6. Indicate the nature of sales accounting by computer bureau. **(10, 11)**

7. Outline the nature of stock accounting by computer bureau. **(12)**

CHAPTER XI

Data Transmission

BASIC CONCEPTS

1. General aspects of data transmission. Data transmission is the movement of information in coded form comprising binary digits (bits) over some kind of electrical transmission system (*see* **10–21, 24–9**). Communication between business units by means of data transmission facilities using either telephone or telegraph lines is increasing. The reason for the increasing use of data transmission rather than voice communication and the normal mail service is due to the expanding use being made of computers in business organisations, especially those with dispersed operating units. This is particularly so with regard to businesses with a centralised computer installation used for processing the data of the various operating units in order to achieve economy in data processing activities and efficient control of business operations.

Instead of despatching data for processing by normal mail services or an internal messenger service, it is much faster to send it by data transmission facilities. The processed data may then be re-transmitted to the originating unit and converted into printed form locally if suitable facilities are available, or, if not, it may be sent through the normal mail service or internal messenger service. Data transmission may be either on-line or off-line, and it is now proposed to outline the characteristics of both communication techniques.

Before proceeding, it is important to appreciate the difference between telephone lines and telegraph lines. The former are referred to as "voice-grade" lines, which allow data to be transmitted at higher speeds than telegraph lines allow (*see* **5**).

2. On-line data transmission. On-line data transmission indicates that the communication lines are connected directly to the computer either by means of a multiplexor or an interface unit (*see* Figs. 55 and 56). The interface unit scans the communication lines frequently to detect those ready to send or receive data. When a line is ready to transfer data the scanning ceases and the channel

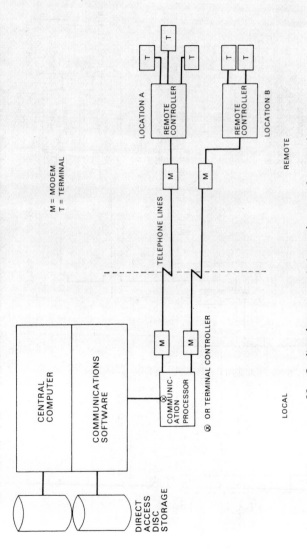

FIG. 55   *On-line data transmission—clusters of terminals*
The multiplexor is located at a distant common point, e.g. Post Office premises or an area office.

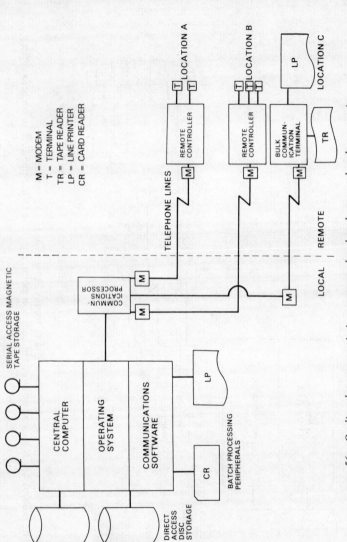

FIG. 56 On-line data transmission system—local and remote batch processing

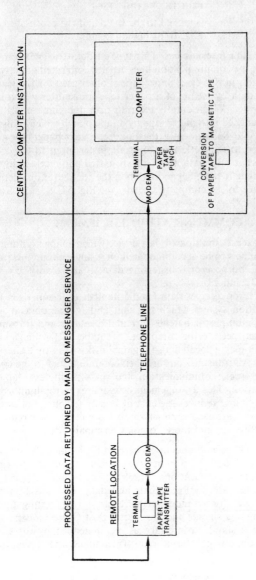

FIG. 57   *Off-line data transmission*

number of the line is signalled to the C.P.U.; if the processor is in a position to accept data, transmission begins.

3. Off-line data transmission. This type of data transmission indicates that the communication lines are not connected directly to the computer. In this case, paper tape is often used for the transmission of data by means of a paper tape transmitter which is a terminal device. When data is received from the communication line, it is punched into paper tape by a tape punch which is also a terminal device. Subsequently, the data recorded in paper tape may be converted to magnetic tape to attain faster input to the computer. Alternatively, data may be transmitted and received in the form of magnetic tape, depending upon the configuration deemed most suitable to the company's needs (*see* Fig. 57).

COMMUNICATION EQUIPMENT

4. Multiplexor. A multiplexor is a device which enables a number of data channels to be accommodated on a single communication line, for the purpose of transferring data to and from the computer (*see* **22** and **23**).

A multiplexor receives data from a number of terminals in the communication system which transmit and receive data at low speed. The multiplexor batches terminal messages and transmits them at high speed to the computer. A number of terminals may share a multiplexor located at a regional office as in time sharing operations. All transmissions are then communicated to the computer by a single communication line via a multiplexor at the central location. This arrangement economises in the number of lines required and reduces the cost of leasing telephone lines.

Multiplexors are used as an alternative to polling which requires dedicated software and more complex terminals (*see* **29**).

5. Modem. The term "modem" is derived from "modulator" and "demodulator" and is an item of equipment connected to each terminal in a communications complex using telephone lines. As telephone lines use analog signals and data terminals transmit signals in digital form a modem is necessary for converting digital signals to analog signals and vice versa. Post Office modems are designed to a standard interface as recommended by the Consultative Committee International Telephones and Telegraphs (C.C.I.T.T.).

6. Front-end and communications processors. These are programmable devices which control the functions of communication systems. They support the operations of a mainframe computer by performing functions which it would otherwise be required to perform itself. The functions include code conversions, editing and verification of data, terminal recognition and control of transmission lines. The mainframe computer is then able to devote its time to data processing rather than data transmissions (*see* Figs. 55 and 56).

COMMUNICATION TERMINALS

Probably the best known data communication terminal is the teleprinter, which transmits data by depressing keys on a keyboard. The data is transmitted along a telegraph line connected to another teleprinter where it is printed (*see* 11). Terminals are now available in many different forms to suit various circumstances (*see* 7–9).

7. Input/output terminals. These are devices used for transmitting or receiving data, and include time-sharing terminals. Some terminals are not connected to the computer and include:

(*a*) paper tape reader for transmitting data;
(*b*) paper tape punch for receiving data;
(*c*) punched card reader for transmitting data;
(*d*) punched card punch for receiving data;
(*e*) magnetic tape units for transmitting and receiving data;
(*f*) printer for receiving data.

Time sharing applications must of course include terminals which are directly connected to the computer, in order to operate by this means. The same considerations apply to real-time systems. In this respect, the terminals are usually visual display units or teletypewriters.

8. Remote batch terminals (distributed processing). Some remote batch terminals are designed as data communication systems for direct communication with a computer or as part of a comprehensive communications network forming a distributed processing system. Such terminals, at various remote locations, communicate with each other for the purpose of transmitting source data and printing documents from the transmitted data. They may also print documents from data prepared locally. Peripheral devices used in such systems include: printer-keyboard, printer, paper tape reader and punch, and card reader and punch (*see* I, **25, 26**).

9. Intelligent terminals. Terminals with processing capabilities are referred to as intelligent terminals and they perform functions which might otherwise be done by the main processor. They may be used for either off-line operations or on-line operations with a host computer.

POST OFFICE DATEL SERVICES

10. Definition of Datel. The Post Office consider data transmission facilities of such importance to commercial, business and industrial undertakings as to merit the provision of a separate group of communications services known as "Datel Services". Datel is a word derived from (Da)ta (tel)ecommunications and the services available are indicated below. It is important to appreciate that it is necessary to obtain permission from the Post Office to connect any communications equipment to Post Office services.

11. Datel 100 Service. This service uses telegraph circuits for the serial transmission of data up to 110 bits per second. Two types of circuit are available either telex (a switched public teleprinter service) or private telegraph circuit. The telex circuits transmit at a maximum speed of 50 bits per second and private circuits at 50 or 110 bits per second. The terminal device used in this service is a teleprinter which produces printed copy and punched tape if required. The equipment may include automatic tape transmitters and re-perforators (a tape punch which punches holes in paper tape to represent the data being received by data signals).

12. Datel 200 Service. This service is designed to allow the duplex serial transmission of data at speeds up to 200 bits per second using either the public telephone network or private speech circuits. This service can also be used for data transmission at a speed of 300 bits per second, but not on a guaranteed basis. Special switching and line concentration facilities can be supplied for data terminals at a computer centre.

13. Datel 400 Service. This service provides one-way data transmission facilities suitable for data collection and telemetry applications. The service enables remote unmanned stations to be "polled" over the public telephone network, and enables the subsequent transmission of digital or analogue data to the central control station. The transmission speed is up to 600 bits per second.

14. Datel 600 Service. This service provides serial transmission of data within two speed ranges, either up to 600 bits per second and between 600 and 1200 bits per second, using either the public telephone network or private speech circuits. Various types of transmission are possible, including transmission in one direction at a time, in both directions but not simultaneously, and in both directions simultaneously, according to requirements.

15. Datel 2400 Service. This service provides for serial transmission of data at a rate of 2400 bits per second employing synchronous both-way transmission, using four-wire private telephone circuits or alternative working over the public telephone network at 600/1200 bits per second.

16. Datel 2400 Dial Up Service. This service is separate from the Datel 2400 Service and is limited to operation over the inland public switched telephone network. It offers synchronous communication facilities at 2400 bits per second or at a reduced rate of 1200 bits per second between any two points on the telephone network in either direction alternately, but not in both directions simultaneously. The customer can switch to an alternative mode of operation which provides for speeds of 600 to 1200 bits per second, and is identical with the fall-back mode of the Datel 2400 Service. Communication between both services is therefore possible in this mode.

17. Datel 4800 Service. This service is for operation on private circuits and the public telephone network. It is expected to become generally available in late 1979 or early 1980.

18. Dataplex System 2 Service. This service complements the existing Dataplex System 1 service. The service consists of a Post Office multiplexing system providing for a mixture of speeds. It uses Time Division techniques (*see* **23**). The transmission speeds which can be provided for full duplex operation are 75, 110, 134.5, 150 and 300 bits per second. The system can accept a combination of any three of these speeds. The channel capacity varies according to the speed being used. At present, the service can, for example, cater for twenty-nine channels at 110 bits per second. Access to the multiplexing equipment can be via the public switched telephone network, private circuits, telegraph circuits or a combination of these.

19. International Datel Services. In the international service, the term Datel has been adopted to refer only to data transmission using the public telephone or telex systems. In addition, data transmissions may be arranged with overseas countries over leased telegraph-type or telephone circuits, provided for a customer's exclusive use. Such circuits may be rented to most locations in Europe and to many points outside Europe, whether or not International Datel Service is available with the country concerned.

TERMS USED IN DATA TRANSMISSION

20. Serial transmission. With this type of transmission, each bit in a character is sent sequentially to the transmission line; by convention the least significant bit is usually sent first, viz.

$$0100011 \rightarrow$$

Speed of transmission is expressed in bits per second.

21. Parallel transmission. In a parallel transmission system, all the bits in a character are transmitted at the same time, viz.

$$\left.\begin{array}{c} 0 \\ 1 \\ 0 \\ 0 \\ 0 \\ 1 \\ 1 \end{array}\right\} \rightarrow$$

Although it appears that seven signals have to be sent to the transmission lines at the same time, in practice special codes are used in order to limit the number of simultaneous signals which need to be transmitted, thereby reducing the technical problems which are introduced when more than one frequency is transmitted at once. Speed of transmission is expressed in characters per second in a parallel transmission system.

22. Frequency division multiplexing (F.D.M.). With frequency division multiplexing a relatively wide band width (range of frequencies available for signalling) is divided into a number of smaller band widths, to provide more channels of communication.

23. Time division multiplexing (T.D.M.). Time division multiplexing is a process whereby a channel which is capable of a relatively high information transfer rate (bits per second) is divided up into a number of time slots to provide a number of lower speed channels. For example, a line capable of carrying 2400 bits per second could, by the use of T.D.M. theoretically be divided into four 600 bits per second channels, or a combination of different speed channels up to a maximum of 2400 bits per second.

24. Synchronous transmission. In this type of transmission, the receiver is kept continuously in step with the transmitter by electronic clocking devices. By this means, synchronisation is maintained in the receipt and transmission of signals.

25. Asynchronous transmission (start/stop). In this type of transmission system, each character is preceded by a start signal which serves to prepare the receiving mechanism for the reception of a character; this is followed by a stop signal which brings the receiving mechanism to rest in preparation for the reception of the next character. Asynchronous transmission may use start and stop elements between blocks of characters rather than between individual characters.

26. Simplex transmission. The transmission of data in one direction only.

27. Duplex transmission. The transmission of data in both directions simultaneously.

28. Half-duplex transmission. The transmission of data in both directions, but not at the same time.

29. Polling. The process of establishing if any terminal in the communication network has a message to transmit. Polling is a continuous process requiring dedicated software and more complex terminals than would be required if using a multiplexor (*see* **4**). The mainframe computer polls each terminal several times each minute to service those with messages to transmit. Messages transmitted by the computer are received by all the terminals in the system but only the terminal to which the message applies displays or prints the message.

PROGRESS TEST 11

1. What do you understand by the term "data transmission"?
(**1**)
2. What are the main purposes of using data transmission facilities? (**1**)
3. Define on-line data transmission. (**2**)
4. Define off-line data transmission. (**3**)

5. Define the following terms used in data transmission:

(a) multiplexor;

(b) modem;

(c) front-end and communications processors. **(4–6)**

6. What are input/output terminals? **(7)**

7. Define the following:

(a) distributed processing;

(b) remote batch terminal;

(c) intelligent terminal. **(8, 9,** *see also* **1, 25, 26)**

8. What do you understand by the term Datel? **(10)**

9. Outline the various Post Office Datel Services. **(11–19)**

10. Define the following terms used in data transmission:

(a) serial transmission;

(b) parallel transmission;

(c) frequency division multiplexing;

(d) time division multiplexing;

(e) synchronous transmission;

(f) asynchronous transmission;

(g) simplex transmission;

(h) duplex transmission;

(i) half-duplex transmission. **(20–8)**

PART THREE

INPUT, OUTPUT AND BACKING STORAGE

CHAPTER XII

Computer Input and Output

INPUT—GENERAL CONSIDERATIONS

Modern electronic computers provide facilities for the input of data for processing by various types of media, depending on the processing requirements of individual businesses.

In general, the various input media may be classified into two main categories—direct and indirect, and the main features of each will now be outlined.

1. Direct input.

(*a*) *Optical:*

(*i*) characters—optical character recognition (O.C.R.) (*see* **3, 4**);

(*ii*) marks—optical mark recognition (O.M.R.) (*see* **5**);

(*b*) *magnetic ink characters*—magnetic ink character recognition (M.I.C.R.) (*see* **6, 7**);

(*c*) *light pen* combined with visual display;

(*d*) *terminal keyboard*, perhaps integrated with a V.D.U., for on-line operations (*see* VIII);

(*e*) *work station keyboard* for direct data entry in respect of small computer systems, i.e. microcomputers and visible record computers (*see* IX).

Input in the form of optical characters or marks and magnetic ink characters recorded on documents is prepared directly in machine-sensible form without the need for the separate source document which is normally used as the basis of data conversion into machine-sensible form.

Direct input has the advantage of reducing data preparation costs, since conversion operations (a feature of indirect input) are eliminated. As a result, data becomes available for processing much more quickly which substantially reduces the total data processing cycle time.

2. Indirect input.

   (a) *Punched card* (*see* **8–11**).
   (b) *Punched paper tape* (*see* **12–18**).
   (c) *Magnetic tape* (*see* XIV, **3–14**).
   (d) *Floppy disc* (*diskette*) (*see* XIV, **36, 37**).
   (e) *Magnetic tape* (*casette*) (*see* XIII).

Data input by means of punched cards is very widely used, for the reason, amongst others, that computer users are often familiar with the characteristics of punched cards from using electro-mechanical punched card equipment.

Punched cards are likely to remain in wide use for a number of years yet, even though direct data entry techniques are becoming more predominant. In comparison with other data entry techniques punched card input predominates in the U.K. There are a number of reasons for this, for instance, punched cards are very durable, which makes them an ideal media for use in the factory and ware-house environment, where they can contend with rough handling. Cards can also be written on which makes them a dual sensible media. They are also used in retail shoe-shops to great advantage as they can be pre-punched with transaction data and stored in the shoe boxes containing the shoes to which the data relates. When the shoes are sold the card is removed from the box providing immediate data for batch processing to update stock status and replenish supplies. The punched card acts as a "turnaround" document in the sense that data already exists for input to the process-ing system.

Perhaps the most widely used alternative methods of data cap-ture in current use are: key-to-tape; key-to-disc and key-to-floppy disc. It has been stated that key-to-floppy disc is the most likely technique to oust the punched card in the future.

Paper tape is often used as an alternative to punched cards, depending upon the choice of computer configuration. Data in this form is often "captured" as a by-product of accounting machine operations for subsequent processing by computer. This technique eliminates the need to punch data into paper tape as a separate operation, thereby reducing the cost of data preparation and speed-ing up the availability of data for processing.

OPTICAL CHARACTERS AND MARKS

Optical characters are designed in a special type fount capable of being interpreted both by humans and by machines (*see* XIII, **14, 15**).

There are two basic O.C.R. founts in use, both of which are approved by the International Standards Organisation:

O.C.R.—A.
O.C.R.—B.

Special ink is not required for printing O.C.R. characters.

Optical characters are sensed by an input device known as an optical character reader which transfers data to the processor.

3. O.C.R.—A. This fount was developed, and is widely used, in the United States. It comprises 66 different characters—alphabetical characters, numbers and symbols—and four standard character sizes (*see* Fig. 58).

4. O.C.R.—B. This fount is the result of the work carried out by the European Computer Manufacturers' Association (E.C.M.A.),

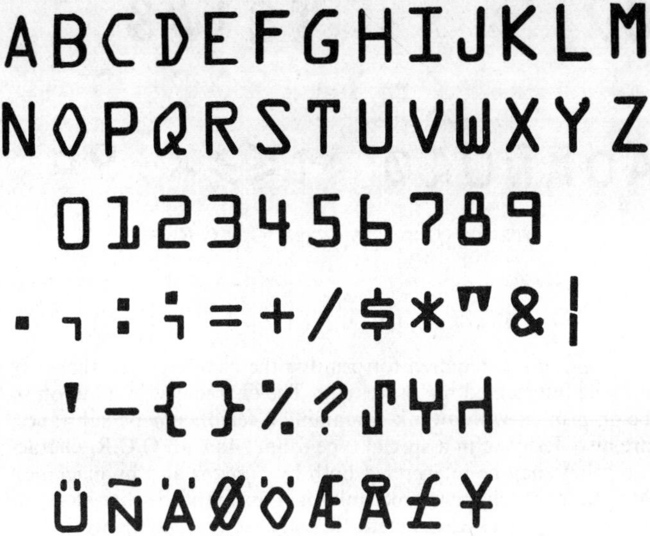

FIG. 58 *Optical characters—O.C.R.—A*

and is widely used in Europe. It comprises 113 different characters and four standard character sizes (*see* Fig. 59).

5. Optical marks (*see* XIII, **16–18**).

An optical mark reader is an input device used for interpreting mark encoded documents and transferring the data to the computer for processing.

```
ABCDEFGH abcdefgh
IJKLMNOP ijklmnop
QRSTUVWX qrstuvwx
YZ*+,-./ yz m åøæ
01234567 £$:;<%>?
89        [@!#&,]
   (=)    "´`^ ~ ˇ
ÄÖÅÑÜÆØ  ↑≤≥×÷°¤
```

FIG. 59 *Optical characters—O.C.R.—B*

MAGNETIC INK CHARACTERS

Magnetic ink is required for printing the characters, so that they may be interpreted for processing. The characters, in addition to being printed with an ink containing a ferromagnetic substance, are also designed in a special type fount. As with O.C.R. characters, they may be interpreted both by humans and by machines. Magnetic ink character recognition is accomplished by an input device known as a magnetic ink character reader/sorter. The technique of M.I.C.R. is mainly used in banking to cope with the enormous task of sorting cheques and updating customers' accounts. It is a more effective method of input than punching a card for each cheque transaction.

There are two M.I.C.R. founts:

E.13B.

C.M.C.7.

6. E.13B. This fount was developed in the United States for the American Banks Association, and has been adopted by British banks (*see* XIII, **19** and **20**).

Each character is made as unique as possible, in order to avoid misinterpretation.

Magnetic ink characters can be overwritten with ordinary ink without affecting their legibility for interpretation by the reader/ sorter.

If any attempt is made to alter a magnetic ink character the subsequent mutilation is detected when the character is being interpreted by the reader/sorter.

The E.13B repertoire consists of ten numeric characters, 0–9, and four symbols to signify the meaning of fields (*see* Fig. 60).

(*a*) *Enlarged.*

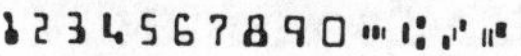

(*b*) *Actual size* (*approximate*)
(*Courtesy of International Computers Limited*)
FIG. 60   *M.I.C.R. characters, E.13B fount*

7. C.M.C.7 (Caractère Magnétique Code). This fount is the continental standard, and although the characters are encoded in magnetic ink their structure is altogether different to E.13B. The characters are formed from a "gapped fount" code, consisting of seven vertical bars.

Each character is identified by the format of the bars, which create a six-bit code. Each bar is separated by a gap; a wide gap equals 1 and a narrow gap equals 0. The M.I.C.R. reader recognises each character by the variable distance between the vertical bars.

The C.M.C.7 repertoire consists of ten numeric characters, 0–9, twenty-six alphabetic characters and five special symbols (*see* Fig. 61).

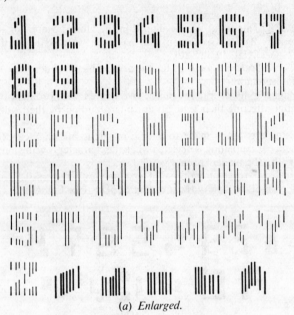

(a) *Enlarged.*

(b) *Actual size* (*approximate*).

(*Courtesy of International Computers Limited*)

FIG. 61   *M.I.C.R. characters, C.M.C.7 fount*

THE 80-COLUMN PUNCHED CARD

The 80-column punched card is produced from a stiff, high-quality paper to avoid the damage which could be caused by frequent handling, and in order to minimise jamming in the card-reading equipment. Data recorded in punched cards are transferred to a computer for processing by an input device known as a card reader.

8. Basic construction of a punched card. A punched card is constructed on the basis of rows and columns, irrespective of the various field layouts which eventually form the basis for designing specific application cards (*see* Figs. 62–4).

(*a*) *Rows.* A card consists of twelve horizontal rows, in the following manner:

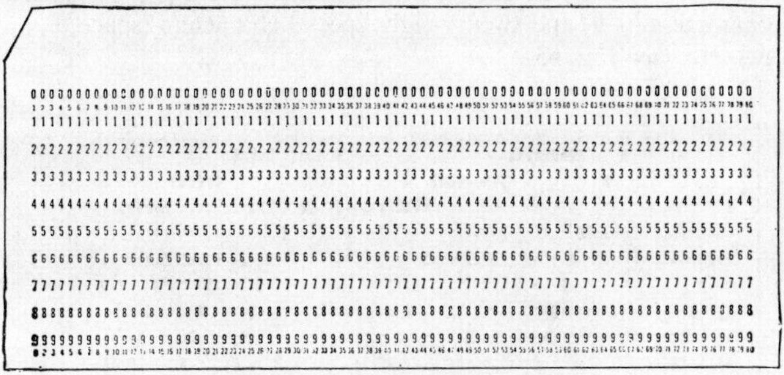

FIG. 62   *A basic punched card*

Alternatives 10 or 12 ⎫
11 ⎬ Zone punch positions.
*0 ⎭
1
2
3
4
5   Numeric punch positions.
6
7
8
9

*The 0 punch position is used both as a zone punch and a numeric punch position.

The rows are referred to as punching positions.

(*b*) *Columns.* The card consists of 80 columns, each of which contains the punching positions indicated above. Each of the card columns is numbered, 1–80, along the bottom edge of the card.

9. Data representation in punched cards. Data is recorded by punching one or more holes in the punching (row) positions in one card column—that is, one column is used to represent one punched character.

Various combinations of holes may be punched to represent either alphabetic characters, numeric characters or special characters.

The combination of holes punched to represent a specific character is based on a punched card code, an example of which is the ICL 64-character code. The 64 characters represented by this code are twenty-six alphabetic characters (A–Z), ten numeric characters (0–9) and twenty-eight special characters (space, £, (,), &), etc. (*see* Fig. 63).

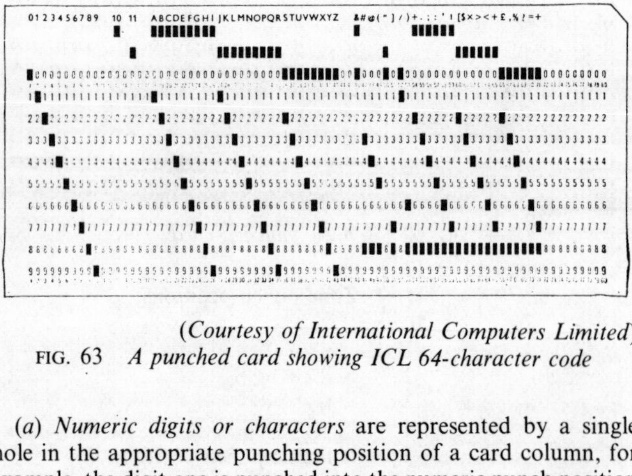

(Courtesy of International Computers Limited)
FIG. 63   *A punched card showing ICL 64-character code*

(*a*) *Numeric digits or characters* are represented by a single hole in the appropriate punching position of a card column, for example, the digit one is punched into the numeric punch position 1, the digit seven is punched into the numeric punch position 7, and so on.

(*b*) *Alphabetic characters* are represented by a combination of two holes, one of which occupies a zone punch position and the other a numeric punch position, for example:

	Zone	Numeric
A is represented by	10	1
B is represented by	10	2
I is represented by	10	9

When the numeric punch positions have been exhausted in combination with a zone punch position, they are used again, but with a different zone punch position, in the following manner:

	Zone	Numeric
J is represented by	11	1
K is represented by	11	2
R is represented by	11	9

(c) *Special characters* may be represented by a combination of two or three holes, which may occupy punching positions as follows:

	Zone	Numeric
& is represented by	10 and 0	—
£ is represented by	0	2 and 8
@ is represented by	—	4 and 8
% is represented by	0	4 and 8

All the punched holes are rectangular or slotted.

(d) The data punched into a card may be *interpreted and printed* along the top edge of the card—each character being located above its appropriate column—for ease of interpretation by operating staff.

10. Card fields. A unit of information in a punched card is known as a "field", and it consists of a number of adjacent columns sufficient to record the number of numerical digits or alphabetic characters required. Examples of card fields are:

(a) customer code number;
(b) stock item code number;
(c) employee number;
(d) quantity;
(e) price;
(f) value;
(g) name and address;
(h) period number;
(i) works order number.

For convenience of the personnel handling the cards and those using the cards, card fields are marked on the card by printed vertical lines. The card columns constituting fields also have a printed heading identifying the data to be punched into the field.

The number of columns in a field is always constant or of fixed length, which means that specific fields always contain the same number of character positions. The size of the field is determined by the maximum number of characters which data may contain. For example, a stock issue for one item may require a quantity field of four columns which can accommodate a quantity up to 9999, whereas other stock issues may be for smaller quantities requiring only two columns, but for simplicity of processing the field is allocated four columns.

The following question will serve as an illustration to demonstrate the design of a punched card field structure for a specific application. The question was set in the I.C.M.A. examinations of November 1978.

As a systems analyst, you have been investigating a sales order entry system and you have decided that the following data will be the required input:

(a) date;
(b) order number;
(c) customer's number;
(d) for each item ordered:
  (i) commodity code;
  (ii) type code;
  (iii) quantity.

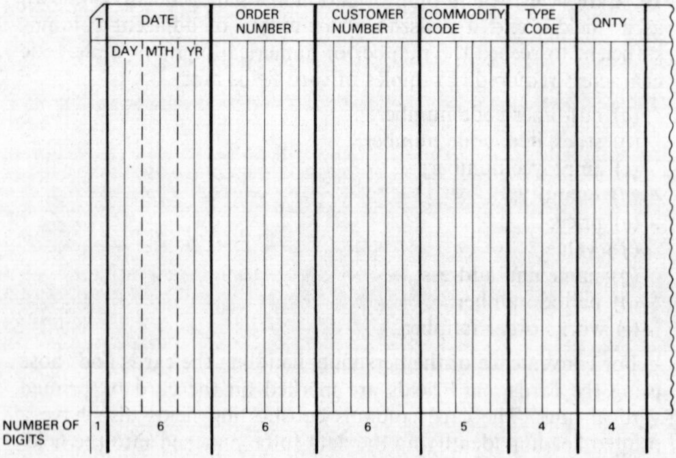

T	DATE			ORDER NUMBER	CUSTOMER NUMBER	COMMODITY CODE	TYPE CODE	QNTY
	DAY	MTH	YR					

NUMBER OF DIGITS: 1   6   6   6   5   4   4

FIG. 64 *Sales order card*

(a) Design the layout of a punched card as an input medium for the above data.

(b) State the validation checks you would specify for the order entry data. What would such checks achieve and why are they necessary?

The solution to part (a) of the question is outlined in Fig. 64 and details providing material for part (b) may be found in VII, **20, 21**.

11. Unit record. A number of related fields punched into a card constitutes a "record". Each master record contained in a file relates to a specific customer, product, stock item or employee, etc. Similarly, each transaction item is recorded separately in a punched card, for example, a stock receipt, a stock issue, an item sold to a customer, the production of a specific product, an operation performed by an employee, etc.

PAPER TAPE: GENERAL CONSIDERATIONS

12. General characteristics. Punched paper tape may be used for input and output of data. When used for input, the paper tape usually contains data relating to current transactions which has been captured during keyboard posting operations by means of a tape punching attachment. In other cases, it is punched from source documents as an alternative to punched cards (see XIII, **3–8**). A paper tape reader is an input device used for interpreting data in paper tape and transferring it to the processor.

Paper tape output, punched under control of the processor is not widely used now.

As paper tape is not so compact as magnetic tape, and access to records is not so convenient as those held in punched cards or on magnetic disc, it is not usually used as a means of backing storage for the retention of master file data.

A spool of paper tape is typically 1 inch (25.4 mm) wide and approximately 700 feet (213.36 m) in length, and may have five, six, seven or eight tracks. Data is represented by means of punched holes across the width of the tape, and the positions in which the holes are punched are referred to as *tracks*. The punched holes conform to a specific tape code for the representation of characters. ICL 1900 series computers use the International Standards Organisation seven-bit code on eight-track tape (see Fig. 65).

The holes representing a character across the width of the tape is known as a "frame", and there are ten frames (characters) to the inch (known as "the packing density").

In addition to the holes representing data, there are a series of small holes along the length of tape known as "sprocket holes" which on early models of paper tape readers were used for tape feed purposes. Modern high-speed readers use the holes for clocking purposes when the tape is being read, and the tape movement is achieved by means of high-speed rollers.

13. Paper tape codes and parity checking. The significance of

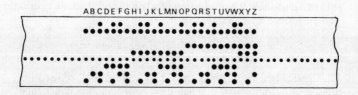

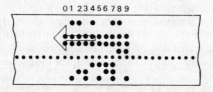

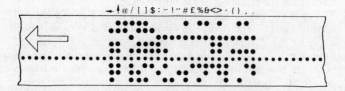

(*Courtesy of International Computers Limited*)

FIG. 65 *The ICL eight-track paper tape code*

whether tape has five, six, seven or eight tracks concerns the number of code combinations possible to represent the range of characters required. In any data processing system, the characters normally required are:

(a) *numeric*—ten characters (0–9);
(b) *alphabetic*—twenty-six characters (A–Z);
(c) *special* characters—various (%, &, £, (,), @, ", :,), etc.

A five-track tape enables only thirty-two characters to be represented, by various combinations of five holes—on the basis that each track position can have a hole punched or not punched, which may be expressed by mathematical notation as follows:

$$2^6 = (2 \times 2 \times 2 \times 2 \times 2 \times 2) = 64$$

It is obvious that numeric and alphabetic characters alone require thirty-six code combinations.

This situation can be resolved by using the same code combinations to represent both numeric and alphabetic characters, differentiated by means of a "shift" code. A "figure shift" code inserted before punching numeric data causes the characters to be interpreted as numeric until a "letter shift" code is sensed. Similarly, all characters following the "letter shift" code will be interpreted as alphabetic until a "figure shift" code is sensed. Effectively, this technique enables sixty-four characters to be represented in five-track tape.

Five-track tape is usually $\frac{11}{16}$ inch (17.46 mm) wide, which is not sufficiently wide for punching codes consisting of six, seven and eight tracks. It is necessary, therefore, to use tape of one inch (25.40 mm) width to accommodate additional tracks, enabling more code combinations to be employed without the need to use "shift" codes.

Six-track tape enables sixty-four characters to be represented by various combinations of six holes which may be expressed mathematically as:

$$2^6 = (2 \times 2 \times 2 \times 2 \times 2 \times 2) = 64$$

Seven-track tape enables sixty-four characters to be represented by various combinations of six holes, the seventh hole or track being used for parity checking.

Eight-track tape enables 128 characters to be represented by various combinations of seven holes, the eighth hole or track being used for parity checking. The mathematical notation in this case is:

$$2^7 = (2 \times 2 \times 2 \times 2 \times 2 \times 2 \times 2) = 128$$

RECORDING DATA ON PAPER TAPE

One of the benefits of using paper tape as a medium for recording data is that the size of fields and blocks of records can be varied. Data punched into cards, on the other hand, require to be of fixed field format and records may not occupy the eighty columns available, which is rather wasteful; more important, the speed with which data is read into the computer is reduced, as the cards pass the reading station of the card reader at a constant speed. The packing of data on paper tape enables data to be input to the computer at a relatively higher speed.

14. Fixed-length fields. It is possible to allocate a specific number of character positions on paper tape in a similar manner to punched cards, irrespective of the number of characters to be recorded in a particular field. For example, if the maximum size of a data field requires six character positions, enabling a quantity to be recorded up to 999 999, then any quantity requiring less than six characters would be recorded as 000125, for instance. The three zeros are termed "insignificant zeros" and occupy three positions which could be occupied by "significant" data, which would increase the speed of input.

15. Variable-length fields. This mode of recording data on paper tape allocates character positions in accordance with the size of the data. Referring to the above example, even though the maximum size of a data field may require six characters enabling up to 999 999 to be recorded, the number 125 would be recorded as such. The insignificant zeros are not punched. This method does, however, require the use of field markers to denote the change of field. In addition, the data requires to be "unpacked" within the computer memory by instructions in the program. The absence of insignificant data enables higher tape input speeds to be attained.

16. Fixed-variable-length fields. This method is a compromise between purely variable and wholly fixed-length working. In general, with this method, descriptive data such as account numbers or stock numbers and similar references are allocated fixed-length fields. Data which is of a variable nature, such as quantities and values, are punched in variable-length format.

ADVANTAGES AND DISADVANTAGES OF PAPER TAPE

17. Advantages of paper tape.

(*a*) Records are punched into tape *one after the other*, unlike punched cards which usually have one record per card; therefore, if a tape is accidentally dropped, the records do not become out of sequence. This is highly probable with punched cards.

(*b*) Records on paper tape may be of *variable length*, which enables character positions to be allocated in accordance with the size of the data, unlike punched cards which have fields of fixed length. Variable-length working is economical in the space occupied by records, and enables data to be read into the computer at a higher speed.

(*c*) Punched tape may be *captured* by means of a tape punch attached to a keyboard accounting machine, which enables selected data to be punched into the tape as posting operations are carried out. This technique eliminates the need to punch tape as a separate operation.

(*d*) Data punched into tape cannot *accidentally be erased*, as is the case with magnetic tape.

(*e*) Paper tape does not take up so much *storage space* as punched cards for the same number of records.

18. Disadvantages of paper tape.

(*a*) It is difficult to *add or delete* records on tape, as a splicing operation is necessary. With punched cards, it is relatively easy as it is only necessary to insert or extract a card.

(*b*) It is only possible to *sort records* on paper tape in the internal memory of the computer, whereas punched cards can be sorted off-line by a mechanical sorting machine.

(*c*) Paper tape input speed is *relatively slow* when compared with magnetic tape. One of the main reasons for this is the packing density of characters—paper tape records ten characters per inch (25.4 mm) of tape, whereas it is possible to record 800 characters per inch of magnetic tape.

(*d*) Verifying paper tape produces a *second tape*, whether or not there are any errors on the original tape. Punched card verification does not necessitate the punching of a second card in most instances. It is only necessary to re-punch cards when errors are discovered, as there is only one record contained in a card, but there are many records in a spool of paper tape.

(*e*) If a spool of tape is lost, then *all the records* contained on the tape are lost, which is more drastic than losing a single punched card.

(*f*) Referring to records on tape is *not so straightforward* as referring to data on punched cards, especially if punched cards are interpreted, as they often are.

OUTPUT

19. Types of computer output. The various types of output from a computer system may be chosen from the following list according to specific requirements:

(*a*) printed;

(*b*) visual display;

(*c*) COM (Computer Output on Microfilm);

(*d*) graphical;

(*e*) punched;

(*f*) magnetically encoded.

20. Printed output. Most systems require printed output in the form of payrolls and invoices and management information, etc. and according to the type of computer in use a large range of printers are available. These include:

(*a*) line printers;

(*b*) matrix printers;

(*c*) band printers;

(*d*) visual record printers;

(*e*) laser printers;

(*f*) teletype;

(*g*) page printing system.

Line printers and matrix printers are referred to as impact printers which print characters by impact onto paper usually by means of a ribbon and print wires or print hammers. Line printers operate at various speed according to the model, i.e. 200, 300, 600, 720, 1500 and 3000 lines per minute. Documentation Incorporated market an impact printer capable of 3000 l.p.m.; the high speed capability is largely due to the machine having an integrated microprocessor controller and lightweight durable alloy hammers; it also has an interchangeable print band. An outline of a matrix printer is provided in IV, **6**; details of a band printer are outlined in IV, **10**; while the features of a visual record printer are provided in V, **9**, (this type of printer is used for recording data on ledger cards).

A laser printer available from Itel International prints on continuous form paper at a speed of 325 lines per second, which is ten times faster than some impact printers.

Teletypes are used as terminals in on-line systems as an alternative to V.D.U.s for transmitting and receiving data. Transmitted data is recorded on rolls of paper and the responses, i.e. the messages from the computer, are also printed.

Honeywell market a system for large volume computer output which is referred to as a Page Printing System capable of printing at 8000, 12 000 or even 18 000 lines per minute. The system also performs perforating, punching, cutting, collating, stacking and addressing. The system is controlled by a minicomputer.

21. Visual display. A V.D.U. has a variety of uses including that of a control unit which enables a computer operator to read program instructions, system messages, keyboard data to be input and master file information (*see* V, **8**). The device may also be used as a terminal for time sharing operations or for retrieving information from computer files in an interrogation system. It may also be used as a data entry device by means of the integrated keyboard. A light pen may be applied for the production of graphs, histograms, drawings, maps and pictures on the screen of a V.D.U. A copy of the data displayed on the screen may be obtained by a copier connected to the V.D.U.

22. Computer output on microfilm (COM). This is a technique which stems the tide of the "paperwork explosion" which has been a feature of computerised batch processing systems in some instances. Very often, the speed with which printed output can be obtained from a computer has been over-exploited and the effects have been to produce too much unnecessary "hardcopy", as it is called.

Computer output by microfilm (COM) is an alternative to printed output and is in the region of ten times faster. COM not only reduces the cost of stationery and storage space for computer printouts, but it is also an information retrieval system. The basic stages of the COM process are outlined below (*see also* Fig. 66).

(*a*) Computer output may be recorded directly onto microfilm by means of a COM recorder connected to the processor—this is for the on-line mode of operation. In its off-line mode, COM is not

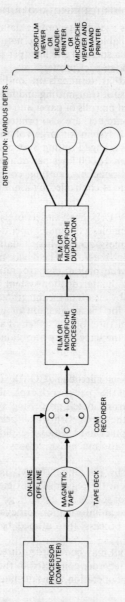

FIG. 66 Computer output on microfilm (COM) or microfiche

directly connected to a computer and images are recorded onto magnetic tape.

(b) The tape deck is connected to a COM recorder which produces images from magnetic tape onto a cathode ray tube (C.R.T.) which are continuously and automatically filmed. This is done through a reduction lens which reduces the image size by a factor of forty-eight. Images are recorded either on 16 mm roll film or 105×148 mm microfiche which can store about 288 computer-sized pages of information which is approximately two million characters. The recorder also adds an index to each image for reference and information retrieval.

(c) The film or microfiche is then processed and used as the negative for the production of copies for distribution to users of the system.

(d) Information may be retrieved by a microfilm viewer, or reader-printer, or a microfiche viewer and demand printer (see Fig. 66).

The use of microfiche is becoming more popular than film. Fiche readers are of a much higher quality than roll-film readers, on a cost-for-cost basis, and they are also less complex. Laser recording techniques are being developed as an alternative to C.R.T. recording and it was recently announced in the publication *Computing* that Kodak Ltd are to launch an off-line laser printer which produces output at the rate of 10 000 lines per minute none of which appears on paper. The reason for this is that "the Komstar Micro-image System", as it is called, uses a laser driven dry heat process to print on to standard microfiche or 16 mm roll film. The on-line version of the system can be connected to any IBM, Itel or Amdahl 370 type mainframe and it is claimed to do the work of ten line printers for the price of one. The printer's microfiche cartridge can accommodate the equivalent of forty-three boxes of continuous stationery.

Debate reported in the *Financial Times* on 4th December 1978, concerned whether or not COM equipment should be "intelligent" and the consensus at the moment seems to be that, ultimately, all COM recorder types will have their own mini- or micro-controller and be linked to the computer they serve like any other peripheral.

COM is used in banking as a solution to providing daily balances of each customer in several thousand branches. Barclays Bank's computers (as reported by *Accountancy Age* on the 26th May 1978) used to print five tons of paper each night. The paper listed all the transactions for all the customers at 3000 branches each day, and the task needed forty printers. The job is now done with nine computer output microfilm units and eighty-five per cent less paper is used.

Each morning before opening, Barclays' branches receive information on the status of all their customers' accounts which are up-to-date as at the close of the previous day's business. The information is received on plastic cards known as microfiche. Prior to using microfiche, the branches had been sent the information on three-part listing paper which was expensive to buy, distribute and store.

23. Graphical. Graphical output in the form of graphs, charts, histograms and diagrams may be produced by a device known as a graph plotter. The technique has a wide range of use in fields such as scientific research, engineering and management information systems. This type of output may also be displayed on the video monitor screen of a microprocessor or even printed out on a teletype terminal in a time sharing system.

24. Punched. Punched output by means of punched cards or paper tape is becoming less widely used as it is being displaced by magnetic media.

25. Magnetically encoded. Output in this form is usually for the purpose of storing updated records and the magnetic media used for the purpose includes flexible discs or, as they are also known, floppy discs or diskettes; standard seven- or nine-track magnetic tape; magnetic tape stored on cassettes; data modules, which are multi-platter (disc) modules; and exchangeable disc packs, etc.

PROGRESS TEST 12

1. Indicate the various input media and methods classifying them into direct and indirect categories.   **(1, 2)**

2. Punching data into cards or paper tape has traditionally been the method for providing computer input.

   (*i*) Name five other methods for providing computer input.

   (*ii*) Describe the procedure involved when creating a card or paper tape input file.

   (*iii*) Comment briefly on one method given in (*i*) above.   **(1, 2(*c*), (*d*), (*e*), 3–7** and *see also* **XIII, 1–8**) [I.A.S. Dec. 1976, Q5]

3. Outline the general characteristics of the following types of computer input indicating the method used for transferring data into the computer for processing:

(*a*) optical characters and marks;

(*b*) magnetic ink characters.   (**3–7**)

4. Indicate the features of an 80-column punched card.   (**8–11**)

5. Give an explanation of the codes that are used to represent data in:

(*i*) punched cards;

(*ii*) magnetic tape;

Your answer should include appropriate illustrations.   (**8–10, XIV, 4**) [A.C.A. June 1978, Q2]

6. The most widely used input media to a computer are punched cards and paper tape. Explain, with appropriate illustrations, the codes that are used to represent numeric, alphabetic and other special characters in each of these media. (**8–10, 13–16**) [A.C.A. Dec. 1976, Q3]

7. Outline the general characteristics of paper tape.   (**12–18**)

8. Outline the various types of output from a computer system.
   (**19**)

9. Indicate the various types of device for obtaining printed output from a computer.   (**20**)

10. Outline the features of computer output by a V.D.U.   (**21**)

11. Define the nature of computer output on microfilm (COM). (**22**)

12. Describe the facilities for providing output from a computer afforded by:

(*a*) a line printer;

(*b*) computer output on microfilm (COM);

(*c*) a visual display unit;

and briefly indicate the applications for which each is suitable.

(*N.B.* A detailed technical description of how these devices operate is *not* required.)   (**20–2**) [A.C.A. Dec. 1976, Q4]

13. Your company has been operating a computer for a number of years and, contrary to initial expectations, the volume of print out has risen dramatically each year.

Describe the system and operational techniques which can be employed to reduce output volumes. (**22**, *see also* XXII, **6**) [I.C.M.A. May 1978, Q3]

14. Indicate the nature of graphical output from a computer.
   (**23**)

15. Outline the nature of magnetically encoded output from a computer.   (**25**)

CHAPTER XIII

Data Preparation and Data Capture

CARD PUNCHING AND VERIFICATION

1. Card punching. Card punching is performed by an operator using a card punch for the purpose of preparing data in machine-sensible form. The punch operator punches data into cards from source documents or specially prepared punching documents. Punching documents are often found to be beneficial in respect of documents from external sources, such as sales orders or purchase invoices which have a high degree of variability in their lay-out, i.e. field sequence. It takes a considerable amount of time to search for data elements to enable them to be punched in the field sequence of the relevant punched card and this slows down the operation considerably.

The punching document ensures high punching speeds by marshalling source data elements into the required field sequence of the punched card. At all times attempts must be made to reduce the time and cost of preparing data for processing by computer because the sooner data is available in machine-sensible form the earlier it can be processed. This also assists in reducing the over-all processing time because total processing time includes the time required for data preparation.

By interchanging keyboards on the card punch, data can be punched in any specific code to suit the needs of the particular computer in use.

2. Card verifying. It is essential to discover punching errors before data is presented for processing and this is accomplished by the verification process. This involves an operator who reads the data contained in source documents, or punching documents, originally used in the punching operation. While reading the data the operator depresses the appropriate keys on the keyboard of the verifier. The verifier does not punch holes however, but compares the hole(s) already punched in card columns with the character keyed on the keyboard. Any difference is detected and the verifier either locks or a red light glows to signal an error condition. The operator then ascertains whether she depressed the incorrect key or whether the original punching was in error. If the verifier operator depressed the wrong key she rectifies this by depressing the correct one and continues by verifying the next column. If the original punching was in error, however, the card is removed from the verifier and returned for re-punching.

Modern card punches assist the verifying process because they enable punching errors to be corrected by means of a duplication feature which automatically re-punches correct columns, leaving only the error columns to be re-punched by the operator. In this way a second error free card is produced which avoids the necessity of having to return cards for re-punching completely after the verification process.

Although verifying is a time consuming process, it is generally regarded as being an essential requirement to avoid the effect of processing incorrect data as this can have drastic consequences apart from the fact that re-processing data is an unproductive activity. It is important to appreciate, however, that verifying does not discover errors on source documents—only punching errors. Source document errors are detected by normal inspection and checking procedures as far as possible but unfortunately all such errors are not detected by this means. Most errors of this type are detected by data validation programs by means of check digit verification, limit and range checks, etc. (*see* VII, **21–6** and Fig. 67).

PAPER TAPE PUNCHING AND VERIFICATION

Paper tape punching may be carried out in a number of ways, but

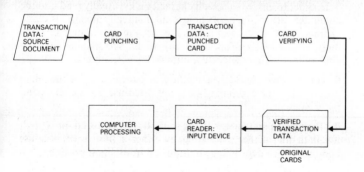

FIG. 67 *Card punching and verifying*

whichever is chosen data will finally be represented by holes in the tape (*see* XII, **12–18**).

3. Methods of punching tape.

(*a*) Hand punch.

(*b*) Automatic punch.

(*c*) On-line tape punch (attached to central processor).

(*d*) Tape punch attachment (attached to keyboard accounting machine).

4. Hand punch. This method is not very effective, as it is very slow and only punches one hole at a time instead of a character at a time. It may be used for punching small lengths of tape while the automatic punches are otherwise engaged.

5. Automatic punch. This type of punch is perhaps the most widely-used method of preparing paper tape for processing by the computer.

The punch consists of the following.

(*a*) A *keyboard mounted on the top of a desk*. The keyboard consists of keys for punching data, function keys, switches and indicator lights for the control of punching.

(*b*) A *punching mechanism*, which punches holes in the tape.

(*c*) A *coding unit*, which translates each key depression into the appropriate code before punching takes place.

(*d*) A *tape code selection* switch.

An operator reading data recorded in source documents depresses selected keys on the keyboard, which causes the data to be punched into the tape.

In order to ensure that each character is eventually read into the computer correctly, a parity hole is automatically punched for each character (series of holes across the tape) in accordance with the mode of parity used (odd or even), which verifies whether each character contains the correct number of holes (bits).

6. On-line tape punch. This method of punching is for recording output from the computer but is not often used in modern computer systems.

7. Tape punch attachment. This method is widely used for capturing data for further processing by either a bureau or in-house computer. The data is captured during transaction posting.

8. Paper tape verifying. In order to ensure that data are correctly punched into tape, it is necessary to verify accuracy usually by the two-tape method.

Data is first punched into an original tape by means of an automatic punch. The tape is then passed to a verifier operator who reads from the same source documents as the operator who prepared the original tape and by means of a verifying machine punches a second tape. The second tape will be free of errors, which is achieved in the following way:

(*a*) The operator *keys in data from the source document.*

(*b*) The data is then *compared automatically* with the data punched in the original tape by means of the reading unit:

(*i*) If the two codes correspond, the punching mechanism punches the data into a second tape.

(*ii*) If the two codes do not correspond, the keyboard locks, which prevents punching in the second tape. A signal light glows, indicating the existence of an error.

(*c*) The verifier operator then determines whether she *depressed the incorrect key or whether the data from the source document was punched incorrectly* in the first instance.

(*d*) The verifier operator depresses the *correct key,* causing the correct data to be punched into the second tape.

(*e*) The verified tape *indicates corrections* by an ink mark which is recorded automatically by the verifier. The ink mark provides a means of visually inspecting tapes for errors made by the original punch operator. If the errors are indicated to the punch operator, it may prevent similar occurrences in the future (*see* Fig. 68).

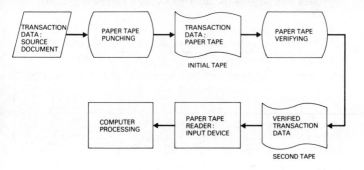

FIG. 68   *Paper tape punching and verifying*

MAGNETIC TAPE ENCODING AND VERIFICATION

Although data may be recorded on magnetic tape by the computer, there are also off-line methods available for recording data on magnetic tape directly without first punching it into cards or paper tape. Methods are also available for converting data to magnetic tape which has been punched originally into cards or paper tape (*see* XIV, 3–14).

9. Keyboard encoding direct to magnetic tape (including verification). A keyboard very similar to that of a standard typewriter is used by the operator, who, reading from source documents depresses appropriate keys on the keyboard, causing the characters to be recorded on seven- or nine-track magnetic tape. For verification, the encoder compares the recorded data when it is keyed in a second time. This system is now being replaced by key-to-disc systems (*see* Fig. 69).

10. Keyboard encoding with C.R.T. display (including verification). This method is more sophisticated than the basic one indicated in **9**, even though a keyboard is used in a similar manner. The special features of this method are as follows (*see* Fig. 70).

(*a*) As the operator keys data from source documents, *it is displayed on a C.R.T.*, thereby enabling her to check her work visually. In this case, data preparation also includes verification.

(*b*) To enable keyboard errors to be reduced, *magnetic tape cassettes* can be supplied which have a special format for display on the C.R.T. as a visual replica of the source document. The operator then keys in the information as if completing a form on

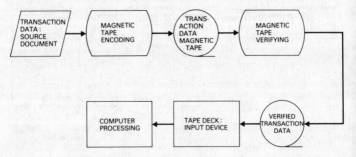

FIG. 69   *Magnetic tape encoding and verifying*

a typewriter. As the data being keyed is displayed in the appropriate data boxes it enables the operator visually to check and correct the data as appropriate before depressing the "send" key, which causes the data to be recorded on to magnetic tape.

(*c*) *Pooling is possible*, whereby a maximum of twelve operators can key into up to four tape drives.

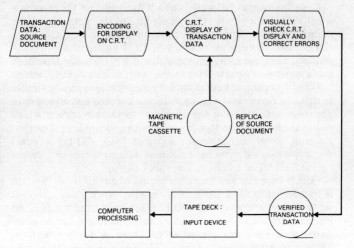

FIG. 70 *Keyboard encoding to magnetic tape with C.R.T. display*

ENCODING OF OTHER MAGNETIC MEDIA

11. Key-to-disc. Key-to-disc systems include a number of key-stations (in the region of twelve to thirty-two) which enables that number of operators at one time to read data from source documents and encode the data into magnetic disc. This is a more efficient method than punching data into cards and is more effective than the alternative method of encoding data to magnetic tape. This type of system is more than a data preparation system because in addition to encoding and verifying data, the system also provides for the validation of data fields, the generation or validation of check digits and the creation of batch totals, all under the control of a read-only program in the memory of the miniprocessor. Some systems are communications-oriented and transmit batches of data to a mainframe computer which may be located at a great distance away, such as another town.

After data has been encoded on disc, verified and validated, etc., records are written to magnetic tape ready for processing by a mainframe computer. The mainframe is then able to process the data which is free of errors and fully validated without having to carry out validation checks which saves valuable processing time.

Key-stations may be located up to 300 metres from the processor which enables them to be strategically sited near to data origination points in factory departments, stores or warehouses, etc.

The essential elements of a key-to-disc system include the key-stations, miniprocessor, magnetic disc drive, magnetic tape deck and a supervisor's console for monitoring the status of the system.

When an operator keys in data, by means of a keyboard similar to that of a typewriter, it is automatically checked and invalid data generates a signal from the processor to the key-station which causes the keyboard to lock, together with an audible or displayed warning. Error correction is facilitated by a V.D.U. or panel display, which indicates the erroneous data by means of a cursor on the V.D.U. or a light on the panel display.

Data is keyed into an entry buffer and when this is full the data is transferred to a defined area of the disc. When a key-station is set to verify the appropriate record is retrieved from the disc and inserted into the key-stations entry buffer so that it can be compared with the same record when keyed in for verification. Differences are displayed on the V.D.U. for correction, either to the original record or the keyed in character by the verifier operator. Records are then moved to an output buffer on disc before being transferred to magnetic tape.

As with all magnetic file media, which can be accidentally erased or overwritten, security measures are necessary and in this instance data is retained on the disc until it has been processed successfully by the mainframe computer. Data is then erased from the disc to provide storage areas for the new batches of data (*see* Fig. 71).

12. Key-to-diskette. A data station is used for recording data on diskettes. As data is entered it is stored in a buffer on the data station and displayed on a screen for the purpose of correcting errors before being recorded on diskette. When data is received it can be recorded to diskette and stored until a further batch of similar data is received. Data is entered by means of a keyboard similar to an electric typewriter. The data station can be set to verify

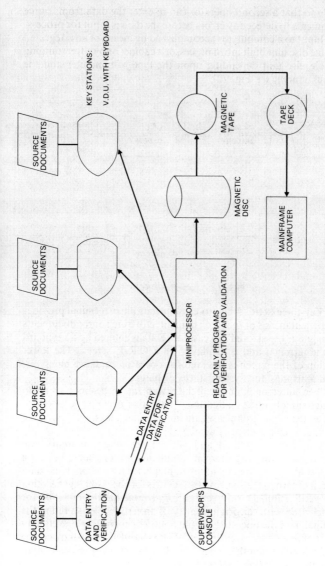

FIG. 71 *Key-to-disc*

mode so that a second operator can re-enter the data from source documents to detect any errors before the data is input for processing. Input to a computer is accomplished by means of an integrated flexible disc unit built into a processor's cabinet or by a freestanding flexible disc unit depending upon the type of computer and the manufacturer (*see* Fig. 72).

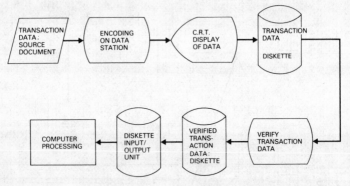

FIG. 72 *Key-to-diskette*

13. Key-to-cassette. A key-to-cassette data entry terminal provides an efficient means of encoding data directly from source documents to magnetic tape stored in a cassette. Data is entered by a keyboard on the terminal and is displayed on a C.R.T. screen. The lower portion of the screen is reserved for operator guidance messages, error warnings and system status displays.

When an error is detected the screen image begins pulsing to attract the operator's attention. When this occurs, the operator presses the keyboard release function key and a message describing the nature of the error is displayed.

Data may be entered and verified according to multi-level formats that are programmed to individual user needs. Within a level, fields are defined by number, name, length and field and data type. The terminal also provides facilities for check-digit generation and verification. During verification, source data is re-keyed for comparison with the original entry. If an error is discovered in the original data the operator has the option of correcting one character or of re-keying the entire field. Data recorded on cassette can be transmitted to another terminal or to a central processor over communication lines (*see* Fig. 73).

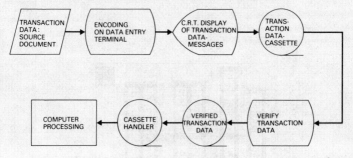

FIG. 73   *Key-to-cassette*

OPTICAL CHARACTER ENCODING AND VERIFICATION

14. O.C.R. character encoding. The printing of characters on documents for optical reading is not so complex as printing magnetic ink characters, mainly because the fount is not so intricate and the use of special ink is unnecessary. It is still necessary, however, to print the characters with a high degree of precision (*see* XII, **3, 4**).

Encoding of characters may be performed in the following ways:

(*a*) *hand printing*, in accordance with specified rules for the formation of characters;

(*b*) by *typewriter* equipped with O.C.R. fount characters;

(*c*) *automatically*, by a line printer fitted with a print barrel embossed with O.C.R. fount characters;

(*d*) by cash registers, adding and accounting machines *equipped with O.C.R. fount characters.*

15. O.C.R. character verification. Unlike characters punched into cards or paper tape, O.C.R. characters are not subjected to a special verification process. It is therefore necessary to subject documents encoded in this special fount to normal checking procedures to ensure that the data is of the required degree of accuracy.

OPTICAL MARK ENCODING AND VERIFICATION

16. Mark encoding. The recording of marks on documents to represent variable data may be performed as follows on p. 204.

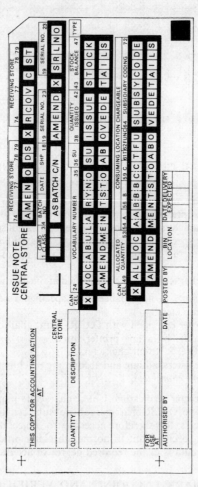

(Courtesy of Computer Power—National Coal Board)
(a) The original form prior to entries
FIG. 74 O.C.R. goods issue note

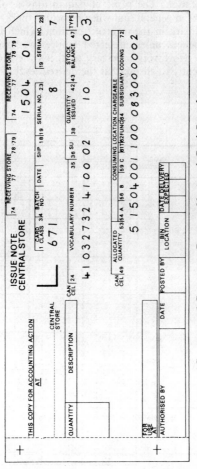

(Courtesy of Computer Power—National Coal Board)
(b) The form after entries have been pencilled in
FIG. 74 *(cont.)*

(*a*) Hand marking using a pencil (*see* Figs. 74 and 75).

(*b*) Automatically by line printer.

17. Mark verification. The same considerations apply as for O.C.R. characters in general, but when recording marks it is very easy to place a mark in the incorrect column, which may have serious consequences unless detected before processing commences. It is therefore very necessary to check the accuracy of marks independently to ensure that the desired level of accuracy is being attained.

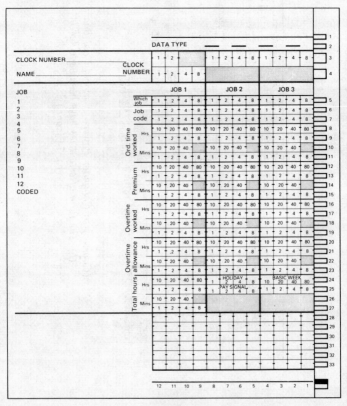

(*Courtesy of Patent Shaft Steelworks Ltd.*)

FIG. 75 *Employee clock-card*

18. Example of O.M.R. combined with O.C.R., demonstrating the use of turnaround documents. The Midlands Electricity Board produces meter reading sheets by computer which contain details printed in optical characters. The meter sheets are used by meter readers who record meter readings (electricity consumed by customers) by marks in pre-designated meter reading columns. The details are then transferred to magnetic tape by optical mark and optical character reading.

The magnetic tape file is then used to produce consumer bills with stubs. These are sent to the consumer who detaches the stub and returns it with the remittance. The stub is then read by an optical character reader and transferred to magnetic tape to provide a file of cash receipts. The cash receipts are then recorded against the consumer record to provide an updated file of consumer details on magnetic tape. Both the meter sheet and the bill stub are turnaround documents as they are initially produced by the computer as an output and subsequently become the basis of input to the computer for further processing. The computer has actually produced its own input data at an earlier output stage (*see* Figs. 76–9).

MAGNETIC INK CHARACTER ENCODING AND VERIFICATION

19. Magnetic ink character encoding. In respect of cheques magnetic ink characters may be encoded when the cheque is printed. The data pre-encoded would include (*see* XII, **6**):

   (*a*) serial number of the cheque;
   (*b*) bank branch number;
   (*c*) customer's account number (*see* Fig. 80(*a*)).

When a cheque is presented to a bank by a customer, the bank encodes the amount of the cheque (*see* Fig. 80(*b*)). The encoding is carried out by a machine known as a M.I.C.R. cheque encoder which has a manually operated keyboard. Alternatively, this may be performed by an encoding machine connected to a keyboard listing machine. When cheque details are recorded on a summary sheet the data is simultaneously encoded on the cheque by the encorder.

20. Magnetic ink character verification. It is necessary to ensure that the accuracy of encoded data is of the required level by

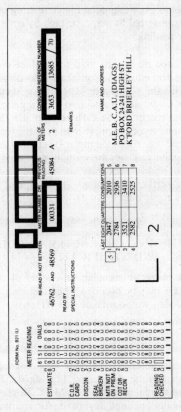

Mark-reading document: payroll

(*Courtesy of Midlands Electricity Board*)
FIG. 76 *Meter reading sheet: O.M.R. and O.C.R.:
Domestic supply*

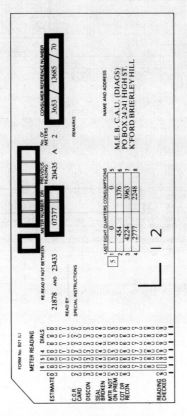

FIG. 77   *Meter reading sheet: O.M.R. and O.C.R.: Offpeak supply*

M·E·B
MIDLANDS ELECTRICITY

M.E.B. C.A.U. (DIAGS)
P O BOX 24 241 HIGH ST.
K'FORD BRIERLEY HILL

ACCOUNT DATE	CONSUMER REFERENCE No
13.12.78	3653/13685/70

FUEL COST DETAILS — See explanation overleaf

CHARGEABLE COST OF FUEL P. PER TONNE	FUEL COST INCLUDED IN BASIC PRICE P. PER TONNE	FUEL FACTOR	FUEL CHARGE (ADDED TO BASIC PRICE) P. PER UNIT
2561	2000	0.00046	0.260

VAT REGISTRATION No 238 5679 21

	METER READINGS PREVIOUS	METER READINGS PRESENT		AMOUNT £
			TARIFF D1 - DOMESTIC SUPPLY	
			STANDING CHARGE	2.92
1	45084	47649	UNIT CHARGE 2565 AT 2.740P	70.28
			TARIFF OP1 - OFF PEAK SUPPLY	
			STANDING CHARGE	0.60
2	20435	22433	UNIT CHARGE 1998 AT 1.260P	25.17

'E' ABOVE INDICATES AN ESTIMATED READING
'C' INDICATES CONSUMERS OWN READING (THE DATE SHOWN OPPOSITE IS THE DATE WE RECEIVED YOUR CARD)
'R' INDICATES METER REMOVED OR PREMISES RE ASSESSED

DATE OF READING OR ESTIMATE	PLEASE PAY THIS ACCOUNT BY	TOTAL AMOUNT DUE
13.12.78	3. 1.79	£ 98.97

PAYMENTS BY POST to MIDLANDS ELECTRICITY BOARD, P.O. BOX No. 18, BRIERLEY HILL, WEST MIDLANDS, DY6 8BL. (further advice on methods of payment is given overleaf)

ENQUIRIES to M.E.B. WHARF LANE, SOLIHULL, WEST MIDLANDS, B91 2JN
TEL. 021-705-6711

A RECEIPT when given by machine to be printed here.

The Post Office, National Giro Centre,
Bootle, Merseyside, GIR 0AA.

MIDLANDS ELECTRICITY BOARD

Date .... 19 ......

BY TRANSFER FROM GIRO ACCOUNT No

DATE BY WHICH PAYMENT IS REQUIRED: 3. 1.79

AMOUNT: £ 98.97

M.E.B. C.A.U. (DIAGS)
P O BOX 24 241 HIGH ST.

CONSUMER REFERENCE No: 36531368570

CREDIT GIRO ACCOUNT No: 400 1001

13Pa
20Ba

SIGNATURE ....

L O I

36531368570 00 A74001001000098973 V

NOTE: 1 *See* Fig. 76
2 *See* Fig. 77

(*Courtesy of Midlands Electricity Board*)

FIG. 78 *Electricity bill with stub: O.C.R.*

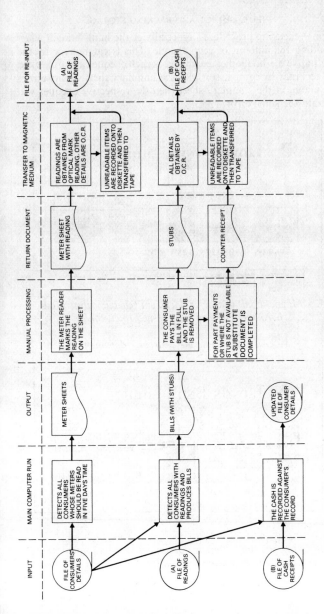

(Courtesy of Midlands Electricity Board)

FIG. 79 Procedure chart: use of turnaround documents in quarterly billing

normal checking procedures, especially at the bank branch when encoding the amount of each cheque. This is catered for by the alternative method indicated above, as each cheque can be checked for accuracy by comparison with the summary sheet. If any errors are made on the summary sheet then the respective cheques will contain the same error.

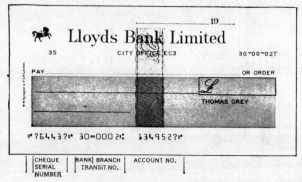

(a) *Magnetic ink character document (cheque) illustrating characters encoded when issued to customer*

FIG. 80   *Magnetic ink character documents*

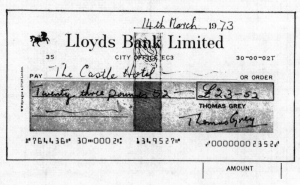

(b) *Magnetic ink character document (cheque) illustrating characters encoded after presentation to bank by customer*

FIG. 80   (*contd.*)

DATA COLLECTION SYSTEMS

21. Features of a data collection system. A data collection system is used for recording and transmitting data from remote locations to either a central point or directly to a computer. When the transmitted data is not input into a computer directly, it is automatically punched into paper tape or punched cards or, alternatively, may be encoded on magnetic tape for input to a computer for processing by an appropriate input device. In general, data collection systems are applied where it is necessary speedily to collect data from dispersed locations within an organisation with a minimum of recording and in a form suitable for processing to obtain the desired information for the control of operations.

Applications include the recording of sales transactions at the point of sale and the recording of production data in respect of factory departments. In respect of a factory data collection system information of a fixed nature may be pre-punched or embossed on punched card or plastic badges. Variable information may be recorded by a keyboard, a set of levers or dials on an input unit.

Punched cards are inserted in a slot on the transmitter, and the contents of the cards are transmitted to a central location after depression of a "transmit" switch. The data represented by dial settings is also transmitted after depression of a transmit switch. Data recorded on a plastic badge is transmitted when the badge is inserted into a badge-reader. The data is then punched or encoded as indicated above, for off-line data collection, or entered directly into the computer for on-line data collection. In respect of on-line operations, the transmitters are connected directly to the computer. By this means the need to convert data into a form suitable for input is eliminated and data is immediately available for processing. Transmitters are strategically sited at dispersed locations throughout the organisation. An example of a data collection system in a steelworks environment is outlined in III, **15** (*see also* III, **14**, VIII, **1**, IX, **3–9**).

22. Retail terminal system. An interesting example of a data collection system is the NCR 280 Retail System. The design of the system allows sales transactions to be recorded in either an off-line data collection environment, or as part of an on-line communication and data processing system. The system consists of retail terminals which increase the speed and accuracy of recording sales transactions. Terminals can operate either as freestanding sales registers or as communication terminals for transmitting and receiving data. They can be connected directly to magnetic tape data collecting units or to an in-store central processor.

A simplified keyboard allows sales staff to record transactions faster and more accurately. An illuminated panel above the keyboard lists the code number and types of transactions to be processed through the terminal. As sales staff enter the transaction code number, the correct sequence of keyboard entries to be followed appears in the display. A series of illuminated instructions on the terminal display guides sales staff through each step of the transactions. The numeric display shows identification codes, the price of each item, sales total, amount tendered and change due to the customer.

As transactions are recorded on the terminal, information is transmitted to a data collector which records data on magnetic tape. The tape reels may be transported to the computer location or the data may be transmitted over telephone lines. Up to fortyeight NCR retail terminals may be connected to a data collector.

An optional feature of the NCR 280 Retail System is a Wand Reader which automatically captures financial, sales and merchandise information at the point-of-sale. A member of the sales staff passes the tag reader over the colour bar-code portion of the merchandise ticket and the retail terminal automatically records the item. Self-checking electronic features built into the tag reader assure that all data is complete and accurate. A tag printer produces the tags which can be read by the wand tag reader. Information on each ticket is printed in readable type as well as in a special code of green, black and white bars. Using the tag reader to record transactions improves customer service by eliminating time consuming keyboard entries and operator errors. This helps in reducing lost sales due to walk-out at checkout points.

In addition to data capture at the point of sale, information can be entered into the system at the point of receipt while taking inventory and while recording store transfers or markdowns.

The Retail System can be extended by means of a Retail Terminal Support System. The support system provides merchandise information throught the day as well as credit control at the point of sale through instant access to local or central credit authorisation files. The support system consists of a control processor, an integrated magnetic tape unit for data collection and communication modules. The control processor collects data from hundreds of retail terminals. Data from the retail terminal support system is transferred to the data processing system for the production of management reports. Data is received either on-line from retail terminals or relayed from data collectors over telephone lines after hours. In multi-store operations, the mutual sharing of data collection facilities and communication lines reduces cost per terminal and reduces information turnaround time. Detailed reports are available to management for prompt action (*see* Fig. 81).

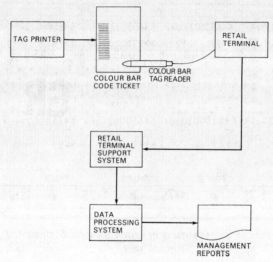

FIG. 81   *NCR 280 Retail system*

KIMBALL TAGS

23. Definition. Kimball tags are special types of price tag used in retailing which contain printed and punched or magnetically encoded information (*see* Fig. 82).

24. Kimball tag applications. Tags are used to improve the control of merchandising by means of automated tag systems which provide automatic facilities for printing and punching information into tags. The tags are then attached to the appropriate merchandise ready for sale. When the merchandise is sold, the tags are removed and the information they contain is converted into paper tape for processing by electronic computer.

A system is also available for recording information contained in tags to magnetic tape in cassettes. The information is then transmitted from remote locations by telephone line to a data centre where the information is received and converted into punched tape or magnetic tape for computer input. This method eliminates mailing delays and provides management reports much more quickly.

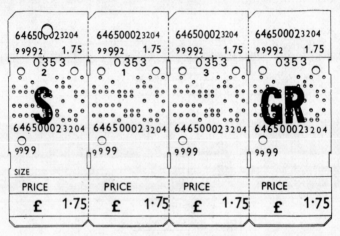

(*Courtesy of Litton Business Systems Ltd.*)

FIG. 82   *Kimball tags*

Machines are available which encode both printed and magnetic language on tags and labels. The magnetic language is easily and accurately read by means of a hand-held magnetic scanning device such as the Datapen reader. By means of the reader information can be automatically captured at the point of the transaction from the magnetically-encoded documents. The encoded documents stay on the merchandise and can be read more than once to record transfers, returns and other inventory data. Such documents have a large capacity for their size, and cannot easily be counterfeited or altered.

Such systems are aimed at capturing and processing data as economically and speedily as possible, in order to provide essential management information for forecasting and control of business operations.

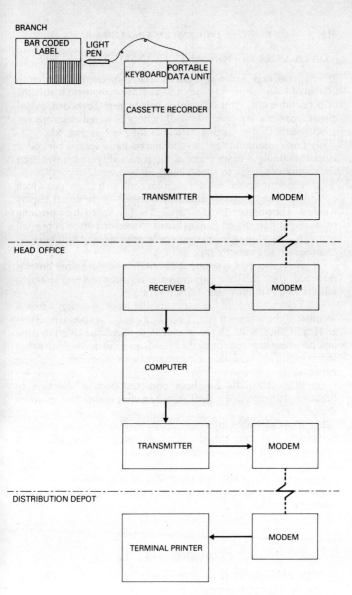

(*Courtesy of J. Sainsbury Ltd*)

FIG. 83 *Supermarket ordering system*

DATA COLLECTION AND TRANSMISSION SYSTEM

25. Supermarket ordering system. The Supermarket ordering system of J. Sainsbury Ltd uses data capture equipment consisting of a portable data unit containing a light pen, keyboard, visual display, cassette tape recorder and battery powered electronics.

The method of collecting data is as follows (*see* Fig. 83).

(*a*) Each commodity in the supermarket has a special bar coded label containing a description of the commodity and a five digit code number unique to that commodity.

(*b*) The store operator scans each bar code with a light pen which optically "reads" the code number for display in the visual display window. The number of cases required is then keyed in by pressing the relevant buttons on the keyboard. An enter button is pressed and the information displayed, code number and quantity, is recorded on the cassette tape.

(*c*) This procedure is continued until the complete store order is recorded, then the data capture units are returned to the transmitters to await automatic transmission.

(*d*) Transmission of data occurs the same evening when a member of the computer staff, operating one of the special receivers at Head Office, will call the branch data telephone to establish a link between the receiver and the branch transmitter. As soon as the link is established the data is transmitted over the public telephone network.

(*e*) When the data has been collected from a selection of branches, the recorded tape from the receiver is then processed by the computer.

(*f*) The debit note information produced is "written" to magnetic tape and transmitted over high speed private lines to a terminal printer at the appropriate distribution depot, where debit notes are printed.

(*g*) The branch order is assembled from the debit notes and the majority delivered to the branch all within twenty-four hours of placing the order.

PROGRESS TEST 13

1. Punching data into cards or paper tape has traditionally been the method for providing computer input.

(*a*) Name five other methods for providing computer input.

(*b*) Describe the procedure involved when creating a card or paper tape input file.

(*c*) Comment briefly on one method given in (*a*) above. **(1–8, see also XII, 1, 2** (*c*), (*d*), (*e*)) [I.A.S. Dec. 1976, Q5]

2. (*a*) Describe three methods of capturing data in a commercial or industrial environment for subsequent input to a centrally located computer.

(*b*) Explain, by reference to the methods you describe, the factors which influence the selection of a particular system of data capture. **(1–25, see also III, 14** and **VIII, 1)** [A.C.A. June 1976, Q3]

3. Indicate two methods of encoding data on magnetic tape. **(9, 10)**

4. Describe the key-to-disc method of data preparation. **(11)** [Based on A.C.A. Dec. 1975, Q1]

5. Indicate how data is encoded and verified in key-to-diskette and key-to-cassette data capture methods. **(12, 13)**

6. Outline the factors concerned with optical character and mark encoding and verification. **(14–18)**

7. Outline the features of magnetic ink character encoding and verification in banking.**(19, 20)**

8. It is proposed to transfer the production and stock control systems in a large manufacturing establishment to a computer. For successful operation of the new system, it will be necessary to pick up data relating to finished and partly finished components from twelve recording points in the factory.
Required:

(*a*) state your recommendation for a method of data capture to suit this particular situation and describe how it would operate;

(*b*) list five advantages that can be claimed for the method you describe. **(21, see also III, 14, VIII, 1, IX, 3–9)** [A.C.A. June 1978, Q3]

9. Indicate the features, method of operating and applications of a data collecting system using retail terminals. **(22)**

10. What are Kimball tags, and in what applications are they used? **(23, 24)**

11. Outline the features of a computer-based supermarket ordering system indicating the type of hardware required. **(25)**

CHAPTER XIV

Backing Storage

INTRODUCTION

1. Definition of backing storage. Backing storage is an extension to a computer's internal storage, and is used for the off-line storage of programs and master files until they are required during processing. When required, they are transferred to the computer's internal storage. In effect, backing storage is a computer's filing system, using magnetic files instead of filing cabinets.

2. Types of backing storage. The details which follow attempt to outline the current methods and developments in computer backing storage.

- (*a*) Methods in general current use:
  - (*i*) magnetic tape (reels);
  - (*ii*) magnetic tape (cassette);
  - (*iii*) exchangeable magnetic discs (hard discs);
  - (*iv*) diskette (floppy discs);
  - (*v*) mini-diskette (mini-floppy discs);
  - (*vi*) integrated discs;
  - (*vii*) data module.
- (*b*) Methods being developed or in limited use:
  - (*i*) bubble memory;
  - (*ii*) laser memory;
  - (*iii*) holographic memory.

MAGNETIC TAPE (REELS)

3. General characteristics. Magnetic tape is widely used for backing storage, and is also used as a means of recording transaction data for input into the computer. Magnetic tape not only allows data to be entered into the computer at very high speeds, but also provides the facility for writing output data to tape at high speed. A further important feature is that it is a very compact means of storing programs and master files.

Magnetic tape in common use is $\frac{1}{2}$ in (12·70 mm) wide and 2400 feet (731·52 m) long, and is held on a reel. A tape deck is used for writing data to magnetic tape from the processor and reading data from tape to the processor. This is accomplished by read/write heads.

4. Magnetic tape codes.

(*a*) Data are recorded as magnetised spots which are known as *binary digits* or "bits".

(*b*) Data are recorded in *parallel tracks* along the length of the tape, the number of tracks may either be seven or nine.

(*c*) The tracks *across the width of the tape* provide one column of data, i.e. one character which may be either numeric, alphabetic or special.

(*d*) A character is represented by a code consisting of a *unique "bit" combination* of 0s and 1s. For example, a seven-track tape may use a code consisting of seven positions of binary notation divided into three divisions, as shown in Table VII (*see also* Fig. 84).

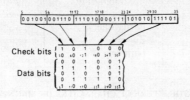

(*Courtesy of International Business Machines Corporation*)
(*a*) *Magnetic tape, seven-track, seven-bit alphameric code.*

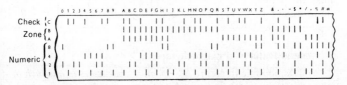

(*Courtesy of International Business Machines Corporation*)
(*b*) *Magnetic tape, seven-track, binary recording.*

FIG. 84   *Types of magnetic tape*

(*i*) One character across the width of the tape may be shown as in Table VIII.

(*ii*) The parity bit check is for ensuring that each character has the correct number of bits (*see* **7** and **8**). The zone bits are used in combination with numeric bits to represent alphabetic or special characters. The numeric bits are assigned the first four binary values of 8, 4, 2 and 1, which are used for representing, in binary coded decimal form, the decimal numeric digits 0–9. Seven-track tape therefore consists of six data tracks and one parity track. Nine-track tape consists of eight data tracks and one parity track for recording bytes.

(*iii*) The coding of various characters may be on the basis shown in Table IX.

An "even" parity check is illustrated in Table IX, whereby all the 1 bits add up to an even number (*see* Fig. 84).

TABLE VII STRUCTURE OF SEVEN-TRACK TAPE CODE

Position	Designation	Number of bit positions
1	Parity check	1
2 and 3	Zone	2
4, 5, 6 and 7	Numeric	4

TABLE VIII STRUCTURE OF CHARACTERS ON MAGNETIC TAPE

	Parity bit check	Zone bits		Numeric bits			
Position on track	1	2	3	4	5	6	7

5. General features of magnetic tape.

(*a*) It is possible to record *800 or more characters in one inch of magnetic tape*, which is equivalent to ten punched cards of 80-column capacity, or alternatively one tenth of an inch (2.54 mm) of magnetic tape can record 80 characters, the equivalent of one punched card. The number of characters per inch of tape is, as we have seen, known as the packing density.

TABLE IX   CODING OF CHARACTERS

	Character	Parity check	Zone		Numeric			
		C	B	A	8	4	2	1
	1	1	0	0	0	0	0	1
Numeric	2	1	0	0	0	0	1	0
	3	0	0	0	0	0	1	1
	A	1	1	1	0	0	0	1
Alphabetic	B	1	1	1	0	0	1	0
	C	0	1	1	0	0	1	1
	%	1	0	1	1	1	0	0
Special	@	0	0	0	1	1	0	0
	,	0	0	1	1	0	1	1

(b) Characters are grouped into *fields*, of which account numbers, names and addresses, quantity, price and value are examples.

(c) Related fields constitute *records*.

(d) Records within a file may be *fixed or variable in length* (*see* **11, 12**).

(e) Records held on magnetic tape are held in *blocks* and the number of records within a block may also be fixed or variable (*see* **9**).

(f) Reels of magnetic tape may be used *repeatedly*:
  (i) old data may be erased and the tape used again;
  (ii) old data may be overwritten by new data.

(g) The process of writing to a magnetic tape which already holds data destroys the data already recorded, therefore *control procedures* are necessary to ensure that current data is not overwritten in error (*see* VII, **13, 14**).

(h) Data on magnetic tape can be *used repeatedly*, because the process of reading tape is non-destructive.

(i) As records held on magnetic tape (especially master files) are normally *in sequence with regard to a particular field* (account number or part number, for instance) the records are stored serially. If it is necessary to access any record for updating purposes, in respect of current input data, then it is only possible to do so by reading all records which precede the required record.

This is known as "serial access", and may be a disadvantage, as searching the tape for the required record can slow down the speed of processing within a specific run, unless each record on the tape has a high frequency of reference during file processing. This is known as the "hit" rate *see* VII, **9**).

6. Uses of magnetic tape. Magnetic tape may be used for a number of different purposes, but in general it is used as a media for input, storage and output. This aspect differs from the use of punched cards and paper tape, which are usually only used as a means of input even though it is possible to use such media for output of an intermediate nature. Specific uses of magnetic tape are indicated below.

(*a*) *Input for processing.* Transaction data may be encoded directly to magnetic tape, thereby dispensing with the need to use punched cards for recording such data. Alternatively, a small computer may be used for converting transaction data in punched cards to magnetic tape for input to a larger, more powerful computer. Very often, data are first punched into cards and input to the computer in random order; they are then validated and written to magnetic tape for further processing to take advantage of magnetic tape transfer speeds and flexibility.

(*b*) *Storage of master files.* Magnetic tape provides a compact means of storing records which are either subjected to updating or used for reference purposes.

(*c*) *Storage of programs.* Computer programs are often stored on magnetic tape, as it provides a fast media for their transfer to the internal memory of the computer in readiness for processing.

(*d*) *Storage of intermediate processing results.* Very often the output from one run is recorded on magnetic tape, which becomes the input for the next run.

(*e*) *Output for conversion.* The output from a powerful computer may be in the form of magnetic tape, which is subsequently converted to printed output by off-line operations to avoid holding up the processor by slow printing speeds.

PARITY CHECKING OF MAGNETIC TAPE CHARACTERS

7. Odd or even parity. When data is being written to magnetic tape, in the form of magnetised spots (bits), an additional magnetised spot is written to each row of spots (representing characters) when necessary to conform to the mode of parity used—"odd" or "even".

Odd parity may be used for seven-track tape, which provides for six data bits per row and one parity bit. When using this parity mode the number of bits representing a character will have a parity bit recorded if they come to an even number, in order to make them add up to an odd number.

When using even parity, the number of bits representing a character will have a parity bit recorded if they come to an odd number in order to make them an even number (*see* **4**(*d*)).

8. Purpose of parity checking. Parity checking is used to ensure that data (in the form of characters) have the correct number of bits written on tape. Parity is automatically checked after being recorded by a read-after-write parity check.

When data is being read into the computer from tape, the parity is again checked and the parity bit is then discarded, as it is not stored in the internal memory. If parity checks indicate invalid characters (incorrect number of bits) then the data are subjected to either re-reading or re-writing and if, after several attempts, the parity check fails, an error is indicated in the data.

RECORDING DATA ON MAGNETIC TAPE

9. Blocking of records. A block of records consists of a number of records which are grouped together without intervening spaces between them, i.e. without inter-record gaps (*see* Fig. 85).

There are a number of ways in which records may be blocked:

(*a*) *Fixed-fixed blocks.* The blocks consist of a fixed number of fixed-length records (*see* Fig. 86(*a*) and (*b*)).

(*b*) *Fixed-variable blocks.* The blocks consist of a fixed number of variable-length records (*see* Fig. 86(*c*) and (*d*)).

(*c*) *Variable-fixed blocks.* The blocks consist of a variable number of fixed-length records (*see* Fig. 86(*b*)).

(*d*) *Variable-variable blocks.* The blocks consist of a variable number of variable-length records (*see* Fig. 86*d*)).

10. Block size. The size of data blocks has a direct bearing on the efficiency with which jobs are run on the computer.

Irrespective of the size of data blocks, a blank length of tape is required between blocks. This is known as an "inter-block gap" and is used to allow the tape to slow down and stop after a block of data has been read or written, and to allow the tape to re-start

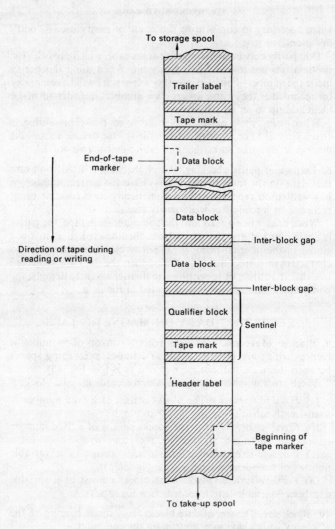

(*Courtesy of International Computers Limited*)

FIG. 85 *Layout of a data file on magnetic tape*

and accelerate to the appropriate reading or writing speed for the next block of data to be input or output.

If data blocks are short, then the deceleration and acceleration of the tape between blocks can exceed the time actually taken in transferring data to and from the computer. In order to eliminate this unproductive time, the block size should be increased as much as the available internal storage locations will allow.

11. Fixed-length records. Fixed-length records consist of fields of a fixed length in a similar manner to fields of data on punched cards. Fixed length implies that the number of character positions allocated to each field of a record is constant, irrespective of the number of character positions required by the data (*see* **9** above). In circumstances when all the character positions are not required,

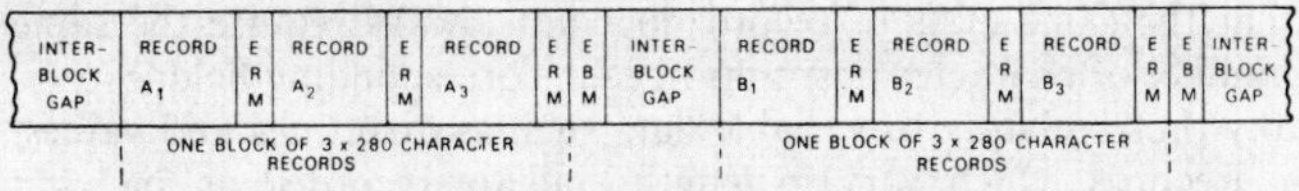

(*Courtesy of International Computers Limited*)
(*a*) *Magnetic tape—"fixed-fixed" blocks*

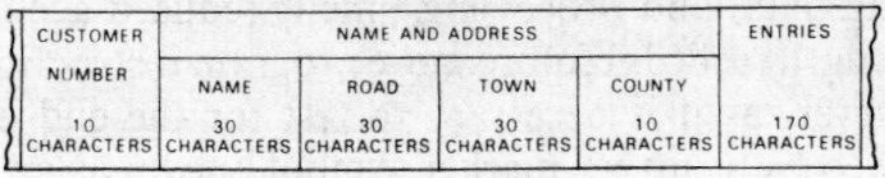

(*Courtesy of International Computers Limited*)
(*b*) *Magnetic tape—fixed-length field*

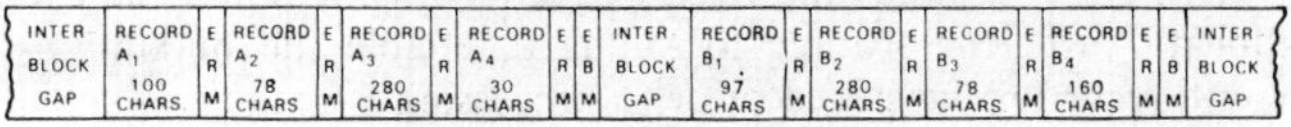

(*Courtesy of International Computers Limited*)
(*c*) *Magnetic tape—"fixed-variable" blocks*

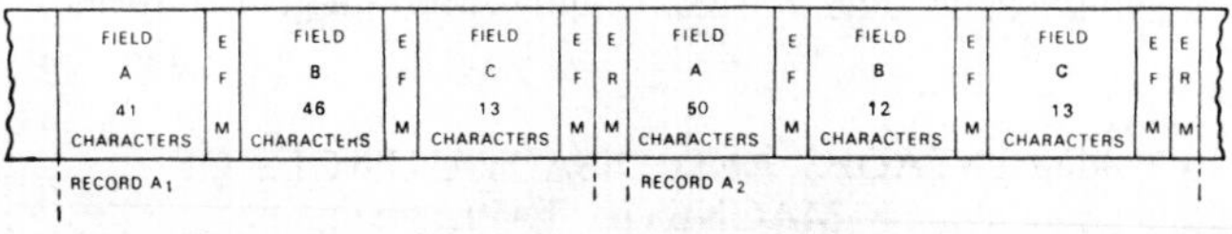

(*Courtesy of International Computers Limited*)
(*d*) *Magnetic tape—variable-length fields*

FIG. 86 *Types of magnetic fields and blocks*

it may be necessary to insert space characters to the right of indicative data, e.g. names and addresses.

Marker symbols are required, in order that the program may detect the end of records and blocks, the following are examples.

(a) *End of record marker* (*E.R.M.*). Indicates that the end of one record has been reached and a new record is to commence.

(b) *End of block marker* (*E.B.M.*). Indicates that the end of one block of data has been reached and a new block is to commence (*see* Fig. 85).

12. Variable-length records. Variable-length records consist of fields of data in which the number of character positions in each field is allocated in accordance with the character positions actually required by the data. This method of recording data recognises that the same class of record does not always require the same number of character positions in each corresponding field, especially those relating to variable data such as quantities and values.

Records which vary in length and are recorded as such on magnetic tape increases the length of tape utilised for significant data. As the efficiency of using tape is increased, so is the speed of transferring data, and processing time is reduced accordingly.

Variable-length records require more program instructions to be written, however, as it is necessary to test for the end of fields. This is achieved by a further marker symbol known as an "end of field marker" (E.F.M.). It is also necessary to indicate the end of records and end of blocks (*see* **11**).

With both variable- and fixed-length records, it is necessary to allocate sufficient storage locations to enable the maximum-length record to be stored prior to processing.

In general, the larger the size of block, the greater will be the amount of data recorded on tape, as the number of inter-block gaps will be fewer. As a result, the transfer of data in and out of the computer memory will be accomplished at a greater speed.

ADVANTAGES AND DISADVANTAGES OF MAGNETIC TAPE

13. Advantages of magnetic tape.

(a) It is perhaps the most widely used form of backing storage, because it is *relatively inexpensive* and has a *large data storage capacity*.

(*b*) It is capable of *transferring* data to and from internal storage at *very high speed*.

(*c*) Data held on magnetic tape can be *sorted by the computer* into the sequence required for updating master files.

(*d*) Transaction data can be *recorded directly on to magnetic tape* by means of magnetic tape encoding machines.

(*e*) Old data may be erased and the *tape used repeatedly*.

(*f*) Records held on magnetic tape do not *take up much storage space* as compared with records held on punched cards.

14. Disadvantages of magnetic tape.

(*a*) It is only possible to *access records serially*, which necessitates the reading of all records until the one required is reached.

(*b*) Input data relating to transactions must always be sorted into the *sequence of the master file* before updating can commence. This is unnecessary with random access devices such as magnetic drums and magnetic disc units.

(*c*) Data can be *accidentally erased or overwritten* unless stringent control procedures are used.

(*d*) Updated information cannot be *written back to the same location* on the same tape. It must be written to a different tape, thus necessitating an additional tape deck. With random access devices it is possible to write updated information to the same storage location.

(*e*) *Visual reading of records* is not possible.

(*f*) *Stringent environmental control* is necessary to eliminate dust and static electricity from the atmosphere, which otherwise could adversely affect the quality of data recorded on the tape, thereby affecting the capacity to read the data accurately.

MAGNETIC TAPE (CASSETTE)

15. General description. Cassette tape is a continuous loop of magnetic tape stored in a container referred to as a cassette. It is easier to handle than conventional reels of magnetic tape as the cassette is easily loaded into the cassette handler. They store data with a recording density of 800 bits per inch serially which is equivalent to 100 bytes per inch. Cassette tapes are available with 282 feet (85·95 m) of recording length. The cassettes used in computer systems are similar in appearance to those used in domestic recorders.

16. Uses of cassette tape. Cassette tape is widely used in small computer systems for the storage of master files and programs. They may also be used for information interchange between different computer systems by communication facilities. In addition, they are used for encoding transaction data from source documents for input to the computer.

EXCHANGEABLE MAGNETIC DISCS (HARD DISCS)

17. General considerations. Disc storage is widely used as a means of backing storage because of its ability to record and retrieve data both serially and by direct access. Direct access is accomplished by directly addressing data locations on the disc surfaces.

In batch processing applications, data may be processed serially, but only those records affected by transactions need to be accessed for updating. Records unaffected by transactions remain unaltered and there is no need to re-write them as is the case with records stored on magnetic tape.

Exchangeable disc packs are so called because they can literally be exchanged when necessary to change over the master files for a new application to be run on the computer.

18. General characteristics. This type of storage is referred to as "hard" discs as the material from which they are made is metal, coated on both sides with a thin layer of magnetisable oxide. A number of discs are combined to form a disc pack. The actual number of discs in a pack varies, some have six, others ten and the capacity varies accordingly from eight to sixty million characters or bytes, for instance.

Disc packs are mounted on a disc drive which rotates the discs. The drive is equipped with read/write heads for reading data from the discs and writing data to the discs.

The discs being outlined have been in existence for some time but are still in use, therefore the details to be outlined generally refer to a basic disc pack of six discs. Each disc is 355·6 mm in diameter. A pack of six discs utilise only ten surfaces for recording data even though there are twelve surfaces in total. Therefore:

(a) top disc—one surface: lower surface only;
(b) four discs—both surfaces: total of eight surfaces;
(c) bottom disc—one surface: upper surface only (*see* Fig. 87(a)).

19. Read/write heads. The transport unit consists of ten read/write heads mounted on arms arranged in pairs. When data transfers take place all the arms move together between discs. Each head is used for reading and writing data from, and to, one disc surface. Each head also has facilities for erasing data.

20. The cylinder concept. For each position of the read/write heads data transfers can be effected from one track on each disc surface. The tracks that can be accessed without head movement are known

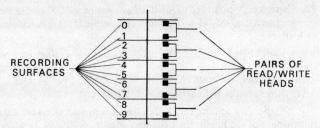

(*Based on data supplied by ICL and reproduced by their kind permission.*)

(*a*) *Exchangeable discs—structure.*

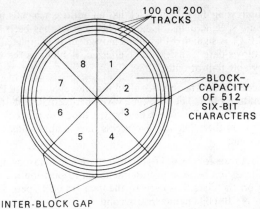

(*Based on data supplied by ICL and reproduced by their kind permission.*)

(*b*) *Exchangeable discs—layout. The capacity of each track = 8 blocks × 512 characters = 4096 characters.*

FIG. 87 *Exchangeable discs*

as a "cylinder". This, of course, is an efficient way of accessing data as delay while waiting for the heads to move into the required position is eliminated. The cylinder is often referred to as the "seek area".

21. Layout of data. Each track is divided in eight equal blocks. Each block is separated by an inter-block gap. The capacity of a block is 512 six-bit characters (*see* Fig. 87(*b*)).

22. Capacity. A cartridge of six discs consisting of 200 tracks per surface has a capacity of 8·19 million characters. This is calculated as follows.

(*a*) Eight blocks of 512 characters per track = 4096 ch. per track.

(*b*) 200 tracks of 4096 characters = 819 200 ch. per surface.

(*c*) Ten surfaces per cartridge = 8 192 000 ch.

It is important to note that as ten surfaces are accessed for each positioning of the heads, the cylinder consists of 40 960 characters which are accessible without further head movement.

Four transports can be attached to a control unit which allows the capacity to be increased to 32.76 million characters.

23. Addressing data. Each track has an address which is used for accessing specific items of data. When a track has been selected the C.P.U. is signalled that head movement is completed, which then allows data transfers to be effected. A block is the smallest addressable unit of data.

24. Access time. The time required for one revolution of the discs is 25 milliseconds. The seek time varies between 30 and 160 milliseconds—that is the time taken by the heads to move from one track to another. The average access time is approximately 97.5 milliseconds.

25. Data transfer speed. Disc transfers are not so fast as magnetic drum transfers because of the time taken to position the moving heads on the discs, but even so the data transfer speed is in the region of 208 000 characters a second.

FILE ORGANISATION—MAGNETIC DISCS: SERIAL

26. Introduction. Although a disc file is a direct access device, it may be organised on a serial basis, whereby records are processed in ascending order of the "key" field. True direct access is not possible in this case, as there are no means of locating a record directly and each record must be accessed in the file sequence to locate the record required, whether or not they are affected by transactions. Serial file processing of discs is therefore similar to processing with magnetic tapes.

It is possible, however, to locate a record directly on a serial disc without having to read each preceding record, by a technique known as "binary chop".

27. Binary chop. The technique first locates the middle record of a file and tests whether the key field is above or below the key field of the record to be located. The process is continued by examining the middle record of the selected half of the file, etc., until the required record is found. The technique saves valuable time in locating records.

FILE ORGANISATION—MAGNETIC DISCS: INDEXED SEQUENTIAL

28. Introduction. This method is a modified version of serial organisation, which allows a sequential file to be processed serially with the facility of direct access to enable inactive records to be by-passed when they are not affected by transactions.

The records are written to the data tracks, in ascending order of key.

It is necessary to compile an index indicating the highest record key in each cylinder and the highest record key in each track.

To access a specific record, the record key is compared with the cylinder index which, by means of a "high or equal" result, indicates the cylinder storing the record. The appropriate track is also determined in a similar way. The tracks are then read sequentially to locate the record required.

29. Overlay. When updating a file organised on an indexed-sequential basis it is normal practice to use the overlay technique. The technique causes an overflow of records on a disc track, and this necessitates allocation to an overflow area. -

30. Overflow area. To overcome the problem of locating records in an overflow area, the cylinder/track index records the highest record key of records stored in the overflow area corresponding to each track indexed.

The presence of the overflow address also indicates whether new file records should be stored in the data area or the overflow area.

It is important to maintain the sequence of records in the file, and it therefore becomes necessary to locate those which are in the data area and in the overflow area, this is achieved by "chaining".

31. Chaining. Using the technique of chaining, a record which has been displaced into the overflow area has its new location recorded within the record which logically preceded it. The displaced record also has the location of the next record in logical sequence. By this means, the sequential order of records is easily traced.

FILE ORGANISATION—MAGNETIC DISCS: OTHER METHODS

32. Partitioned file. With this method of file organisation, each record is located by reference to an alphabetic directory or index, which is useful for storing and locating sub-routines.

33. Random file organisation. Records are not stored in any organised sequence (random), and so general rules for retrieving records cannot be applied. Random organisation requires the use of a full index or an address generation system.

With randomly organised files, it can take much longer to locate records than with a sequential file.

VIRTUAL STORAGE

34. Concept of virtual storage. Some recently launched computers are incorporating a new storage management technique known as "virtual storage". The technique increases the apparent capacity of internal storage by an amount many times its actual capacity. Concurrent processing of several programs, that would otherwise exceed the main internal storage capacity is made possible.

35. Mode of operation. Virtual storage uses magnetic discs which are used to store programs required for processing. This is instead of loading them to internal storage (main storage), which is the normal method employed.

In order that the main storage available is used in the most efficient manner, the technique splits the program into small segments called "pages". Only those pages which are required for processing are called into main storage at one time. The remainder of the program stays in virtual storage.

The addresses within a page refer to virtual storage locations and when transferred to main storage the addresses must refer to main storage locations before processing can be executed. It is necessary, therefore, to effect address translation, which is achieved by a hardware-assisted table look-up (*see* XXV, 7).

DISKETTES

36. Diskette (floppy discs). Diskettes are used for storing master files, operating systems and application programs in smaller computer systems. They are also used for encoding transaction data for input to a computer and for receiving output from a computer. Diskettes are light in weight and non-rigid in construction which is why they are referred to as "floppy" discs. This is in distinction from the exchangeable discs made from metal which are referred to as "hard" discs. The "floppy" nature of the discs makes them suitable for mailing to a central computer without risk of damage.

Diskettes are housed in eight inch (approximately 200 mm) square covers or sleeves and may be single- or double-sided, single or double density. The single density discs have a capacity in the region of 243K bytes (equivalent to approximately 3000 punched cards) and the double density a capacity in the region of 486K bytes. The data transfer speed is in the region of 31K bytes per second. NCR tend to define these discs as flexible discs whereas the term diskette was originated by IBM.

This method of data recording and storage has tended to be used instead of the more traditional methods in some cases, but it is considered to have a challenger in the form of bubble memory (*see* **42**).

37. Mini-diskette (mini-floppy discs). Mini-diskettes are smaller versions of those indicated above being approximately $5\frac{1}{4}$ inches (approximately 133 mm) square and stored in a cover or sleeve. These minis tend to be used on microcomputers and have a capacity in the region of 89K bytes. The data transfer speed is about 125K bits per second which is equivalent to approximately 16K bytes per second.

INTEGRATED DISCS AND DATA MODULES

38. Integrated discs. Some modern small computers have integrated discs stored in the same cabinet as the processor and memory. The discs are mounted in a pull-out unit and a single spindle unit holds one fixed two-surface disc and one removable two-surface disc. Each disc has a capacity of approximately 4.9 million bytes and a transfer speed in the region of 312 kilobytes per second.

39. Data module. This is a multi-platter disc unit with in-built read/write heads housed in a transparent plastic case. This differs from standard disc systems whereby read/write heads are part of the disc drive. The data module is more expensive than the standard disc pack but the drive is correspondingly less expensive. Disc surfaces are kept cleaner and if a head crash occurs the consequences are localised compared with standard disc packs where head crashes can be more drastic.

Up to 140 million bytes can be stored on a dual-spindle unit with a transfer speed up to 885K bytes per second.

ADVANTAGES AND DISADVANTAGES OF DIRECT ACCESS STORAGE

40. Advantages.

(*a*) Any item of data can be directly addressed depending upon the method of the file organisation used.

(*b*) High data transfer speed.

(*c*) Input data can be input in random order (without the need for sorting).

(*d*) Discs may be used for real-time remote enquiry systems.

(*e*) Latest discs have a high storage capacity.

(*f*) Data may be erased and new data recorded on data tracks.

(*g*) Different discs or disc units are not required for updating records as the existing records may be amended by overwriting.

(*h*) Sub-routines, tables and rates may be called in as required during processing.

41. Disadvantages

(*a*) Storage devices are rather expensive.

(*b*) Data may be accidentally erased or overwritten unless special precautions are taken.

(*c*) Problems of locating overflow records on discs.

(*d*) Relative complexity of programming.

(*e*) Some discs have a lower storage capacity than magnetic tape.

DEVELOPMENTS IN BACKING STORAGE

42. Bubble memory. This type of memory is being developed for use as mass memory and a possible replacement for disc files. The bubbles may be thought of as cylindrical magnets which are formed from magnetic regions called "domains" after the application of a critical bias magnetic field value. The bubbles are created on memory chips with capacities of 92K or 256K. Rockwell has launched a bubble memory system with a megabyte of storage and a module with a capacity of one megabit.

Developments are taking place to reduce the size of the bubble or magnetic domain to less than two microns to enable one megabyte of memory to be stored on to a chip not greater than about half a cubic inch (approximately 80 mm³) in over-all size.

Strings of bubbles allow streams of bits carried by the bubbles to become a series of electrical pulses providing output from the bubble memory.

43. Laser memory. A new mass storage device has been developed by Philips Data Systems which takes the form of a 12 in (294 mm) plastic disc on which information is recorded and read by a laser. The capacity on each side of the disc is 500 megabytes of data—a total of 1000 megabytes which is equivalent to half a million A4 sheets of information.

Due to the method of recording employed—a process of burning holes with a diode laser-plastic discs can only be written on once which, in effect, makes it a write/read only memory. It is estimated, however, that there will be an erasable laser memory by 1980.

44. Holographic memory. This is an optical memory system whereby a pattern is recorded on a photo-sensitive plate by mixing laser light from a reference beam and laser light scattered from the object bearing the information to be recorded. The data in the hologram is effectively "smeared" over the whole of the plate. A degree of redundancy is built into the system so that dust and scratches on the emulsion have little effect on the recorded information.

Data in the reconstructed image are arranged as an array of dots —one dot for each "bit". Information may be read out by directing a laser beam in to the hologram so that the reconstructed image falls on to a photodiode array on a silicon chip. At present the main limitation is that information on a holographic store is generally fixed and is presently of value for storing large amounts of fixed information such as machine instructions.

PROGRESS TEST 14

1. Define what you understand by the term "backing storage", and indicate the types of backing storage either in current use or in the process of development. **(1, 2)**

2. Indicate the general characteristics and uses of magnetic tape. **(3–14)**

3. Give an explanation of the code that is used to represent data on magnetic tape. **(4)** [Part of A.C.A. June 1978, Q2]

4. Define the following terms:

(a) Parity checking   (d) Overflow area
(b) Binary chop   (e) Chaining
(c) Overlay   (f) Virtual storage

(7, 8, 27, 29–31, 34–5)

5. What are the advantages and disadvantages of using magnetic tape files as backing storage, compared with the use of magnetic disc files? **(13, 14, 40, 41)** [I.A.S. Dec. 1976, Q2]

6. (a) Explain the following terms as they relate to the organisation and processing of files held on magnetic discs:

(i) cylinder;

(ii) overflow.

(b) What advantages do discs have over magnetic tapes as file storage media? **(13, 14, 20, 30, 40, 41)** [A.C.A. June 1978, Q4]

7. Outline the nature of cassette tape and its uses. **(15–16)**

8. Outline the general characteristics of exchangeable magnetic discs (hard discs). **(17–35)**

9. Explain the basic principles relating to the organisation of data on a disc pack and describe the indexed sequential method of file organisation. **(26–33)** [A.C.A. Dec. 1975, Q2]

10. Outline the nature of diskettes. **(36–7)**

11. Define the following terms:

(a) Integrated disc   (d) Laser memory
(b) Data module   (e) Holographic memory
(c) Bubble memory

(38–9, 42–4)

PART FOUR

IMPLEMENTING A COMPUTER

CHAPTER XV

Analysis and Development of Computer Systems

ESSENTIAL FACTORS FOR SUCCESSFUL IMPLEMENTATION OF A COMPUTER

1. Feasibility study. A computer cannot be plugged in and away she goes, as it were—its successful implementation depends upon a number of factors amongst which is the need to conduct a thorough "in-depth" feasibility study. Management must make a decision on the basis of a feasibility study report either to implement or not to implement a computer. Whichever decision is made can have far reaching effects on the future efficiency of the business.

The correct decision is crucial because it is possible to make an incorrect decision in either of two instances. In the first instance management may decide not to implement a computer when they should or, in the second instance, to implement a computer when they should not. The consequences of failure to implement a computer when it is necessary is a reduction in administrative efficiency. On the other hand, the consequences of implementing a computer when it is not needed is chaos as systems will be disrupted, unnecessary costs will be incurred and organisational changes will be made needlessly.

A number of important considerations concerned with conducting a feasibility study are summarised below.

(*a*) *Objectives of study.* At the outset it is important that the objectives of the study should be clearly defined in order that the study team have a clear understanding of the requirements of the study. The objectives may be to determine if all or some of the following factors are feasible using a computer:

(*i*) reducing the number of staff in specific administrative functions because of cost;

237

(*ii*) avoiding the need to increase clerical staff because the calibre of staff required is in short supply;

(*iii*) improving the flow of information for management;

(*iv*) providing problem solving facilities for management;

(*v*) improving cash flows by producing invoices and statements of account earlier;

(*vi*) reducing the cost of processing each unit of data;

(*vii*) streamlining accounting routines;

(*viii*) providing the means for effective systems integration;

(*ix*) improving the accuracy of information and data on business documents.

(*b*) *Choice of areas for improvement.* In order to achieve the designated objectives it is necessary to select the areas of the business most likely to achieve them. Possible areas may be chosen on the following basis:

(*i*) those involving procedures which process a large volume of data, forms or documents;

(*ii*) those involving procedures with a high proportion of repetitive operations;

(*iii*) those involving procedures with a large number of clerical staff;

(*iv*) those involving procedures which suffer from delays due to bottlenecks in processing perhaps due to insufficiently planned procedures, inadequate methods of processing or high-volume posting or calculating operations.

(*c*) *General considerations of a feasibility study.* A number of important factors must be taken into account before any conclusions can be established and before the feasibility study report is presented to management. They include the following aspects:

(*i*) the alternative types of computer configuration available;

(*ii*) the availability of standby facilities in case of breakdown of the computer;

(*iii*) business trends and their likely impact on data processing commitments;

(*iv*) the extent to which the organisation would need restructuring with the advent of a computer;

(*v*) the availability of experienced computer personnel, systems analysts and programmers, etc.;

(*vi*) the feasibility of using a computer bureau instead of installing an in-house computer;

(*vii*) the feasibility of using several microcomputers instead of a mainframe computer;

(*viii*) the incidence of redundancy in respect of clerical staff;

(*ix*) the time necessary to develop computerised systems;

(*x*) the need for computer appreciation courses for management and staff.

(*d*) *Cost considerations of using a computer.* Some of the elements of cost which must be considered include:

(*i*) the cost of purchasing or renting a computer perhaps compared with the cost of using a computer bureau;

(*ii*) the cost of developing computer systems;

(*iii*) the cost of computer accommodation;

(*iv*) the cost of recruiting and training computer staff;

(*v*) the annual cost of operating the computer system;

(*vi*) the comparative costs of alternative methods of processing;

(*vii*) the cost of writing off current equipment;

(*viii*) the availability of finance to purchase a computer system;

(*ix*) the cost of obtaining finance to purchase a computer system;

(*x*) the cost of converting master files to magnetic tape or disc.

(*e*) *Expected benefits of using a computer.* The possible benefits are numerous if computers are planned and used effectively. Some typical benefits are summarised below:

(*i*) more effective administrative procedures and accounting routines;

(*ii*) more timely and relevant information for management decision making and control;

(*iii*) improved cash flows by earlier production and despatch of invoices and statements of account or revision of product prices or maintenance contract terms;

(*iv*) more effective control of stocks;

(*v*) more optimal solutions to administrative problems such as production planning and capital budgeting;

(*vi*) increased level of systems integration providing economy and increased efficiency;

(*vii*) improved forecasting techniques;

(*viii*) facilities for simulating business operations before embarking on costly changes to the physical systems concerned;

(*ix*) random enquiry facilities for the retrieval of information on demand;

(*x*) real-time control of key operations.

(*f*) *Feasibility study in an organisation possessing a computer.*
When a computer already exists in the organisation it is still necessary to conduct a feasibility study for any proposal to computerise a business system. The objectives and stages of feasibility study for a proposed system may be based on the following outline of action to be taken:

(*i*) define objectives of system to be studied;

(*ii*) define objectives of the feasibility study (see (*a*));

(*iii*) collect facts relating to the current system, including: types and volume of input, types and volume of output, frequency of processing, time for performing each main activity, number of staff employed on the system, type of files used, number of records in files, frequency of referring to files, frequency of updating files, file activity ratio ("hit rate"), problem areas and operating costs, etc.;

(*iv*) anticipate system development costs, including costs of file conversion;

(*v*) estimate run times;

(*vi*) anticipate costs of computer operations;

(*vii*) assess expected benefits (*see* (*e*));

(*viii*) prepare feasibility study report;

(*ix*) submit and discuss report with appropriate management;

(*x*) make decision to computerise and proceed with more detailed systems analysis if management consider proposals satisfactory; otherwise continue with existing system perhaps with minor modifications.

2. Top management support. The time, effort and finance required for the initial implementation and development of computerised systems may deter the most enlightened managers unless the feasibility study report makes refusal difficult. This is a further pointer to the value of an accurate feasibility report. It is imperative for top management—the board of directors and functional managers—to show interest at the outset, otherwise projects will have little chance of success once a computer is installed.

Any dissension on the part of top management will filter through the organisation to the lower management levels and this in itself will detract from the successful implementation of systems. Departmental managers in charge of systems to be computerised will not, in all probability, provide the required level of support to systems staff which is so essential for the efficient operation of new systems. User departments need to participate in the design of systems with which they are concerned and for which they are responsible.

3. Education and training programme. The reason for any lack of enthusiasm on the part of management may be ignorance of computers—or even fright—and this should be dispelled by means of a short induction course. Such a course may be conducted by internal systems staff if any are already employed in the organisation or, if they are not, selected managers and staff may attend a computer manufacturer's or college based computer appreciation course. The contents of a computer appreciation course may consist of the following:

(*a*) definition of a computer;
(*b*) the place of the computer in the organisation;
(*c*) duties of systems analysts and programmers;
(*d*) responsibilities of the data processing manager;
(*e*) outline of computer applications;
(*f*) benefits of using computers related to present systems if relevant;
(*g*) data preparation methods;
(*h*) processing techniques, batch, on-line, real-time and multiprogramming, etc.

4. Communication. Before a computer is implemented within the organisation the fact that this is under consideration should be communicated to all personnel, particularly those who are likely to be the most affected once a computer becomes operational. This course of action will dispel distorted rumours circulating within the organisation which could have a damaging effect on morale.

It is also necessary to communicate company policy with regard to possible redundancies when systems are transferred to the computer. Of particular importance are the arrangements to be made for retraining staff and possible redeployment.

In most companies it will be the responsibility of the managing director to formally communicate these factors and he should also stress the importance of obtaining the fullest co-operation of staff in the difficult transition period ahead, in respect of systems development and changeover.

5. Recruitment of effective data processing staff. A computer will only be as efficient as the personnel who manage, develop systems and program the computer. It is essential to obtain the services of an effective data processing manager who, first and foremost, should be a good manager. He should have a wide knowledge of business systems particularly of the business in which he is employed and due to this essential requirement he is often appointed from within the business. Former organisation and methods specialists and line managers have been appointed to the post of data processing manager on the basis of their knowledge of key systems in the organisation.

The data processing manager should have a considerable knowledge of computers, particularly of the model in use, or about to be implemented, but he need not be an expert in programming. He is responsible for interpreting and executing the policy of the Steering committee, planning, organising, co-ordinating and controlling projects to ensure they achieve objectives (*see* VII, **34**).

Systems analysts should be recruited from within the organisation whenever possible to take advantage of their knowledge of the business which is of extreme importance for the development of computer systems. They must be aware of the needs of the operating functions and departments particularly the purpose and objectives of the systems they operate. This is the reason why O. & M. investigators often become systems analysts when a computer is implemented into a business.

A systems analyst must have many talents and be capable of viewing the business as a total system and yet be able to analyse it into its constituent elements (sub-systems). He must be able to appreciate the interactions which occur between sub-systems and the effects computerisation is likely to have on them. He should design systems without unnecessary complexity as the simpler the design the more effective they are likely to be (*see* **19, 20**).

Programmers are required who are capable of writing simple, efficient programs. Unnecessary complexity in programs is likely to increase computer running time and produce documents and reports which are too complex for system needs. This situation requires a high degree of co-ordination between programmers and systems analysts to ensure that ambiguity does not enter into programming as this will result in systems failing to meet their objectives.

6. Data processing steering committee. A steering committee should be formulated with responsibility for appraising the viability of computer projects, to ensure they are cost effective and would be of benefit to the business as a whole, to optimise corporate performance rather than functional performance. Such a committee enables the data processing needs of the business as a whole to be co-ordinated with other functional activities within the framework of corporate plans.

Membership of a steering committee should consist of representatives of the various functions which will be affected by the installation of a computer into the business. The committee is likely to be chaired by the chief executive, which would enable him to have an overview of proposed computer projects and assess whether they accord with the future strategy and policy of the business. The interest of functions in a typical manufacturing business would probably be represented by the production controller, stock controller, chief accountant, sales manager, chief buyer and of course the data processing manager. The D.P. manager is then in a position to be aware of company policy and can interpret its requirements more objectively before executing the needs of such policy.

7. Systems implementation. Before a new computer system is implemented it may be necessary to conduct "pilot" runs with test data to ensure that the system achieves its defined purpose and objectives. Programs must of necessity be subjected to trial runs with test data, consisting of both valid and invalid data for the purpose of ensuring that the program can contend with all possible eventualities. Corrections are then made either to the programs or the system, which are then subjected to further trials. When the situation appears to be satisfactory "parallel" running of the new system and the existing system can commence. The results produced by both systems can then be compared and any notable differences investigated and corrected. This is a "fail-safe" procedure as it would have drastic consequences on the business if the old system was dispensed with before the new system had proved to be satisfactory. It is not unknown for "bugs" to appear after parallel running has been dispensed with even after detailed trials have been conducted.

See Fig. 88 illustrating the stages of implementing a computer.

8. Monitoring performance. Computer systems must be monitored to detect any deviations from planned results and performance, so that suitable amendments can be effected and staff subjected to further training if necessary.

9. System updating. The term updating is sometimes referred to as maintenance in the context of ensuring that a system meets current requirements. Systems must be adjusted for the needs of change either for fundamental reasons, e.g. the introduction of V.A.T. or for systems development in respect of integration or the introduction of on-line processing. When packages are used, amendments

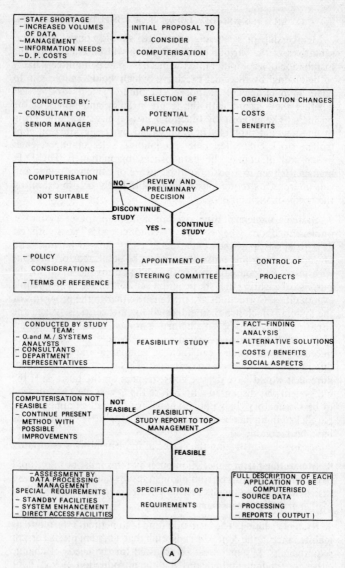

FIG. 88 *Flowchart illustrating the stages of implementing a computer*

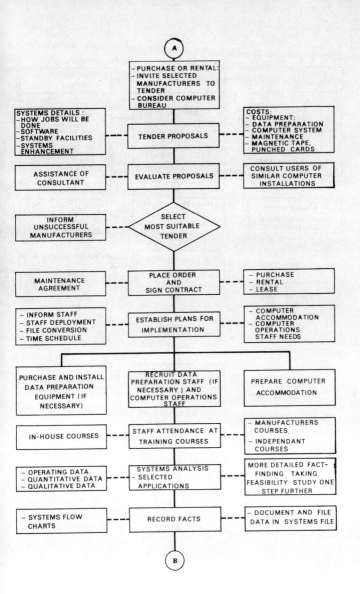

FIG. 88 (*contd.*)

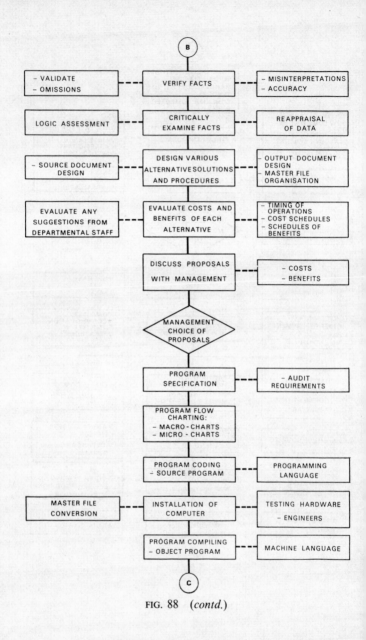

FIG. 88 (contd.)

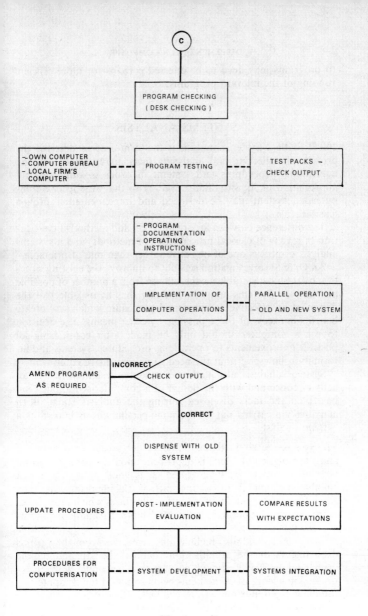

FIG. 88 (*contd.*)

to programs may need to be effected perhaps for more efficient running of the relevant programs.

SYSTEMS ANALYSIS

10. Definition. Systems analysis is the term used to describe the process of collecting and analysing facts in respect of existing operations, procedures and systems in order to obtain a full appreciation of the situation prevailing so that an effective computerised system may be designed and implemented if proved feasible.

The difference between an organisation and methods investigation (a review of clerical procedures and methods) and a systems analysis project is one of objective rather than one of principle.

An O. & M. investigation sets out to improve the existing situation by the most suitable means, chosen from a number of possible alternatives. Systems analysis, however, has as its objective the design of an effective computerised procedure which will create benefits in excess of those possible by other means. The decision to use a computer should only be made after considering all possible improvements to operations, procedures, systems and information flows, without the need to use expensive equipment.

Systems analysis also embraces systems design, which is an activity concerned with the design of a computerised application based on the facts disclosed during the analysis stage. Both activities are carried out by the same person who is known as a *systems* analyst.

11. Systems analysis team. Some projects require a team of analysts, the size of which is dependent upon the complexity and type of system to be investigated. It is good policy to recruit suitable personnel from existing staff, as it is important that they should have a sound knowledge of the business which often takes many years to obtain in sufficient depth to analyse systems effectively.

The team should also include representatives from the various departments of the organisation that will be affected by the investigation. This approach ensures that personnel with an intimate knowledge of the systems being reviewed for computerisation have the opportunity to record facts which may otherwise be overlooked and which are important for the effective design of the computer system.

After the project is concluded the personnel on secondment go back to their department (unless recruited for systems work on a full-time basis due to their experience) and take an active part in the newly installed computerised system. By this means the best results are obtained, as personnel who have been brought into the picture are more likely to co-operate and accept the changes which have been implemented.

STAGES OF SYSTEMS ANALYSIS

12. Systems analysis and O. & M. In general, the same stages of investigation are conducted for a systems analysis project as for an O. & M. investigation. The main differences are the types of document used for recording facts (in some respects) and the greater depth of analysis which is required with regard to the number and type of characters contained in documents, records and reports.

During the design stage, however, the technical details differ greatly because an O. & M. investigator may assess the viability of using word processing equipment instead of normal typing services, for instance. A systems analyst, on the other hand, will be concerned with the best way of designing the system in accordance with the characteristics of the computer configuration installed or to be installed.

The reader is referred to the author's HANDBOOK, *Organisation and Methods*, which covers the stages of conducting a systems investigation in depth. It is now proposed to deal with those aspects which have a direct bearing on the facts required prior to computerising a procedure or system. It is emphasised, however, that the basic stages of collecting, recording, verifying and examining the facts are common to any type of systems investigation as are the types of facts collected in respect of resources used, operating data, quantitative data, qualitative data, operating costs, organisation structure of application areas, company policy and external influences, etc.

The principal methods of obtaining facts include interviewing personnel; observing activities which can be performed in a number of ways including visual and photographic methods; use of questionnaires or by inspection and examination. The interview method of collecting facts is widely used as it enables facts of situations not visible by observation to be obtained and also enables activities and the use of forms to be explained.

DOCUMENT ANALYSIS FORM
Reports and Intermediate Documents

PROJECT _____ DATE _____

COMPILED BY _____

1. IDENTIFICATION
Invoice as despatched to customers (retail only) following an approved order for goods. Form No. 18236/M.

2. DISTRIBUTION AND USE
Top copy. Sent to customer via outgoing mail office - window env.
2nd copy. Internal transfer in daily batch of documents to Sales Ledger Dept, Manager Mr. A. Smith. Posted to appropriate a/c and filed in chronological order (see Block diagram 36/8).
3rd and last. Retained in Invoicing Dept. for later matching with warehouse delivery advice (See Block Diagram 23/2).

3. FREQUENCY
Issued daily not more than 2 days from receipt of accepted order.

4. SEQUENCE
By Invoice Number. Number pre-printed on Invoice Pads.
Supervisor keeps manual record of daily beginning and finish numbers.
Copy 2 sorted to customer number sequence by Accounts Dept. and filed Cust No. within date. Copy 3 kept in Invoice Number within date.

5. ELEMENTS OF DATA
Account details typed from order with exception of Cust. No. which is rubber stamped on to order by coding clerk. See Grid Chart 4/102 for breakdown on items.

6. VOLUME
Present 1,000 maximum daily. Non-seasonal. Estimated to increase to 4,000 daily within 3 years.

7. FORMAT
Need to re-design although same elements of data. Disc. rates need not be pre-printed on new form-computer can print.

8. SPECIAL CONSIDERATIONS
Possibility of standard Invoice for all customers - check.

(Courtesy of International Computers Limited)
(a) Example of document analysis form.

FIG. 89 Types of analysis documentation

OUTPUT ANALYSIS CHART

JOB 1/A : TEAM A   PREPARED BY :

DATE : 7/3/74

Data Fields

N = Numeric
A = Alpha
A/N = Alpha/Numeric

	Data Field	Max.	Aver.
1	CUSTOMER No.	N/5	5
2	TRAVELLER	N/2	2
3	BRANCH	N/3	3
4	NAME & ADDR (INVOICE)	A/N 86	58
5	NAME & ADDR CONSIGNEE	A/N 80	50
6	DATE	N/6	6
7	ORDER No.	N/8	5
8	CODE No./ITEM DESCRIPTION	A/N 66	44
9	QTY ORDERED	N/4	4
10	PRICE	N/6	4
11	EXTENSIONS	N/8	5
12	VAT	N/5	4
13	CASH DISC	N/5	4
14	GROSS	N/9	6
15	NET	N/9	6
16	CREDIT LIMIT	N/5	5
17	CURRENT A/C BAL	N/9	6
18	1 MONTH A/C DETAILS	N/80	36
19	TRAN SALES MTHLY VALUE	N/9	6
20	BRANCH SALES...	N/10	7

Field Size in Characters

	OUTPUT DOCUMENTS	1	2	3	4	5	6	7	8	9	10	11	12	13	14	15	16	17	18	19	20
O.	INVOICES	R	R	R	R	S	C	S	R	R	S	R	C	C	C	C	C				
O.	CREDIT CONTROL REPORTS	R	R	R			C											R	R	R	
O.	A/C QUERIES	R	R	R	R		C											R	R	R	
M.	STATEMENTS	R	R	R	R		C												R	R	
M.	TRADE REPORTS (A)			R			C			R	R								R		
M.	CREDIT STANDING REPORTS			R			C														
P/Q	PRICE CHANGES & OTHER NOTICES	R	R	R	R		C	LETTER FORM NARRATIVE PLUS NEW PRICES, CHANGE OF VAT, ETC.													
M.	TRADE REPORTS (B)	R	R	R			C						C		C						
M.	COMMISSION TAB		R	R					R	R	R									C	C
Q.	QUARTERLY ABSTRACT		R																	C	C

R = Record   S = Source   C = Computed

(Courtesy of International Computers Limited)
(b) Example of output analysis chart.

FIG. 89 (*cont'd.*)

In general, the stages of investigation are as follows:

(*a*) define the problem;
(*b*) plan the project;
(*c*) collect the facts;
(*d*) record the facts;
(*e*) verify the facts;
(*f*) examine the facts.

It is now proposed to outline the specific aspects which are of particular importance in the analysis of systems for computerisation.

13. Specific aspects of systems analysis. Apart from collecting facts as indicated above, there are other specific points to be considered in a systems analysis, as follows.

(*a*) Collect specimens of all documents used in the system.
(*b*) From the documents collected prepare:
  (*i*) grid or X chart (*see* **14**);
  (*ii*) document analysis form—input (*see* **16**);
  (*iii*) document analysis form—output (*see* **15**);
  (*iv*) file analysis form (*see* **17**);
  (*v*) output analysis chart (*see* **18**, Fig. 89(*b*));
  (*vi*) clerical procedure chart;
  (*vii*) procedure narrative.
(*c*) Analyse the system and separate essential from non-essential elements.

RECORDING TECHNIQUES USED IN SYSTEMS ANALYSIS

14. The grid or X chart. This chart is used to define the relationships which exist between the various documents in a system. It is very useful when used in combination with document classification to determine the relationship between input and output documents.

The chart also assists the identification of unnecessary documents and elements of data.

In addition, the chart is useful for establishing which documents can be combined or those which may have the number of copies reduced.

The relationship between the various documents is indicated by an X in the relevant box.

15. Document analysis form—output. This form assists the analysis of the documents in the existing system and provides information for the design of a new system (*see* Fig. 89(*a*)).

A document analysis form should be prepared for every document in the existing system and for documents required in the new system which do not exist in the present system.

The form is essential for describing the output from the system, and includes the following information.

(*a*) *Identification* of the form:

    (*i*) form title;

    (*ii*) form number.

(*b*) *Distribution* and use. Each person who receives a copy of the output (report) should be interviewed and the following facts established:

    (*i*) job title, function and responsibility;

    (*ii*) reason for receiving the report;

    (*iii*) information used from the report;

    (*iv*) action taken from the report;

    (*v*) additional information required;

    (*vi*) information not required;

    (*vii*) suitability of report layout;

    (*viii*) establish whether copy is filed, passed on or destroyed (for subsequent follow-through if necessary).

(*c*) *Frequency of issue:*

    (*i*) daily;

    (*ii*) weekly;

    (*iii*) monthly;

    (*iv*) quarterly;

    (*v*) annually;

    (*vi*) on request.

(*d*) *Elements of data and their sequence:*

    (*i*) control keys or fields, e.g. customer account number, etc.;

    (*ii*) filing sequence, e.g. invoice number, customer account number, pre-printed number on pads of documents, etc.;

    (*iii*) reason for preparing the report in a specific sequence;

    (*iv*) identify the source of each element of data shown on the report;

    (*v*) elements of data produced during processing and the manner of their production;

    (*vi*) maximum, average and minimum size of each element of data and its percentage occurrence.

(*e*) *Volume:*

    (*i*) maximum and average number of documents;

(*ii*) maximum and average number of lines of data per document;

(*iii*) assess growth rate for elements of data and reports together with seasonal variations.

(*f*) *Format:*

(*i*) consider if the layout of the document requires amendment or whether suitable in the existing format;

(*ii*) assess whether all the data need be pre-printed or whether suitable for printing by the line printer.

16. Document analysis form—input. This form is useful for describing the source documents within the system, that is those documents which contain basic data to be input for processing.

The information contained on the analysis form may consist of the following.

(*a*) *Identification:*

(*i*) form title;

(*ii*) form number.

(*b*) *Purpose* of the document.

(*c*) Where *originated* and by what means:

(*i*) allows a check to be made for duplication of documents;

(*ii*) determines the extent to which various similar documents may be combined;

(*iii*) the content of similar documents may be rationalised;

(*iv*) enables an assessment to be made on the adequacy of the present methods of preparation;

(*v*) an assessment is made to ensure if it is originated in the best possible location under the circumstances.

(*d*) *Elements of data* and their *sequence:*

(*i*) description of each data field;

(*ii*) sequence of each data field;

(*iii*) pre-printed fields;

(*iv*) fields which may be required but not presently included;

(*v*) size of each of the fields indicated, specifying whether fixed or variable length, maximum, average and minimum size of each field;

(*vi*) an indication of the percentage of occurrence of each field is useful for assessing the average size of the complete input data for each transaction, which is an important aspect in the design of punched cards for input.

(*e*) *Volume:*

(*i*) maximum and average number of source documents;

(*ii*) possible future changes in volume;

(*iii*) seasonal variations in volume.

(*f*) *Frequency of preparation:*

(*i*) at present;

(*ii*) foreseeable or prospective changes in frequency.

(*g*) *Files affected* by the input:

(*i*) determine the type of file affected by the input (transaction) and the applications concerned;

(*ii*) assess the adequacy of the file organisation and content of records compared with the fields contained in the source document.

17. File analysis form. This form is used for defining the construction of files and may contain the following information.

(*a*) *Identification:*

(*i*) file name;

(*ii*) application in which used.

(*b*) *Purpose* of the file.

(*c*) *Records constituting the file:*

(*i*) maximum, average and minimum size of each record;

(*ii*) names of different records contained in the file;

(*iii*) percentage occurrence of each type of record in the file.

(*d*) *Volume* of records in the file:

(*i*) maximum, average and minimum number of records contained in the file;

(*ii*) maximum and average transaction volumes affecting the file;

(*iii*) assess future size of file;

(*iv*) indicate future volumes of transactions affecting the processing of the file;

(*v*) indicate seasonal variations of transactions affecting the processing of the file.

(*e*) *File organisation:*

(*i*) sequence of records;

(*ii*) control key;

(*iii*) adequacy of present sequence;

(*iv*) suitability of present keys.

18. Output analysis chart. This chart assists in examining the outputs from the current system to establish the information content of reports, their source and the relationships which exist between source documents and reports.

The chart is constructed as follows (*see* Fig. 89(*b*)).

(*a*) Output documents are listed down the left-hand side of the chart.

(*b*) Information fields contained in reports are listed along the top of the chart.

(*c*) The type of character contained in fields is classified as follows:

    (*i*)   N   = numeric.

    (*ii*)   A   = alphabetic.

    (*iii*) A/N = alpha/numeric.

(*d*) Information fields derived from records are indicated by the designation R, and those derived from source documents by S.

(*e*) Information fields derived from calculations are indicated by the designation C.

(*f*) The maximum and average field size in characters is also indicated.

(*g*) Appropriate designations are entered in columns at the point of intersection of the document column and the appropriate information field.

(*h*) Fields marked R must be contained in master records.

(*i*) Fields marked S are the transaction details which must be contained in source documents.

SYSTEMS DESIGN

19. Objectives of systems design. The design of a computer-based system (and any other type of system) is a creative task which has as its objective the implementation of a system creating benefits and improvements superior to those achieved by other methods.

The system must therefore be designed so that basic business documents and reports are produced as effectively as possible in accordance with the needs of the business.

Provision should be made for automating decisions of a routine nature whenever possible, which may be incorporated in the program in the form of standard formulae, thereby assisting the various levels of management by freeing them from routine decision-making.

During the process of designing a system, it should be borne in mind that the system(s) under review should not be considered in isolation from other systems, as many systems are inter-related either by the need for basic information or by the output from one system being the input to other systems (*see* XX, **7**).

The processing requirements of the total system—the organisation—should be considered, even though it may be decided to design separate systems—"sub-systems"—initially. Even so, the separately designed systems should be planned in such a way that they may be developed with a minimum of amendment and disruption at a later date after gaining experience in the design and processing of separate applications (*see* XXIII, **20, 21**).

20. Essentials for the effective design of systems. A well-designed system should take into account the following factors:

(*a*) production of the desired information, at the right time, in the right amount, with an acceptable level of accuracy and in the form required at an economical cost;

(*b*) incorporation of checks and controls which are capable of detecting and dealing with exceptional circumstances and errors;

(*c*) need to minimise the cost and the time spent on recording source data;

(*d*) need to minimise the cost and the time spent on data preparation;

(*e*) need to minimise the cost and the time spent on processing data;

(*f*) effective safeguards for the prevention of fraud;

(*g*) effective security measures in order to avoid loss of data stored in master files;

(*h*) efficient design of documents and reports;

(*i*) efficient design of computer runs;

(*j*) design of suitable coding systems to aid identification, comparison, sorting, verification and the elimination of ambiguity;

(*k*) policy matters and their effect on business systems;

(*l*) legal matters and their relationship with business systems;

(*m*) adequate handling of exceptions to normal situations. While a system can be designed to process all possible variations or exceptions on a computer, this may create a considerable degree of complexity in programming and extend processing time to an unacceptable level. Consequently it may be more efficient to design clerical systems instead of computer systems to handle them.

SYSTEMS SPECIFICATION

21. Purpose of a systems specification. The systems analyst having developed a computer based system must specify in writing the features and operating requirements of the application. Initially it is presented to management for their scrutiny and approval prior to implementation. The document also provides a programmer with the details he requires for writing the programs for each run. It also provides formal documentation for system updating and general reference. It is the counterpart of a procedure manual prepared by O. & M. staff.

22. Structure of a systems specification. A typical systems specification may be arranged into six sections as follows.

(*a*) Introduction:

    (*i*) terms of reference;

    (*ii*) objectives;

    (*iii*) expected benefits;

    (*iv*) annual operating costs, development costs and annual equipment costs.

(*b*) Systems definition:

    (*i*) written description of system embracing clerical and computer procedures;

    (*ii*) system flowcharts, procedure charts and computer run charts.

(*c*) Equipment:

    (*i*) schedule of equipment required to operate the system including ancillary equipment for data preparation;

    (*ii*) possible alternative equipment.

(*d*) Detailed specification:

    (*i*) input specification and layout;

    (*ii*) output specification and layout;

    (*iii*) file record specification;

    (*iv*) source document specification and layout.

(*e*) Program specification:

    (*i*) details of test data and testing procedures;

    (*ii*) checks and controls.

(*f*) Implementation:

    (*i*) file conversion;

    (*ii*) parallel running and pilot schemes during program and system testing;

    (*iii*) preparation of job procedures for user departments;

    (*iv*) preparation of job procedures for data preparation and computer departments

23. Block diagram. A block diagram is sometimes referred to as a "system outline" or "system function" diagram. The diagram is used to outline the whole system in respect of inputs, files, processing and outputs independent of operation details.

The computer is not shown in such a diagram, as it is only required to show the flow of information through the system and the output produced.

24. Systems flowchart. This chart is prepared from the block diagram and introduces the computer, which is shown as a box. The chart is mainly designed to illustrate the flow of documents around the computer and the processing performed by the computer.

Some essential aspects of its construction are:

(*a*) the name of each department concerned with the system is recorded along the top of the flowchart;

(*b*) inputs to the system are shown on the left-hand side of the chart;

(*c*) outputs from the system are shown on the right-hand side of the chart;

(*d*) processes are shown by the appropriate symbol in the relevant column, and contain a reference code;

(*e*) each symbol contains a brief description;

(*f*) symbols are connected by lines and arrows.

25. Procedure narrative. A procedure narrative is a written description of the new system, and expands the restricted details shown on the systems flowchart. The narrative and systems flowchart combined form the most important part of the initial specification presented to the chief programmer.

26. Computer run chart. Computer run charts are prepared from the systems flowchart, and show the sequence of computer operations to be performed.

The chart expands the detail of each computer box on the systems flowchart showing inputs, files and outputs relevant to each run.

It is good practice to support the chart by a written description of the processing stages (*see* **37, 38** and Figs. 100–7).

27. Clerical procedure chart. This type of chart is also prepared from the system flowchart and outlines the clerical operations necessary to support computer operations.

28. Computer procedure flowchart. This is the most detailed flowchart prepared by the systems analyst during the design stage, and is used to support the written program specification.

It is used to show the sequence of operations and decisions in a computer procedure.

The chart is prepared from the computer run chart (*see* Figs. 108, 109, 111, 113, 114, 116, and 117).

29. Output specification and layout. When designing the output from the system, it is necessary to consider the needs of the user in order that the output should serve a useful purpose. The size of a document and/or report must not be decided upon without first considering the limitations of the equipment used in their production.

For each printed output it is necessary to consider the following aspects.

(*a*) Use *standard planning chart* for indicating:
   (*i*) system identification—name and number;
   (*ii*) program name and number;
   (*iii*) number of print lines per sheet;
   (*iv*) maximum size of fields;
   (*v*) field content;
   (*vi*) lateral and vertical spacing requirements.
(*b*) Prepare a *written description of the output* in respect of:
   (*i*) purpose of document or report;
   (*ii*) number of copies;
   (*iii*) type of stationery, e.g. size, pre-printed or blank and quality;
   (*iv*) special considerations;
   (*v*) distribution;
   (*vi*) frequency of issue (allied to frequency of computer run).
(*c*) Provision of samples (*see* I, **7**).

30. Input specification and layout. It is necessary to consider both the original source document and the input media to the computer.

Source documents are the forms used for the initial recording of data and they are usually pre-printed. The design of such documents should take into account the layout of the punched card or other media used for input so that data fields appear in the most convenient order for transcription—that is, punching or encoding.

Data of a fixed nature, that is non-variable, can be pre-printed to avoid unnecessary entry of details each time the form is compiled.

If computer input is by means of punched cards, then the cards should be printed with the title of the fields in accordance with those on the source document required for input.

It must not be overlooked that some source documents are originated outside the business, which means that their design cannot be changed. In such cases a punching document may be designed to assist the punch operator when preparing cards for computer input.

A dual-purpose or mark-sensed card may be classified as a source document and input media (*see* I, **3**).

Source document specifications contain the essential elements recorded on the input document analysis form together with any amendments that are deemed necessary (*see* **16**).

Samples of source documents and input media must be provided.

31. File record specification. The construction of files is based on the information recorded on the file analysis form, suitably amended for the needs of the computer system (*see* I, **4, 5**, Fig. 90).

The following details are extremely important in the design of files for computer processing.

FILE RECORD SPECIFICATION					PAGE 1
FILE NAME Sales ledger file		VALUE OF IDENTIFICATION SALESLEDGER			BLOCKING 25 records
SEQUENCE Home/Export Customer code, date, Invoice No.		ESTIMATED NO. OF RECORDS 10,000			SECURITY G.F.S.
RECORD NAME FIELD DESCRIPTION	DATA RECORD DATA NAME	PICTURE	OCCURS	TOTAL CHS	FIELD POSITION
	LEDGER				
Record type	RT	XX		2	1–2
Date	DATE	DDMMYY 9(6)		6	3–8
Home/Export	HE	X		1	9
Customer code	CUST	X(4)		4	10–13
Invoice number	INVNO	9(5)		5	14–18
Description	DESC	X(10)		10	19–28
Line number	LINE	9(5)		5	29–33
Value	VALU	Pence 9 (8)		8	34–41

(*Courtesy of Charles Richards Fasteners Limited*)

FIG. 90 *File record specification*

(a) Specification for *all files*:

    (*i*) medium to be used;

    (*ii*) file name;

    (*iii*) labels;

    (*iv*) size of records—maximum and average;

    (*v*) names of different records contained in the file;

    (*vi*) sequence of records;

    (*vii*) block size—unit of transfer—applicable to magnetic files;

    (*viii*) field names, descriptions, field lengths and maximum values.

(b) Specification for *card files*:

    (*i*) card types;

    (*ii*) punching code.

(c) Specification for *magnetic tape files* (*see* XIV, **3–12**).

    (*i*) packing density and gap size;

    (*ii*) number of reels constituting the file;

    (*iii*) file security arrangements (*see* VII, **14**);

    (*iv*) retention period.

(d) Specification for *direct access files* (*see* XIV, **17–39**):

    (*i*) method of storage—random, serial, sequential, partitioned or indexed sequential;

    (*ii*) method of access—random, serial, sequential, selective-sequential or partitioned.

It is important to note that the method of storage refers to the manner in which the file is organised and the method of access refers to the manner of referencing, updating or amending the file.

    (*iii*) Bucket size.

DECISION TABLES

32. Use and construction of decision tables. Decision tables are used in the process of analysing the factors involved in a problem, which necessitates defining the conditions specific to the problem and the actions to be taken when the various conditions arise.

A computer program written for a specific application must provide for branching to appropriate parts of the program when specified conditions in data are discovered after testing.

A decision table enables the branching requirements of a program to be precisely specified.

Decision tables may be used to assist the preparation of a

complicated flowchart to ensure that all conditions and actions have been catered for and that cause and effect relationships are clearly visible.

A decision is divided into four parts (*see* Figs. 91, 93, 94, 96):

(*a*) condition stub $\left.\right\}$ condition statement;
(*b*) condition entries

(*c*) action stub $\left.\right\}$ action statement.
(*d*) action entries

The condition stub and condition entries define the conditions to be tested.

The action stub and action entries define the actions to be taken dependent upon the outcome of the testing.

The "rules" consist of a set of outcomes of conditions tests, together with the related actions.

A decision table may be prepared from a procedure narrative by underlining all conditions present with a solid line and all actions with a broken line. The conditions and actions are then recorded on the decision table.

The features of a decision table are as follows.

(*a*) Each condition and action stub contain a limited entry, that is to say an entry complete in itself.

(*b*) The entry part of the table in respect of the condition stub indicates if a particular rule satisfies the condition.

(*c*) The entry part of the table in respect of the action stub indicates the action required in respect of the condition entry.

Figure 91 is related to the stock control computer procedure flow-chart illustrated in Fig. 113, showing an analysis of the action required for types of transaction.

(*d*) Three symbols are used in the condition entry part of the table:

(*i*) Y (yes), if the condition is satisfied.

(*ii*) N (no), if the condition is not satisfied.

(*iii*) - (hyphen), if the condition is not relevant to the rule.

(*e*) In the action entry part of the table an **x** is recorded to signify a required action. If no action is required the column is left blank.

33. When to prepare a decision table. As a general rule, a decision table may be prepared when the number of rules multiplied by the number of conditions equals six or more.

34. Decision table and flowchart problem (1). The reader may now wish to attempt the following question from the November 1976 examinations of the I.C.M.A.

Stockists Limited calculates discounts allowed to customers on the following basis:

Order quantity	Normal discount %
1–99	5
100–199	7
200–499	9
500 and over	10

RULES	RECEIPT	ISSUE	ORDER	POSITIVE ADJUSTMENT	NEGATIVE ADJUSTMENT
	1	2	3	4	5
CONDITION STUB	CONDITION ENTRIES				
TRANSACTION – RECEIPT?	Y	N	N	N	N
TRANSACTION – ISSUE?	–	Y	N	N	N
TRANSACTION – ORDER?	–	–	Y	N	N
TRANSACTION – POSITIVE ADJUSTMENT?	–	–	–	Y	N
TRANSACTION – NEGATIVE ADJUSTMENT?	–	–	–	–	Y
ACTION STUB	ACTION ENTRIES				
ADD TO STOCK	X			X	
DEDUCT FROM STOCK		X			X
ADD TO QUANTITY ON ORDER			X		
DEDUCT FROM QUANTITY ON ORDER	X				
ADD TO STOCK AVAILABLE				X	X
DEDUCT FROM STOCK AVAILABLE		X			X

FIG. 91 *Limited entry decision table*

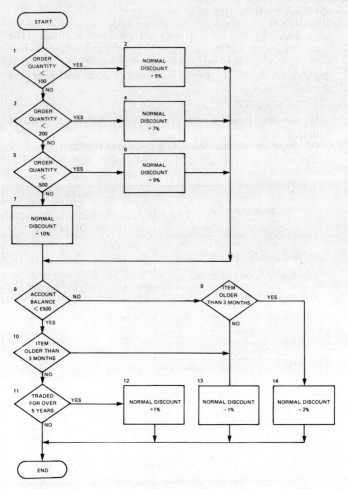

(Courtesy of Major R. S. Couder, RAPC Training Centre)

FIG. 92   *Flowchart problem*

These discounts only apply if the customer's account balance is below £500 and does not include any item older than three months. If the account is outside both of these limits, the above discounts are reduced by 2 per cent. If only one condition is violated, the discounts are reduced by 1 per cent. If a customer has been trading with Stockists Limited for over five years and conforms to both of the above credit checks then he is allowed an additional 1 per cent discount.

You are required to:

(a) construct a limited entry decision table illustrating the above situation; and

(b) draw a flowchart illustrating the above situation.

The solution to this question is illustrated in Figs. 92 and 93.

CONDITION STUB	RULES				
	1	2	3	4	5
	CONDITION ENTRIES				
ORDER QUANTITY? (SEE FIG. 92)					
ACCOUNT BALANCE < £500?	Y	Y	Y	N	N
ANY ITEM > 3 MONTHS?	Y	N	N	Y	N
CUSTOMER > 5 YEARS?	–	Y	N	–	–
ACTION STUB	ACTION ENTRIES				
STORE NORMAL DISCOUNT RELEVANT TO QUANTITY	X	X	X	X	X
APPLY NORMAL DISCOUNT RELEVANT TO QUANTITY			X		
APPLY NORMAL DISCOUNT +1%		X			
APPLY NORMAL DISCOUNT −2%				X	
APPLY NORMAL DISCOUNT −1%	X				X

FIG. 93   *Decision table problem*

35. Decision table and flowchart problem (2). For additional practice in the preparation of decision tables and flowcharts the reader may wish to attempt the following question which was set in the

June 1976 examinations of the Institute of Accounting Staff (I.A.S.).

A soft drinks manufacturer sells to three sales outlets,

(a) supermarkets and large departmental stores
(b) retailers
(c) hotels and catering establishments.

Dependent upon the sales outlet and the value of sales, the following chart indicates the discounts allowed to customers.

Supermarkets and large departmental stores: Discount Allowed %

For orders less than £50	5
For orders £50 and over but less than £100	8
For orders £100 and over	10

Retailers:

For orders less than £50	3
For orders £50 and over but less than £100	7
For orders £100 and over	10

					RULES				
CONDITION STUB	1	2	3	4	5	6	7	8	9
	CONDITION ENTRY								
OUTLETS									
S & L	Y	Y	Y	N	N	N	N	N	N
RETAILER	—	—	—	Y	Y	Y	N	N	N
HOTEL & CATERING	—	—	—	—	—	—	Y	Y	Y
ORDER VALUES:									
< £50	Y	N	N	Y	N	N	Y	N	N
≥ £50 < £100	—	Y	N	—	Y	N	—	Y	N
≥ £100	—	—	Y	—	—	Y	—	—	Y
ACTION STUB	ACTION ENTRY								
DISCOUNT ALLOWED									
3%				X					
4%							X		
5%	X								
7%					X				
7½%								X	
8%		X							
10%			X			X			X

FIG. 94 *Decision table problem*

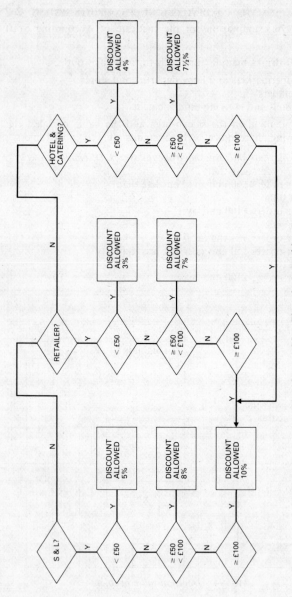

FIG. 95 *Flowchart problem*

Hotels and catering establishments:

For orders less then £50	4
For orders £50 and over but less than £100	$7\frac{1}{2}$
For orders £100 and over	10

(*a*) From the information given, construct a "limited entry" decision table and flowchart.

(*b*) What advantages are there from the use of decision tables?

NOTE: The question has been slightly amended.

The solution to the question is outlined in Figs. 94 and 95.

36. Decision table and flowchart problem (3). As this is a practical subject and may be usefully employed in a number of situations to solve logical problems relating to business systems it is considered that a further problem would serve a useful purpose. The question which follows was set in the June 1977 examinations of The Association of Certified Accountants (A.C.A.).

The following is a description of the procedure for dealing with delivery charges for goods bought from **AB Ltd**:

For the purpose of determining delivery charges, customers are divided into two categories, those whose Sales Region Code (S.R.C.) is 50 or above, and those with an S.R.C. of less than 50.

If the S.R.C. is less then 50 and the invoice amount is less than £1,000, the delivery charge to be added to the invoice total is £30. But if the invoice value is for £1,000 or more, the delivery charge is £15.

If the S.R.C. is equal to or greater than 50 and the invoice total is less than £1,000, the delivery charge is £40. For invoices totalling £1,000 or more, however, the delivery charge is £20.

Required:

(*a*) prepare a decision table of the above procedure;

(*b*) prepare a flowchart of the above procedure.

NOTE: The question has been slightly curtailed.

The solution to the question is outlined in Figs. 96 and 97.

FLOWCHARTING COMPUTER APPLICATIONS

The purpose of this section is to illustrate by means of flowcharts (computer run charts) a number of widely-used computer applications.

In general, computer applications consist of "runs" and

	RULES			
	1	2	3	4
CONDITION STUB	CONDITION ENTRY			
SALES REGION CODE ≥ £50	Y	Y	N	N
INVOICE AMOUNT ≥ £1000	Y	N	Y	N
ACTION STUB	ACTION ENTRY			
DELIVERY CHARGES:				
ADD £15 TO INVOICE TOTAL			X	
ADD £20 TO INVOICE TOTAL	X			
ADD £30 TO INVOICE TOTAL				X
ADD £40 TO INVOICE TOTAL		X		

FIG. 96   *Decision table problem*

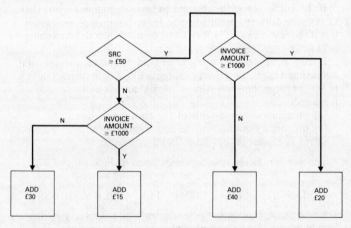

FIG. 97   *Flowchart problem*

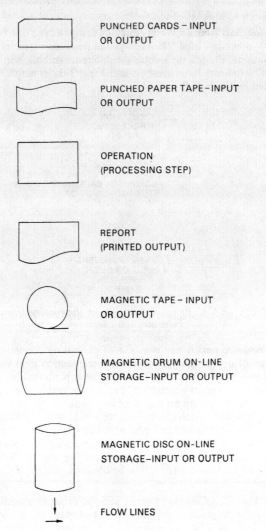

FIG. 98 *General flowchart symbols for the construction of computer run charts*

PUNCHED CARDS – INPUT
OR OUTPUT

PUNCHED PAPER TAPE – INPUT
OR OUTPUT

OPERATION
(PROCESSING STEP)

REPORT
(PRINTED OUTPUT)

MAGNETIC TAPE – INPUT
OR OUTPUT

MAGNETIC DRUM ON-LINE
STORAGE – INPUT OR OUTPUT

MAGNETIC DISC ON-LINE
STORAGE – INPUT OR OUTPUT

FLOW LINES

"routines", and it is now proposed to indicate some of the more important considerations (*see* **38**).

37. Flowchart symbols. When designing computer run charts, flow-chart symbols are used. The various computer manufacturers and the National Computing Centre use different symbols, but Fig. 98 serves to indicate basic symbols and Fig. 99 the symbols recommended by the N.C.C.

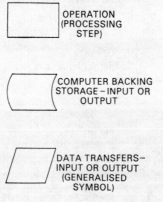

OPERATION
(PROCESSING
STEP)

COMPUTER BACKING
STORAGE – INPUT OR
OUTPUT

DATA TRANSFERS–
INPUT OR OUTPUT
(GENERALISED
SYMBOL)

FIG. 99   *N.C.C. flowchart symbols for the construction of computer run charts*

38. Computer run. A run is a unit of processing consisting of a number of operations applied to each transaction item within a batch (*see* **26** and Figs. 100–7). Each item is processed in accordance with a program which loops back to the next item after completing the processing on the preceding item.

It is normal for each run to have its own program consisting of a series of instructions to be performed on each transaction item.

The number of operations performed in a single run should be as high as possible, and it is necessary to consider the following factors which have a bearing on the constituent elements of each run.

(*a*) The *size of internal storage* and the capacity available for storing the program, which may consist of many instructions.

(*b*) The *feasibility of segmenting programs* and storing the various segments in direct access backing storage devices to be called in when the previous segment has been completed. This technique overcomes the non-availability of internal storage for storing the whole program.

(*c*) The *number of devices* (such as magnetic tape units or printers) required in a run should be no more than those which comprise the computer installation.

(*d*) The *complexity of the run* in respect of the number of different activities to be performed (such as calculating, printing and updating) within the run.

(*e*) The ability of the run to deal with *exceptions and errors* within the data being processed.

39. Processing routine. A routine may form all or part of an application consisting of a number of computer runs usually interconnected by the output from a preceding run forming the input to the succeeding run. For example, the output from a wages calculation routine includes the updating of the payroll master file which forms the input to the next run for printing payslips and pay envelopes (*see* Fig. 100).

40. Applications. An application consists of a complete job processed on the computer, examples of which are:

(*a*) Payroll preparation, including payslips and updating of tax and earnings records (*see* Fig. 100).

(*b*) Payroll master file amendment (*see* Fig. 101).

(*c*) Sales invoicing (*see* Fig. 102).

(*d*) Sales ledger updating, including the preparation of statements of account, list of overdue accounts and list of all accounts (*see* Fig. 103).

(*e*) Stock control, including stock updating and preparation of a stock schedule including notification of items requiring to be re-ordered (*see* Figs. 104 and 105).

(*f*) Integrated stock control, sales invoicing and sales ledger updating (*see* Fig. 106).

(*g*) Integrated nominal ledger (*see* Fig. 107).

Figures 100–107 illustrate the computer runs required for processing the applications listed above.

41. Integrated nominal ledger application. Figure 107 illustrates the computer runs for an integrated nominal ledger system which may be performed by a nominal ledger package providing for the production of profit and loss statements, balance sheet and variance reports. The latter is achieved by incorporating budgetary control

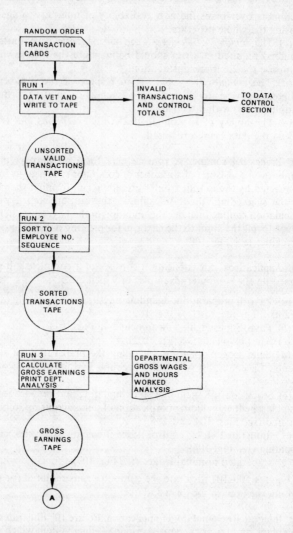

FIG. 100 *Computer run chart—payroll system* (*using magnetic tape backing storage*)

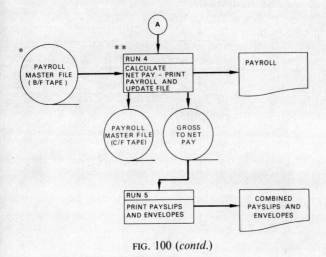

FIG. 100 (*contd.*)

* This file contains details for printing payslips. Alternatively, a separate tape may be produced.

** The program for this run also performs P.A.Y.E. calculations.

Rates are punched into the cards because of the high variability of pay rates and the absence of direct access backing storage for reference files.

The transaction cards show

Hours worked—normal including time rates.
Hours worked—overtime including premium time rates.
Bonus details including bonus rates.

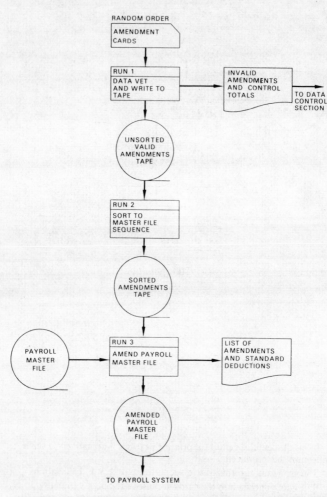

FIG. 101 *Computer run chart—payroll master file amendments*

Piecework details including piecework rates. Amendment cards show new starters, leavers, pay adjustments, changes to P.A.Y.E. code numbers and changes to standard deductions.

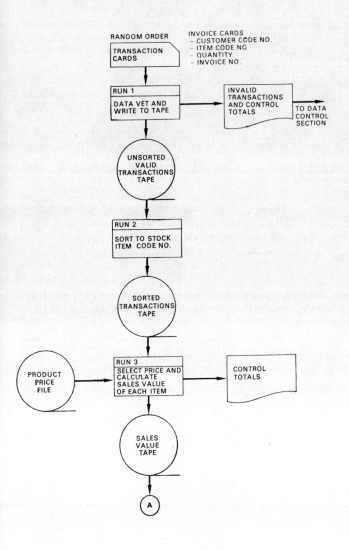

FIG. 102 *Computer run chart—sales invoicing procedure*
(part of sales accounting system)

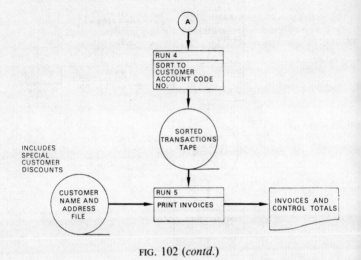

FIG. 102 (*contd.*)

The product price file includes standard discount and VAT rate. The sales value tape may be used subsequently for sales analysis.

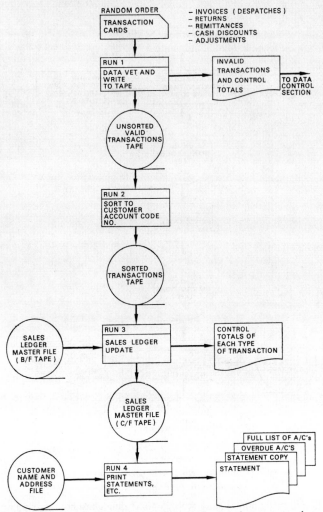

FIG. 103 *Computer run chart—sales ledger updating procedure (part of sales accounting system): monthly processing*

Instead of invoice cards, the sales value tape from the invoicing procedure would be used if sales invoicing and the sales ledger are computerised. Similar considerations apply if cash remittances are computerised.

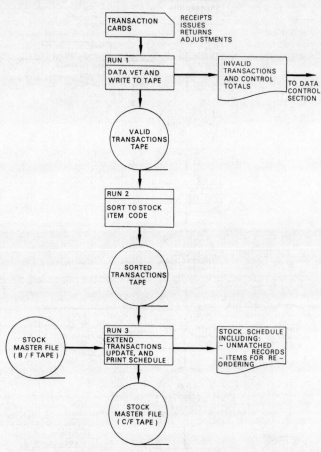

FIG. 104   *Computer run chart—stock control system (using magnetic tape backing storage)*

Separately printed stock schedules (including unmatched records) and re-order schedules may be produced from re-runs after setting sense switch. All stock records must be re-written to a new magnetic tape master file, even those records for which there are no current transactions.

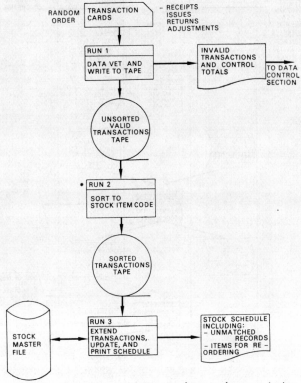

FIG. 105 *Computer run chart—stock control system (using magnetic disc backing storage)*

* It is advisable to sort transactions into the sequence of the master file, even though the appropriate records are directly addressable, to minimise processing time by having all item code transactions grouped together. For logic reasons, it is also preferable for receipts to precede issues, etc.

Stock records for which there are no current transactions do not require re-writing to a new magnetic disc master file, which is essential for magnetic tape systems. Stock records for which there are current transactions are updated by overwriting the existing data on the same magnetic disc master file.

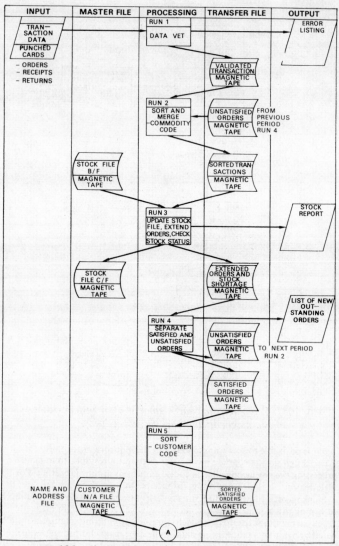

FIG. 106 *Computer run chart—integrated stock control, sales invoicing and sales ledger system* (*using N.C.C. symbols*)

The system outlined assumes that complete processing is carried out once a month. In practice, certain parts of the processing may be performed daily, weekly or monthly.

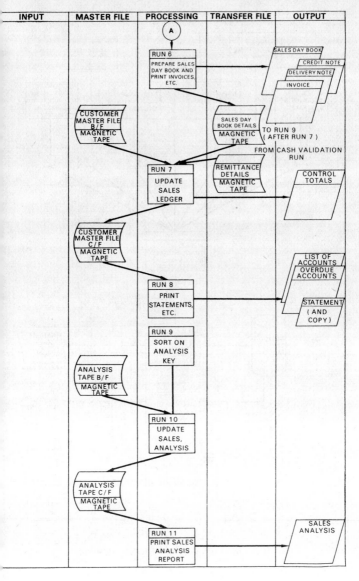

INPUT	MASTER FILE	PROCESSING	TRANSFER FILE	OUTPUT

FIG. 106 (*contd.*)

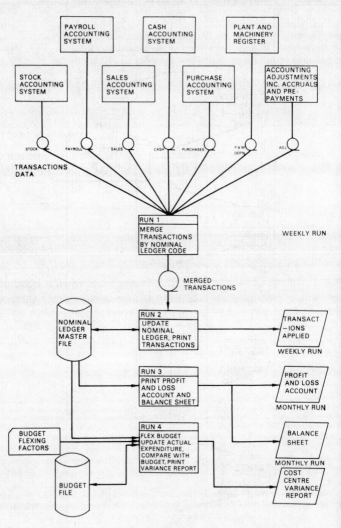

FIG. 107 *Integrated nominal ledger flowchart*

and budget flexing. Other forms of nominal ledger applications may not be so comprehensive and incorporate only sales and purchase transactions. Yet other applications may not produce profit and loss statements or balance sheets but restrict their output to accounts schedules or trial balance for the preparation of final accounts and balance sheet by normal accounting methods.

Run 1. Input is derived from data produced by the separate computer applications in respect of stocks, payroll, sales, purchases, plant and machinery including depreciation, accruals and pre-payments, accounting adjustments and cash. The data on the transaction files is deemed to have been validated in the relevant runs of the appropriate applications. The run is concerned with consolidating all nominal ledger data on relevant nominal ledger codes.

Run 2. The input to this run is the consolidated file from run one. This run is for the purpose of updating the nominal ledger master file and printing out a list of transactions applied for the purpose of providing an audit trail. The master file is stored on disc to facilitate direct access to relevant nominal ledger records.

Run 3. At the end of the month the nominal ledger master file is used for printing a profit and loss account and balance sheet.

Run 4. The nominal ledger master file records are input together with a budget file and budget flexing factors. The budget file is updated with actual expenditure for the period to obtain the cumulative expenditure to date for comparison with budgeted expenditure. This provides the basis for printing out a cost centre variance report.

BENCHMARK TESTS

42. Benchmark tests defined. Benchmark tests are used to assess the performance of different computer systems for the selection of the system which best fits the requirements of the businesses' data processing commitment. The tests are applied to representative data and processing functions such as reading and writing records, sorting operations and multiplication, etc. The actual times obtained can be compared with manufacturers' published performance data for evaluating the various computer systems under consideration. Tests are conducted by benchmark programs which also provide valuable information in respect of the amount of internal storage used during processing.

43. Advantages of benchmark tests. These are summarised below:

(*a*) assists in selecting the most suitable computer system for a businesses' data processing requirements;

(*b*) performance data is known in advance which assists in formulating job schedules;

(*c*) the cost and performance of different computer systems may be compared for establishing cost effectiveness.

44. Disadvantages of benchmark tests. These are summarised below:

(*a*) the problem of defining a representative workload for establishing performance data;

(*b*) the time involved with conducting such tests.

DATA PROCESSING STANDARDS

45. Types and purpose of standards in general. There exist many types of standards for many different purposes covering procedural regulations, forms and paper sizes, screw sizes, electrical and building standards, flowcharting symbols and terminology in various professions; such as the Terminology of Management and Financial Accountancy, of the I.C.M.A. Standards are contained in army manuals, British Standards and International Standards, etc.

Standards attempt to provide a code of practice or to reduce variety thereby providing a framework of best practices and the basis for rationalisation.

46. Standards and data processing. It follows that standards should be adopted in data processing activities for the purpose of providing a code of practice. In this respect it is prudent policy to adopt standard practices for the preparation of systems documentation and the operation of data processing systems. Of particular importance is the adoption of a Data Processing Standards Manual containing details in respect of:

(*a*) the contents and format of a systems specification (*see* **21, 22**);

(*b*) computer operating instructions;

(*c*) program preparation and documentation;

(*d*) program testing procedures;

(*e*) validation procedures;

(*f*) systems evaluation procedures.

A manual of this type provides the means for familiarising new systems staff with the code of practice required and assists in the recognition of the design philosophy adopted by their predecessors. The manual also provides the means for staff training and continuity of systems development. It would also be of great assistance for inter-disciplinary communications if data processing terminology was standardised because a variety of terms are used to define similar aspects.

CODING SYSTEMS

47. Purpose of coding systems. Code numbers are allocated systematically to specific entities on a planned and co-ordinated basis in order to provide a unique identity of customers, stocks, expenditure items, suppliers and employees, etc. A code number is a compact means of defining a specific entity as only a few digits are required rather than lengthy descriptions. Descriptions are still required however for the purpose of describing items on despatch notes, sales invoices and purchase orders, etc. Such descriptions are complementary to code numbers and they must, of course, be matched by validation checks. Code numbers are referred to as "key" fields on transactions and records.

Computer processing systems in particular utilise code numbers for locating specific records on master files and matching them with transaction data prior to updating the records.

48. Centralised control of coding systems. It is good practice for series of code numbers to be planned and allocated centrally to avoid conflict. If this is not done, duplicated code structures could be implemented causing chaos in the identification of various transactions types. This could be overcome to some extent, however, by validation checks on the type of transaction. Systems staff usually accept responsibility for the design of coding systems as it is an integral element of systems design.

49. Important features of coding systems. The following summary will serve to indicate the main factors to consider for effective coding systems.

(*a*) *Uniqueness*—Each entity should have a unique unambiguous code number for specific identification.

(*b*) *Useful purpose*—Code numbers in general serve a useful purpose as they assist sorting of transactions which can be done much faster by computer than any other method. It is also much easier to sort by numeric codes than alphabetic descriptions. Code numbers also facilitate the comparison of data items, perhaps for matching purposes, either for updating master files or for comparing actual and budgeted expenditure, etc.

(*c*) *Compactness*—Code numbers require fewer digits or characters than descriptions which complement each other but at the same time allows descriptions to be abbreviated in certain instances to eliminate redundancy, i.e. unnecessary characters. For example, "FASTENER" may be abbreviated to "FSTNR" by eliminating the vowels.

(*d*) *Meaningful*—Although not always possible or desirable, specific parts of a code when relevant should relate to particular facets of the item to which it relates, e.g. size, shape, type, location and specification of component parts held in store (*see* **50**).

(*e*) *Self-checking*—Codes should contain self-checking facilities when necessary in the form of check digits for validation purposes (*see* VII, **22–26**).

(*f*) *Expansibility*—Codes should facilitate expansion by allowing flexibility in the coding structure to allow insertions by leaving gaps between blocks of code sequences.

(*g*) *Standard size*—All codes of a given type relating to a specific entity should contain the same number of digits to facilitate field checks.

50. Faceted code. Each position in the code number has a specific meaning, for example, if it is required to develop a code for basic raw materials used in manufacturing it may be based on the following structure.

Type of material—1st digit
   1—Steel
   2—Copper
   3—Brass
Section—2nd digit
   1—Rod
   2—Strip
   3—Sheet
Size—3rd digit
   1 ⎫
   2 ⎬ Appropriate range
   3 ⎪ of sizes
   4 ⎭
Location in stores—4th digit
   1 ⎫
   2 ⎬ Appropriate storage
   3 ⎪ location
   4 ⎭

51. Serial code. Sequences of code numbers may be allocated to specific types of record or to identify specific entities. No information is conveyed by the code number itself. For example, a range of numbers may be allocated for departmental codes, expenditure codes, stock codes, customer account codes, etc.

These code numbers may be applied in the following way.

(*a*) Departmental code:

Direct
    1—Press shop
    2—Machine shop
    3—Assembly shop
    4—Finishing shop
    5—Inspection shop
Indirect
    6—W.I.P. stores
    7—Finished product stores
    8—Consumable stores
    9—Toolroom
    10—Maintenance department

(*b*) Expenditure codes:

Operating labour:
    20—Tool setters
    21—Labourers
    22—Shop clerks
General operating overheads:
    25—Scrap
    26—Rectification
    27—Waiting time
    28—Shift premium
    29—Small tools
    30—Consumable materials
    31—Lubricants
    32—Works stationery

(*c*) Combination of codes may be used as follows:

    1/29—Press shop/small tools
    9/31—Toolroom/lubricants
    10/20—Maintenance department/tool setters

52. Block coding. A block is set of serial or code numbers analysed into smaller groups which may be based on some general characteristic of the entities, for example:

Steel rod	0001–0170
Steel strip	0171–0340
Steel sheet	0341–0500

Copper rod	0550–0670
Copper strip	0671–0840
Copper sheet	0841–1000

Brass rod	1050–1200
Brass strip	1201–1400
Brass sheet	1401–1550

PROGRESS TEST 15

1. Why is a computer feasibility study necessary? Describe the cost information that you would expect to find in a feasibility report. **(1)** [I.A.S. June 1976, Q1]

2. A feasibility study is the investigation an organisation undertakes of its various activities to establish whether or not the use of electronic data processing equipment can be justified.

Required:

(*a*) list the factors which may prompt a firm to institute such a survey;

(*b*) outline the stages of a typical study in a medium-sized organisation. **(1)** [A.C.A. June 1975, Q8]

3. Outline and comment on the objectives and various stages of a feasibility study for a proposed business system. You are to assume a medium-sized organisation that already has sufficient computing power to cover its foreseeable needs. **(1 (*f*))** [A.C.A. Dec. 1978, Q6]

4. The list of unsuccessful computer installations is a long one and there is no doubt that many organisations are disappointed with the way their computer projects have developed. What, in your opinion, are the principal reasons for the failure of computer projects? **(1–9)** [A.C.A. June 1976, Q6]

5. Regardless of its technical excellence, a computer based system should be economically viable.

(*a*) List the circumstances which may lead to erosion of planned profitability in such systems.

(*b*) To ensure effectiveness, what steps would you take to plan and control:

(*i*) the selection, and

(*ii*) the implementation of additional processing tasks? **(1–9)** [I.C.M.A. Nov. 1975, Q3]

6. Your company is planning to introduce a computer system and you have been asked to design a two-day introduction course for existing staff employed outside the proposed data processing department.

Prepare a report for your managing director stating what you would expect such a course to achieve and the topics you would include. **(3)** [I.C.M.A. Nov. 1975, Q5]

7. The use of a computer is being considered by your company.

(*a*) Commencing with the preliminary survey, list all the steps you would recommend to be taken and briefly describe each of these steps. You are to assume the ultimate purchase of a computer.

(*b*) The decision to go ahead is then taken. Summarise the remaining steps concluding with the systems evaluation. (Fig. 88) [I.C.M.A. Nov. 1974, Q7]

8. Indicate what you understand by the term systems analysis, and state its purpose. **(10)**

9. When should a systems survey or study take place? Summarise (*a*) the main steps, and (*b*) the work involved, in a systems study. Assuming that you are a project leader conducting a systems study covering all commercial activities in a company, who would you include in your study team and why? State the industry for which your selection would be suitable. **(11–18)** [I.C.M.A. June 1971, Q6]

10. Outline the stages of a typical O. & M. assignment. How does systems analysis differ from O. & M.? **(12)** [A.C.A. Dec. 1975, Q4]

11. Fact finding is an important part of the systems analysis process.

(*a*) Explain why fact finding is important.

(*b*) List the principal methods of obtaining facts, describing the advantages and disadvantages of each method. **(12)** [I.C.M.A. May 1978, Q5]

12. Outline the main stages in the development of a systems project and briefly describe the work carried out by the systems analyst at each stage. **(12–40)** [A.C.A. June 1978, Q6]

13. Identify, describe and briefly evaluate the techniques of fact finding and fact recording available to both the systems analyst and

an O. & M. officer when investigating a system within an organisation. **(12, 13)** [A.C.A. June 1975, Q5]

14. Assume that you are a systems analyst with XYZ Ltd. A computer has been installed and satisfactory computerised payroll and sales accounting systems are now in operation. It has been agreed that the next project will be to transfer the company's raw material stock control system to the computer. Outline the main stages through which you would expect the project to pass. It is not expected that any additional computing equipment will be required. **(12–40)** [A.C.A. Dec. 1976, Q5]

15. What criteria relating to effective systems design should guide a systems analyst when formulating proposals for a computer-based system? (Assume that the systems analyst works in a company where a computer has already been acquired). **(19, 20)** [A.C.A. Dec. 1975, Q5]

16. A systems investigation usually produces a systems specification or systems definition.

(a) What are the main contents of a systems specification?

(b) What are its purposes?

(c) To whom is it directed? **(21, 22)** [I.C.M.A. Nov. 1976, Q5]

17. (a) Explain the reasons for preparing a fully detailed systems specification.

(b) Tabulate the essential contents of a systems specification. **(21, 22)** [A.C.A. Dec. 1978, Q4]

18. Describe decision tables and discuss their use in systems analysis. What relationship have decision tables to flowcharts? **(32, 33)** [I.C.M.A. Nov. 1972, Q5]

19. The master file of a company's payroll is held on magnetic tape. Details obtained from clock cards are punched into cards.

(a) Draw a systems flowchart of the computer runs necessary to produce the output required and to update the payroll master file.

(b) Annotate briefly each stage to show its purpose.   (Fig. 100) [I.C.M.A. May 1975, Q3]

20. (a) Draft the systems flowchart for a computer-based payroll system. Assume punched card input and magnetic tape backing storage.

(b) Provide notes to your flowchart explaining the activity that is taking place at each stage of the system.   (Fig. 100) [A.C.A. June 1978, Q1]

21. (a) Draw a system flowchart showing the main programs

which would typically be required in a computer-based stock control system.

(*b*) Give, and briefly explain:

(*i*) Five examples of transaction or amendment data which would normally be input into such a system.

(*ii*) Five examples of the kind of reports you would expect the system to produce, also indicating their frequency. (Figs. 104–6, X, **12**) [A.C.A. June 1975, Q6]

22. Indicate the factors which must be considered in the design of computer runs. (**38**)

23. (*a*) Construct the systems flowcharts to show the processing runs for a nominal ledger system.

(*b*)(*i*) Specify the input and indicate which input could probably be automatically provided by other computer systems.

(*ii*) List the validation checks you would apply to the input. (**41** and Fig. 107) [I.C.A. Nov. 1973, Q4]

24. Benchmark tests are widely used for testing the performance of computers. What is meant by a benchmark test? In what circumstances are they used and what are their advantages and disadvantages? (**42–4**) [I.C.M.A. May 1976, Q3]

25. What are "Data Processing Standards"? Describe the main kinds of standards and explain their importance to the effective running of a computer department. (**45, 46**) [A.C.A. December 1976, Q8]

26. (*a*) Briefly list the main sections and contents of a typical data processing standards manual.

(*b*) In what ways do data processing standards assist in the effective operation of a computer department? (**45, 46**) [A.C.A. June 1978, Q7]

27. An important factor in the operation of all data processing systems (manual, mechanised or computerised) is the type of coding employed within the organisation. What factors determine the design of effective coding systems? Illustrate your answer with examples from your own experience. (**47–52**) [I.C.M.A. Nov. 1976, Q1]

28. Within the context of a data processing system, discuss the need for, and the advantages to be gained from, the use of a meaningful accounting code. (**47–52**) [I.A.S. Dec. 1976, Q6]

CHAPTER XVI

Computer Programs

ELEMENTS OF COMPUTER PROGRAMMING

1. Computer instructions. Each operation performed by a computer (on transaction data relating to a specific application) is in accordance with a pre-defined instruction.

Each instruction defines a basic operation to be performed, identifies the address of the data to be processed, the location of the data affected by the operation and the input or output device to be used. The complete set of instructions necessary to process a job is known as a "program".

Instructions are of five basic types as follows.

(*a*) *Arithmetic/logic*. Add, subtract, multiply, divide, shift, round-off, collate and compare, etc.

(*b*) *Data transfer*. Read from input, read to output, read a character, read a word, read a block of data, print a line, transfer data to different locations in the memory, etc.

(*c*) *Conditional branch or jump*. The presence of specific conditions in the data being processed is established by a comparison of data factors or the testing of a counter which causes the computer to branch or jump to the next appropriate instruction.

(*d*) *Unconditional branch or jump and loop*. When it is necessary to execute an instruction which is not the next in sequence in the internal memory, this is achieved by an instruction known as an unconditional branch or jump. This provides the means of creating a loop in the program for executing a common sequence of instructions repeatedly to various units of data. *See* Table X, Figs. 108, 109, 111–14). A loop is terminated by a conditional branch after effecting a test.

(*e*) *Counter*. A counter is a memory location (unit of storage) used for the purpose of storing a control parameter for automatically controlling a processing sequence. A counter may be set with a specific number which is decremented by "1" after each event being controlled. The counter may then be tested to detect whether it reads "0", for instance. If a "0" is detected then a

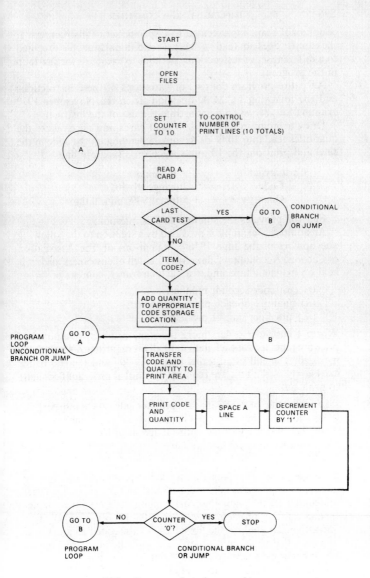

FIG. 108   *Program flowchart problem*

conditional branch is executed to a specific set of instructions. If the counter does not read "0" then a conditional branch is executed to a different set of instructions, perhaps to execute a further loop in the program.

An entire program consists of variations of these instructions and the following I.C.M.A. question set in the November 1972 examinations serves to demonstrate the use of the instructions.

Draw a program flowchart to read cards and accumulate the quantities read into 10 fields in core, depending on the code in the card and print out the 10 totals, each on a separate line.

Card layout	Columns
Code	1–2 (range 01–10)
Quantity	3–5 (max. 999, min. 001)

Fig. 108 provides the solution to this question.

An additional example is provided by a solution to the following question set in the June 1976 examinations of The Association of Certified Accountants: data from a batch of customers' orders is held on magnetic tape and, for each customer, consists of:

 (*i*) customer account number;
 (*ii*) quantity of each product ordered;
 (*iii*) price per unit of product.

Where a customer orders more than one product, quantity and price are repeated for each item until all his requirements have been included. The end of customer marker is "0" and the end of file marker is " – 1". You are required to draft a program flowchart to print out:

 (*a*) the value of each separate product sale on each order;
 (*b*) the total amount to be charged to each customer;
 (*c*) the total value of the entire batch of orders.

Fig. 109 provides the solution to this question.

2. Stages of program preparation. Before programming can commence, each problem must be analysed and program flowcharts prepared using program flowchart symbols to determine the logical aspects of the problem (*see* Figs. 108–111, 113, 114). Each operation indicated on the flowchart is then coded as an instruction on a coding sheet in accordance with the programming language being used (*see* **3–5**). The "source" program, as the initial program is called, is then punched into cards (one card per instruction) and is then input to the computer for assembling or

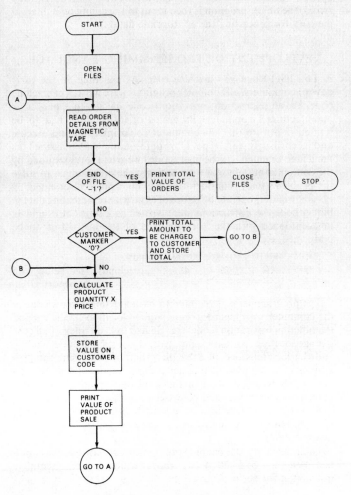

FIG. 109 *Program flowchart problem*

compiling (*see* XVII, **11–17**) into a machine code "object" program by appropriate software (*see* Fig. 119). After eliminating any errors, the object program is then input to the computer's internal memory for processing the appropriate data.

DEVELOPMENT OF PROGRAMMING LANGUAGES

3. Low-level language—machine code. At one time, in the early days of computers, all computer programs were written in machine code, i.e. an instruction (operation) code specific to a particular manufacturer's computer. Programs of instructions had to be written in a form that the computer could interpret and execute and accordingly this type of programming was classified as "machine-oriented" as the instructions were in a form required by the computer but not in a form to assist the programmer to solve the problems under consideration, i.e. not "problem-oriented".

As computers operate by pulses of electricity representing data in binary code the instructions were written as a series of 0s and 1s in accordance with the "bit" pattern of the instruction to be performed, e.g.

00101	00110	10100	00100	(binary).
5	6	20	4	(decimal) (*see* below and Appendix II).

The programmer was required to have a detailed knowledge of the computer with regard to core storage locations, registers and the function (operation) code, etc. He had to keep track of all core storage locations for data input, working areas, output assembly, and the locations occupied by the program. However, the programmer's task is now made easier as these functions are performed automatically by software in the form of translation programs known as "assemblers and compilers".

As program instructions were written as a series of 0s and 1s far removed from basic English, it was classified as low-level language programming.

Later developments enabled programs to be written in a simplified form, e.g. 5. 6. 20. 4 (*see* above) which is a representative instruction for performing:

> Add the four digit number in core store location
> six to the four digit number in core store location
> twenty and store the sum in core storage location
> twenty. (Add = 5)

However, not all computers used the same function or operation code, or indeed the same instruction format, which meant that a programmer probably had to learn a different function code and the operating details of another type of computer if he changed his job.

4. Low-level language—assembly code. To overcome these difficulties and to avoid the laborious task of writing programs in machine code, each computer manufacturer devised his own assembly code or assembly language. The advantage of an assembly language is that it enables a program to be written much more easily, at the same time allowing the same degree of flexibility that was available when writing programs in machine code. This means that programs can be prepared much more quickly than is possible with machine code, without the sacrifice of machine-running time when processing a job, which is not so with the high-level languages to be discussed later.

An assembly language enables program instructions to be written in mnemonic or symbolic code, that is in pseudo-code (a language which is not machine code). Programs written in this type of language are known as "source" programs and they have to be translated into a machine code program by a programming aid (software) known as an "assembler" (*see* XVII, **11–14**). After assembling, the object program is input each time the job to which it relates is to be processed. The process of writing instructions in mnemonic or symbolic code is known as "autocoding".

Instead of writing 5 for "add" and possibly 10 for "compare", the programmer writes "ADD" and "COM" in accordance with the symbolic code for a particular computer. Also, instead of specifying actual storage addresses (core storage locations) symbolic addresses are indicated in each instruction, i.e. OLDBAL, which is the symbolic address for "old balance".

An instruction in assembly language, for a single-address type computer, would take the form:

LDX 1 OLDBAL.

This instruction means "load the item of data named 'OLDBAL' to accumulator 1". The assembler automatically assigns a core store location to OLDBAL, which is indicated in the object program.

Assembly languages are still rather complex, and generally the number of instructions which have to be written are still the same as for machine code programming unless "macro-coding" is used. Such a language is also biased towards the machine rather than the problem (*see* XVII, **11, 14**, Fig. 120 for an example of an assembly code program).

5. High-level languages. In order to simplify and speed up the preparation of programs, a number of high-level languages have been developed which are problem-oriented rather than machine-oriented. Examples of high level languages are as follows.

(*a*) ALGOL. An algebraic language for scientific programming using algorithms. The name ALGOL is an abbreviation for *ALGO*-rithmic *L*anguage.

(*b*) FORTRAN. An algebraic language used for preparing instructions in the form of arithmetic formulas. The name FORTRAN is an abbreviation for *FOR*mula *TRAN*slation.

(*c*) COBOL. A language which uses basic English-style statements for the writing of instructions applicable to business data processing. The name COBOL is an abbreviation for *CO*mmon *B*usiness-*O*riented *L*anguage (*see* **15–19** for an outline of Cobol and an example of a Cobol program).

(*d*) BASIC-Beginners All purpose Symbolic Instruction Code (*see* VIII, **22**).

High-level languages are not so efficient with regard to machine running time as those written in an assembly language. The reason for this is that a language such as Cobol produces generalised sets of instructions from basic Cobol statements whereas an assembly language allows the programmer more flexibility in determining the series of instructions to achieve the desired results. It goes without saying that tasks may be processed in a number of ways, some of which are more or less efficient than others, and this is where the skill of the programmer comes to the fore.

PRINCIPLES OF PROGRAMMING

In order to illustrate the basic principles of programming for a digital computer it is proposed to use a hypothetical machine code first of all, followed by an illustration of an assembly language (*see* Fig. 120) and then conclude with an outline of Cobol (*see* **15–19**).

It is important to appreciate that some computers use a "two-address" type of instruction and others use a "single-address" type of instruction.

6. Two-address instructions. Many data processing operations are involved with two data factors, for example in multiplying two numbers, dividing one number into another, adding two numbers, comparing two numbers and transferring data from one area of core store to another, all involving two data addresses.

A two-address instruction comprises the following:

(*a*) Function or operation code—indicates the operation to be performed.

(*b*) A address—the address of the "operator" data factor.

(*c*) B address—the address of the "operand" data factor.

(*d*) Extra character—indicates the number of digital positions in the data to be processed.

7. Hypothetical machine code. Each computer has a unique machine code for each type of operation to be performed, which must be specified in the instruction. A hypothetical machine code is outlined in Table X.

8. Example of a program consisting of hypothetical machine code instructions. The subject of the example is a simplified stock updating procedure which is outlined in Fig. 111.

9. "Add-to-storage" concepts. Two-address computers are often referred to as "add-to-storage" or "add-to-memory" machines, because the result of addition replaces the previous contents of the B address in internal storage locations instead of in a special accumulator, as used with single-address computers (*see* Fig. 112).

For example, if it is required to add the contents of the A address to the contents of the B address, then the instruction would be written as follows:

Assume:

Contents of A address are 12345 in core storage locations 201–5.
Contents of B address are 45678 in core storage locations 301–5.
Extra character–5.

The instruction would be written as follows:

5   205   305   5

The address of each operand is referred to as 205 and 305 respectively, that is in the high-order position, but they could have been referred to as 201 and 301 in the low-order position.

When the two operands are added, the sum will be stored in the location of the B address, destroying the previous contents through over-writing.

The arithmetic unit in this type of computer adds only one digit at a time in each of the data factors (operands) and because of this is called a "one-digit-adder".

TABLE X   HYPOTHETICAL MACHINE CODE

Operation code	Operation	Details
1	Read a card	The contents of a punched card will be read by the card reader and placed in the A address specified (and other adjacent core store locations according to the number of columns of data). The B address is not required.
2	Print	The contents of the A address will be printed by the line printer. The B address is not required.
3	Transfer	The contents of the A address specified will be transferred to the B address specified.
4	Multiply	The contents of the A address (the multiplicand) will be multiplied by the contents of the B address (the multiplier) and the product will be stored in the location specified by the B address.
5	Add	The contents of the A address will be added to the contents of the B address and the sum retained in the location of the B address.
6	Subtract	The contents of the A address will be subtracted from the contents of the B address and the remainder retained in the location of the B address.
7	Loop	A conditional transfer for processing the next record in a batch. The B address is not required. The A address indicates the address of the next instruction to be processed if it is not the next in sequence, i.e. loop back to "read a card".

TABLE X   HYPOTHETICAL MACHINE CODE (*cont.*)

Operation code	Operation	Details
8	Test for last card	A test for the purpose of indicating if the last card has been processed. The B address is not required. The A address indicates the address of the next instruction to be processed if the last card has been read—this is usually an instruction to "stop". If the last card has not been read then the next instruction in sequence is processed.
9	Branch	A conditional transfer or jump in accordance with the result obtained from a comparison of two or more data factors. The B address is not required. The A address indicates the address of the next instruction to be processed if it is not the next in sequence.
10	Stop	This instruction causes all processing to cease, that is after all transactions and records have been processed. This is executed after conducting a test to see if the last transaction or record has been processed and the result indicates that they have. No A or B address is necessary as the test instruction directs the program to the address of the "stop" instruction.
11	Punch a card	The contents of the A address will be punched into a card by a card punch connected to the processor. The B address is not required. (*See* **8** and Figs. 111 and 112.)

(*a*) *Operation code requirements* (*see* Table XI).

TABLE XI OPERATION CODE

Operation code	Operation
1	Read a card
2	Print a line
3	Transfer
4	(Not used)
5	Add
6	Subtract
7	Loop
8	Test for last card
9	(Not used)
10	Stop
11	Punch a card

(b) *Program coding* (*see* Table XII (refer to Figs. 111 and 112 for details of each instruction)).

TABLE XII PROGRAM CODING

Instruction number	Operation code	Operands	
		Address A	Address B
1	1	001	—
2	8	143	—
3	3	007	025
4	5	012	025
5	6	017	025
6	3	001	085
7	3	025	091
8	11	085	—
9	2	085	—
10	7	133	—
11	10	—	—

Instruction 8 in Table XII will effect output punching from core store addresses 085 to 095, similarly, instruction 9 will effect printing from the same core store locations.

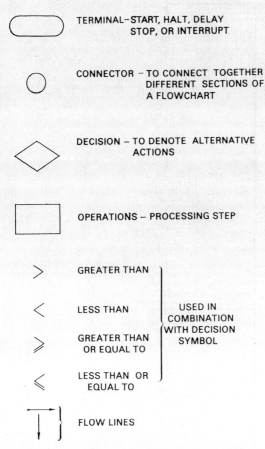

FIG. 110 *General program (computer procedure) flowchart symbols (for the construction of computer flowcharts)*

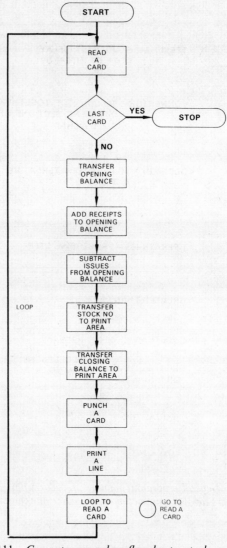

FIG. 111   *Computer procedure flowchart—stock updating application* (*outline*)

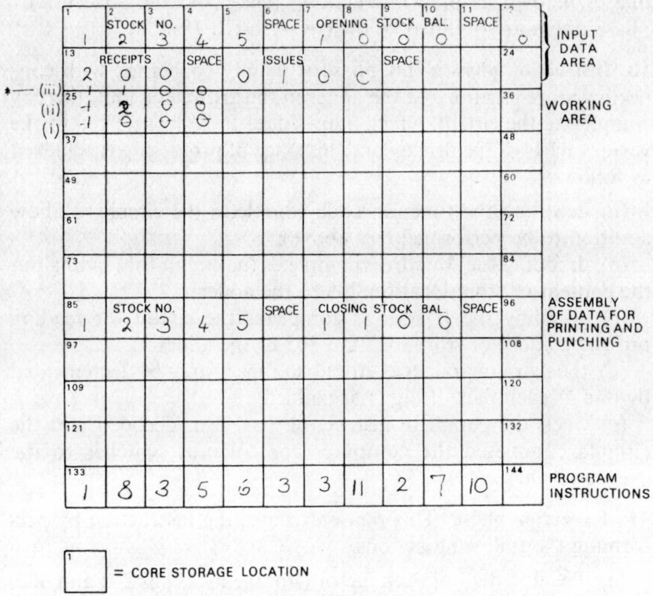

= CORE STORAGE LOCATION

* (i) Transfer of opening stock balance.
  (ii) Contents of storage after adding receipts.
  (iii) Contents of storage after subtracting issues.

FIG. 112 *Diagram illustrating utilisation of internal storage—stock updating application*

If it is necessary to retain the previous contents of the B address for any reason then the "add" instruction must be preceded by a data transfer instruction so that the contents of the B address may be retained in a different store location.

The processing of instructions is carried out in two distinct phases, known as the "instruction" phase and the "execution" phase; these are outlined below (*see also* III, **19**).

10. Instruction phase. This phase is mainly concerned with connecting store locations to the adder in the arithmetic unit, thereby completing the circuit, which allows data to be transferred to the various parts of the processor. This stage of processing is achieved as follows:

(*a*) decoding the function code completes the circuit to allow addition to be performed (*see* above);

(*b*) decoding the A address completes the circuit for reading out the content of store location 205 to the adder;

(*c*) decoding the B address completes the circuit for reading out the content of store location 305 to the adder;

(*d*) the extra character is stored so that it may be decremented by one as each pair of digits are added;

(*e*) when the complete instruction has been decoded and the circuits completed the computer control unit switches to the execution phase.

11. Execution phase. This phase executes the instruction by performing the following actions.

(*a*) The first digit of each factor (storage locations 205 and 305) are added together and the sum stored in location 305.

The content of 305 will be 3 with 1 to carry which is held in the adder. The extra character is decremented to 4.

(*b*) The same procedure is carried out with store locations 204 and 304, 203 and 303, 202 and 302, and 201 and 301 consecutively, carrying forward any carry at each addition and decrementing the extra character by 1 until it is reduced to 0.

(*c*) When the above point is reached, the operation is complete and processing is switched to the instruction phase for carrying out the next instruction.

12. Single-address instructions. This type of instruction comprises the following:

(*a*) function code—indicates the operation to be performed;

(*b*) accumulator (X)—specifies the accumulator to be used to store one of the operands to be used by the instructions;

(*c*) address (A)—the second operand with which the instruction is concerned.

This type of instruction may also include a modifier field which may be zero or may contain the address of an accumulator whose content may be used to modify the operand address indicated in (*c*) above. However, this aspect has been omitted here for simplicity.

If it is required to add the contents of one store location to that of another store location and store the result in a different location, this may be achieved in the following way.

Assume:
Function code for "store" is 6.
Function code for "add" is 5.
Function code for "load" is 3.
Contents of store address 1000 is 111.
Contents of store address 2000 is 039.
The answer to be placed in store address 3000.

It is important to appreciate before proceeding that this type of computer can only perform arithmetic operations in special store locations known as accumulators, which in effect take the place of the B address in two-address computer instructions. The instruction therefore only requires one address to be specified —the A address.

The accumulator is a special-purpose store for receiving data to be processed and the results of processing from the adder/subtractor.

Each program instruction is held in a word of storage. The instructions to achieve the desired results are:

Instruction:

1 3 X 1000—load the contents of store location 1000, i.e. 111, to accumulator X.

2 5 X 2000—add the contents of store location 2000 to the content of accumulator X, i.e. 39 added to 111 producing 150.

3 6 X 3000—store the content of accumulator X, i.e. 150, in store location 3000.

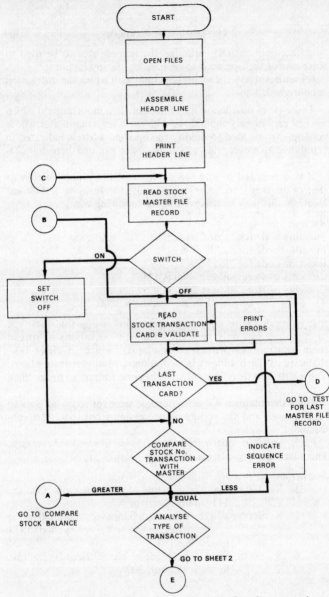

FIG. 113 *Computer procedure (program) flowchart—stock control (illustrating the use of program switches)*

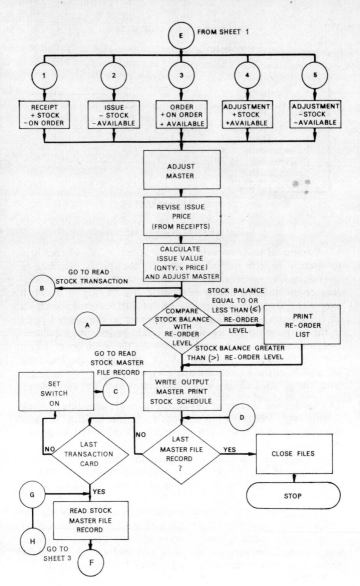

FIG. 113 (contd.)

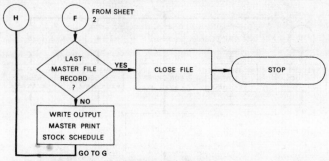

FIG. 113 (*contd.*)

PROGRAM SWITCHES

13. Purpose of program switches. The insertion of switches in a program is to indicate to the computer the specific sequence of instructions to be processed, according to the varying circumstances encountered during processing. The setting of a switch avoids the need to write separate sets of instructions for each set of circumstances, but directs the computer to the desired point in the program for processing the relevant instruction sequence.

The setting of a switch may simply be the insertion of 1 in a specific location of storage. After an operation requiring the switch in the set condition it may be unset by subtracting 1 from the switch location, which converts it to 0 (the unset state).

14. Application of program switches. Figure 113 illustrates a stock control computer procedure flowchart which is designed to show the application of switches in a program, together with loops and branches.

Two files are processed in conjunction with each other—the stock master file, which may be assumed to be recorded on magnetic tape, and the transaction file, which may be assumed to be a file of punched cards.

The files are in stock number sequence and it is necessary to update the stock master file records with transactions which affect them such as receipts, issues, orders and adjustments. A switch test is inserted between the instruction to read a stock master file record and the instruction to read a stock transaction card.

At this point in the program, the switch is unset or "off" to allow one transaction card to be read into memory. A test for "last transaction" is inserted to determine the next course of action but of special interest is the "compare" instruction which compares the stock number of the transaction with that of the master. If the result of the test is "equal", it is then necessary to analyse the type of transaction before adjusting the master. After completing the processing on the transaction the next transaction is read in (assuming each time that the last transaction has not already been processed). If this transaction is greater than the master in respect of the stock number, then it is not to be applied to the current master in memory. The new transaction is held in memory and the program "jumps" to compare the stock balance of the previous stock number being processed.

The updated master record is then written to magnetic tape and a line printed on the stock schedule. A test is then made to determine whether the last master file record has been processed and if not a further test is performed to determine if the last transaction card has been read. If the test results in "no", then the switch is set to "on" and a jump made in the program to read in the next stock master record. As the switch is "on" a transaction card is not read (it is already held in memory) and the next instruction to be executed is "compare" stock numbers and the switch is set to the unset state to allow a further transaction to be read in if necessary.

If, after testing to determine if the last master file record has been processed it transpires that it has not but that the last transaction card has been processed, then a branch is made to a small section of program for the purpose of completing the processing of the master file without the need to go through the main part of the program.

The switch when on effects an unconditional transfer, through an instruction having an operation code stipulating this requirement. The address part of the instruction specifies the location of the "compare" instruction. To turn the switch off, the operation part is changed to "no operation" which causes the next operation in sequence to be executed—"read a transaction".

The reader may now like to attempt the following question set in the I.C.M.A. December 1971 examinations.

Draw a program flowchart to update a stock master file held on a magnetic disc in item reference order. The input to update the master file includes receipts and issues and is held on magnetic tape which has been sorted by a previous program into the following sequence:

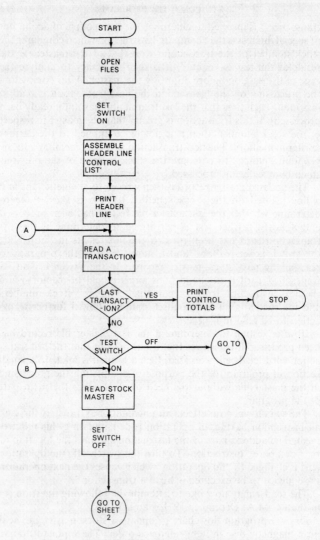

FIG. 114 *Program flowchart problem*

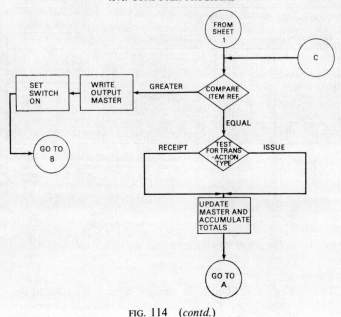

FIG. 114   (*contd.*)

(*a*) item reference;
(*b*) receipts;
(*c*) issues.

The control totals are the only items to be printed by this program.
    Fig. 114 provides the solution to this question.

FLOWCHART EXERCISES

The following question was set in an I.A.S. examination.
    Illustrate by drawing a program flowchart, the logic to be applied
to produce the results shown in the last two columns of Fig. 115,
if the record was held on a computer-based file.

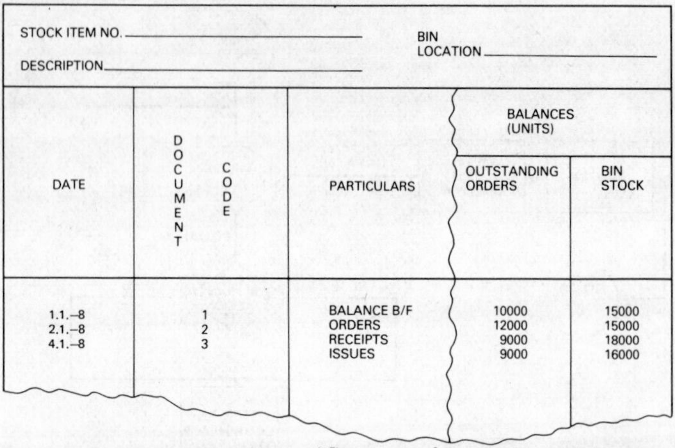

DATE	D O C U M E N T	C O D E	PARTICULARS	OUTSTANDING ORDERS	BIN STOCK

STOCK ITEM NO. _____

DESCRIPTION _____

BIN LOCATION _____

BALANCES (UNITS)

DATE	DOCUMENT	CODE	PARTICULARS	OUTSTANDING ORDERS	BIN STOCK
1.1.–8	1		BALANCE B/F	10000	15000
2.1.–8	2		ORDERS	12000	15000
4.1.–8	3		RECEIPTS	9000	18000
			ISSUES	9000	16000

(Courtesy of I.A.S. June 1978, Q8)

FIG. 115   *Extract of information appearing on a stock master card*

SOLUTION:

The missing information is the number of units in respect of the various transactions, i.e. orders, receipts and issues. It is necessary to obtain the missing units by deduction, i.e. logical assessment. Units ordered increase O/S orders; receipts reduce O/S orders and increase bin stock and issues decrease bin stock. The details are shown in Table XIII.

TABLE XIII   MISSING TRANSACTION INFORMATION

Date	Document Code	Particulars	Transaction (Units)	Balances (Units) O/S Orders	Bin Stock
1.1.–8	—	Balance B/F	—	10000	15000
1.1.–8	1	Orders	2000	12000	15000
2.1.–8	2	Receipts	3000	9000	18000
4.1.–8	3	Issues	2000	9000	16000

The program flowchart required to show the logic to be applied to produce the results shown in the last two columns, if the record was held on a computer based file is shown in Fig. 116.

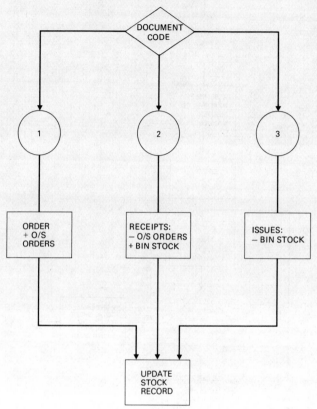

(*Courtesy of I.A.S. June 1978, Q8*)

FIG. 116   *Simplified program flow chart*

The following question was set in the I.A.S. examinations of June 1977 and it outlines a typical data processing procedure which should demonstrate to the student the logical aspects involved in defining the steps required to produce the required output.

Input.
A card file is fed into the card reader, data punched in the following fields:

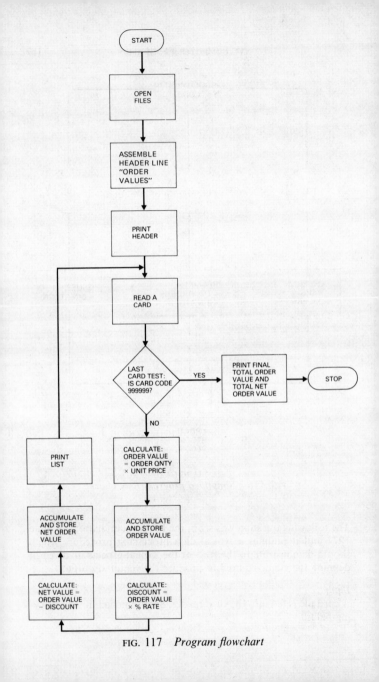

FIG. 117 *Program flowchart*

Card columns   1–6 Product Code

   ,,   ,,   7–11 Order No.

   ,,   ,,   12–14 Order Quantity

   ,,   ,,   15–17 Unit Price

   ,,   ,,   18–19 Discount (%)

Processing.

Order value = Order quantity × Unit price

Discount   = Order quantity × Unit price × $\dfrac{\% \text{ Discount}}{100}$

Net value   = Order value − Discount

Output.

A listing under the following headings is required:

Product No.	Order No.	Order Quantity	Unit Price	Order Value	Net Order Value
xxxxxxx	xxxxx	xxx	xxx	xxxxxxx	xxxxxxx

The listing should provide a final total order value and total net order value.

Note: The last card will have 999999 punched in card columns 1–6 and blanks in all other fields.

Draw a **PROGRAM** flowchart to show the steps required to produce the output required. The solution is given in Figure 117.

ELEMENTS OF COBOL
(COMMON BUSINESS-ORIENTED LANGUAGE)

Cobol is a high-level language, designed to assist the task of programmers by enabling them to write programs much more simply compared with what is involved in writing programs in assembly code. Simplicity is achieved by writing Cobol statements which approximate to English-style statements instead of operations in symbolic code. It is for this reason that Cobol is classified as a high-level language.

Cobol is "problem-oriented" rather than "machine-oriented", as it is designed to assist the programmer in the solving of problems rather than providing for the type of instructions required by the computer for executing processing steps. Programs written in Cobol must be translated into machine code instructions and this is achieved by a software translation program known as a compiler (*see* XVII, **15–17**).

The details to follow should be read in conjunction with the Cobol program illustrated in Fig. 118.

COBOL PROGRAMMING FORM

PROBLEM: STOCK UPDATING APPLICATION PAGE 1 OF 5
PROGRAMMER: A.S. BAKER DATE 6/3/72
IDENTIFICATION (73–80) PUNCH UNLESS SPECIFIED
PAGE NUMBER (1 2 3) PUNCH UNLESS SPECIFIED

```
PAGE SERIAL CONT A   B   C
000010 IDENTIFICATION DIVISION.
     2 PROGRAM-ID. PROG-1
     3 AUTHOR. A S BAKER.
     4 REMARKS. PROGRAMMING STOCK UPDATING
     5 DATE 29 FEBRUARY 1971.

   100 ENVIRONMENT DIVISION.
     1 CONFIGURATION SECTION.
     2         SOURCE-COMPUTER. HONEYWELL SERIES-200 MODEL-110
     3         OBJECT-COMPUTER.
     4                 HONEYWELL SERIES-200 MODEL-110
     5                 MEMORY SIZE 12288 CHARACTERS
     6                 ASSIGN OBJECT-PROGRAM TO CARD-PUNCH.
     7 SPECIAL-NAMES.
     9         PAGE IS HOF.
    20 INPUT-OUTPUT SECTION
    21 FILE-CONTROL.
    22     SELECT PRINTA ASSIGN TO PRINTER.
    23     SELECT TRANIN ASSIGN TO CARD-READER.
    24     SELECT TRNOUT ASSIGN TO CARD-PUNCH.
    25 DATA DIVISION.
    26 FILE SECTION.
```

RE-ORDER QUANTITY ______ NAME OF COMPANY ______

FIG. 118 *Stock updating application:* COBOL *programming form*

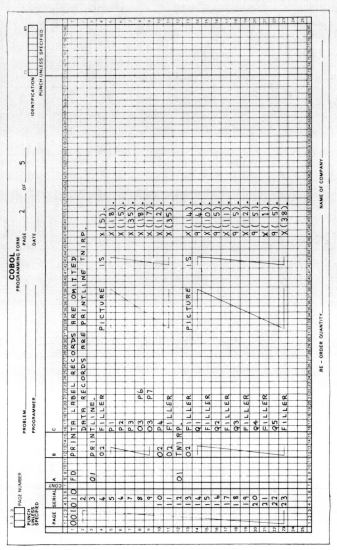

FIG. 118 (contd.)

FIG. 118 (*contd.*)

COBOL PROGRAMMING FORM

```
       PROCEDURE DIVISION.
START.  OPEN INPUT TRANIN
        OPEN OUTPUT TRNOUT
        OPEN OUTPUT PRINTR.
HEADER. MOVE SPACE TO PRINTLINE WRITE PRINTLINE BEFORE ADVANCING HOF
        MOVE ZERO TO COUNTER.
        WRITE PRINTLINE BEFORE ADVANCING 2 LINES.
        MOVE "WESTBROMWICH LTD" TO P1
             "STOCKUPDATING FOR WEEK ENDING" TO P3.
             DATIN TO P4.
        WRITE PRINTLINE BEFORE ADVANCING 2 LINES
        MOVE "STOCK NO." TO P1
             "OPENING BAL" TO P2
             "RECEIPTS" TO P6
             "ISSUES" TO P7
             "CLOSING BAL." TO P4.
        WRITE PRINTLINE BEFORE ADVANCING 2 LINES
        ADD 6 TO COUNTER.
READ-1. READ TRANIN AT END GO TO SUMUP
        IF INP IS EQUAL TO "IEOF" GO TO SUMUP
```

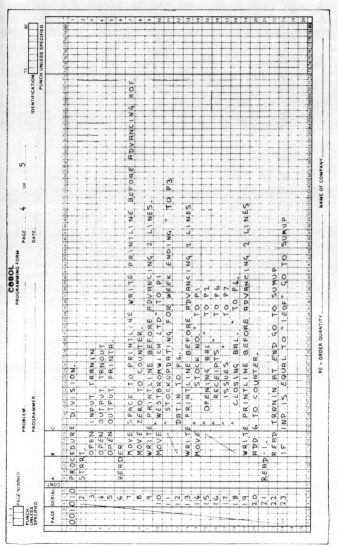

FIG. 118 (contd.)

COBOL
PROGRAMMING FORM

PAGE 5 OF 5

PAGE NUMBER

PUNCH UNLESS SPECIFIED

IDENTIFICATION 73

PUNCH UNLESS SPECIFIED

PROBLEM

PROGRAMMER

DATE

PAGE	SERIAL	CONT	B	C
000240	24		SHIFTI.	
	25			MOVE BALIN TO GRAFT
	26			ADD RECIN TO GRAFT GIVING GRAFT
	27			SUBTRACT ISSIN FROM GRAFT GIVING GRAFT(NEWBAL)
	28		SHIFT2.	
	29			MOVE STNOIN TO Q1 MOVE STNOIN TO STNOOT
	30			BALIN TO Q2
	31			RECIN TO Q3
	32			ISSIN TO Q4
	33			GRAFT TO Q5 MOVE GRAFT TO BALOUT
	34		BOPOUT.	
	35			WRITE TNIRP BEFORE ADVANCING 2 LINES ADD 2 TO COUNTER.
	36			IF COUNTER IS EQUAL TO 38 PERFORM HEADER.
	37			MOVE SPACE TO PRINTLINE.
	38			WRITE TRNOUT. MOVE SPACE TO TRNOUT.
	39			GO TO RERD-1.
	40		SUMUP.	
	41			CLOSE OUTPUT PRINTR.
	42			CLOSE OUTPUT TRNOUT.
	43			CLOSE INPUT TRANIN.
	44			END COBOL.

RE – ORDER QUANTITY

NAME OF COMPANY

FIG. 118 (contd.)

15. The four divisions of Cobol. Cobol programs are structured in four divisions:

(*a*) identification division;
(*b*) environment division;
(*c*) data division;
(*d*) procedure division.

16. Identification division. The purpose of this division is to identify the program by means of the following details:

(*a*) program name and number;
(*b*) programmer's name;
(*c*) application to which the program belongs;
(*d*) date program was written.

17. Environment division. The purpose of this division is to describe the computer system to be used to compile the source program and execute the object program. Details of each section are as follows.

(*a*) *Configuration section:*
    (*i*) source computer;
    (*ii*) object computer;
    (*iii*) memory-size statement to indicate the store capacity available;
    (*iv*) device to be used for storing the object program.

(*b*) *Special names.* Names assigned to sense switches and the channels of the paper tape loop on the printer. An example is HOF (Head of form) used to obtain alignment of printer on the next page.

(*c*) *Input–output section—file control.*
    (*i*) Names of files assigned by programmer. Examples are:
PRINTA: programmer-assigned name for defining print assembly area in internal storage.
TRANIN: programmer-assigned name for input transactions.
TRANOUT: programmer-assigned name for output.
    (*ii*) Hardware device assigned to each file. The assigned hardware devices are printer, card reader and card punch.

18. Data division. The purpose of this division is to describe the data to be processed.

(*a*) *File section.* For each file named in (*c*), (*i*) above, it is necessary to define the following details for storage allocation:
    (*i*) File name.
    (*ii*) Record name.

(*iii*) Layout of the record, indicating for each field the name, location, size and format.

Type of character is shown as follows:

9 = Numeric characters.
X = Alphameric characters.

The size of fields and their format is shown as follows:

Item number 9 (5) = five numeric characters. Spare (unused) character positions X(11) = eleven spaces filler.
Item name X(10).

(*iv*) Location of storage for input and output is indicated by assigned data names.

The statement "PRINTA label records are omitted" means that the printer does not require a file identification.

The statement "Data records are printline TNIRP" indicates the next data format line. The name TNIRP is the programmer-assigned name for this purpose.

The designations P1 and P2, etc., are subdivisions of the print-line and are set up by the programmer in the file section to enable him to insert printing items into parts of the printline quickly and accurately without the need to transfer large amounts of data through internal storage.

The name INP is the programmer's name for identifying the input file. The input entry defines the input fields by means of names assigned by the programmer (the names are limited to six characters):

STNOIN = Stock number input (four numeric characters).
BALIN = Brought forward balance input (five numeric characters).
RECIN = Receipts input (five numeric characters).
ISSIN = Issues input (five numeric characters).

The name OUP is the programmer's name for identifying the output fields:

STNOOT = Stock number output.
BALOUT = Carried forward balance output.

All the data fields are assigned internal storage locations by the compiler.

(*b*) *Working storage section.* This section is used for defining the size, format, and content of every counter, storage area, or constant value used by the program.

"Counter" may be used for controlling the number of lines printed on each page.

DATIN is the programmer-assigned name for the data, which may be entered by the operator either by means of the console type-writer or by a call card.

GRAFT is the assigned name for the internal storage location to be used as a working area.

19. Procedure division. The purpose of this division is to specify the processing steps to be performed on the data described in the Data division. This division is divided into paragraphs by the programmer, each of which contains procedure statements (expressed in English words and sentences) constituting a specific routine. Special "reserved" words are used for specific operations which may not be used for names assigned by the programmer.

START defines the hardware devices to be made available for input and output—in this case card reader, card punch and printer.

HEADER deals with the setting up and printing of headings on the printer.

READ 1 is concerned with reading in of transaction data.

SHIFT 1 is concerned with moving data to the working areas of storage and the statements may be translated as follows:

"Transfer the opening balance (brought forward balance) of stock from the input area of storage to the assigned working area. Add the receipts into stock to the brought forward balance in the assigned working area. Subtract the issues from stock from the total held in the assigned working area to produce the new stock balance (carried forward balance)."

SHIFT 2 is concerned with moving the required data to the assigned output area of storage.

BOPOUT is the name assigned by the programmer for output requirements; in this case, the data indicated in SHIFT 2 is punched out and printed on a stock schedule. The instruction "go to READ-1" is a loop in the program to read in the next transaction. The reference to 38 indicates the number of lines per page.

"Move space to printline" clears data from the output area when it has been output, in readiness for the next item.

SUMUP is the assigned name for closing the files at the end of processing. Referring to READ-1, a test is made to see if the last card has been read and this is indicated by means of a card at the end of the pack which is punched with IEOF in the first four columns which causes the program to branch to SUMUP.

EMULATION

20. Definition. Emulation is the technique of processing whereby programs written for a particular computer are emulated by a different computer thereby eliminating the need to re-write programs for different computers. The technique is made possible by the provision of hardware facilities and special programs.

Prior to the inception of this technique, changing over to different computer models necessitated the re-writing of programs for the new model installed, which was a costly and time-consuming activity.

21. Hardware facilities for emulation. The main hardware facility required for emulation is a device known as "read-only" storage, which is a unit consisting of a number of perforated instruction cards. The instructions in the cards are classified as micro-programs and each line of perforations controls the flow of data for one machine code instruction. Special perforated cards are used to achieve program compatibility between different computers. The read-only storage unit is built into the hardware of the computer.

22. Emulator program. Emulation requires the read-only storage facility to be linked with a memory resident emulator program to execute instructions in the language of the previous computer. For each instruction, control of the program is effected by read-only storage until it cannot handle a specific operation, at which time control is passed to the emulator program which executes the operation in the mode of the new computer. At the completion of the operation, control is passed back to the read-only storage for the next instruction to be processed.

23. Internal storage requirements. The computer emulating a different computer requires a greater amount of internal storage because of the need to store the emulator program.

24. Efficiency of emulation. The efficiency of emulated programs will usually be comparable to that of the previous computer but the full capabilities of the new computer will not be achieved to the same extent as with specially written programs.

PROGRESS TEST 16

1. Illustrate by drawing a program flowchart, the use of the following programming techniques:

(a) a conditional jump;
(b) an unconditional jump;
(c) a loop;
(d) a count. (**1** and Fig. 108) [I.A.S. Dec. 1974, Q4]

2. Write explanatory notes on the following programming terms:

(a) instruction format;
(b) macro instruction;
(c) conditional branch;
(d) data division, as used in Cobol. (**1, 3–6, 18**, *see also* XVII, **13, 15**) [A.C.A. June 1978, Q5]

3. Write explanatory notes on the programming term "branching". (**1, 3–6**)

4. Illustrate by means of a systems flowchart, the stages involved in producing a working computer program from the original program specification. (**2** and Fig. 119) [I.A.S. June 1977, Q5]

5. What do you understand by the following terms:

(a) source program;
(b) object program?

Give an account of how these two kinds of program are related and explain the steps in preparing a fully tested object program. (**2**) [I.C.M.A.]

6. List sequentially the main steps taken by a programmer preparing an operational computer program for a new application, and comment on each step. (**2** and Fig. 119) [I.C.M.A. Nov. 1976, Q3]

7. Outline what you understand by a low-level machine code programming language. (**3**)

8. Outline what you understand by a low-level assembly code programming language. (**4**)

9. What is a high-level programming language? (**5**) [I.C.M.A.]

10. (a) What are the characteristics of, and what advantages are claimed for, high level programming languages?

(b) Outline, with the aid of a diagram, how a program written in a high level language becomes a machine code program ready for operational use. (**5** and Fig. 119) [A.C.A. June 1975, Q7]

11. What is a two-address-type instruction? (**6**)

12. Define the following terms:

(*a*) instruction phase;

(*b*) execution phase. **(10, 11)**

13. What is a single-address-type instruction? **(12)**

14. What is the purpose of using program switches? **(13, 14)**

15. Define the meaning of the term emulation in the context of electronic computers. **(20–4)**

CHAPTER XVII

Software

GENERAL CHARACTERISTICS OF SOFTWARE

1. Definition. Software is the term used to describe program support which enables computer hardware to operate effectively.

A computer system consists of both hardware and software, and it is only by the intelligent combination of both that the best results are obtained. Hardware is a collection of machines which can only perform tasks when directed to do so by the software.

Software enables a general-purpose computer configuration to be transformed into a special-purpose system for carrying out a unique series of tasks for a number of different applications.

In general, software consists of the programs used by a computer prepared either by the manufacturer or user, but, specifically, the term embraces the operating systems and application programs supplied by the computer manufacturer.

2. Types of software. Software is available for various purposes:

   (*a*) sub-routines (*see* **3** and **4**);

   (*b*) utility programs (*see* **5** and **6**);

   (*c*) executive and operating systems (*see* **7** and **8**, and VIII, **10, 14**);

   (*d*) diagnostic routines (*see* **9** and **10**);

   (*e*) assemblers (*see* **11–14**);

   (*f*) compilers (*see* **15–17**);

   (*g*) application packages (*see* **18–24**);

   (*h*) communications software (*see* VIII, **5**).

The general characteristics of each of these types of software will now be considered.

SUB-ROUTINES

3. Definition. A sub-routine is a section of a main routine (a program for a specific application) which is incorporated into the application program, as required, to perform a series of basic instructions. They are called in from backing storage when necessary unless incorporated during program assembly or compilation (*see* **13**).

4. Advantages of using sub-routines. Sub-routines consist of instructions to perform tasks which are common to many different applications and their inclusion avoids the necessity of writing them specially for each application. This facility provides economy in the use of programmer's time, which may be used more productively for non-routine programming requirements.

UTILITY PROGRAMS

5. Definition. Utility programs or service programs are provided by the computer manufacturers to perform tasks which are common to all data processing installations.

6. Tasks performed by utility programs. In general, the following types of task are performed by utility programs.

(*a*) Sorting data.
(*b*) Editing output data.
(*c*) Converting data from one recording medium to another:
    (*i*) card to tape: reel or cassette;
    (*ii*) card to disc or diskette;
    (*iii*) tape to printer;
    (*iv*) tape to disc or diskette.
(*d*) Dumping of data to disc or tape.

EXECUTIVE AND OPERATING SYSTEMS

7. Definition. The ICL 1900 series of computers, for example, have a program known as Executive permanently held in the internal working store of the computer. This is a master program, loaded prior to the commencement of processing, which performs tasks of a supervisory nature.

Operating systems may be used as extensions to Executive programs in order to reduce the extent of the operator's activities, to increase the extent to which programs are handled automatically and to provide access to the processor for on-line enquiry operations.

8. Tasks performed by Executive. As mentioned above, this master program operates in a supervisory capacity in a similar manner to a human supervisor, but in this respect the role of supervisor is automated. Some of the tasks performed by this program are:

(*a*) communicating with computer operator by means of the console unit or typewriter;

(*b*) loading and unloading of programs;

(*c*) supervising multi-programming operations, including:

(*i*) supervising the running of each program;

(*ii*) allocating control to each program according to its priority and the operating state of its peripheral units;

(*iii*) protecting each program's working store from overwriting;

(*d*) allocating peripherals to programs and checking their availability;

(*e*) controlling and monitoring all information transfers;

(*f*) warning the operator when peripheral units require attention;

(*g*) automating the logging of time relating to computer operations.

For other aspects of operating systems *see* VIII, **10, 14**.

DIAGNOSTIC ROUTINES

9. Definition of diagnostic routine. A diagnostic routine consists of aids for the automatic discovery of programming errors. Without such aids errors would either be overlooked, in which case the program would not achieve its purpose, or the discovery of errors would take much longer.

10. Types of diagnostic routine.

(*a*) PLAN Symbol Analysis assists in the discovery of errors in programs written in PLAN (*P*rogramming *LA*nguage *N*ineteen hundred series (ICL)) by printing a list of symbolic names with their references.

(*b*) TRACE prints for each successful instruction the instruction address and its machine code, thereby assisting the programmer to trace the true sequence of operations.

ASSEMBLER

11. Definition. This is a program which translates a "source" program, written in an assembly or programming language, into a machine code "object" program.

The translation process is performed by the computer itself, and this is known as "automatic programming".

12. Purpose. The purpose of such a procedure is to simplify and speed up the task of programming by enabling the programmer to write programs in a language much simplified compared to that used for writing programs in machine code. Therefore, instead of writing a program which is immediately compatible to the computer, a program is written which is more compatible to the programmer for solving the problem and the computer is used for the conversion of the program to one which it can interpret and execute.

13. Translation. The assembler translates symbolic or mnemonic function codes into the equivalent machine codes and symbolic address into actual internal store locations. Each mnemonic instruction is normally converted into a machine code instruction on a one-for-one basis, but it is possible to use the technique of "macro-coding", which enables a complete sub-routine to be incorporated into the object program by means of writing a single "macro-instruction". Once again, the objective is to simplify the task of programming.

14. Object program. The term object program is used to define the program which is generated by the translation process and which is then used for processing the data of a specific application. The term source program is self-explanatory, as it is the original program written for processing the data of a specific application but which is not directly usable by the computer.

After translation, the object program is retained either in punched cards (one card per instruction), punched paper tape, magnetic tape or magnetic disc. In addition, a print-out is produced by the line-printer of both the source and the object program instructions, for comparison and error checking. It is also possible to have a print-out of diagnostics as an aid to error checking. (*See* Fig. 119 for an outline of the translation process of source to object program; *see also* Fig. 120.)

COMPILER

15. Definition. This is a program which translates a source program, written in a high-level language, into a machine code object program (*see* Fig. 119).

A compiler performs the task of assembling the object program, but is generally more complex than an assembler because each source program instruction in a high-level language such as Cobol

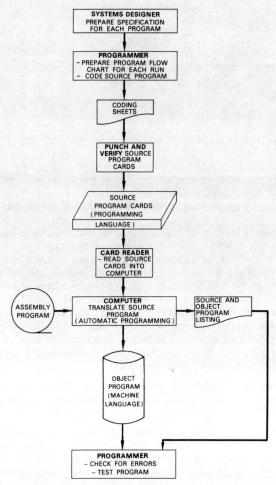

FIG. 119 *Flowchart illustrating the assembly process—*
source to object program

```
SEQ  PGLIN LABEL   OPCD  OPERAND                                          A/C VI-M13    SFX CT       LOCN  INSTRCTN A-ADD B-ADD  .FLAGS

0001               CTL   1    4SSS1                                                                                            .    S
0002 0101  CARDIN  DA    1X19,G        ALLOCATION  AND                                               210  00228                .
0003 0102  PARTNO        1,4             DEFINITION OF                                                213                        .
0004 0103  OLDBAL        5,9               CORE FOR                                                   218                        .
0005 0104  RECPTS        10,14         CARD INPUT AREA                                                223                        .
0006 0105  ISSUES        15,19                                                                        228                        .
0007 0107  PCHOUT  DA    1X9,G         ALLOCATION AND                                                 230  00238                 .
0008 0108  PARNO2        1,4             DEFINITION OF                                                233                        .
0009 0109  NEWBAL        5,9               CORE FOR PUNCH OUTPUT AREA                                 238                        .
0010 0111  WKAREA  DCW   #5           WORK AREA FOR CALCULATIONS                                      244                        .
0011 0113          ORG   *&X00&1      ORIGINATE AT 01 LOCATION                                        301                        .
0012 0114  PRTOUT  DA    1X56,G         PRINT OUTPUT AREA                                             301  00356                 .
0013 0116  HEADA   DC    @NCE@              PRINTER HEADER                                 3          360                        .
0014 0117          DCW   @PART NO   OLD BALANCE  RECEIPTS  ISSUES   NEW BALA@             50          410                        .
0015 0120  START   MLC   HEADA,PRTOUT&55           MOVE HEADER TO PRINT                    7          411  M360356    360   356  .
0016 0121          W     PRTOUT                      WRITE PRINT AREA                      8          418  M%Y1301W %Y1       301  .
0017 0122          CS    PRTOUT&55               CLEAR PRINT AREA                          4          426  /356       356        .
0018 0123          CC    J                         SKIP A LINE                             2          430  FJ                    .
0019 0124  READ    R     1,CARDIN                READ A CARD                               8          432  M%G1210R %G1       210  .
0020 0125          MLC   OLDBAL,WKAREA        MOVE OLD BALANCE TO WORK AREA                7          440  M218244    218   244  .
0021 0201          A     RECPTS,WKAREA           CALCULATIONS                              7          447  A223244    223   244  .
0022 0202          S     ISSUES,WKAREA                                                     7          454  S228244    228   244  .
0023 0203          MLC   WKAREA,NEWBAL        SET UP PUNCH AREA WITH                       7          461  M244238    244   238  .
0024 0204          MLC   PARTNO,PARNO2           NEW BALANCE & PART NO.                    7          468  M213233    213   233  .
0025 0205          P     1,PCHOUT             PUNCH A CARD                                 8          475  M%G1230G %G1       230  .
0026 0206          MLC   PARTNO,PRTOUT&8            ASSEMBLE                               7          483  M213309    213   309  .
0027 0207          MLC   OLDBAL,PRTOUT&20            PRINT LINE                            7          490  M218321    218   321  .
0028 0208          MLC   RECPTS,PRTOUT&31               IN                                 7          497  M223332    223   332  .
0029 0209          MLC   ISSUES,PRTOUT&40           PRINT OUTPUT                           7          504  M228341    228   341  .
0030 0210          MLC   NEWBAL,PRTOUT&51              AREA                                7          511  M233352    233   352  .
0031 0211          W     PRTOUT                     PRINT A LINE                           8          518  M%Y1301W %Y1       301  .
0032 0212          CS    PRTOUT&51            CLEAR PRINT AREA                             4          526  /352       352        .
0033 0213          CC    J                    SKIP A LINE                                  2          530  FJ                    .
0034 0214          BLC   HALT                 LAST CARD TEST                               5          532  B541A      541        .
0035 0215          B     READ                 LOOP TO READ A CARD                          4          537  B432       432        .
0036 0216  HALT    H     HALT                 STOP                                         4          541  .541       541        .
0037 0217          END   START                PROCESSOR CONTROL SIGNAL                                     411        411        .
                        END OF LISTING                                                        1 SEQUENCE ERROR
```

FIG. 120 *Stock updating application: source program and object program listing (computer output from line printer)*

generates a number of machine code instructions, i.e. a macro-instruction generates a number of micro-instructions.

As a result of the increased complexity, the compiler is larger in terms of the translation instructions it contains, and this produces a problem of internal storage capacity, as a large amount of storage is required to accommodate the compiler during the compilation run. It is sometimes necessary to compile a program on a computer which is different to that on which the compiled program will be run on account of this factor. As a matter of interest, this is the reason for stating the source computer and object computer in a Cobol program (*see* **XVI**, **17**(*a*)).

16. Purpose. Compiling is performed for similar reasons as for assembling—to reduce the complexity and time involved in writing programs.

17. Storage requirements. to give some idea of the core storage required, for both assembling and compiling, it must be appreciated that during translation the internal store must hold the source program, the compiler or assembler and the resulting object program.

APPLICATION PACKAGES

18. Definition. Application packages are "ready-made" programs designed in a standardised way for applications which are common to many users. A package consists of discs, cards or reels of magnetic tape containing program instructions for the particular application, a manual for information regarding the application and its use and supporting documentation.

19. Sources of application packages. Packages are often obtained from the manufacturer of the computer being used and are part of the program support service which is essential for efficient operation of the computer installation. Some manufacturers supply application packages without additional charge and this is referred to as a "bundled" package, meaning that hardware and software support is all-inclusive. Other manufacturers supply software (including application packages) on an "unbundled" basis, meaning that all software is charged separately, i.e. not included in the cost of the installation.

Packages are also available from computer bureaux and software houses, and which source to choose depends upon the availability of the type of package required from the computer manufacturer, how effectively each package produces the desired results, and the relative costs.

20. Types of application package. Computer manufacturers have many different types of package available, which may be used in original form if compatible with a user's requirements or may be modified to the specific requirements of a particular user.

Application packages include programs for commercial, scientific, mathematical and technical use.

(*a*) PERT—*P*rogram *E*valuation *R*eview *T*echnique. Used for planning and monitoring large-scale complex activities.

(*b*) SCAN. An adaptive stock control system using short-term forecasting techniques, variable re-order points and variable re-order quantities.

(*c*) PROMPT. A production control system including production analysis, stock management, factory planning and control, together with control of purchasing.

(*d*) PROSPER. A financial planning system which includes the evaluation of risk.

(*e*) COMPAY. A *com*pany *pay*roll system. (*See* IX for examples of application packages.)

21. Compatibility of package programs. Although the purpose of using package programs is to provide ready-made programs common to many users' systems this is not so straightforward as it may at first appear. In the first instance, optional modules must be selected and assembled together to facilitate the specific requirements of a particular user. In other instances a package may not be suitable without writing additional programs on an "own coding" basis. Packages are usually developed for specific computer models and may need to be modified to be compatible with other models which can increase processing time causing a loss of efficiency. Therefore although a package may be compatible with a system's requirements it may not be compatible with regard to hardware.

Some of the points indicated may be clarified by the following I.C.M.A. data processing question—November 1973, question 5. "Your company has a small computer with disk storage. You are planning to use it for payroll, using a package program that you have used in another installation."

Draw up an implementation programme to the "take on" stage.

Factors to consider regarding the compatibility of a package program used in another installation are summarised as follows.

(a) Compatibility of package to computer system installed.
   (i) Is the package disc compatible?
   (ii) Does a relevant assembler or compiler exist?
   (iii) Were both installations from the same manufacturer?
(b) Variations in system requirements.
   (i) Does the package generally conform to the payroll system requirements?
   (ii) Is it feasible to modify the package and if so what time and cost factors will be involved to effect the modifications?
   (iii) Is it feasible to modify the payroll system to conform to the characteristics of the package?
(c) Package efficiency.
Will it be more efficient to use the package compared with a different package or writing a special payroll program? Assess run timings.
(d) Cost of using package.
Will it be more economical to use the package compared with the cost of developing a special payroll program? This factor will require consideration of whether the package is free of charge or whether it is subject to a hire charge. Assuming the package is deemed to be compatible and feasible the implementation programme may be summarised as follows:

(a) check characteristics of package;

(b) modify package system to provide for minor variations;

(c) assemble or compile object program.

Usually done by the supplier rather than the user.

(d) correct errors;

(e) test program with test data and compare with pre-calculated results;

(f) correct errors;

(g) further testing with test data and compare with pre-calculated results;

(h) if results of tests satisfactory run program with live data.

22. Advantages

(a) Programmers are able to concentrate on new application programs for which there are no suitable packages available or on the development of existing programs.

(b) It is possible to rationalise the numbers of programs being written for applications which are common to many users, which from a national point of view is very important as it optimises the use of scarce resources, i.e. skilled programmers.

(c) Computer applications can be implemented much earlier than is possible when programs are written specially for specific jobs.

(d) No extra costs are incurred when packages are obtained on a "bundled" basis.

(e) The preparation of fewer programs reduces the number of programmers required.

23. Disadvantages.

(a) Package programs may require more computer processing time than specially written programs, since they have been prepared in a more generalised way to suit the needs of many users.

(b) It is sometimes difficult to obtain packages suitable for specific users' needs, and this may cause modification problems.

(c) Programmers will not gain the same level of experience if they do not write all the programs used within a business.

24. Development of application packages.
Packages are becoming more acceptable than they were, due to an increase in the level of co-operation between package designers and prospective users.

Packages are being sponsored by official organisations and trade associations for specific industries in order to achieve rationalisation in the number of different programs being used for similar purposes.

The search for programs written for specific applications for use on similar applications by other users has been rationalised by the National Computing Centre by means of its *National Computer Program Index* service. A prospective user of a particular type of program specifies his requirements to the N.C.C. who, from their files, advise the enquirer of the existence and source of suitable programs together with general details. It is then up to the prospective user to contact the source for further technical and financial details.

25. Other support services—"turnkey" operations. Although this service is not solely related to software it does involve the provision of software as well as hardware. Turnkey services may be defined as "the supply and installation of a computer system in such a complete form that the user need only 'turn a key' as it were to commence using the system". Such a service is provided by external consultants. The user figuratively turns a key to gain access to the system for whatever purpose it is designed. This requires the initial identification of a client's needs, the selection of the most suitable hardware (computer system) and the relevant elements of software support. The service covers systems design, program coding, testing and debugging until the system is suitable for handing over to the client.

A business with very little data processing experience using sophisticated machines, or no computer specialists on the staff, would find this service of the utmost benefit as it would enable the changeover of systems to be accomplished by experts without too much involvement by management.

PROGRESS TEST 17

1. Numerous support facilities and services can be bought by organisations with data processing requirements. Typical of the services available to them are the following:

   (*a*) generalised software systems;
   (*b*) specific software support;
   (*c*) bureaux services;
   (*d*) turnkey services.

Describe for each of the above categories the nature of the service offered, stating an example of where an organisation could find its use advantageous.   (**1–20, 25**, *see also* X) [I.C.M.A. Nov. 1978, Q2]

2. (*a*) Define "software".

(*b*) Briefly describe and indicate the purpose of THREE main kinds of software which are normally in use in a computer installation. **(1–24)** [A.C.A. Dec. 1976, Q6]

3. Define and indicate the use of the following types of software:

(*a*) sub-routines;

(*b*) utility programs. **(3–6)**

4. An essential element of computer software is the operating system provided by the manufacturer. Describe what is meant by an operating system, its importance and the facilities typically provided with an operating system for a third generation computer. **(7, 8** and VIII, **10, 14)** [I.C.M.A. May 1973, Q4]

5. Define and indicate the purpose of "diagnostic" routines. **(9, 10)**

6. What is an "assembler"? **(11–14)**

7. What is a "compiler" and how does it differ from an "assembler"? **(15–17)**

8. Define and state the aims of a high-level language compiler. What are the advantages and disadvantages of using a high-level language compiler? **(15–17)** [I.C.M.A.]

9. A company with 700 employees and labour cost analysed over 80 headings has decided to use a standard package program to process its payrolls and provide the labour cost analysis. What is a package program, and what are the advantages of using one? **(18, 22)** [I.C.M.A.]

10. From what source can application packages be obtained? **(19)**

11. Outline the various types of application package available. **(20)**

12. (*a*) What points should be considered in evaluating application packages currently available for payroll systems in a particular company?

(*b*) List the sources from which you could expect such packages to be obtained. **(19, 21)** [I.C.M.A. Nov. 1976, Q2]

13. What are the relative disadvantages of using package programs? **(23)**

14. Outline the purpose of the National Computing Centre's *National Computer Program Index* service. **(24)**

CHAPTER XVIII

Financial and Economic Aspects of Computers

A computer involves considerable capital expenditure, which must be justified in a similar manner to other items of a capital nature. It is therefore essential to obtain an adequate return on the investment to ensure that it is an economically viable proposition. It is important that the return is as high as possible and should at least be commensurate with the normal return on the whole of the capital employed in the business.

INITIAL COSTS OF IMPLEMENTING A COMPUTER

The initial costs of introducing a large mainframe computer into an organisation are considerable, as the content of the cost schedule outlined below shows. No attempt has been made to quote cost figures, as these vary a great deal according to individual circumstances in a business and the computer configuration installed.

1. Computer accommodation.

(*a*) Conversion of existing premises or the construction of new premises.

(*b*) Installation of air-conditioning equipment (not generally applicable to mini and microcomputers).

(*c*) Office furniture and equipment.

2. Hardware.

(*a*) Central processor.

(*b*) Input, storage and output devices.

(*c*) Data preparation equipment.

(*d*) Data transmission terminals.

3. Software.

(*a*) Purchase or hire of application packages.

(*b*) Utility programs. (If software support is on a bundled basis no charges are incurred.)

4. Staff training.

(*a*) Management computer appreciation courses.

(*b*) Courses for systems analysts and programmers.

(*c*) Courses for computer operators.

(*d*) Training of data preparation staff—magnetic tape encoding, card or paper tape punching, etc.

5. Feasibility study. Conducting initial investigations by internal staff and consultants.

6. Parallel operation. Operating old and new data processing system during the proving period.

7. File conversion. Converting master files of the existing system to those of the computer system.

8. Program writing and testing. Although this is a continuing activity rather than a "once-only" task it is included for completeness. Computer time is often hired for this purpose from a local firm having a computer installation similar to the one to be implemented.

9. Master file recording media.

(*a*) Punched cards.

(*b*) Magnetic tape reels.

(*c*) Exchangeable disc packs.

ANNUAL OPERATING COST

The annual operating costs of a computer installation may typically consist of the following items.

10. Computer accommodation.

(*a*) Annual depreciation charge for premises specially constructed.

(*b*) Annual depreciation charge for air-conditioning equipment.

11. Hardware.

(*a*) Annual depreciation charge of purchased machines and equipment, or alternatively annual rental or leasing costs.

(*b*) Cost of maintenance contract.

12. Computer operations—general expenses.

(a) Usage of punched cards or reels of paper tape.

(b) Additional reels of magnetic tape.

(c) Training courses.

(d) Printer output stationery.

(e) Electric power for running computer installation.

(f) Hire of computer time for standby purposes.

13. Computer operations—personnel (payroll and other related costs).

(a) Data processing manager.

(b) Senior systems analyst.

(c) Systems analysts.

(d) Chief programmer.

(e) Programmers.

(f) Operations supervisor.

(g) Chief computer operator.

(h) Computer operators.

(i) Master file librarian.

(j) Data preparation supervisor.

(k) Punch and verifier operators or magnetic tape encoding operators.

(l) Control and scheduling supervisor.

(m) Control clerks.

(n) Secretarial staff.

14. General administrative expenses.

(a) General supplies.

(b) Forms and stationery.

(c) Telephone.

(d) Service agency fees.

(e) Travelling expenses.

(f) Insurance.

(g) Inter-departmental charges—net.

(h) General establishment charges—cleaning, lighting and heating.

(i) Subscriptions and publications.

ACCOUNTING TREATMENT OF INITIAL COSTS

15. Introduction. When deliberating the course of action to be taken in the accounting treatment of initial expenditure, whether of a capital or revenue nature, when a computer is introduced into the organisation, a number of factors should be considered:

(*a*) whether the expenditure represents a *tangible asset* which may be shown on the balance sheet;

(*b*) the *time involved with asset accounting* in respect of writing off depreciation annually and maintaining records;

(*c*) the whole of the expenditure of a capital nature may be written off in the first year for taxation purposes. The benefit obtained is, of course, a reduced liability for the payment of corporation tax.

Although expenditure may be written off in the first year for tax purposes it may be written off over a number of years in the books of account. When the whole of the expenditure is written off in the first year in the books of account it is still usual, for cost comparison purposes, to include notional depreciation charges in operating statements, which is particularly important when assessing the annual operating costs of a computer.

16. Treatment of specific items. The expenditure incurred in the construction of new premises for accommodating the computer and for data preparation activities could be written off over a number of years, as value is unextinguished for some considerable time. The same considerations apply in respect of air-conditioning equipment.

Alterations to existing premises, unless representing an increase in value, is normally treated as revenue expenditure and written off in the first year.

Office furniture is perhaps best written off, to avoid the necessity of maintaining asset records, etc.

The expenditure of conducting a feasibility study, file conversion, staff training, program writing, program testing and parallel operation should be classified as revenue expenditure and written off in the first year.

Computer hardware (when purchased) represents unextinguished capital expenditure and may, if required, be written off over a specified number of years. It is not unusual, however, for such expenditure to be written off in the first year for taxation purposes.

CRITERIA FOR ASSESSING THE ECONOMIC VIABILITY OF A COMPUTER

17. Cost effectiveness. It is often considered that cost savings are essential for ensuring the economic viability of a computer. It goes without saying that cost savings should always be strived for and the usual way in which this factor is assessed is to compare the annual operating costs of the new or proposed computer system with those of the current system. If the comparison proves unfavourable then an erroneous decision may be made not to proceed with the new system proposal because all relevant factors have not been considered. An important factor, that has not been taken into account, is the benefits which the new system is capable of achieving compared with those of the current system. The golden rule to apply is "if the value of benefits exceeds the cost of obtaining them—then it is a viable proposition".

In such cases it is possible to increase annual operating costs to those currently incurred without being concerned, especially if the cost of the present system is lower than it should be. This may occur in some instances because of outmoded systems which fail to achieve current requirements in respect of work volumes or providing output at the right time—in such instances the systems may be said to be inefficient. As an example, invoices and statements of account may be running several weeks late resulting in an inadequate cash flow which is a critical factor in the efficient running of a business.

When operating cost reductions are considered feasible, they may not materialise immediately owing to the necessity of operating both the old and new systems concurrently, that is in parallel, until the results obtained from computer operations are proved to be satisfactory.

Initially, costs may increase due to the need to employ additional staff to run both systems side-by-side, afterwards cost reductions may be achieved when the old system has been dispensed with (*see* XXVI, 1).

18. Speed and volume factors. Due to the phenomenal speed with which a computer can process data, a much higher volume can be processed in a specified time than is possible by other methods. In such cases, even though the annual operating costs of a computer application may exceed those of the previous system, the cost of processing each unit of data is likely to be lower.

The speed of processing is particularly important if the previous system was overloaded, as additional staff would be required to cope with increasing volumes and the use of a computer obviates the need for this course of action. Even with additional staff, however, it is doubtful, in many instances, if the work could be accomplished in a suitable time scale. Once again this is where the speed of the computer comes to the fore as management information is often required speedily, without unnecessary delay, for control purposes.

19. Accuracy of information. Management not only require timely information but also reliable information and this is facilitated by a computer as error detection routines are incorporated in computer programs. Such routines are referred to as validation checks (*see* VII, **21**). Information produced by a computer is generally more reliable than that produced by clerical systems as human fallibility is eliminated to a great extent. Once a program has been written incorporating appropriate checks then errors are disclosed automatically. A clerk may be distracted by environmental conditions such as the need to answer the telephone or the need to discuss work problems with a colleague. In such circumstances concentration is lost and errors often get overlooked and remain undetected. This is not to say, however, that clerical systems do not incorporate checks and controls, indeed they do, but the automatic checking facilities provided by computer programs may be said to be superior.

Undetected errors in data not only affect internal operations but external operations also which can have economic consequences on the business. Inaccurate control data, for instance, can cause management to make incorrect decisions because the real situation is not disclosed in the data. Similarly, it is possible to order ten times the quantity of materials required by the erroneous insertion of an additional nought in the order quantity on the purchase order form.

20. Problem solving and decision making. (*See* XXVI.)

21. Tangible benefits. In a business known to the author, a number of tangible benefits were obtained from the use of a computer and, in addition, the selection of projects suitable for computerisation presented no problems as the benefits possible of achievement were very obvious.

(*a*) *Maintenance contracts.* The firm in question has a very large number of products to service under the terms of maintenance contracts. From time to time the contracts are subjected to price amendments and this factor caused an appreciable processing problem because of the magnitude of the task. One disadvantage was the loss of income due to the protracted period for processing the price changes. The computerised procedure enabled price adjustments to be speedily processed and customers were notified much earlier. This enabled additional funds to be generated as well as increasing the income of earlier trading periods by an amount which would not otherwise have been realised if customers had not been charged with the new contract terms during that period.

(b) *Marketing*. The same firm accomplished an increase in sales by using the computer for printing a large volume of pre-paid post cards which were sent to customers indicating that their machines had been installed a specified number of years and that they were due for replacement. A wide coverage of such customers was normally a very time-consuming task, involving searching records and the subsequent preparation of post cards, but the computerised technique using a software enquiry package enabled the task to be performed much more efficiently.

For additional benefits possible of achievement by computerised techniques and applications the reader is recommended to refer to XXVI, 1–4.

PROGRESS TEST 18

1. Summarise the initial costs of implementing a computer. (1–9)

2. As an assistant to the chief accountant of a manufacturing company, you are asked to prepare a statement showing the estimated costs and savings expected to result from the computerisation of the existing manual/mechanical system. Using suitable headings, illustrate how you would present this information. (NOTE: No figures are required.) (1–14, 17) [I.A.S. Dec. 1976, Q1]

3. (a) Tabulate, under main headings, the principal types of expenditure to which you consider the costs of running a computer department should be allocated.

(b) What benefits might an organisation gain from a newly installed computer installation. (1–21) [A.C.A. June 1978, Q8]

4. Summarise the annual operating costs of a computer installation. (10–14)

5. Outline the accounting treatment of the initial costs of implementing a computer. **(15–16)**

6. Indicate possible benefits which may be obtained from using a computer. **(17–21)**

CHAPTER XIX

Methods of Financing the Acquisition of a Computer

GENERAL CONSIDERATIONS

1. Methods of financing. There are basically three methods of financing the acquisition of a computer: purchasing, renting and leasing. Of the three, renting a computer from the manufacturer seems the most favoured, but whichever method is selected the decision must only follow careful consideration of a number of factors.

2. Factors to consider in choice of method.

(*a*) The *net cost* of the computer over the period of time it is installed, compared with the alternative methods of financing.

(*b*) The extent to which the model of computer being considered will *satisfy the data processing needs* of the business for a specific period of time (taking into account the degree of change envisaged in the business and the incidence of technological obsolescence).

(*c*) The availability of *sufficient funds* for investing in a computer by outright purchase.

(*d*) The *competing demands* on limited financial resources for other alternative investments.

(*e*) The *tax allowances* available.

(*f*) *Experience* of using electronic computers for business data processing.

PURCHASING A COMPUTER

3. Purchasing considerations. If sufficient cash resources are available internally or it is possible to obtain a loan, and it can be foreseen that the computer under consideration will be suitable for the data processing needs of the firm for ten years or so, then generally purchase would be the best method of acquisition.

On the other hand, if there appears to be a more important use for the funds available, or it can be foreseen that the computer would only be effective for the data processing needs of the business for three or four years, then it would be unwise to purchase.

It is necessary to consider the problem of disposing of a computer at a reasonable price in the second-hand computer market or obtaining a suitable trade-in allowance, and the relative profitability of alternative investments.

In instances where experience has not been obtained in operating electronic computer systems, first-time users may find it more beneficial to rent rather than purchase a computer, as capital losses would not be sustained in the event of premature disposal.

It may sometimes be beneficial in the case of first-time users to take the longer-term point of view, appreciating that the desired benefits may not be achieved until the computer operating staff have gained experience and learned from any initial mistakes.

The longer-term point of view also appreciates that the effect of technological obsolescence may be more than compensated for eventually by the increased level of effectiveness of operating the obsolete computer, on the premise that it is of greater benefit to operate a less effective tool skilfully than a more sophisticated tool unskilfully.

Another important point to remember is that it is not ownership that is of paramount importance, but the effective use of a computer for increasing the level of business efficiency, profitability and overall effectiveness.

When purchasing a computer, it is necessary to obtain a maintenance and service agreement from the manufacturer, which constitutes a separate charge.

4. Advantages of purchasing a computer.

(a) *Tax allowances* are available on capital expenditure, which reduces the actual cost of purchasing a computer.

(b) It is *cheaper to purchase* rather than to rent or lease a computer *in the long term*.

(c) A computer, when owned, may be *disposed of* at any time.

(d) Additional charges for *excess running hours* are not incurred, as is the case when renting a computer.

(e) The *funds generated* on disposal of a computer are a cash inflow which reduces the actual amount paid for the computer.

(f) A computer is the property of the business, and may be shown as *an asset in the balance sheet*.

(g) No *fixed monthly cash outflows* occur, as with a rental or leasing agreement.

5. Disadvantages of purchasing a computer.

(*a*) The risk of *technological obsolescence.*

(*b*) The liquidity of a company is reduced due to the *outflow of funds* for purchasing the computer.

(*c*) If the computer is purchased by funds obtained from a loan a *liability* is incurred on the *balance sheet* (that is, of course, offset by a corresponding asset). Interest is also payable on the loan.

(*d*) Reduction of funds available for *alternative investments.*

(*e*) *Capital losses* will be incurred if the computer is disposed of prematurely.

(*f*) *Less than optimum benefits* may be obtained from investing in a computer if previous experience of operating computers has not been obtained.

6. Assessment of net purchase cost.
When purchasing a computer, or any other capital equipment, it is important to appreciate that the initial capital outlay does not constitute the net purchase cost. The calculation of net purchase cost should take into account a number of factors as follows.

	£	£
(*a*) Initial capital outlay (including installation cost).		x
Add:		
(*b*) Interest payable on a loan obtained to purchase the computer (if appropriate).		x
Less:		x
(*c*) Expected proceeds from disposing of the computer at the end of its systems or useful life.	x	
(*d*) Tax allowances on capital outlay (at the current rate of corporation tax).	x	
(*e*) Interest earned on tax allowances (assuming the funds generated by the increased level of retained profits are effectively invested).	x	x
NET PURCHASE COST		x

7. Discounted cash flow concepts.
All the above factors constitute cash flows, items (*a*) and (*b*) are cash outflows, and items (*c*), (*d*) and (*e*) are cash inflows.

As the cash flows occur during different time periods, it would be beneficial to subject them to a discounted cash flow procedure

(D.C.F.), using the net present value technique. By this means, a more accurate comparison of the alternative methods of financing a computer is possible.

It will be appreciated that purchasing a computer involves a cash outflow at the beginning of the period (this may be indicated as year 0) of the total capital sum. On the other hand, rental and leasing charges involve periodic cash outflows. It is, of course, the difference in the timing of the cash flows which is of importance and which affects their present value. Similarly, the tax allowances, interest on tax allowances and the amount received from disposal of the computer, all occur at different time periods.

"Net present value" is a technique which requires all cash flows to be "discounted" at an appropriate rate of interest (the normal rate of return on assets employed within the business, for instance) in accordance with the period of time in which the cash flows occur. After "discounting", each cash flow is expressed in terms of its present value (*see* below) and it is then necessary to deduct all "present value" cash inflows from the present value of cash outflows. The result obtained is the net present value.

The basis of the technique may be explained by a simple example, e.g. if it is possible to receive £1 now instead of in one year's time then its present value would be higher because if the £1 was invested at a rate of interest of 10 per cent then it would be worth £1.10 in one year's time. Conversely, the present value of £1 receivable in one year's time would only be £0.9091, because if this amount was invested at a rate of interest of 10 per cent then it would be worth £1 after one year (£0.9091 + £0.0909).

On the same basis, present cash outlays are more costly than future cash outlays and this must be taken into account when assessing the present net value or net cost of renting or leasing a computer, compared with outright purchase. This may be explained by a further example, e.g. £1 to be paid in one year's time has a present value of £0.9091 and if this amount was invested now, it would produce £1 in one year's time.

It may be assumed that if a computer is not purchased, but rented or leased instead, the funds retained in the business will be profitably employed and earn the rate of return which is used as the discounting factor in the present value calculations. If this is not so then £1 payable in one year's time is no different to £1 payable now except for possible erosion due to inflation, in which case rental or leasing of a computer has the particular advantage of being a hedge against inflation, as the terms remain unchanged during the period of the agreement (*see* below for a more detailed example).

RENTING A COMPUTER

8. Renting considerations. Most manufacturers of computers provide rental agreements, and this method seems to be the one mainly used by their customers for acquiring a computer.

Rental agreements are generally obtainable for two, five or seven years, with a standard period of two years.

The main advantage of acquiring a computer by this means is that it does not require a large initial capital outlay, thereby leaving the company's liquidity position unchanged. A further advantage is that the effect of technological obsolescence is minimised, as it is possible to exchange the existing computer for a later model and enter into a new agreement. It is not so necessary to exchange a computer completely these days, however, because of the modular concept, which enables systems to be enhanced (additional internal storage or more powerful peripherals) on site, thereby increasing the power of the existing computer.

It is generally advisable to rent a computer, rather than purchase one, if it seems probable that a completely different model will be required within three years or less. If a computer is purchased under such circumstances, then it is highly probable that high capital losses would be sustained on disposal.

Rentals are usually payable monthly and the rental charge remains unchanged during the period of the agreement, thereby providing a hedge against inflation. It is usual, however, to vary the rental charge according to the number of hours the computer is in operation during each month.

Manufacturers usually cover the capital cost of the computer over four years' rentals and as a result the monthly rental charge (exclusive of maintenance) is $\frac{1}{48}$ of the capital cost. Therefore, for a computer costing £48 000 the rental charge would be £1000 per month (as a general approximation).

The discounted cash flow principle may be applied to these cash flows, and in order to highlight the incidence of "discounting" a further example may prove helpful (*see* **7**).

(*a*) Assume for simplicity that the "discounting" is performed on an annual basis rather than on a monthly basis.

(*b*) Assume the rate of interest is 10 per cent.

(*c*) Other cash flows are excluded for simplicity (*see* **7**).

(d) Present value calculations are as follows.

Year	Annual rental (12 × £1000) £	Present Value Factor*	Present Value of rental charges £
1	12 000	0.9091	10 909.2
2	12 000	0.8264	9916.8
3	12 000	0.7513	9015.6
4	12 000	0.6830	8916.0
	48 000	Net present value of cost outlays	38 758
			(rounded up)

* The present value factors may be obtained from published tables but may easily be calculated.

The calculations clearly indicate that the true cost of deferred payments is much less than the actual payment, providing, as stated earlier, that the funds retained in the business by such deferred payments are profitably employed.

In addition to the monthly rental charge, the manufacturer charges a separate amount for maintenance and service, which is usually added to the rental charge.

9. Assessment of net rental cost. When renting a computer, it is important to appreciate that the actual rental payments do not constitute the actual cost of rental. The calculation of net rental cost should take a number of other factors into account.

	£	£
(a) Actual rental payments (excluding maintenance charges as these are also applicable if the computer is purchased).		x
Less:		
(b) Interest earned on retained capital (the additional capital outlay which would have been expended on purchasing the computer. If the technique of discounted cash flow is applied, however, this factor is automatically allowed for).	x	
(c) Tax allowances on rental payments (at the current rate of corporation tax).	x	
(d) Interest earned on tax allowances (assuming that the funds generated by the increased level of retained profits are effectively invested).	x	x
NET RENTAL COST		x

10. Advantages of renting a computer.

(*a*) *Tax allowances* are available in respect of rental payments, which reduces the actual rental charges paid.

(*b*) As rental charges remain unchanged during the period of the rental agreement, *a hedge against inflation* is created.

(*c*) As a computer may be exchanged for another model a *hedge against technological obsolescence* is ensured.

(*d*) The company's *liquidity position* is not affected drastically as a large amount of capital is unnecessary.

(*e*) *Normal lines of credit* remain unaffected, whereas it may be necessary to obtain a bank loan to purchase a computer.

(*f*) Available funds may be used for *alternative investments*, which otherwise may not be considered.

(*g*) *Losses may be minimised* if it is found necessary to dispense with the computer prematurely.

11. Disadvantages of renting a computer.

(*a*) It is *more expensive* to rent than to purchase or lease a computer in the long term.

(*b*) *Rental charges are not reduced after an initial period*, as are leasing charges.

(*c*) Additional charges are made for operating hours which *exceed a specified number*.

(*d*) The monthly rental charge is a *fixed cash outflow*, which must be met.

(*e*) A computer may be *re-possessed* for failure to meet rental charges.

(*f*) A computer *never becomes the property* of a business.

LEASING A COMPUTER

12. Leasing considerations. The leasing of a computer is normally effected through a finance house, which generally provides leasing terms for periods of three to five years, although longer leasing periods of seven years are available.

The lessee selects the computer required, and negotiates with the supplier the details of cost, delivery and installation in the normal way as if he is going to purchase the computer directly. When the computer is installed at the lessee's premises the supplier's account is paid by the leasing company (lessor). The lessee then commences to pay leasing charges to the lessor.

The main difference between leasing and renting a computer is that leasing charges are calculated differently, and usually provide for a longer primary period, say seven years compared with two years for rental. In addition, leasing charges tend to be lower than rental charges during the primary period, with the added advantage that the leasing charges are reduced to a nominal level if the lease is renewed after the primary period.

It is generally advisable to lease, rather than to rent or purchase a computer if it seems likely that a different computer will be required within four or five years, as compared with three years for rental and ten years for purchase. These periods are only approximations, and are given to provide some guidance in formulating a decision.

The leasing charge is usually payable monthly, and the amount remains unchanged during the primary period, thereby providing a hedge against inflation. The same charge is made, however, regardless of the number of hours the computer is in operation each month, which is not the case with renting a computer from a manufacturer.

Leasing a computer does not require a large capital outlay, which avoids the necessity for obtaining a loan or reducing the funds available which may be used for other purposes.

When leasing a computer, it is necessary to negotiate a separate maintenance agreement with the manufacturer, as this is not provided for by the lessor.

It is advisable to apply discounted cash flow principles to the cash flows, in order to make a clear comparison with the alternative methods of acquiring a computer.

The assessment of net leasing cost is calculated in a similar manner to that outlined for the net rental cost.

13. Advantages of leasing a computer.

(a) *Tax allowances* on leasing payments, which reduces the actual leasing charges.

(b) As leasing charges remain unchanged during the primary period, a *hedge against inflation* is provided.

(c) If the lease is *renewed* after the primary period, the leasing charges are greatly reduced.

(d) Although the leasing period is normally longer than a rental period, there is still a *degree of flexibility* present, for keeping up to date with technological developments by exchanging the computer if and when necessary. Leasing is very much more flexible in such circumstances compared with the situation when a computer has been purchased.

(*e*) A large capital outlay is unnecessary, thereby leaving the *liquidity position and lines of credit unimpaired*.

(*f*) Funds which might otherwise have been utilised in purchasing a computer are *available for alternative investments*.

(*g*) Leasing *charges are more favourable* than rental charges.

(*h*) No additional charges are made if *operating hours exceed a specified number*.

(*i*) The *residual value* of old equipment may be allowed for in the terms of the lease for new equipment.

14. Disadvantages of leasing a computer.

(*a*) The *primary period* for a lease is usually *longer* than a rental agreement.

(*b*) A computer never becomes *the property* of a business.

(*c*) A computer may be *re-possessed* for failure to pay leasing charges.

(*d*) The monthly leasing charge is a *fixed cash outflow*, which must be met.

PROGRESS TEST 19

1. Discuss the factors you would consider important when evaluating whether to buy or lease a computer. (**1–7, 12–14**) [I.C.M.A.]

2. Outline the relative advantages and disadvantages of purchasing a computer. (**4, 5**)

3. Indicate the relevance of discounted cash flow concepts when evaluating whether to buy, rent or lease a computer. (**7, 8**)

4. Indicate the relative advantages and disadvantages of:

(*a*) renting a computer;

(*b*) leasing a computer. (**10, 11, 13, 14**)

PART FIVE

GENERAL SYSTEMS CONCEPTS AND MANAGEMENT INFORMATION SYSTEMS

CHAPTER XX

Systems Theory and Concepts

DEFINITION OF SYSTEMS THEORY AND SYSTEMS

1. Definition of systems theory. Systems theory may be defined as "the concepts and philosophy which provide the theoretical framework for the development of all types of systems including business systems, control systems, management information systems (M.I.S., *see* XXIII), mechanical systems and electronic systems, etc." Systems theory is based on general systems theory. It is now proposed to outline a number of important concepts relevant to the development of business systems in general and M.I.S. and control systems in particular.

2. Definition of a system. "A system may be defined as a combination of interrelated elements, or sub-systems, organised in such a way as to ensure the efficient functioning of the system as a whole, necessitating a high degree of co-ordination between the sub-systems, each of which is designed to achieve a specified purpose."

If one considers the human body, it is made up of a number of related sub-systems which are interrelated and interdependent and which, as a whole, form a very powerful system which automatically adjusts its behaviour according to its environment. The human body is an adaptive system which consists of a basic framework in the form of a skeleton, a nervous system, a brain, senses relating to taste, sight, hearing and touch, as well as limbs for walking and holding objects; all co-ordinated by the central nervous system actuated by the brain.

The human body reacts to its environment in a number of ways, for instance, by shivering to keep warm when it is cold or stopping at a kerb before crossing the road.

3. The business as a system. In the context of a business organisation the production function is a sub-system within the environment of a total system consisting of integrated physical and control systems. The production sub-system itself consists of smaller sub-systems in the form of machines (mechanical sub-systems) which are also inter-related with the machines' operators.

There also exist work-handling sub-systems which may be either human or automatic and the power supply sub-system, all of which interact with each other to form the hub of business operations. Physical sub-systems are governed by control or administrative sub-systems such as production control, quality control, cost control, stock control and budgetary control, etc. Information for control is generated by separately structured data processing sub-systems which are an essential element of management information sub-systems.

4. Business systems. A business system may be defined as a combination of related sub-systems consisting of a series of operations arranged in a logical sequence to achieve a particular purpose as efficiently as possible. Such systems should be standardised whenever possible and should be integrated as far as possible to achieve economy in data processing.

5. System resources. Business systems require resources to enable them to operate in the same way that a factory requires resources and, what is more, the nature of the resources required are similar for both factory and administrative systems. The difference, of course, is in the manner of their use. The major resource is finance because this is an "enabling" resource for obtaining the other resources essential to the effective operation of systems. These resources are personnel, office space, machines and equipment and business forms and documents.

6. System elements. All systems, particularly data processing systems and M.I.S. consist of five basic elements, i.e. input, processing, storage, output and control. These elements are outlined in II. The following details outline the nature and content of the various elements in respect of a stock control system.

    (*a*) *Input.*

Source data	*Document containing source data*
(*i*) Receipts into store	Goods received note copies
(*ii*) Issues from store	Issue notes

(*iii*) Orders placed on   Order copies
suppliers
(*iv*) Stock reserves   Stock reserve notes
(*v*) Stock adjustments   Stock adjustment notes
(*vi*) Revised stock control   Stock revision notes
levels, re-order level and
quantity
(*vii*) Returns to supplier   Returns to supplier notes
(*viii*) Returns to store   Returns to store notes
(*ix*) Excess issues to   Excess issue notes (initiated by
standard   presentation of scrap notes)
(*x*) Parts lists   Compiled from product specifi-
          cation sheets
(*xi*) Revisions to parts   Modification notes to product
lists   specification sheets
(*xii*) Standard prices of   Standard price schedule
materials and parts

(*b*) *Processing and preparation of control information.*

(*i*) Batch source documents by type of transaction.

(*ii*) Allocate batch numbers and control totals.

(*iii*) Record batch details in control register.

(*iv*) Sort transactions to stock number sequence.

(*v*) Record standard prices.

(*vi*) Calculate standard value of transactions.

(*vii*) Revise stock control levels, re-order level and quantity of appropriate stock items.

(*viii*) Update stock record cards for each item with transaction data including the calculation of stock balance, free stock, orders placed and outstanding, and stocks reserved for special orders or jobs.

(*ix*) Compare stock balance with re-order level for each stock item.

(*x*) Compile re-order schedule.

(*xi*) Compile other stock reports and statistics.

(*c*) *Output.*

(*i*) Updated stock record card file.

(*ii*) Re-order schedule.

(*iii*) Stock schedule indicating orders placed, stocks reserved, stock shortages and stocks available (free stocks).

(*iv*) Report of stock losses.

(*v*) Report of obsolete, dormant and slow-moving stock.

(*vi*) Report relating to stock statistics, including number of

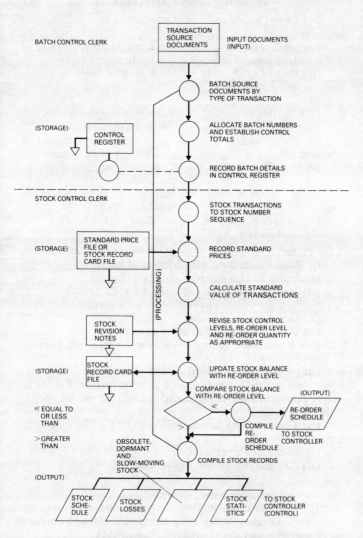

FIG. 121 *Stock control system outlining common elements of systems*

weeks' stock of major items, average stocks (quantity and value), stock turnover ratios (usage to average stocks held), stock trends and comparisons with previous periods and objectives.

(*d*) *Control:* The stock controller interprets the information disclosed in the reports and discusses the situation with the supplies manager (supplies controller) and materials controller. They in turn recommend a suitable course of action to remedy any adverse situations disclosed in the reports. The stock controller has a functional relationship with the chief storekeeper on matters relating to the stores.

(*e*) *Storage:* In this instance, storage consists of storing the master files, including stock records cards and parts lists (*see* Fig. 121).

SYSTEM RELATIONSHIPS

7. Input/output relationships. In many cases systems have a direct relationship because, in many instances, the output from one is the input to another, even though they may be administered as separate systems. This may be due to the way in which the systems were initially developed, but in many instances input/output relationships have been the basis for integrating such systems to take advantage of administrative efficiency which larger systems often achieve (*see* XXIV, **4**).

8. Open systems. Open systems are those which interact with their environment either for the collection of information on which to base strategy, or for conducting business transactions with suppliers, customers, the general public, departments, trade organisations, etc. Such systems adapt to changes in the environment in order to survive, which requires speedy reaction to competitive situations and other threats in the most effective way. Open systems include man, biological, organisational and business systems.

9. Closed systems. These are systems which do not interact with their environment either for the exchange of information or business transactions. Such systems are self-contained and business systems do not conform with this category as they interact with their environment to a great degree as no business exists in a vacuum.

NOTE: The reader should not confuse open and closed systems as indicated above with open-loop and closed-loop systems which are control systems (*see* XXII, **13–17**)

10. Control relationships. Control systems are often separately structured from the systems which they control, for instance, the production control system controls production quantity and the quality control system controls the quality of production. In a similar manner, the cost control system controls the cost of production, and so on. These control systems are basically administrative systems for monitoring the results and modifying the state of the physical systems to which they relate.

TABLE XIV   INTERCONNECTING ACTIVITIES AND ELEMENTS—
EXTERNAL ENVIRONMENT

Basic activity	Interconnecting element
1. Orders despatched to supplier by purchasing department	Information flow
2. Materials and parts despatched to customer's goods receiving section	Physical
3. Advice of delivery by means of delivery notes accompanying goods	Information flow

Table XV outlines the inter-relationships within the internal environment of the business as follows.

TABLE XV   INTERCONNECTING ACTIVITIES AND ELEMENTS—
INTERNAL ENVIRONMENT

Basic activity	Interconnecting element
1. *Goods receiving section*	
(a) Receives materials and parts from supplier	Physical
(b) Validates delivery by reference to copy order	Control
(c) Validates quantity received with delivery note and copy order	Control
(d) Validates quality of items received by inspectors located in receiving section	Control

Basic activity	*Interconnecting element*
(e) Prepares goods received notes, reject notes and shortage notes	Recording source data
(f) Despatches copies of documents to purchasing department	Information flow
(g) Despatches items received to stores accompanied by a copy of goods received note (assuming no direct deliveries to production departments, etc.)	Physical and information flow

2. *Stores*

(a) Stores materials and parts in designated locations	Physical
(b) Records receipts on bin cards	Recording basic data
(c) Despatches goods received notes to Stock Control	Data flow

3. *Production and service departments*

(a) Prepares issue notes for material and parts requirements	Recording source data
(b) Despatches issue notes to stores	Data flow

4. *Stores*

(a) Issues materials and parts requirements to production and service departments	Physical
(b) Records issues on bin cards	Recording basic data
(c) Despatches issue notes to Stock Control	Data flow

5. *Production and service departments*

Utilisation of materials and parts for production and other purposes	Physical

6. *Stock Control*

(a) Collects and batches goods received notes and issue notes	Data preparation
(b) Despatches batches of notes to Data Control	Data flow

Basic activity	*Interconnecting element*
7. Data Control	
(a) Checks batches of documents for errors, assigns batch control numbers, calculates control totals and records in register	Control
(b) Despatches batches of documents to Data preparation section	Data flow
8. Data Preparation	
(a) Converts source data into suitable input media for processing by computer	Data conversion
(b) Despatches input media to Data processing room	Data flow
9. Data Processing	
(a) Processes data to produce desired output—stock schedules, reports and error lists	Data processing
(b) Despatches schedules, reports and error lists to data control	Information flow
10. Data Control	
(a) Records receipts in control register	Control
(b) Investigates and corrects errors	Control
(c) Despatches stock schedules and reports to stock control	Information flow
11. Stock Control	
(a) Examines schedules and reports for aspects requiring attention	Control
(b) Informs supplies manager of items which require replenishment	Information flow

Basic acitivity	*Interconnecting element*

(c) Informs material controller of stock shortages, reserved and free stocks, stock losses, dormant and obsolete stocks (appropriate action taken) — Information flow

12. *Stores Audit*
  (a) Checks items in stock and compares the quantity of each item with stock schedule — Control
  (b) Investigates deviations — Control
  (c) Prepares audit report for Chief internal auditor — Information flow
  (d) Informs Stock controller of deviations and provides advice regarding adjustments deemed necessary (appropriate action taken) — Information flow

13. *Stock Control*

  (a) Prepares stock adjustment sheets and collates them into batches — Recording source data and data preparation
  (b) Despatches batches to data control (basic procedure is then performed as indicated in 7–10) — Data flow

14. *Computer operations audit*
  (a) Audits all aspects of data processing activities to ensure that documented procedures are being adhered to, etc. — Control
  (b) Checks for fraudulent conversion — Control
  (c) Prepares audit report for chief internal auditor (appropriate action taken) — Information flow

11. Interconnecting activities and elements. The details contained in Tables XIV and XV relate to the interconnecting relational elements of the stores sub-system with other sub-systems. It will be apparent that the stores function is related to the external and internal environment either directly or indirectly. In particular the stores is related to the purchasing system, goods receiving, production, stock control, data control, data preparation, data processing, stores audit and computer operations audit.

The interconnecting element may be of various types relating to physical and control relationships, information flow, data recording, data flow or data conversion, etc. Figure 122 outlines the basic relationships.

12. Coupling and decoupling of systems (integration and disintegration). If systems are over integrated they may become too complex to understand and operate and if one part of the system ceases to function correctly this may cause the system as a whole to deteriorate and perhaps cease to function completely. This creates unacceptable delays and disruption to those parts of the system (sub-systems) which are unable to function because of the absence of the necessary inputs from other related sub-systems.

When systems are decoupled it is easier to administer them in some cases as they become less complex and more flexible which enables them to react to random influences as they occur without too much disruption. Decoupling may re-create the former situation whereby systems existed separately on a functional basis but were co-ordinated by the chief executive for the achievement of overall objectives. Each functional sub-system has more independence even though they are still inter-related in reality, but loosely connected for administrative convenience. Each functional executive must apply initiative to achieve functional objectives but there must also exist a high degree of co-operation between the various sub-systems to avoid sub-optimisation for the business as a whole. The efficiency with which systems are designed and integrated plays a large part in their success or failure.

CLASSIFICATION OF SYSTEMS

13. Planning systems. The purpose of some systems is to plan the operations of other systems. Planning is primarily concerned with the allocation of resources to specific tasks and the setting of performance standards. A plan establishes the guide lines for future

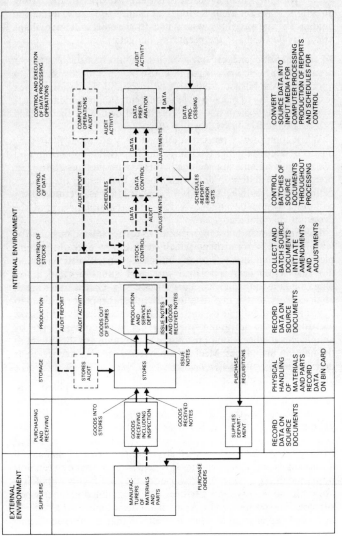

FIG. 122 *Relationship of sub-systems—stores and other functions*

action without which a business is likely to drift in the wrong direction. Plans set a course for the business to follow, under the guidance of the navigator, who is usually the chief executive. Plans also provide the basis for preparing budgets.

14. Mechanistic and organic systems. A mechanistic system or organisation structure is rigid in construction and is designed to operate on the basis of standardised rules and regulations which restrict its ability to react to its environment. If non-standard situations arise the system may not be able to deal with them which causes a complete breakdown of the system.

When computer systems are designed, they are usually tested by means of decision tables to ensure that all possible conditions and the relevant actions are included in the computer program. The program is then able to deal with all eventualities on the basis of defined rules (*see* XV, **32–6**). If any condition was overlooked the computer would be unable to deal with the situation until the program was modified.

It is well known that stable conditions do not exist in business for long, as the environment in which the business operates is completely fluid and interacts on the business. A mechanistic system is not sufficiently flexible to deal with such situations and is not able to adapt to the new circumstances easily. On the other hand, an organic system or organisation structure is geared to respond to environmental influences and is able to redefine its objectives according to the prevailing circumstances. It accomplishes this by an efficient re-allocation of resources and retuning of the system to the new circumstances. Mechanistic systems are also referred to as deterministic systems (*see below*).

15. Deterministic systems. Deterministic systems are mechanistic in nature and this type of system has been contrasted with an organic system to define the difference in their behaviour. It is now proposed to consider other characteristics of a deterministic system. In general, this type of system enables the output generated from specific inputs to be predicted without error. This equally applies to a computer program. Business and economic systems do not come into this category however as they are highly unpredictable. Mechanical systems perform in a pre-defined manner when subjected to specific inputs. As an example, a centre lathe behaves in a predictable manner when a specified gear is engaged (input) as it will process material at a defined speed therefore the rate of output is known. It is important to appreciate that the state of such a system can only be assessed when it is working smoothly without malfunctions and is continually under control. If wear occurs in the machine's parts then it will change its state to a probabilistic system (*see below*).

16. Probabilistic system. Business and economic systems are of a probabilistic nature as they are subjected to random influences from the internal and external environment. It is this factor which prevents their state being predicted precisely; it is only possible to assess their probable behaviour as the effect of random variations or influences cannot be predicted with any great degree of accuracy. Indeed the occurrence of random influences themselves cannot be predicted to any great extent. The state of such systems can therefore only be defined within specified limits even when they are subject to control because stocks of raw materials, parts and finished goods, for instance, are influenced by changes in demand and variations in supply. Stock control systems are implemented to detect and control such variations on a probability basis.

Similarly, production activities are subjected to random variations in respect of manpower availability and level of productivity achieved, machine breakdowns and material supply, etc. Production planning and control systems are implemented to detect and control such variations in order to minimise their effect on the achievement of desired states.

The quality of production also varies randomly due to inconsistency in the quality of raw materials, human error and faulty machine operation. Quality control systems are designed to detect and correct such situations. At a higher level, top management cannot be sure of the outcome of any specific strategy as it is not certain what actions will be taken by competitors, suppliers, customers and the government in the future, as this depends upon the vagaries of the international economic climate at any point in time.

In general, probabilistic systems are of a stochastic nature as it is not certain what outputs will be achieved from specific inputs because it is not possible to ascertain what events will occur outside the direct control of a system which will steer it away from its desired direction or state (*see* XXII, **22, 25**).

17. Adaptive (self-organising) system. This type of system is dynamic as it responds to changing circumstances by adjusting its behaviour on a self-organising basis. The system alters its inputs as a result of measuring its outputs. It attempts to optimise its performance by monitoring its own behaviour. This class of system includes animal, human and organisational systems. It is of course imperative for a business to adjust its state dynamically otherwise it would not overcome threats to its existence. This also relates to the animal world where it may be said to be the "survival of the fittest" especially in their natural domain. Animals need to use their sensory functions to the full to detect environmental situations either to their advantage or disadvantage. It would be an appeasement of their hunger if they reacted at the right time to the availability of the right type of food in the environment. On the other hand, if the situation was reversed and they did not react to the situation where they were being hunted then the outcome could be a failure to survive.

Computerised systems such as stock control are often adaptive as changes in demand are sensed and responses are speedily implemented to change the state of the system to avoid the following.

(a) Overstocking and the related consequences of high average stocks, which increases the investment in stocks over the desired level, increased interest on capital, increased depreciation due to prolonged storage, increased obsolescence due to a complete fall off in demand and the increased costs of storage facilities.

(b) Stock shortages, which generate loss of orders or disrupt the flow of production, causing under-utilisation of resources, underabsorbed fixed overheads and loss of profits on units not produced and/or sold (see XXI, 16).

A computerised stock control system would also adjust the re-order level as a result of changes in demand to avoid re-ordering materials at a previously established re-order level. If this did not occur, then in a situation of reducing demand, a replenishment order may be placed as a result of an automatically produced re-order list which would increase the level of stock to an even higher level than required (see (a) above).

In the event of increasing demand, a failure to adjust the re-order level would mean that the program would not replenish supplies in accordance with the new circumstances and stock shortages would occur (see (b) above).

Adaptive systems are often classed as cybernetic systems and these are discused in XXII. In respect of functional, total and management information systems in general the reader is referred to XXIII.

PROGRESS TEST 20

1. Define systems theory.   **(1)**

2. Define the term "system".   **(2–4)**

3. Specify the resources required to enable business systems to function.   **(5)**

4. Outline the nature of the various elements in a stock control system.   **(6)**

5. Indicate the nature of system input/output relationships.   **(7)**

6. Define "open" and "closed" systems.   **(8, 9)**

7. What are control relationships?   **(10)**

8. Outline the interconnecting elements between systems.   **(11)**

9. One of the pitfalls a system designer must avoid is that of sub-optimality.

(*a*) Define what is meant by sub-optimality and explain how it might be avoided.

(*b*) Give a practical example of sub-optimality.   **(12, 17**, *see also* **XXI, 6)** [I.C.M.A. Nov. 1978, Q4]

10. Indicate important considerations concerned with coupling and decoupling of systems.   **(12)**

11. Specify the features of:

(*a*) planning systems;

(*b*) mechanistic and organic systems;

(*c*) deterministic systems;

(*d*) probabilistic systems.   **(13–16)**

12. Define deterministic and probabilistic systems. Give an example of each and explain in what circumstances, if any, a system may change from deterministic to probabilistic or vice versa.   **(15, 16)** [I.C.M.A. Nov. 1976, Q7]

13. Define the nature of adaptive (self-organising) systems.   **(17)**

CHAPTER XXI

Goals and Objectives of Systems

OVER-ALL OBJECTIVES, UNITY OF DIRECTION AND CORPORATE OBJECTIVES

1. Over-all objectives and unity of direction. In order to ensure that systems being developed conform with corporate requirements it is essential for O. & M. and systems analysts to have a clear and unambiguous appreciation of the objectives of the business as a whole. If this factor is not taken into account systems will be out of balance with each other and unity of direction will not be achieved. A "total systems approach" is necessary so that the inter-active elements of related systems are clearly identified to ensure the achievement of corporate objectives.

Analysts must be aware of the economic purpose of the business, the types of products marketed and the markets aimed at before they can be in a position to assess the relevance of the objectives of individual systems. The objectives of particular systems are not simply assumed by analysts, they are established by discussion with management who must agree them before system development gets under way.

2. Corporate objectives. Whenever possible corporate objectives should be specified in precise meaningful terms. It is then possible to assess the deviation, if any, from the desired achievement by comparing actual results with planned performance. Typical corporate objectives may be defined in the following way:

(*a*) required rate of return on sales;

(*b*) required rate of return on assets employed;

(*c*) required rate of annual growth in respect of sales, earnings per share, market value of shares;

(*d*) maintaining existing capital gearing ratio;

(*e*) reducing cost of products by a stated amount;

(*f*) increase profitability of specified product groups by a defined amount;

(*g*) eliminate products with a contribution less than a defined amount;

(*h*) increase market share of specified products by a defined amount;

(*i*) increase the turnover rate of stocks and W.I.P.;

(*j*) develop new markets—home and export;

(*k*) improve customer satisfaction with respect to price, quality, delivery, credit terms and after-sales service;

(*l*) improve cash flows.

SYSTEM AND SUB-SYSTEM OBJECTIVES

3. System objectives. The objectives of particular systems must be determined within the framework of corporate objectives as indicated above. Production planning systems must ensure that production flows smoothly to achieve a given utilisation of assets so that a higher level of production facilitates a higher level of sales, and a higher level of profit, which achieves a higher rate of return on assets employed in the production process. This factor is also the basis of achieving a specified rate of annual growth in respect of sales—assuming of course that all production is capable of being sold. If production bottlenecks are removed then the turnover rate of W.I.P. is increased and a reduction of product costs is possible because a higher level of production reduces the fixed costs per unit. This assists in attaining increased product profitability.

The objective in respect of customer satisfaction is partly satisfied by efficient production planning as delivery promises will be more likely to be achieved. Customer satisfaction may also be achieved by an effective sales accounting system by ensuring that customers' orders are dealt with efficiently and special orders notified to the product design office without delay. Improved cash flows may also be achieved by speeding up the preparation of invoices and statements of account.

Marketing systems also have an important part to play in developing new markets, improving after-sales service, developing an effective pricing policy and ensuring that orders are received for the most profitable products.

4. Sub-system objectives. A sub-system may be defined as a departmental activity within the framework of a functional activity. Individual departments are set objectives within the framework of functional objectives and accordingly they may be defined as sub-objectives. The factory objective to reduce production costs may be achieved by a sub-analysis of factors which will achieve this

requirement and accordingly sub-objectives may be as shown in
Table XVI.

TABLE XVI PRODUCTION DEPARTMENT SUB-OBJECTIVES

Sub-objective	Monitored by:
Increase machine utilisation by 5 per cent to 85 per cent	Factory management and production planning and control
Reduce idle time from 2 per cent to 1 per cent of total production time	Factory management and production planning and control
Reduce labour turnover from 15 per cent to 5 per cent	Factory management and personnel department
Increase operator performance to an average of 120 per cent from present 110 per cent	Factory management and work study department
Reduce scrapped output to 5 per cent of good production from present 8 per cent	Factory management and quality control department

As a further example Table XVII outlines the system objectives
and sub-objectives of a sales department processing incoming
customers' orders. It may be assumed that the control of finished
stock is the responsibility of the sales department.

The objectives indicated above form part of the over-all marketing strategy which may include objectives to increase the market
share of defined products and their profitability. Product profitability is also dependent upon the factory objectives outlined in
Table XVI.

MOTIVATIONAL INFLUENCES AND CONFLICT OF SYSTEM GOALS

5. The influence of the human element on objectives. When management set business objectives they must never ignore the fact that
people are involved in their achievement and very often organisational objectives may not correspond with the objectives of

TABLE XVII   SALES DEPARTMENT OBJECTIVES AND
SUB-OBJECTIVES

System objective	Sub-objective
Improve customer satisfaction	Reduce delivery time of orders by five days
	Ensure that special orders are notified to the product design office the day they are received
	Ensure that orders are acknowledged and delivery dates quoted within two days
	Improve accuracy of quoting delivery dates—margin of error must not exceed one week
Optimise stock levels	Minimise stock shortages, by more sophisticated stock control and demand forecasting techniques, to 95 per cent confidence level. Reduce average inventory by 10 per cent

the personnel which form the organisation. A great deal depends upon the motivational influences which exist, if any, and their value to individuals. Incentive schemes are often linked to objectives as a motivating influence but, even so, targets may be set at a level which personnel consider too high, regardless of the monetary inducement which may be available. Other motivating elements may be considered such as a greater participation in decision-making in order to stimulate job interest but even this will have varying reactions from individuals. Some personnel may require a less demanding working environment, increased leisure time, more welfare facilities or, perhaps, higher status. These are socio-technical factors involving consideration of social sciences with respect to the behavioural aspects of people at work.

With automated systems it is possible to predict what outputs will be achieved from specified inputs but such systems require programming and people are not susceptible to being programmed as automatons. Perhaps the answer lies in the area of effective leadership, fair deals, good communications and recognising that people are human beings.

6. Conflict of system goals (sub-optimality). In a manufacturing-and marketing-oriented business, conflict of system goals causing sub-optimality may occur because the two major functions, although interdependent, may have different system goals. In respect of the manufacturing function or system, if standard products are produced the factory manager may wish to produce the longest possible runs to reduce the cost per unit. This would be accomplished by spreading fixed manufacturing costs over a greater volume of production and minimising the setting-up costs which are associated with change-overs to different product lines. The marketing system, however, may wish to obtain orders regardless of minimum quantity considerations on the basis that any order is better than no order. This situation causes conflict of system goals and must be resolved by top management in accordance with company policy.

A further example of conflict of system goals is outlined in the following I.C.M.A. data processing examination question set in the November 1976 examinations given below.

The production plan for a company, which was agreed by the board of directors after consideration of all factors, calls for 10 000 units each of products X, Y and Z, to be produced each week. However, to obtain longer production runs and lower production costs per unit, the production manager decided to produce 30 000 units of each product every third week.

Discuss the conflict of system goals inherent in this situation, in the context of the systems approach.

The answer to this question needs careful consideration of the implications outlined in the situation, as the over-all production level is the same but it would affect other operational aspects of the business. The production plan calls for a steady pattern of production no doubt to optimise the over-all business objectives in respect of stock policy, production costs and sales demand. The production manager's decision is in conflict with the agreed system goals and may have repercussions as follows.

(*a*) The level of demand for each of the products obviously requires a steady, consistent level of production of 10 000 units of each product weekly.

(*b*) The decision to produce 30 000 units of each product every third week may defeat the production manager's goal of reducing the production cost per unit. This would be the situation if the product assembly lines and related machine processes had to be re-set every third week. This would not be necessary on the basis of the board's agreement to produce 10 000 units of each product each week as resources would be geared up accordingly. The production manager's decision would probably cause idle facilities to be incurred in the weeks that two of the products were not in production. If idle facilities were not incurred to a great extent there would be a certain level of disruption on change-overs.

(*c*) The production manager's decision would increase the level of stock as the board's agreement would tend to minimise stock holding requirements. Accordingly, there would be an increase in the level of capital tied up in stocks and increased costs of storage, etc.

(Refer to **1** of this chapter for further details of over-all objectives and unity of direction).

PROGRESS TEST 21

1. State the importance of defining over-all objectives in the achievement of "unity of direction". **(1)**

2. Define the nature of typical corporate objectives. **(2)**

3. Specify the nature of system objectives. **(3)**

4. Outline the nature of sub-system objectives. **(4)**

5. What is the relevance of the human element in the achievement of objectives. **(5)**

CHAPTER XXII

Control Theory

BASIC ELEMENTS OF CONTROL

1. Definition of control system. A control system may be defined as a "control loop" superimposed on another system having a different purpose, e.g. the production system, which is controlled by the production control system (*see* XX, **10**). Control is for the purpose of detecting variations in the behaviour of a system so that control signals can be communicated to the appropriate manager. He is then in a position to effect changes to the system he is managing, so that it reverts to the desired state and so achieves its objectives (*see* **25**). Many administrative systems are control-orientated but they do not effect control directly—this is the prerogative of the manager concerned.

2. Basic elements of control. The basis of control in business systems consists of the following elements.

(*a*) *Planning.* The determination of objectives or parameters, standard time for an operation, level of production activity required, level of sales required, expenditure allowed, performance level required, etc.

(*b*) *Collecting facts.* The collection and recording of data in respect of actual time taken, level of production achieved, level of sales achieved, expenditure incurred, actual performance level, etc.

(*c*) *Comparison.* The comparison of objectives with actual results for the purpose of indicating variances from planned performance in the various spheres of business operations, and inform-ing the relevant manager of significant deviations (variances).

(*d*) *Corrective action.* Action is taken by the relevant manager (effector) to maintain a state of homeostasis (*see* **25**) or to revise plans.

3. Control and the Pareto Law. An important factor for effective control is the application of the Pareto Law which, in general, states that many business situations have an 80/20 characteristic. for example, 80 per cent of the value of items in stock is represented by 20 per cent of the items. Therefore, the degree of control may be reduced by concentrating control on the 20 per cent high-value items, especially for controlling the total value of items held in stock.

Less rigid control procedures may be applied to the remaining 80 per cent of the items. Similarly, key production materials and parts may consist of 20 per cent of the total range held in stores, therefore tight control must be applied to these items, which should reduce the number of failures to report crucial stock situations, especially if the importance of the 20 per cent is stressed sufficiently and independent checks applied to the stock records, perhaps by the stock controller or auditor.

4. Threshold of control system. The measurement of a systems output by a sensor may be defined as the keystone of control because it is the point at which control begins and is, in fact, the threshold between the physical system and the related control system. For example, the output from the factory is measured and used as a basis of control by the production control system.

5. Control interface. The communication of data from a physical system to its related control system is a means of connecting the two systems and may be defined as "the control interface". This may be accomplished by strategically sited data collection devices forming a factory data collection system. The data is then communicated to a computer for processing. The communication device is in fact the interface in this instance. In a more basic system the provision of source documents, such as progress tickets, to the control system serves the same purpose and may be classified as the control interface.

6. Control based on the exception principle. As can be seen above, control is often based on deviations from planned performance which is referred to as "management by exception". This concept is extremely important to business control as it allows management to grasp essential facts more speedily and to correct adverse trends much sooner, owing to the fact that only significant factors are reported on. Economy is accomplished in saving on the time required to compile reports either by normal clerical methods or by computer printout. Redundancy of information is eliminated—a feature of detailed schedules in some cases, as, very often, too much information is provided for the control process. Also, detailed schedules often leave the task of filtering essential requirements to management which slows down the process of corrective action and corrective action may not be taken at all as it is very easy for a manager to overlook essential facts in the hurly-burly of daily routine (*see* **31**).

Examples of control techniques using the exception principle are budgetary control and standard costing. Budgetary control compares actual with budgeted results periodically for the purpose of reporting to the relevant manager significant variances for their attention. Whilst budgetary control is used for controlling over-all business results, the control of costs relating to products in respect of direct material and direct labour is achieved by standard costing.

7. Requisite variety. Business systems consist of combinations of inter-related variable elements and it is the number of such elements which creates difficulty in designing effective control systems. The number of elements is a measure of a system's inherent variety and the greater the number of elements, the greater the degree of complexity.

A control system needs to be designed with the same degree of variety as the system it is to monitor, in order to allow for all possible conditions likely to arise in the operation of the system. This is a very important feature of control systems, particularly so with regard to computer-based systems, as the range of variety must be fully catered for, so far as it is economically viable to do so, as programs must contain the necessary instructions for processing data according to its classification or significance.

Before coding a computer program for a specific application a program flowchart is normally prepared which itself may be based on a decision table. The decision table is compiled to ensure that all conditions relating to data, and all necessary actions relating to such conditions, are taken fully into account during processing. The flowchart is a means of establishing the logic of computer operations and the establishment of their completeness to achieve a desired result. A decision table is therefore an aid in the preparation of a flowchart which is, in its turn, an aid to program coding (*see* XV, **32–6**).

These factors are particularly relevant to computerised exception reporting applications such as automatic stock re-ordering and credit reporting (*see* Fig. 113).

The effectiveness of control is dependent upon the extent to which the variable elements in the system to be controlled have been predicted and, if not included in the computer program (when relevant), are catered for by other control procedures.

CYBERNETIC CONTROL

8. Definition of cybernetics. The subject of cybernetics is important for control systems of all types and the basic concepts apply equally to business control systems and to man and machine systems. Cybernetics may be defined as "the science of communication and control in man and machine systems". The term is derived from the Greek word "Kybernētēs", the derivative of the Latin word *gubernator*, which in English may be translated as governor or controller.

9. Cybernetic control process. The cybernetic control process is identical to the process of control based on exception reporting, i.e. management by exception. The basic elements of the cybernetic control process may be analysed as follows:

(*a*) *Reference input.* The use of resources are planned to achieve a defined objective(s) and appropriate control parameters are established to assist their achievement. The parameters are outlined in **2**(*a*) and are referred to as "reference inputs".

(*b*) *Sensor (measurement of controlled variable).* Operations are undertaken and data in respect of a system's outputs are measured by a sensor which indicates the actual state of the system, i.e. the magnitude of the output signal. The measured output is referred to as the controlled variable. A sensor may be a mechanical, electronic or manual data recorder depending upon the nature of the system being controlled.

(*c*) *Feedback.* The output signal is then communicated by the process of feedback to the control system.

(*d*) *Comparator.* The comparator compares the output signal (the actual state of the system) with the desired state (the reference input). The difference between the two states is a measure of the variance or error. A comparator may be a control clerk (stock control clerk, cost clerk, budgetary control clerk), an automatic device in a machine or a computer program.

(*e*) *Error signal.* The error is signalled (communicated) to the effector.

(*f*) *Effector.* The effector adjusts the controlled variable by modifying the input of resources perhaps to increase or decrease the level of production in accordance with status of the error signal + or −. This action is to modify the behaviour of the system to achieve the reference input and obtain a state of homeostasis (*see* **25**). The effector may be a manager or supervisor in the case of

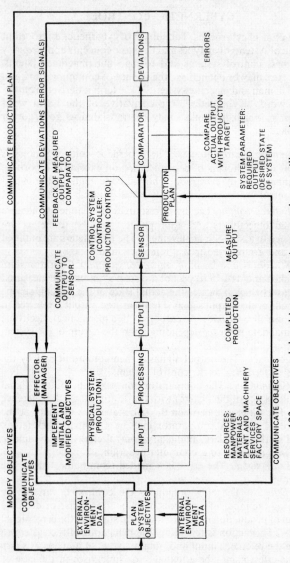

FIG. 123 *A manual closed-loop production control system illustrating cybernetic concepts*

business systems or an automatic device in a process control system.

(*g*) *Modification of reference input.* It may be found that the reference inputs of a system are inaccurately defined, invalid or out of date and require to be modified to conform to the true situation.

The elements outlined are illustrated in Fig. 123 which portrays a manual closed-loop production control system.

FEEDBACK

10. Features of feedback. An important feature of cybernetics is feedback, which is the communication of a systems-measured output to a comparator for the detection of deviations (errors) (*see* Fig. 123).

The *Watt governor* is usually regarded as the first man-made feedback mechanism for controlling the speed of an engine.

The governor has weighted arms mounted on pivots, so that they are free to rise by centrifugal force as they revolve.

The arms turn at an increasing speed as the engine speed increases. The arms operate a valve which admits energy to the engine. The arms rise higher as the engine speed increases and the valve is closed proportionately thereby reducing the amount of energy supplied to the engine which tends to limit its speed.

If the engine fails to attain a given speed the arms are so positioned that the valve is opened more, admitting more energy until the required speed is reached. The required output (defined engine speed) is achieved by self-regulation as the input to the engine is adjusted by its own output on the feedback principle.

Self-regulation is not usually possible with business systems as the deviations from a required performance must be observed by a human being in the control system or by a computer program. Action to achieve the desired state of homeostasis (*see* **25**) must be taken by a manager after being notified of the deviations from the required state of the system. If the controller of the system fails to observe the deviations, then no effector action can take place. Even when deviations are noted and communicated to an effector he may fail to take the appropriate action.

Feedback is essentially an output signal causing error signals to be generated as the basis for adjusting the input to a system which, in respect of an automatic control system such as the Watt governor, is achieved by an in-built control mechanism.

11. Negative feedback. Most business control systems are "negative" error-actuated systems as the actual behaviour of the system is compared with the desired behaviour and the differences are detected as positive deviations (errors) and action is effected in the opposite direction to counteract them. For example, if the actual output from a production system is lower than the planned output, the difference between them would be detected as an error below standard. Corrective action would then be taken to increase output to the desired level which would necessitate an adjustment in the opposite direction to the error—an increase in production. The signal(s) which modify the behaviour of a system is not feedback but the result of feedback (*see* **10**).

12. Positive feedback. The characteristics of some types of system are such that the detected deviations need to be amplified. The process of amplification in telecommunications is defined as "a unidirectional device which creates an enlargement of a waveform".

Amplification applies to servo-mechanisms whereby a small manual force is detected and amplified to achieve a defined purpose. For example, a small manual force applied to aircraft controls is detected and amplified to the force necessary to adjust the control surfaces.

If unfavourable deviations detected in business systems were amplified, corrective action would not be achieved as the errors would be amplified and cause the systems to deteriorate until they went completely out of control.

In situations causing favourable deviations in business systems there is a case for their amplification or an adjustment to the control parameters. For example, if a lower-priced material was used in production instead of the standard material at a higher price, then the material cost of production would be lower. This situation assumes that the alternative material is suitable for its purpose and may be considered for further use thereby amplifying the deviations. For policy reasons it may be considered prudent to maintain the original standard for a while. Alternatively, the parameter (standard) may be amended immediately, in which case the deviation will disappear completely and will not be subjected to amplification as the desired state of the system has been modified.

OPEN-LOOP SYSTEM

13. Basic characteristics of open-loop systems. The basic characteristic of an open-loop system is that it does not contain the element of feedback. Without feedback, a system does not provide for the sensing of measured outputs for comparison with the desired outputs. Such a system does not therefore contain the element of control at all.

14. Example of open-loop system. A basic type of open-loop system could be a domestic hot-water system without a thermostat, in which case there would be no automatic regulation of the water temperature. In such a case the heater would have to be switched off manually when the desired temperature was attained.

If the heater was switched off prematurely then the desired temperature would not have been reached or, if the heater was switched off a little late, the temperature of the water would be too high. Such a system is not effective.

Within a business, control of stocks by a stock control system would not be in existence, in which case storekeepers would have to report stock shortages as they occurred which, of course, is a little late in the day to obviate the consequences of such circumstances. In addition, excessive stocks may not be noted until the year-end stocktaking by which time it is too late to take effective action to minimise losses when the excess stocks are written off or disposed of below cost.

CLOSED-LOOP SYSTEM

15. Basic characteristics of closed-loop systems. An essential element of a closed-loop system is the communication of measured outputs to the control system—feedback. Such a system is defined as a closed-loop, which is a basic requirement of cybernetic systems.

Many closed-loop systems are self-regulating as they contain a built-in control mechanism, for example, the Watt governor and the thermostat in a domestic water-heating system.

Business systems containing integrated control systems performing continuous monitoring activities are also closed-loop systems as they contain the essential element of feedback (*see* Fig. 123 and Fig. 124).

16. Automatic closed-loop business systems. Computers are widely used for business data processing applications and the computer programs often contain in-built control functions. For example, a stock control application includes the processing of a transaction

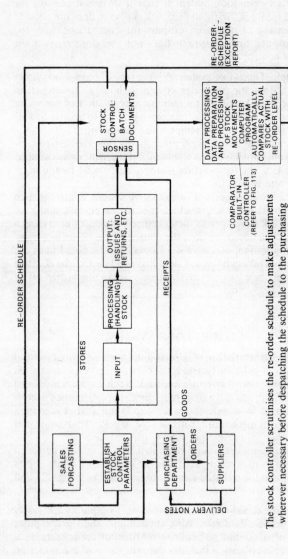

The stock controller scrutinises the re-order schedule to make adjustments wherever necessary before despatching the schedule to the purchasing department

FIG. 124 *An automatic computerised closed-loop stock control system (outline only)*

file and the updating of the stock master file for the purpose of calculating the new stock balance for each item in stock.

The program may also provide for the comparison of the actual quantity in stock with the maximum permissible stock and print out an "excess stock" report for management control. The program may also incorporate automatic stock re-ordering whereby the actual quantity in stock of each item is compared with the re-order level. When the balance in stock is equal to, or less than, the re-order level a re-order list may be printed which is despatched to the purchasing department for the placing of purchase orders. Alternatively, a purchase order may be printed by the computer line printer which would reduce the lead time for the replenishment of supplies.

If, however, the balance in stock is greater than the re-order level no action is effected and the computer continues with the basic routine. The program may be defined as a built-in controller and the computer system a closed-loop system, as the actual state of the system is compared with the desired state and exception reports automatically printed (error signals) (*see* Figs. 104, 105, 113, 124).

17. Manual closed-loop business system. Manual control systems are widely used in business and, providing they contain feedback, may be classed as closed-loop systems. Indeed, to be classed as a control system at all feedback must be incorporated (*see* Fig. 123 above).

With regard to a manual stock control system, a stock control clerk is required to observe the stock status of each item, usually when updating the master record with current transactions, and trigger off the re-ordering procedure as necessary. However, through lack of concentration or interruptions, the clerk may fail to observe items which require to be re-ordered and no action will be effected to replenish supplies for stock requirements. This is the danger of a manual control system, as human beings are not infallible.

Failure to take action either to reduce excessive stocks or re-order supplies may have drastic consequences. In the first instance, excessive stocks lock up capital unnecessarily, increase interest charges, stock handling costs and the cost of storage facilities. On the other hand, failure to obtain supplies may create stock shortages and production delays, creating excessive idle time, under-absorbed fixed overheads, loss of profit on products not produced and possible loss of future orders (*see* XX, **17**).

The solution to such a problem may be the employment of conscientious clerks who fully understand the consequences of their failure to report on situations requiring action. The incorporation of checking facilities such as random or spot checks may also provide the means of detecting previously unobserved situations.

DELAY FACTOR

18. Time-lag between physical event and information flows. If as a result of feedback unfavourable deviations are detected and action taken to eliminate them, the ultimate result will depend upon when the action was effected. Careful consideration must be given to the time-lag between a physical event and the information flows informing the effector of the event. For instance, if an unfavourable production output is detected and action is taken too late to alter the situation, then it is out of phase because the state of the system has probably changed in the meantime and action is taken to remedy a situation which no longer exists. This is referred to as the "delay factor" and such circumstances cause systems to hunt or oscillate around the desired state (*see* **22**).

In the circumstances outlined, if production failed to meet the desired target, action would be taken to increase production but if the necessary adjustment was delayed it is possible that, in the meantime, production has taken an upward swing. The result of the delayed action to increase production would tend to increase production even more, perhaps to a greater level than is warranted by the previous shortfall.

An adjustment may then be effected to reduce production but by this time production may have taken a downward swing and the delayed action would decrease production below the desired level thereby amplifying the situation.

19. Amplification and damping. The principles outlined show that if action to remedy a situation is delayed then the result achieved is of a positive feedback nature, whereby deviations are amplified instead of being damped down. What was meant to be negative feedback becomes positive feedback.

20. Practical example. In order to demonstrate the above principles and concepts Table XVIII outlines the actual production output in five different weeks, the delayed information flow in respect of each week's output, the "corrective" action taken, and the

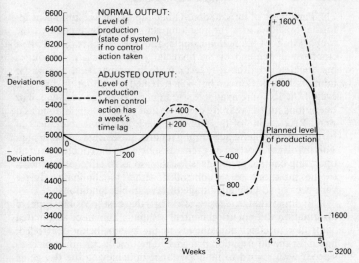

FIG. 125   *Effect of time-lag in an oscillating system*

resulting output. The table should be studied in conjunction with
Fig. 125.

TABLE XVIII   RESULT OF TIME LAG BETWEEN PHYSICAL EVENT
AND INFORMATION FLOW

Week 1	Week 2	Week 3	Week 4	Week 5
Normal output −200	Normal output +200	Normal output −400	Normal output +800	Normal output −1600
	Information received for week 1	Information received for week 2	Information received for week 3	Information received for week 4
	Corrective action +200	Corrective action −400	Corrective action +800	Corrective action −1600
	Adjusted output +400	Adjusted output −800	Adjusted output +1600	Adjusted output −3200

21. Timeliness of information. Other aspects of the timing of information flows and the resulting action may be related to the preparation of annual accounts and the Balance Sheet of a company at the end of the financial year. These are, of course, historical and, although delay in their preparation should be minimised, no action can be taken to remedy the situation disclosed even if the facts are available within one day of the year-end. The operations for the year are complete and what is done is done as it were. Recognition of this situation has led to the development of periodical short-term accounting reports, statements and statistics. This involves reporting on events as soon after the conclusion of an operating control period as is feasible, so as to effect adjustments to the situations being controlled, either to eliminate adverse variances or to take advantage of favourable conditions.

It is important to appreciate that the best possible type of information will not affect control without a human or automated controller to effect adjustments to the system being controlled, based on the information provided. The time factor must be considered with regard to its importance in achieving the degree of control required. For example, if information in respect of scrapped production is not reported early enough, no remedial action can be taken to stop production and to remove the cause of the scrap. It becomes necessary to introduce quality controllers to monitor the quality of production at strategic locations in the production processes. By this means, production may be stopped when it is discovered that the acceptable level of quality is not being achieved. Quality control charts are normally employed for monitoring the quality of production. By this means, corrective action may be taken to remove the cause of the scrap and so ensure that production achieves the desired level of quality (the desired state of the system).

22. Hunting or oscillating. Business activities hardly ever achieve a steady state as they are subjected to random influences both from the internal and external environment (*see* XX, **16**). This causes results, or the level of performance, to fluctuate above and below the average or normal state. For example, stocks of materials attain an over-all average level, but vary on a day-to-day basis, which is a normal state of affairs. It is extreme variations which must be controlled, as these cause a system to "hunt" or "oscillate" around its standard or normal state, corrective action being effected as a result of feedback. The effect of negative and positive feedback in an oscillating system is shown in Figs. 126 and 127.

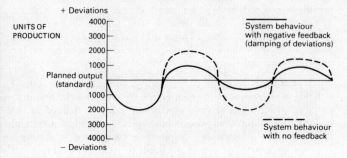

FIG. 126   *Effect of negative feedback in an oscillating system*

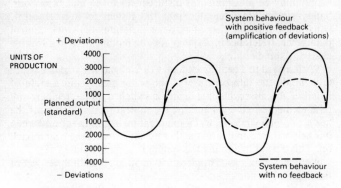

FIG. 127   *Effect of positive feedback in an oscillating system*

23. Buffeting. Unusual disturbances to a system's behaviour are caused by "buffeting" and this results in fluctuating system states, i.e. a tendency to "hunt" or "oscillate" and deviate from the desired course. For example, a strong cross wind on a motorway will buffet a motor vehicle, causing it to deviate sharply from the desired direction. The driver of the vehicle must apply corrective action to remedy the effect of the cross wind, usually by the application of negative feedback, i.e. steering in the opposite direction to the wind. *See also* **22** and **25**.

24. System tuning. When a car engine is out of tune it does not run smoothly and is said to be out of tune. To improve its performance it must be retuned, and the same considerations apply to business systems as they also require retuning from time to time to accord with current circumstances. This is the reason systems studies take place, to modify the operations performed in a system or the method employed.

25. Homeostasis. Systems, to be effective, must maintain a state of balance, which requires the elimination of unnecessary "hunting" or "oscillating". The term "homeostasis" may be defined as the process of holding steady or "balancing" the output of a system, i.e. the "controlled variable", despite disturbances and "buffeting". It is the process of restoring a system to its desired state when subjected to changing environmental conditions (*see* **22** and **23**).

In a stock control system, unusual variations in demand and supply may be interpreted as disturbances to normal behaviour. Safety stocks are integrated into the system to overcome this situation, but in the case of extreme variations the stock control parameters (reference input) may require modification to allow for changing trends.

With regard to a heating system, a thermostat situated in a water tank holds the termperature of the water steady—in a state of balance—because when the heater is switched on the temperature rises to the desired level and the thermostat then switches off the heater. After a while the water temperature begins to fall and when it is below the desired level the thermostat switches the heater back on. This action maintains the system in a steady state.

A further example of homeostasis is outlined in **10** in respect of the Watt governor.

26. Response time. This term is usually used in the context of computing systems and is a measure of the time elapsed from making a request for information and the time it takes for the computer to respond. A clerical information system may react too slowly to requests for information which is one of the reasons why M.I.S. are often computer-orientated. In real time systems a computer must respond to changing circumstances as they occur in order that the system may be effectively controlled (*see* III, **14**, and VIII, **4, 7**).

COMMUNICATION THEORY

Before defining specific aspects of communication and noise in the narrow sense of everyday business activities, it is important to appreciate the wider concepts involved in communication.

All systems contain the element of communication, especially closed-loop systems providing the basis of feedback. Communication may therefore be defined as the provision of information on which to base a decision to control the state of a system (*see* Fig. 123).

27. Elements of communication. The elements of communication may be described by an example from telecommunications: a wireless operator using a morse key transmits messages to a distant location where they are received by another wireless operator who records the messages.

The elements of such activities are as follows.

(*a*) *Information source*. Originator of message wishing to convey information to another person.

(*b*) *Message*. Details of situation on message pad.

(*c*) *Transmitter*. Wireless operator transmitting message by means of morse key connected to transmitting set.

(*d*) *Signal*. The signal produced by the transmitting set when the morse key is depressed.

(*e*) *Receiver*. Wireless operator receiving message by means of a receiving set and earphones and writing message on a message pad.

(*f*) *Information destination*. Receipt of message by addressee (*see* Fig. 128(*a*)).

28. Elements of communication in cost control system. In order to relate the elements of communication outlined above to a business environment, a cost control system is used as an example: it is desired to communicate the incidence of scrap production to the cost control system.

(*a*) *Information source*. Inspector responsible for informing cost office of scrap production.

(*b*) *Message*. Details of scrap recorded on scrap notes (source documents).

(*c*) *Transmitter*. Distribution of scrap notes by messenger service.

(*d*) *Signal*. Delivery of scrap notes to cost office.

(*e*) *Receiver*. Cost clerk receiving scrap notes.

(*f*) *Information destination*. This may be the cost clerk receiving the scrap notes, or the cost controller after the cost clerk has processed the scrap notes (*see* Fig. 128(*b*)).

29. The noise element in communications. Noise is a telecom-

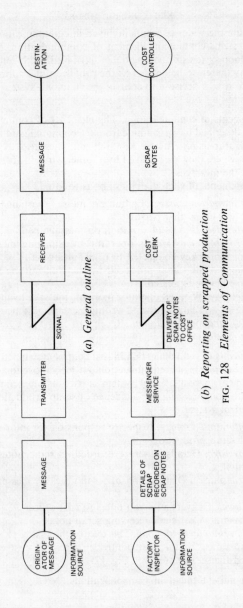

(a) General outline

(b) Reporting on scrapped production

FIG. 128 Elements of Communication

munications term which indicates the presence of unwanted signals in electrical and electronic devices. In the context of data communication, noise is any disturbance to the transmission of the required signal which causes the signal being received to differ from the signal transmitted. In the business control context, this implies that as the effective control of business is dependent upon accurate information, the incidence of noise is likely to distort the information being received by either the controller or the effector. Consequently the state of a system may be misinterpreted as a result of the distorted information, and incorrect action to remedy the situation may be applied.

In general terms, noise alters the content of a message received from that which is meant to be conveyed. This situation can arise simply by misinterpretation of the context of a message, the use of terms not understood by the recipient (jargon), the presence of static on the line during a telephone conversation, too much padding in a report which tends to hide the essential facts, and inadequately worded communications, etc.

30. Redundancy and the noise factor. The element of redundancy is often incorporated into communications to overcome the problem of noise. Redundancy refers to the addition of bits, characters or digits to ensure that messages are received correctly or that the correct record is being processed. Examples of redundancy are as follows.

(*a*) The spelling-out of a value in addition to presenting it in the normal way, i.e. £20 (twenty pounds).

(*b*) The inclusion of a parity bit (binary digit) in addition to the bit combination of a character in coded form. The parity bit is an additional 1 bit which is included in character codes punched into paper tape or encoded on magnetic tape either for data transmission or data transfer in computer operations. The parity bit is inserted automatically by the data preparation equipment, and is for the purpose of checking that data is being transferred or transmitted free of corruption. A 1 bit is added to ensure that the 1 bits accord either to an even number count or to an odd number count, depending on the mode in use (*see* XIV, **7, 8**).

(*c*) Quite frequently in computer data processing applications, check digits are used to ensure the accuracy of stock numbers and account numbers prior to processing. A check digit is a number which is added to such numbers for the purpose of producing a "self-checking" number. A check digit has a unique mathematical relationship to the number to which it is added. The editing routine of a computer program performs check digit verification and data is rejected as invalid when the check digit derived is any other number than the correct one (*see* VII, **22–6**).

31. Redundancy and management reports. Redundancy incorporated in management reports tends to overshadow the essential facts. For example, a complete listing of cost-centre budgeted and actual expenditure, although conveying all the facts, does not in fact convey a clear appreciation of the situation directly. The manager concerned is required to establish the significance of each of the items listed by going through the list item by item comparing each budgeted and actual expenditure amount to determine those which require his immediate attention.

If reporting is restricted to items with significant variations of actual expenditure from budgeted expenditure, then a greater impact is made and the recipient of the report can speedily respond to the situation disclosed. In the complete listing indicated above, the significant details were not highlighted and in fact the essential requirement, the disclosure of variances, was not included. In such a case, the control system is inefficient, as a complete listing in such a case is an obstacle to the clear understanding of the situation.

PROGRESS TEST 22

1. Define the nature of a control system. (**1**)

2. The concept of control occupies an important place in systems theory and is a major part of the function of the management accountant.

(*a*) List the basic elements of control and discuss how these are implemented in an effective control system.

(*b*) Describe the safeguards which must be incorporated in systems design to ensure the continued effectiveness of a control system. (**2, 8**) [I.C.M.A. May 1978, Q1]

3. What is the significance of the Pareto Law to the effective control of systems? (**3**)

4. State your understanding of the following terms:

(*a*) threshold of control system;

(*b*) control interface. (**4, 5**).

5. "Control is often based on deviations from planned performance which is the basis of 'management by exception'—a very

important management concept." Discuss this statement. **(6)**

6. Define the term "cybernetics" and indicate its incidence to exception reporting. **(8, 9)**

7. Outline the elements of the cybernetic control process. **(9)**

8. A company operates a stock control procedure which has the essential features of a closed-loop system, comprising:

(*a*) stores, dealing with the physical receipt, holding and issue of materials;

(*b*) a stock control office which:

   (*i*) is supplied with copies of goods received notes, requisitions and return to store notes;

   (*ii*) maintains stock records;

   (*iii*) establishes parameters for stock and re-order levels, incorporating future usage data from the production control department;

   (*iv*) originates purchase requisitions as required;

(*c*) a purchasing department.

You are required to draw an outline flow chart of the system described, showing the necessary major information flows and linkages. Identify on your chart the three points in the system which function as sensor, comparator and effector. (Fig. 124 may be used as the basis for the solution) [I.C.M.A. May 1977, Q4]

9. Define the nature of feedback **(10)**

10. Define and discuss the characteristics of negative and positive feedback in relation to information systems. Give an example of each. **(11, 12)** [I.C.M.A. May 1976, Q2]

11. Define the nature of "open-loop" and "closed-loop" systems. **(13–17)**

12. The quality of management information is directly related to its timing.

(*a*) Discuss this statement, with particular reference to:

   (*i*) the different purposes for which the information may be required; and

   (*ii*) the relative merits of speed versus accuracy in each case.

(*b*) Explain in what ways the timing of information flows should be taken into account when designing information systems. **(18–21, 26** *see also* XVIII, **18, 19)** [I.C.M.A. May, 1977, Q3]

13. Explain the following system terms:

(*a*) hunting or oscillating;	(*d*) homeostasis;
(*b*) buffeting;	(*e*) response time.
(*c*) system tuning;	**(22–6)**

14. Indicate the basic elements of communication both in telecommunications and the normal business environment. **(27, 28)**

15. Define what is meant by "noise" in communications. **(29)**

16. "Redundancy is very often incorporated into business communications to overcome the problem of noise but can on occasions create noise." Discuss this statement. **(30, 31)**

CHAPTER XXIII

Concepts of Management Information Systems

MANAGEMENT INFORMATION SYSTEM (M.I.S.) DEFINED

1. Basic requirements. It has already been stated that a management information system embraces data processing systems, control systems and decision making based on the facts communicated by the control systems (*see* I, **1**). Referring to the data processing element, a highly organised data processing system is essential for collecting, recording and converting data into machine-sensible form (in some instances), prior to processing the data. Such activities require well-defined systems which emanate from efficient systems design. These systems often produce information for management as a by-product of processing accounting data rather than as a primary product in its own right (*see* XXIV, **8, 9**).

The objectives of M.I.S. include the provision of information to all levels of management at the most appropriate time, at an acceptable level of accuracy and at an economical cost. Such information is used in the decision making process for modifying the state of systems by taking appropriate action while the state of the system is current and not historic. It is pointless adjusting the controls of an aircraft after it has crashed.

An essential requirement of an M.I.S. is feedback which is the process of communicating a system's measured outputs to the control system which generates control signals to an effector—normally a manager in respect of business systems (*see* XXII, **9**). It is this factor which allows the state of a system to be modified as stated above (*see* Fig. 129).

2. On-line interrogation facilities. Some computer-orientated management information systems have on-line facilities which allow managers to gain access to information by means of interrogation (direct access) terminals. The terminals are connected to a central processor by means of communication lines. Requests for

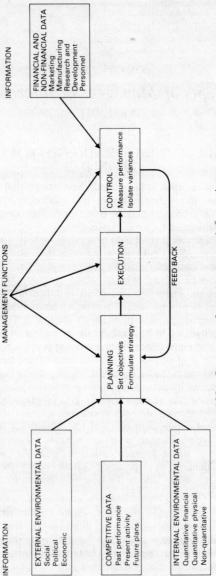

FIG. 129 *Structure of a management information system*

information are activated by keying in messages on the terminal keyboard and the computer responds interactively by retrieving the information required from backing storage (information files) and printing or displaying the results on the terminal screen depending which type of terminal is used. This facility enables managers to obtain information on demand when they need it rather than when it is possible to supply it from batch processing operations. Batch processing does not provide the user with on-line facilities; all data processing and production of information is obtained from the computer system which is manned by specialist staff (*see* VII and VIII).

DATA RELATING TO BUSINESS OPERATIONS

3. Data is not information. It is important to appreciate that "data" is not an alternative term to "information". Data is the term used to define facts relating to business operations (*see* I, **8**), which do not serve any useful purpose until they have been converted into a more meaningful form by means of data processing operations (*see* **1**).

4. Input element. Data is the input element of a data processing system and as such is the means of generating information after it has been subjected to validation checks, sorting, calculations and comparison with other related data. Such comparisons may include actual cost data compared with standard cost data or actual expenditure compared with budgeted expenditure. From this type of comparison variances are calculated, i.e. differences, from standards or budgets. This is the basis of exception reporting (*see* XXII, **6**).

5. Collection of facts. In its original form data is merely a collection of facts recorded on source documents in readiness for data conversion, prior to batch processing operations. It is perhaps interesting to note that the smallest unit of data is a binary digit, or "bit", which is a 0 or 1, the basis of coding characters in binary code for processing by computer, i.e. machine code.

INFORMATION RELATING TO BUSINESS OPERATIONS

6. Purpose of information. Information is essential for planning and controlling business operations both at the strategic and tactical level of management. Information is playing an ever increasing part in the day-to-day management of business as it provides the means for assessing the results of specific courses of action. It also supplies the facts with which to steer business operations along the correct glidepath by making tactical adjustments to control surfaces in order to achieve a safe landing, i.e. achieve its desired objectives. It also enables management to assess uncertainty and reduce the element of risk in decision-making.

To serve a useful purpose, information must be meaningful and understood by the recipient who must appreciate its significance and the action to be taken as a consequence of receiving it. If it does not serve a useful purpose there is a good case for not producing it and deploying the resources used to other more productive purposes. To be useful, information must inform the recipient of a situation with which he is concerned to enable corrective action to be taken, if appropriate, to modify the system to attain its desired state. Even if no action is taken this is quite in order providing the information indicates that no action is necessary as the manager is fully aware that the situation is satisfactory—he does not have to ponder if he needs to take any action, a state which the absence of information would engender.

7. Output element. Information is the output element of a data processing system which may be displayed visually on a screen by means of a V.D.U. or printed out as a report on a computer systems printer.

8. Information from time sharing systems. By means of time sharing systems users are linked to a central computer by terminal which enables managers, accountants and corporate planners to develop information for themselves by means of modelling systems. This facility enables the user to access a computer on an on-line basis to develop business models relating to capital investments requiring a D.C.F. approach for their evaluation (*see* XIX, **7**), and models regarding projected profit and loss statements and balance sheets which may be subjected to "what if" facilities to establish the outcome of changing specific variables and constraints in respect of levels of activity and cost factors, etc. (*see* XXVI, **5–7**).

9. Incomplete information. It may not be economical to produce all the information needs of management but it is essential that managers are aware of the extent and importance of any information not provided. The manager is then in a position to assess the inherent risk in making decisions without the information, and can act accordingly. Managers should be aware that it is not possible to make precise decisions on the basis of incomplete facts and this is where their managerial intuition comes to the fore.

10. Importance of information. Information is the lifeblood of business and is playing an ever increasing part in the day-to-day management of business—it is becoming a highly valuable business resource both for planning and control. Business managers are increasingly becoming confronted with complexity because of growth, and, in this instance, complexity arises due to the size of the business unit and the interactions between various factors, increasing volumes of transactions and diversity of operations. Competition is also becoming much more critical in many instances, particularly from overseas manufacturers—one only needs to consider cars, motor cycles, cameras, calculators and hi-fi equipment—which requires management to develop alternative strategies based on market intelligence, i.e. information.

Technological developments requires management to become responsive to change because it is imperative to adopt the latest technology in many cases, in order to maintain operational efficiency as a means of warding off competitive threats. There is also the need to comply with changing government policies and legislation. All of these situations require the provision of vital information so that management can react at the right time with the most suitable strategy for the prevailing circumstances.

11. Desirable properties of management information. These properties are summarised below:

(*a*) must serve a useful purpose;

(*b*) must be relevant to the responsibilities of specific managers to enable them to control operations effectively;

(*c*) must contain an appropriate level of detail for the level of management;

(*d*) must relate to current circumstances as outdated information is not only useless but dangerous as wrong decisions may be made; dynamic information systems rather than static systems are essential;

(*e*) must have an acceptable level of accuracy—not necessarily complete accuracy;

(*f*) must be available at the right time to comply with the response time needs of the system being controlled;

(*g*) must be based on the exception principle when appropriate;
(*h*) must be produced at an acceptable level of cost;
(*i*) must be easily understood;
(*j*) must avoid unnecessary redundancy.

PLANNING INFORMATION

12. Futuristic information. Information for planning purposes is futuristic, predictive or forward looking and attempts to assess the future situation on the basis of trends and forecasts derived from the use of forecasting techniques.

This type of information is produced by planning systems (*see* XX, **13**), and is required at two basic organisational levels—the strategic level and the tactical level. Information for planning is generally obtained from the external environment but internal environmental data is also essential and it is used for responding to change at the right moment of time in order to remain profitable on the one hand and to survive on the other (*see* Fig. 129).

13. Information for responding to change. Responding to change at the right moment requires information which is obtained by adopting an analytical approach in an attempt to foresee events which will necessitate change to particular business systems. Managers need to adopt an outwards-looking, rather than a narrow, inwards-looking stance, so that they may have a panoramic view—instead of a mere foreground snapshot—of the business environment. Only by this means will they see the wood for the trees, and only in this way will business systems be tuned to changing circumstances. Indeed, only in this way will the purpose and objectives of systems be redefined.

14. External environmental information. This source of information is for the purpose of identifying threats and opportunities which may arise and to which management must respond either to maintain the business on a steady keel or to navigate new waters according to circumstances. This source of information provides information in respect of the following factors;

(*a*) main competitors' share of market;
(*b*) new market opportunities, the third world countries, for instance;
(*c*) national economic growth rate compared with internal growth rate;
(*d*) state of labour market (manpower resources);

(e) possible threats to continuity of supplies in respect of crop failures or political issues in respect of pay awards, etc.;

(f) technological developments and their likely effect on the business: microtechnology, for instance;

(g) trends in the rate of inflation;

(h) world economic climate;

(i) trends in demand and consumer preference;

(j) likely level of interest rates—the cost of funds for investment in capital projects;

(k) impending government legislation. (See Fig. 129).

15. Internal environmental information. This source of information outlines the profile of the internal environment which may affect future courses of action in accordance with company policy and constraints which may limit desired courses of action, e.g. because of a low liquidity position and manpower problems. These factors would be particularly relevant in respect of capital investment projects for expansion. Information from this source provides the following factors in respect of the state of the company:

(a) type of product manufactured and sold or merely distributed as in the case of a wholesale food warehouse;

(b) type of market—home/export/wholesale/retail/consumable/capital;

(c) share of market obtained;

(d) state of labour relations;

(e) quality/cost effectiveness of products;

(f) profitability of company compared with other companies in same industry;

(g) liquidity of company;

(h) turnover rate of assets in relation to sales;

(i) sales turnover;

(j) discount policy;

(k) credit policy;

(l) types of process;

(m) main functions;

(n) stock policy;

(o) investment level in research and development;

(p) organisation structure-grouping of activities/centralised or decentralised operations. (See Fig. 129.)

16. Strategic planning information. Information for strategic planning is provided by top level systems (see XXIV, **8**), which aim at assisting management in exploiting a company's major strengths and overcoming weaknesses, whilst continuously searching for new opportunities either to ensure the survival of the business in the critical environment which exists, or to achieve a desired rate of growth and profitability.

Business strategy is concerned with how a company means to achieve its objectives which must include an assessment of risk and uncertainty as well as constraints on any proposed course of action as indicated above. The degree of risk involved in various courses of action must be evaluated by such techniques as risk analysis.

The determination of a suitable strategy to achieve the long range objectives of the business is dependent upon obtaining sufficiently accurate information on the company's specific strengths and inherent weaknesses in addition to general environmental information as outlined above (*see* **14** and **15**).

It should be appreciated that the longer the planning period the more information becomes a matter for conjecture and judgement —but even this is better than no assessment of the future at all. It is much better to have some idea of the direction in which the company can steer, or desires to steer, and be aware of the obstacles to be overcome in the process.

Strategic decisions often have long range consequences especially when concerned with the development of new products, the building of new factories and warehouses or the extending of existing premises to provide additional capacity for manufacturing. It is also important to obtain market intelligence information for assessing the extent of future competition to enable products to be redesigned or methods of production to be improved so as to reduce costs and selling prices, thus warding off the effects of such competition.

Long range planning requires long range forecasting which is a systematic information gathering activity of a continuous nature embracing the company as a whole. By this means changes in the economic, technological, financial, sociological and legislative environment in which the business operates are continuously under review. This enables a business to react dynamically in order to contend with threats which endanger the achievement of its objectives, or to take advantage of new opportunities (*see* Fig. 129).

17. Operational planning information. Information for operational planning is obtained by expanding the quantified strategic objectives in respect of production, sales, expenditure and stocks, etc. into detailed plans for the achievement of the strategic plan. Such plans normally take the form of budgets and production and sales programmes, based on information derived mainly from forecasts or from judgment.

The factors to consider include the planning of an effective organisation structure, product-market development planning, resource development planning, capital planning and operational planning. Such plans are concerned with the tactics to be employed to facilitate the attainment of strategic objectives and are prepared by functional managers responsible for the achievement of specified objectives in respect of sales, production, finance and purchasing, etc. The managing director is responsible for ensuring that all the detailed plans are co-ordinated within the framework of company policy and the over-all strategic plan.

CONTROL INFORMATION

18. Programmable information. Information of a control nature is more programmable, as control systems are designed to produce information in respect of operational achievements. A great deal of information in this category is obtained from budgetary control and standard costing systems, whereby comparisons are made with budgeted or standard data and actual achievements. The differences or variances are the basis of exception reporting (*see* **XXII, 6**). These requirements may be built into computer programs as they are structured on the basis of standardised rules. Routine decision making may also be computerised in a similar manner (*see* **XXVI, 4**).

19. Tactical control information. Examples of this type of information may be summarised as follows (*see* Fig. 129).

(*a*) Gross profit to sales—analysed by product or product group.

(*b*) Net profit or contribution to sales—analysed by product or product group.

(*c*) Net profit to capital employed.

(*d*) The extent of deviations from budgeted sales, analysed as follows:

    (*i*) price variance;

    (*ii*) mix variance;   } volume variance.

    (*iii*) quantity variance; }

(*e*) Material price and usage variances.

(*f*) Labour rate and efficiency variances.

  (g) Stock turnover ratios.
  (h) Average investment in stocks compared with budget.
  (i) Value of slow-moving and obsolete stocks.
  (j) Departmental activity ratios.
  (k) Departmental usage of capacity ratios.
  (l) Departmental analysis of cost of scrapped production.
  (m) Departmental analysis of ratio of cost of scrapped production to cost of good production.
  (n) Departmental analysis of labour turnover.
  (o) Cash flow statements.
  (p) Overhead expenditure variances.

FUNCTIONAL AND TOTAL INFORMATION SYSTEMS

20. Functional information systems. Most business organisations are structured on a functional basis whereby each function is controlled by a functional specialist to obtain the benefits of specialisation. When a business first comes into existence it is often a one-man concern and most of the information relating to business transactions is stored mentally by the proprietor. The proprietor may of course supplement his memory by maintaining simple records of items ordered and sold, how much he owes and how much he is owed, etc.

When a business expands the proprietor delegates responsibility for the control of specific functions to his assistants who eventually become managers in their own right as the business grows. Delegation is necessary since it is not possible for the proprietor to effect direct control over all the functional activities as he did previously. In these circumstances each manager develops his own functional systems and information files, often in isolation from other functional systems also developed in isolation. It is this situation which causes the objectives of the various functions to conflict with each other creating sub-optimisation of the business activities as a whole. *See* XXIV, **5**, for further considerations of developing functional systems.

21. Total information systems. A total information system is by definition a single all-embracing system, i.e. a completely integrated system, covering all business activities (*see* XXIV, **4**). Such a system is, in most instances, more idealistic than a practical reality due to the inherent complexity of business organisations necessitating a detailed knowledge of system relationships and their interdependence.

It is also necessary to establish the information requirements of functions and the information flows between functions. Partial integration of systems is possible and desirable and the structure of business systems may consist of groupings of integrated systems each consisting of a number of related sub-systems, e.g. order processing, credit control, invoicing, sales ledger updating, stock ledger updating and stock replenishment, etc.

The objective of integrated or total systems is increased administrative efficiency which is largely achieved by eliminating the shortcomings of functional systems. The expected benefits of integration include:

(*a*) data input once only, thereby avoiding duplication of data recording and processing;

(*b*) elimination of copying errors, which arise when copying common data onto several documents for various functional requirements;

(*c*) elimination of duplicated files, in each of the functions requiring access to common information;

(*d*) elimination of out-of-phase information files, which arises when systems are functionalised.

Integrated systems are often developed on the basis of output/input relationships whereby the output from one system provides the input to another related system.

Such systems need to be computer orientated because of the highly complex inter-relationship of data flows that must be processed in an acceptable time-scale and stored for ease of retrieval for effective decision making. A highly sophisticated management information system of the type outlined may contain the following features.

(*a*) *A comprehensive databank*, containing details in respect of company objectives expressed in terms of budgets and standards embracing finance, sales, production, stocks, costs and manpower, etc. (*see* XXV).

(*b*) *Real-time processing capabilities*, whereby physical events are updated in the computer's backing storage as they occur, thereby providing up-to-date information for remote access on a random basis by authorised personnel of the organisation. When interrogated, the system may present the information requested either on a teletypewriter or visual display unit. Data transmission facilities are necessary for direct access to the computer from geographically dispersed operating units and for the transmission of the requested information (*see* III, **14**).

(*c*) *Current and cumulative operating results* may be compared automatically with budgets and standards, held in the data bank, for the calculation of variances for inclusion in management reports compiled on the basis of the exception principle and printed out by a printer.

(*d*) The application of *operational research techniques* such as "simulation" may be applied, so that the behaviour of such systems as stock control and production control can be assessed by means of models and the results used to guide management in making decisions without the need to incur the costs of physical alterations to such systems to find out how they react to specified changes which may otherwise be necessary (*see* XXVI).

(*e*) Time-sharing facilities may be incorporated for multiple access to the central computer by a number of authorised personnel for various purposes (*see* VIII, **17–22**).

(*f*) Multi-programming facilities may also be provided whereby several application programs may be processed simultaneously, using the computer more effectively in consequence (*see* VIII, **13–16**).

PROGRESS TEST 23

1. Indicate the basic requirements of a management information system. (**1**)

2. A large manufacturing company is contemplating the installation of a computer based interrogation system for use by top management and some functional specialists, notably the financial and management accountants.

(*a*) Explain the general features of interrogation systems and how they would be of service to users.

(*b*) What are the major hardware and system design features necessary for an interrogation system to operate effectively? (**2, 8**) [I.C.M.A. May 1978, Q2]

3. The output of a management information system is, by definition, information. Define information and discuss ways in which a company might assess the value of information to be produced by a new management information system. (**3–19,** I, **9**) [I.C.M.A. May 1978, Q6]

4. (*a*) Explain the difference between "data" and "information".

(*b*) List with brief comments, five of the desirable properties of information produced for management.   (**3–19**) [Part of A.C.A. June 1976, Q1]

5. Indicate the purpose and importance of information.   (**6, 10**)

6. Indicate the nature of:

(*a*) futuristic information;

(*b*) information for responding to change;

(*c*) external environmental information;

(*d*) internal environment information;

(*e*) strategic planning information;

(*f*) operation planning information;

(*g*) programmable information;

(*h*) tactical control information.   (**12–19**)

7. Although the overall objective in the design of management information systems is the optimisation of the system as a whole, other factors are also of considerable importance. Discuss these other factors.   (**20**, *see also* XXIV, **4**)

8. Define the nature of:

(*a*) functional information systems;

(*b*) total information systems.   (**20, 21**)

CHAPTER XXIV

Development of Management Information Systems

ESTABLISHING THE INFORMATION NEEDS OF MANAGEMENT

1. Discussion. When information systems are being developed analysts must appreciate that some managers do not appreciate what their information needs are, or even what information is available. In such circumstances, it is the duty of systems analysts to discuss with each manager the specific problems encountered within his area of responsibility, the decisions which have to be made, the information provided to assist him in making decisions, any information required but not provided, the interpretation of reports and how to use them effectively.

To illustrate this point, a business man was concerned about his company making losses so he decided to implement a computer to analyse business transactions to provide management information. The business man was quite pleased with the information provided, even though the business continued to make losses, because he knew precisely where the losses were being made—rather a negative situation but at least the business man was better informed than previously.

2. Informal information. Managers often receive information informally, rather than from formal documentation. If these factors are overlooked when developing a computerised M.I.S. they will not be provided for in the system specification and consequently the system will be doomed to failure at the outset.

THE APPROACH TO THE DEVELOPMENT OF M.I.S

3. Management information approach. Systems are often developed for routine administrative requirements rather than for management information purposes. This situation may require a reappraisal of priorities in some circumstances to decide which should come first—routine business documents, or information for decision making and control.

The routine administrative activities of a business must of necessity be provided for as no organisation can operate without records of transactions and basic documents in the form of pay-slips, orders and invoices, etc. On the other hand, effective management of a business relies on efficient control of operations and making the right decisions at the right time. Information is, of course, required to accomplish these requirements.

4. Total systems approach. Some systems are developed on the basis of a "total systems" approach or philosophy. The approach recognises that all business systems are related to each other to a greater, or lesser, extent. This must be so because the business as a whole is a complete system, a corporate entity, comprising all the functional systems.

The "total systems" philosophy recognises the relationships and inter-dependence of systems, particularly as the flow of information throughout a business transcends arbitrary functional demarcation lines which are structured for administrative convenience. This approach enables a number of related sub-systems to be integrated to form a larger system. This offers a number of advantages, e.g. with regard to an integrated computer system, data are entered as input to a system only once and all relevant records are updated automatically. By this means data can be retrieved according to functional information needs, especially if the integrated system is supported by an integrated file structure—a database.

Fundamental changes may be required for administering integrated systems as they become inter-functional systems, rather than loosely connected functional systems. This factor must be recognised, since a greater degree of co-ordination and co-operation between managers is essential to ensure smooth operation, free of inter-functional conflict. It must not be overlooked, however, that the co-ordination of functional activities is one of the prime responsibilities of a managing director or general manager.

A computer will probably be necessary to process the data of integrated systems to facilitate their response-time needs in respect of information for effective control and the need to process large volumes of data speedily and accurately (*see* XXII, **26**).

This implies that it may only be the larger type of business which can afford a high degree of systems integration due to the cost

of the computer configuration needed to support this data processing commitment. Looking at this point in a different way, it may
also mean that it is only the larger business which needs a high
degree of integration of systems for reasons of efficiency, because
size often generates systems complexity due to the many inter-
relationships which exist between functions and systems. Large
firms tend to be structured in a very detailed functional manner
with a high degree of specialisation, it is this factor which may
cause problems of integration, particularly as a compromise may
be necessary with regard to individual functional objectives so that
the objectives of the business as a whole are optimised rather than
those of individual functions (sub-systems). Once integration has
been developed, however, the benefits may be enormous.

A smaller business may not require a high degree of systems
integration due to less complexity in its operations but, on the
other hand, the systems may be much more simply combined than
is possible for the larger business.

The "total systems" approach requires a detailed analysis of all
business systems in order to define the relationships between
inputs, files and outputs as well as types of information and the
frequency with which it is required by specific managers for control
and decision making. The business must be looked upon as a
complex communications network, which indeed it is, as one only
has to consider the most elementary data or information inter-
changes which occur even in the smallest business. The very task
of collecting facts and defining their relationships is formidable in
itself, but the design of integrated systems, providing for all
functional needs, is even more formidable.

Systems can only operate effectively if they are fully understood
by managers and staff and integration can detract from this due to
the greater complexity of such systems. Of course, Rome was not
built in a day and this implies that systems integration should be
developed on an evolutionary basis rather than a revolutionary
basis.

A further important factor is the need to integrate systems in
such a way that they operate smoothly and achieve the desired
objectives as effectively as possible. This also implies their development on a modular basis for full integration at a later date (*see*
XXIII, **21**).

5. Functional (piecemeal) systems approach. The development of
systems on an unplanned, unco-ordinated basis is known as the

piecemeal approach. Such an approach is for the purpose of developing individual functional systems, or systems to deal with specific types of problems. Although this may achieve functional optimisation the business as a whole will perform at less than full effectiveness as there will be a clash of objectives of the various functions (*see* XXIII, **20**).

Various functional systems may require information of a common nature which is often stored in separately structured functional files. Apart from duplication of files the danger is that files of some functions may be updated regularly, and others less regularly, causing conflict when the information from the various sources is compared either for control or decision-making.

This approach does not consider the interdependence of systems and views each system as if it existed in a vacuum which, indeed, it does not. The over-all result will achieve a whole galaxy of systems which are connected to each other in reality but this fact is not recognised when they are being developed. It is a matter of not letting the right hand know what the left hand is doing to some extent. Such systems must be steered in a common direction by the chief executive exercising one of the elements of management, that of co-ordination.

6. Input to output approach. This approach considers a system from the input stage together with the processing operations and file references necessary to produce defined outputs. This may appear to be quite logical on the face of it as data must first of all be input to a system before it can be processed to produce a desired output in the form of a document or report.

The disadvantage of this approach is that output can only be produced on the basis of the data available, rather than the data that should be available, for processing. The data currently captured in the system may not relate to the true output requirements in respect of particular elements of information, whether on a basic document, such as an invoice, or a profitability report, for instance.

7. Output to input approach. From the foregoing comments it would seem more appropriate to develop systems from back to front, which on the face of it seems to be the wrong way round. It must be appreciated, however, that to obtain a defined output, it is necessary to assess the "ingredients" that must be used to produce it. Only in this way will the "plum pudding" be of the correct recipe, i.e. specification. The data to be input for processing can only be defined after establishing the specific output required.

8. Top-down approach. This approach is the development of top-level systems initially, for the purpose of supplying management with information relating to the strategic aspects of business. This is in distinction to information for the tactical control of operations. The top-level systems are then supported by operational systems at the departmental level hence the term "top-down".

Operational systems are developed subsequently to top-level systems which is the opposite to the normal approach of developing the lower-level systems initially and then building upwards.

9. Bottom-up approach. This approach develops systems from the operating level upwards, which is the reverse direction to that indicated above. In fact, as stated, this is the normal approach, most systems being implemented at this level because it is less difficult to define data flows and relationships. The information needs of management are then provided for by enhancing the departmental or functional systems by the addition of processing routines for analysing data as a basis for producing reports. The reports are then used by management for strategic planning, decision-making and control.

This approach puts more emphasis on the provision of detailed information in respect of activities to the operating management level so that they are in a position to make tactical decisions. Only in this way can they be provided with the means of achieving the objectives for which they are responsible.

10. The database approach. The development of database philosophy provides the means for providing all the information requirements of a business and of the various levels of management within the business. The development of a database must, of necessity, specify the information needs of all levels of management.

An essential requirement of a database is not merely to store data but also to provide an effective means of retrieval by all personnel authorised to access the database. The objective of a database is to provide reliable, up-to-date, unambiguous data on demand.

A database may be defined as a collection of structured data supporting the operations of the business as a whole or, which is most likely, major areas of a business. It may also be defined as a computer-based centralised management information system (*see* XXV).

CORPORATE INFORMATION ADVISER

11. Responsibilities of information adviser. Particularly in the larger type of organisation the post of corporate information adviser may well be considered a necessary requirement. He would be a specialist in respect of managing the information resources and requirements of the business in the same way that other managers control the use of resources connected with their activities.

The responsibilities of the post are envisaged as far-ranging, embracing all aspects of information ranging from that required for initial planning and policy formulation to the provision of information for the tactical control of operations embracing all functions: sales, production, purchasing, stock control, finance and accounting, research and development, personnel, etc. If a business is developing a database the information adviser may have the title of database administrator (*see* XXV, **13, 14**).

12. Co-ordinating element. An information adviser would act as a catalyst for generating all the information needs of the business and collecting information to produce cohesive reports, fully intelligible by their recipients. He should act in a consultative capacity and should conduct discussions with managers throughout the organisation for defining their specific information needs.

After the discussions have been concluded, meetings should be arranged with the data processing manager and organisation and methods manager to outline current and future information requirements. The outcome would be the establishment of priorities for the development of specific systems to produce particular information. Such systems may be computer-oriented or clerical-oriented or a combination of both depending upon volumes of data to be processed, response time needs for control and other relevant factors.

When systems are developed and ultimately implemented they should be monitored by the information adviser to ensure they are achieving their defined purpose and operating smoothly and efficiently.

THE APPROACH TO IMPROVING THE FLOW OF INFORMATION IN A BUSINESS

13. The question "What?" This question may be used in a number of ways as follows.

(*a*) *What information is available at present?* A schedule of forms, reports and schedules and specimens of each may be compiled for the purpose of preparing a procedure map—sometimes referred to as a forms specimen chart—for displaying the forms used in a system and the information flows between them.

(*b*) *What information could be made available?* Indicate the forms, reports and schedules which could be made available from data currently collected.

(*c*) *What information should be made available?* The relevant information needs of each manager are established after discussions have taken place. This provides the basis for designing new information flows and files using existing methods or computerised methods if feasible.

14. Why? This question may be used in the following way.

(*a*) *Why is the information necessary?*

(*b*) *What would be the result on the business if information presently provided was eliminated or prospective new information not provided?*

These questions assist in establishing whether information has a valid purpose.

15. Who? This question may be used as follows.

(*a*) *Who receives the information?* A circulation list may be compiled showing the recipient of each report.

(*b*) *Who could receive the information to advantage?* A list of managers who would find the information useful is prepared.

(*c*) *Who should receive the information?* A list is compiled of all managers for whom the information is essential for the control of operations. This is in distinction to those managers who could usefully use the information but not to the same extent—it may be useful as background information.

16. When? This question may be used for the purposes outlined below.

(*a*) *When is the information supplied or available?* Details are required of the frequency of supplying reports or the day in each week or the number of days after the month end, etc.

(*b*) *When could the information be supplied or be made available?* It is established whether the information could be provided sooner if necessary.

(*c*) *When should the information be made available?* This establishes the time of the day, week or month the information is needed and whether it is required before or after specific operations. This depends upon the nature of the information, whether required predominantly for planning or control purposes.

17. Where? This question may be posed as follows.

(*a*) *Where is the information originated?* This establishes the venue—country, county, town, government, competitor, customer, supplier, branch office, branch factory, head office—originating the information.

(*b*) *Where could the information be originated?* Possible alternatives are investigated, including considerations whether distributed or centralised origination of information is desirable, i.e. whether centralised computer processing or distributed processing systems are required (*see* I, **23–6**).

(*c*) *Where should the information be originated?* This establishes the most suitable point of origination or location, i.e. section, department, function, activity, office, factory. This considers the use of point-of-sale recording by communications-oriented retail cash registers and factory data-collection systems which provide efficient ways of capturing transaction data as events occur.

18. How? This question may be used in the manner outlined below.

(*a*) *How is the information supplied?* This establishes whether the information is provided formally, informally or verbally; as a printed report, displayed on a V.D.U., as a detailed report or as an exception report.

(*b*) *How could the information be supplied?* Possible alternatives are considered including printed reports from a computer system, display on a V.D.U. on demand, formally by report, informally by observation, etc.

(*c*) *How should the information be supplied?* The most suitable method is established after discussion with all interested parties and after studying the results of feasibility studies (*see* XV, **1**) and the specific circumstances of each case.

THE COSTS AND BENEFITS OF PRODUCING INFORMATION

19. Control of data processing costs. In the same way that manufacturing costs are controlled in a well organised factory, so must the costs incurred in processing business data be controlled. Only in this way can information be produced economically. It is necessary, therefore, to subject data processing activities to the same measures of control to which factory operations are submitted, i.e. production planning and control, quality control, budgetary control and cost control. If data processing is allowed to proceed haphazardly, then the ultimate costs will be too high for the benefits being obtained in most cases.

It is usual in the factory to establish the most suitable production method and this is determined on the basis of economic viability, taking into account volume, speed of output, quality needs, cost per unit produced, etc. Within the data processing environment it is pointless implementing expensive machines in order to speed up the processing of data if, on the one hand, the reduction in processing time is not essential and if, on the other hand, the volume of data to be processed is insufficient for the application of more sophisticated processing methods. One might say, "Do not use a sledgehammer to crack a walnut", or, what is more to the point, do not use an expensive computer system when a biro in the hands of an efficient clerk will do the trick.

It is often necessary to compromise with regard to the timeliness and cost of data processing, as the presentation of reports earlier than needed will only add to costs, not benefits. Although it is often difficult to evaluate the cost of processing each unit of data, it is essential to make an assessment of several alternative methods to enable comparative costs to be compiled so that the most suitable method may be implemented.

The costs incurred in producing information by a computer may be summarised as follows.

(a) Initial systems analysis and design.
(b) Program flowcharting and coding.   } Initial systems development
(c) Program testing and parallel operation.
(d) Operations:
   (i) data collection;
   (ii) data recording;   } Data capture
   (iii) data preparation and verification;
   (iv) data validation;
   (v) processing runs;
   (vi) computer printouts;
   (vii) distribution of reports.

20. Benefits of producing information. Some attempt should be made to evaluate the benefits derived from the information produced by the data processing system. If benefits can be evaluated in monetary terms this is an advantage, because it is then possible to compare the value of benefits with the cost of obtaining them. In general, if the value of benefits exceeds the cost of supplying the information, then it is an economical proposition.

It is often difficult to assess benefits directly, and it becomes necessary to approach the problem from a different viewpoint, by attempting to establish what would be the consequences of not having the information. For example, a failure to report on items of materials or parts which had reached their re-order level could cause production delays. In this case, if a section of five operatives producing a particular product was held up for lack of materials or parts (owing to failing to re-order them) then each day's delay, assuming each operator is paid £15 per day, would cost £75 due to unproductive time. This example pre-supposes that the operatives could not be engaged on other productive work which, of course, may not be the case. In addition to direct labour losses, the fixed production overheads would be under-absorbed and the normal profit margin would also be lost.

As a further example, if a direct labour performance report, analysing the performance of each operator in a department, was not provided it would not be possible to improve the performance of the department as no information would be available to the departmental manager to indicate relevant control action. In order to assess the benefits of such a report it may be possible to compare the performance achieved in the department both with and without the information. The difference in performance may then be evaluated and compared with the cost of providing the report—if the value of the benefits exceed the cost of producing the report then it may be said to be a viable proposition.

INFORMATION AND THE LEVEL OF MANAGEMENT

21. Top management. As a general guide, the higher the level of management to whom information is provided, the more it must relate to strategic aspects for future planning and policy determination. This type of information is derived from the use of forecasting techniques and the assessment of uncertainty and risk to provide a basis for effective decision-making.

Of course, top management must be kept informed of current results in all areas of the business so that they may apply appropriate control action as circumstances dictate. This type of information requires to be in summarised form for speedy interpretation, usually in the form of exception reports. They are not concerned with details relating to each function or department, an over-all appreciation is sufficient to direct their attention to key factors.

22. Operating or departmental management. The operating level of management require more detailed information in respect of their area of responsibility for day-to-day control of operations and operational decisions. In this respect a department or section manager would require to know the efficiency of performance of each operator under their control or the number of units scrapped analysed by operation, cause and cost. Similarly, a credit controller would require to know each customer who had exceeded credit limit so that appropriate action can be taken to remedy the situation. In a similar manner, a stock controller requires to know the status of each item in stock so that he is aware of stock shortages, excessive stocks and stock which require to be replenished.

INFORMATION RELATED TO THE TYPE OF BUSINESS

23. General information. Most businesses will require similar types of information particularly that which relates to the internal environment. Such information relates to employee details regarding type of job, salary, qualifications, positions held, etc. Most manufacturing-type organisations require information on stock status, the progress of orders through the factory, production costs and variances from budgets, etc. Sales organisations require information in respect of product profitability, performance of sales representatives, sales by area and other market intelligence.

24. Specific information. According to the type of business, specific types of information are required to assist in the effective control of the particular class of operation undertaken in order to achieve defined objectives. Specific examples are provided below.

(a) Car manufacturer:
 (i) extent of competition from overseas manufacturers;
 (ii) technological developments;
 (iii) current styling techniques;
 (iv) success of productivity deals;
 (v) share of market obtained compared with that required.
(b) Tour operators:
 (i) status of hotels in various countries and resorts;

(*ii*) medical facilities and health hazards in various countries;

(*iii*) political unrest in specific countries detrimental to particular holiday centres;

(*iv*) expected level of future costs of package holidays, i.e. accommodation and aircraft charter;

(*v*) availability of holiday accommodation at all times.

(*c*) Stock brokers:

(*i*) movement of share prices (share index);

(*ii*) state of money market;

(*iii*) economic climate;

(*iv*) climate in particular industries.

(*d*) Building societies:

(*i*) clients overdue with mortgage repayments;

(*ii*) balances on customer investment, share and mortgage accounts;

(*iii*) likely trend in interest rates and its effect on investment in building society funds;

(*iv*) likely level of house prices in future;

(*v*) Government policy in respect of housing programmes and restrictions on mortgages.

PROGRESS TEST 24

1. Specify the factors to be considered when establishing the information needs of management. (**1, 2**)

2. Outline the various approaches to the development of management information systems including:

(*a*) management information approach;

(*b*) total systems approach;

(*c*) functional (piecemeal) systems approach;

(*d*) input to output approach;

(*e*) output to input approach;

(*f*) top-down approach;

(*g*) bottom-up approach;

(*h*) database approach. (**3–10**)

3. Although the over-all objective in the design of management information systems is the optimisation of the system as a whole, other factors are also of considerable importance. Discuss these other factors. (**4**, *see also* XXIII, **20**)

4. Outline the nature of the responsibilities of an information adviser. (**11, 12**)

5. What approach may be made to improving the flow of information in a business?   (13–18)

6. Outline the costs and benefits of producing information. (19, 20)

7. Discuss important aspects in respect of:

(a) information and the level of management;

(b) information related to the type of business.   (21–4)

CHAPTER XXV

Database and Management Information Systems

DATABASE DEFINED

1. What is a database? A database or databank may be defined as a collection of structured data supporting the operations of the whole or major areas of a business. It may also be defined as a centrally located data file providing the foundations of a computer based management information system.

The concept of a database means something very specific and the collection of data must have certain qualities. The following definition was given by Floyd Johnson of Honeywell-Bull at an NCC conference on databases in 1973. "A non-redundant collection of all data serving one or more defined business applications, that data being structurally linked to and permitting access to all other data in that collection for which a natural or logical business relationship has been defined to exist, however complex."

An essential requirement of a database is not merely to store data efficiently but also to provide an effective means of retrieval. The objective of a database is to provide reliable up-to-date unambiguous information on demand. The centralisation of information in itself serves no purpose but if it can be retrieved more efficiently than is otherwise possible then the data structure of a business may be rationalised.

The term "data" in the context of a database refers to a collection of data elements which, when related in a logical manner, provides meaningful information.

A database to be of any use at all must be maintained in an up-to-date condition. In a large volume situation, such as the Driver and Vehicle Licensing Centre operations, this can present a formidable task regarding the number of transactions to be effected each day.

Similarly, file maintenance creates an additional work load for dealing with the deletion of obsolete, and the addition of new, records in respect of employees, customers and suppliers, etc.

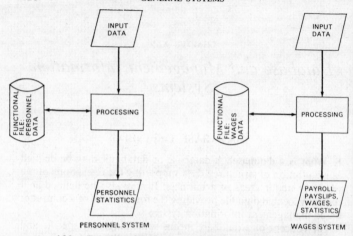

FIG. 130   *Functional (sub-system) approach to file structures*

2. Essential considerations for setting up a database. Traditionally, functions have developed their own files to support their specific operations. Such files are used for reference purposes or are updated with transaction data in order to provide the latest status of stocks, customer and supplier balances, etc. Such files often consist of records containing common data elements which are duplicated in several functional files. This situation creates redundancy as the same data elements in each of the files are updated separately. The personnel function, for instance, maintains a file of employee records containing data elements in respect of employee, name, address, number, marital status, department number, grade and rate of pay, etc. Similar data elements are also stored on the payroll file used in the preparation of wages and maintaining a record of earnings and tax. An input of current transaction data is required to each application to update relevant data elements (*see* Fig. 130).

A database system aims at eliminating such duplication of storage and updating and providing the means for retrieving data elements for each of the application requirements in the required combinations. All data relating to a specific subject, employees in this case, is then consolidated rather than fragmented within several functional files (*see* Fig. 131).

When separate files are maintained with common data elements some are out of phase with others, which is due either to different

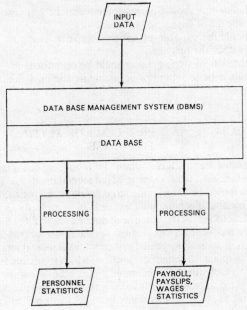

FIG. 131 *Database approach to file structures—integrated files*

updating cycles or frequencies or even omitting to update a file completely.

Important factors related to the use of databases are summarised below:

(*a*) data should be input once only;

(*b*) redundant data should be eliminated;

(*c*) data should be capable of being speedily retrieved;

(*d*) files should be easy to maintain;

(*e*) files should be expandable;

(*f*) access to files should be restricted to authorised users by the use of passwords;

(*g*) restart and recovery procedures are necessary;

(*h*) selective print-outs should be provided for the specific information requirements of managers;

(*i*) provision should be made for batch and on-line processing;

(*j*) new data structures should be capable of being incorporated into the database;

(k) distinction should be made between the physical and the logical storage of data;

(l) should be capable of contending with changing circumstances within the business;

(m) the cost of storing data should be optimised;

(n) should be self-monitoring including the provision of audit trails.

STRUCTURE AND PROBLEMS OF SETTING-UP A DATABASE

3. Integrated file structure. A database is built-up on an integrated file structure basis to serve the needs of several functions. The ideal situation would be to have one large database serving the needs of the business as a whole but this leads to complexity in defining data relationships. A database need not be a single file, however, as it is often practicable to implement several small databases serving the needs of several integrated systems, that is several sets of functional groupings, in respect of functions which have direct relationships with each other. For example a sales accounting system may be integrated to provide for invoicing and stock control. A product file would provide data elements in respect of product code and description, cost price, selling price, V.A.T. rate, stock balance, history of stock movements, etc. A customer file would provide data elements in respect of customer code number, name, address for invoicing and address for delivery if different to the invoice address, credit limit, account balance age analysis, sales history. The product file would enable stock schedules and re-order lists to be printed out on demand. The customer file would enable lists of account balances, accounts which had exceeded credit limit, age analysis of account balances, profitability reports and statements of account to be printed out as required.

4. Problems of setting up a database. One of the problems of setting up a database for systems integration purposes is the classification of data elements as each must be allocated a data name for identification purposes. Data elements may be known by different names in the various functions and a data classification scheme is therefore essential before a database can be got off the ground. A data dictionary consisting of data definitions, characteristics and inter-relationships is therefore very necessary.

It is also necessary to specify data requirements for various functional needs, as indicated in the examples outlined previously, with regard to the personnel/payroll application and the integrated sales accounting system. The logical data relationships must also be defined. Only by this approach is it possible to design effective file handling methods, which must take into account the operating needs for accessing data rather than the manner in which data is physically stored.

DATABASE MANAGEMENT SYSTEM (D.B.M.S.)

5. What is a database management system? It is a highly complex software package for creating, updating and extracting information from a computer-oriented database. There are a number of D.B.M.S. packages available amongst which are those listed below.

(*a*) ADABAS—Adaptable Data Base Management System (Software A.G.).

(*b*) BDMS—Burroughs' Data Management System.

(*c*) DMS 1100—Univac Data Management System—1100 series.

(*d*) IDS—Integrated Data Store (Honeywell).

(*e*) IMS—Information Management System (IBM).

(*f*) RAMIS—Random Access Management Information System (Mathematica).

(*g*) System 2000—Product of Management Research International.

(*h*) TOTAL—Product of Cincom Systems.

6. Examples of a D.B.M.S. package. As an example, the IDS package of Honeywell is a D.B.M.S. using Cobol as a host language, which provides users with a simplified and easy to use method for record processing using mass storage random access devices. It is a general purpose system which can be used to build a variety of databases ranging from a simple file serving an individual application up to and including a complex integrated database serving an entire business.

The package contains the following elements.

(*a*) Data Description Language (D.D.L.). (Providing extensions to the Cobol Data Division.)

(*b*) Data Manipulation Language (D.M.L.). (Providing extensions to Cobol Procedure Division.)

(*c*) A translator which operates in conjunction with the Cobol compiler.

(d) Run-time software.

(e) Support utilities.

(f) User documentation.

The Data Description Language (D.D.L.) allows records to be defined and fields within records to be named and the type of field specified, i.e. whether numeric, alphabetic or alphanumeric. In addition, the D.D.L. is used to specify the required logical links so that a hierarchy or network of records can be established.

The Data Manipulation Language (D.M.L.) provides the processing instructions which allow programs operating under a D.B.M.S. to store, find and retrieve data records on the database. This adds to the processing capabilities of a Cobol procedure division.

Supporting utility programs assist in creating and loading the database, maintaining and auditing the database, etc.

7. Storage aspects. Direct access storage devices such as discs have made the use of databases possible particularly by means of the technique of "virtual" storage. The technique increases the apparent capacity of internal storage as programs are split into "pages" and only those which are required for processing are called into the internal memory. The remainder of the program remains on disc storage—virtual storage—until required.

Virtual storage is necessary in most database systems because of the large storage capacity required for D.B.M.S. software especially when it includes data communication facilities for on-line processing (*see* XIV, **34, 35**).

Discs also allow pointer techniques to be used which is required when dealing with overflow conditions on the disc tracks, so that records can be located when they are out of sequence. This applies to index sequential and random file organisation. Discs may also have chained records either within a file or in other files. By this means it is possible to build up logical relationships between non-contiguous records.

STRUCTURAL DATA RELATIONSHIPS

8. Data elements. In the every day use of our language it is well known that characters make up words. Words in the context of data processing may be classed as "fields" or data elements such as a customer's account number, quantity ordered, price, and value, etc. A series of related data elements constitute "records".

From this it can be seen that logical relationships exist between data elements which may be very simple or complex. In setting up a database it is essential to be aware of all such relationships. It is also important to appreciate logical relationships before making changes to particular data elements otherwise disruption will occur as certain functions will not be able to access data elements in the form they are required.

The Database Task Group (D.B.T.G.) initially recognised the three generally accepted definitions of structural data relationships as:

(a) sequential list structures;
(b) tree structures;
(c) complex network structures.

It was also considered that the totality of data in a business may be a combination of all three.

9. Sequential list structure. A structure in which each element is related to the element preceding it and the element following it.

10. Tree structure. A hierarchical structure in which each element may be related to any number of elements at any level below it but only one element above it in the hierarchy.

11. Network structure. Similar to a tree structure but with the important exception that any element may be related to any number of other elements. This type of structure closely represents the logical data relationships which exist in the world of business.

12. Sets. The D.B.T.G. concept of "sets" may be used to define the structures indicated above. The concept of sets is fundamental to understanding any file management technique related to "lists".

(a) A set is a collection of named record types.
(b) Any number of sets may be defined in a database.
(c) A set must have a single "owner" type, i.e. a master record relating to a department for instance.
(d) A record type may be "owner" of one or more sets.
(e) A record type may be a "member" in one or more sets, e.g. details of employees may be a "member" of a personnel department set and a manufacturing department set.
(f) A record may be both owner and member but in different sets.
(g) A set must have a specified set order.

THE DATABASE ADMINISTRATOR

13. The database administrator as a co-ordinator. As the whole concept of a database is to rationalise business systems by the integration of such systems it follows that the data needs of an organisation must be co-ordinated at a very high level. This is basically the responsibility of a database administrator who may not yet exist in many organisations. Nevertheless someone has no doubt been vested with such responsibilities, perhaps a senior member of the systems staff.

When data is common to two or more applications then programmers are not allowed the freedom they previously enjoyed to name data elements and subject them to processing independently of other application requirements. This is where the database administrator assumes command, as it were, because he must consider the data needs of the several applications under consideration for consolidation into a database.

14. Duties of a database administrator. He must first of all be conversant with business policy and strategy, particularly for the long term, as the very fabric of a business is dependent upon an efficient and effective management information system of which a database is a fundamental part—the roots of such a system in fact. He should play an active part in the planning of information systems particularly with regard to feasibility studies.

He should be an expert in all file management techniques and be able to advise management and system planners of the capabilities and shortcomings of various file management systems with regard to the application under review. It is essential that he liaise and consult with project teams with regard to the development of design specifications, program specifications, systems documentation and programs, etc. It is imperative that he monitor the implementation of a database ensuring that time and cost constraints are adhered to. It is of extreme importance the administrator ensures that system objectives are achieved. Also of importance is that the initial preparation and maintenance of a data dictionary should be the responsibility of a database administrator, as this is essential for the success of a database system.

PROGRESS TEST 25

1. Define your understanding of the term "database", indicating its relevance to management information systems. **(1–14)**

2. Outline the essential considerations and problems concerned with setting up a database. **(2, 4)**

3. What is a database management system? **(5, 6)**

4. Define your understanding of the term "database administrator". **(13, 14)**

CHAPTER XXVI

Use of Computers in Management Information Systems

DATA PROCESSING AND MANAGEMENT REPORTS

1. Data processing. Quite often a computer is installed for the purpose of processing data relating to business transactions, in order to produce business documents such as invoices, statements, payslips and payrolls and purchase orders as well as updating master records. The master records contain historical data relating to employees' earnings, amounts purchased from suppliers together with the amount owing to them, sales to customers and amounts outstanding, and balances of items held in stock, etc. In addition, transaction summaries and error reports are printed out (*see* Figs. 100–7).

The basic purpose of using a computer in this way is to cater for the processing of high-volume, routine transactions and to reduce the cost per unit of data processed.

In the past, computers were installed to obtain the benefit of a reduction in the number of staff employed, but this was not always achieved, since although some clerical jobs were eliminated (by transferring them to the computer) others were created for staffing the computer installation. In some instances, staff numbers were reduced, but this did not necessarily apply to total payroll costs as the computer operations personnel often commanded higher salaries.

2. Management reports. The present tendency is to extend computer applications to the preparation of management reports, as it is possible (because of the vast processing speed of the computer) to prepare them in a more appropriate time-scale for the control of operations and decision-making than is possible by other means. Reports for the different levels and functions of management may be generated as follows.

(*a*) *Management accounting.* Cost centre overhead variances may be printed out automatically by the computer. This is achieved by making a comparison of the budgeted expenditure (held in backing files or data banks) with the actual expenditure incurred, which is input to the computer, and assessing the difference or variance. This technique provides the basis for issuing reports on the cost of operations to cost centre controllers so that they can take appropriate action as indicated by the results. This is known as "exception" reporting, but the important point is that it is done automatically by means of the computer program.

By means of computer-based predictive models, in addition to assessing variances from the past period it is also possible to predict the variances that will be incurred in the following operating period unless appropriate management action is taken to eliminate adverse variances.

(b) *Sales management.* Although the activities outlined below may be classed as management accounting activities, they are indicated as "sales management" because of the special nature of the contents of the report. In this instance, if sales budgets are held in backing files, in terms of quantity and value for each product group, by sales area, customer and representative, then they may be compared with the actual results achieved and the variances printed out to form the basis of control reports for action by sales management.

By means of computer-based predictive models it is possible to project future sales if no management action is taken to alter the present trend.

(c) *Production management.* This level of management may be supplied with more detailed and timely reports (relating to the operations for which they are accountable) with which to effect control, so that improvements may be achieved in order to attain company objectives.

The types of report which may be supplied are as follows.

(*i*) Operator performance ratios   —Daily.

(*ii*) Quantity and cost of scrap analysed by product   —Daily.

(*iii*) Cost of consumable supplies and variances from budget   —Weekly.

(*iv*) Output variances by product   —Weekly.

(*v*) Cost of overtime and shift working   —Weekly.

(*vi*) Departmental overheads
(*see* (*a*) above)   —Monthly.

MANAGEMENT PLANNING AND DECISIONS

3. Management decisions. Certain classes of decision can be computerised or automated, and are known as routine or "structured" decisions because they are made on the basis of standardised rules. This class of decision is usually made by the operating level of management, therefore, if managers have fewer routine decisions to make they are able to spend more time on problems of an "unstructured" type which do not conform to standardised rules for their solution. The computer when used in this way is a very valuable tool of management but does not in any way change the real functions of management.

A notable example is that of stock control—for instance, when items held in stock have reached a pre-defined re-order level a list may be printed out in order that supplies may be replenished. It is also possible to design a system which would print a purchase order (from data held in backing files) thus eliminating a clerical operation at the same time. This technique eliminates the need to scan files by a human being, thereby reducing the risk of overlooking any item of stock due to be replenished. If items to be re-ordered were overlooked, then production delays might be encountered or supplies might have to be purchased in an emergency at increased cost (*see* XVI, **13, 14**).

A further example relates to the issue of works orders. It is possible to issue works orders automatically (under computer control) in a pre-determined sequence after the completion of each previous order in the queue. This system requires the installation of data recorders in the works for the purpose of transmitting data, relating to each order completed, to the central computer in order that files may be updated and new orders issued.

4. Management planning and problem solving. It is sometimes found that a misconception arises in the use of a computer, in as much as it is considered necessary to have high-volume routine processing needs as a pre-requisite for its installation. However, the more sophisticated applications must not be overlooked, especially in the area of planning and problem-solving. In this respect, the computer becomes a real tool of management if used for complex situations such as the following:

(*a*) *Capital budgeting.* This technique involves using the computer to assist management in making decisions with regard to the alternative courses of action which are possible when seeking to maximise the return from investments of a capital nature (e.g. choosing a particular machine from a range of similar machines, each having different capital and operating costs). It is necessary to make assumptions with regard to future cash flows, therefore this element of uncertainty must be provided for on a probability basis. It is also necessary to "discount" future cash flows (by means of an appropriate interest rate) to "present" values in order to allow for the difference in timing of cash flows of the possible alternative investments. Discounting is necessary, as the returns to be received in the future are not worth so much as returns currently obtained, because of the interest which could be earned on re-investment. Cash flows must take into account tax allowances and tax on profits earned (or expected) in respect of each alternative. When using the "present value" concept for investment appraisal, the choice is usually made on the basis of the investment which provides the highest "net present value". It is in performing this type of calculation that the computer is eminently suitable, because of its speed of operation. From the information printed out by the line printer, management can select the investment which seems most suitable. The information is presented much more quickly by the computer than is possible by other means because of the laborious nature of the calculations.

(b) *Demand forecasting.* By means of demand forecasting, it is possible to assess the changing pattern of demand for goods and, by feeding appropriate data to the computer, it is possible to adjust the stock control parameters, e.g. the quantity to re-order at a pre-determined re-order level to allow for the changing circumstances.

This technique enables working capital locked up in stocks to be reduced because, through the increased level of control, it is possible to reduce stock levels, especially if re-ordering is automatic.

An additional advantage is that storage space and costs may be reduced as a result of the improvement in control.

(c) *Budget preparation.* The preparation of budgets can be a difficult task because of the large number of variables which must be co-ordinated to form the master budget. The master budget is very rarely accepted by management in the first instance, consequently budget amendments are necessary for the establishment of corporate objectives. Budget amendments may require changes being made to sales quantities which generate a host of other amendments to sales costs and margins, production quantities, stocks and manpower requirements, etc. Changes to these variable factors can be processed very speedily by the computer and provide an amended master budget much more quickly than by other methods, especially those of a purely clerical nature. The computer can also process varying quantities of particular budget elements, e.g. sales or production quantities and the related income, costs and profits in order to develop a series of alternative budgets for use in corporate planning.

(*d*) *Production scheduling.* The computer may be used to prepare production plans, in the form of schedules, much more speedily than by clerical methods. Also when amendments are necessary it is possible to make them very quickly by means of the computer. Amendments to one part of the production plan may have a chain effect on the remainder and it is this aspect which makes the task so laborious when using clerical methods.

It is also possible to prepare a series of alternative plans very quickly by means of the computer, thus enabling management to select the most suitable plan for implementation.

Production plans prepared by a computer are usually more reliable and as a result delivery dates are more realistic, resources are utilised more effectively, the number of planning staff is reduced and the throughput of jobs is speeded up.

The scheduling technique used depends to a great extent upon the type of production undertaken, i.e. whether one-off projects such as a bridge, a power station, a ship or a motorway are predominant, which requires the application of a network planning technique. The network plan may be printed out by the computer either in the form of a printed schedule or in graphical form. If batch or mass production techniques are used then linear programming or queueing theory may be applied.

BUSINESS MODELS AND SIMULATION

5. Business models. One approach to solving specific problems inherent in particular business systems is to construct a model of the system. Variables and constraints in business systems are represented in models symbolically in the form of algorithms or algebraic equations. By this means they may be subjected to statistical or mathematical analysis in order to observe their behaviour when subjected to changing variables. This then enables optimum solutions to particular problems to be obtained. This is actually experimenting with models as an aid to studying real life situations and is less costly and speedier than experimenting with the real life system itself. Different combinations of variables may be fitted into the model and the results observed.

As an example, a model of a stock control system may be prepared for experimentation purposes perhaps to optimise the investment in stocks. Variations in lead time and usage rates may be established from historical information and applied to the model, progressively changing the variables one at a time. It will then be possible to observe:

(a) the number of occasions when items would be out of stock;

(b) the number of occasions the maximum stock level may be exceeded;

(c) the average investment of working capital in stocks for varying stock levels;

(d) the effect on stock levels through changes in safety stock levels, re-order levels, order quantities, lead times and usage rates.

When a computer is used to process the data several years' operations may be obtained within a matter of hours.

One problem associated with the construction of models for complex systems is the need to ensure that variables and constraints are representative of the real life situation. Only in this way will a model react in a similar way to the real situation.

Models are often over-simplified because of the difficulties encountered in identifying all variables and their relationships. Models are dynamic in the sense that they can be used repeatedly to predict the results of different situations when different values are assigned to variables. It is possible to construct models very accurately but assign inaccurate values to variables which prevents accurate results from being obtained in respect of a systems behaviour.

6. Simulation. When experimenting with a model the behaviour of the real life system is being simulated. In some instances, however, a system cannot be specified in precise algorithms because the system behaves in a non-predictable manner, i.e. it is a stochastic or probabilistic system. In such instances, historical data or estimated values have to be collected regarding the frequency with which events occur and Monte Carlo techniques are used to simulate the random behaviour of the system.

The situation applies during the development of a computer-based communications system, as it is necessary for the system designer to simulate the behaviour of the proposed system. This is undertaken in order to assess the traffic density in respect of terminals in order to evaluate system performance as it is necessary to know the average time it takes to handle messages, the number of messages handled in various time periods, the number of messages waiting for service in a queue, etc.

The results of the simulation will assist in determining the number of telephone lines required to avoid bottlenecks on the one hand and the possibility of terminals sharing lines on the other without impairing the level of service required.

This type of simulation is facilitated by simulation models in the form of computer programs which are designed to behave in a similar manner to the real-life system. It is not always necessary to write simulation programs as packages are available for the purpose.

7. Modelling package. A modelling package is a suite of application programs designed to cover a wide range of business needs with regard to financial and corporate planning and forecasting, etc. A package, in general, provides a model-building language, model-running language, report generator language, "What if?" facilities and a statistical sub-system for data analysis.

The language used to describe the model is often quite straightforward and is easily learned by the person who is not a computer specialist which allows models to be run on a computer by accountants, corporate planners and managers in general. It must be stressed however that the results obtained from running a model can only be as good as the construction of the model in the first instance. The results can also only be used as a guide to decision-making; it does not make the decisions.

The model running language is also relatively straightforward as it is recognised as a problem solving aid not an exercise in programming skills. By modelling facilities the user can manipulate models and study alternative strategies which to some extent extends the user's knowledge of the business and the inter-relationship of variables, constants and contraints which must be built into the model.

A financial modelling package for "system ten" users is available from Dataskil, ICL's software house. It is called Prosper Ten and provides facilities for budgeting, forecasting, costing and investment analysis. With this package, chief accountants, financial directors and managing directors can run modelling systems in their own offices with a minimum system ten configuration.

A simple financial model and the result of running the model on

```
?PERIODS, = 6
?HEADINGS '1ST QUARTER' '2ND QUARTER' '3RD QUARTER'
?HEADS FROM COL 4 '4TH QUARTER' 'TOTAL YEAR' % OF SALES
?COLUMN 5 = SUM OF COLUMNS 1 TO 4
?COLUMN 6 = 100 X COLUMNS 5 / COLUMN 5 (LINE 1)
?ADD LINE 1   'SALES' 100, 125, 150, 175
?ADD LINE 2   'MATERIAL COST' = .35 X 'SALES'
?ADD LINE 3   'LABOUR COST' = .20 X LINE 1
?ADD LINE 4   'OTHER DIRECT' = 10 ÷ .03 X LINE 1
?ADD LINE 5   'GROSS PROFIT' = 'SALES' - SUM OF LINES 2 TO 4
?ADD LINE 5.5
?ADD LINE 6   'G A COST' 10, 12, 14, 15
?ADD LINE 7   'SELLING EXPENSE' = 4 ÷ .05 X  SALES
?ADD LINE 8   'DEPRECIATION' 4,4,4,4
?ADD LINE 9   'PROFIT BEF TAX' = LINE 5 - SUM OF LINES 6 TO 8
?ADD LINE 10  'INCOME TAX' = .52 X 'PROFIT BEF TAX' MINIMUM 8
?ADD LINE 11  'PFT BEF TAX' LINE 9 - LINE 10
?REPORT 1 LINES 1 TO 11, COLS 1 TO COL 6 'SAMPLE INCOME STATEMENT'
                                                         'QUARTERS'
?INDENTIFICATION 'SAMPLE RUN'
```

FIG. 132   *Financial model*

LINE NO	NAME	1ST QUARTER	2ND QUARTER	3RD QUARTER	4TH QUARTER	TOTAL YEAR	%S OF SALES
	SAMPLE INCOME STATEMENT						
	QUARTERS						
1.0	SALES	100	125	150	175	550	100
2.0	MATERIAL COST	35	44	52	61	192	35
3.0	LABOUR COST	20	25	30	35	110	20
4.0	OTHER DIRECT	13	14	14	15	56	10
5.0	GROSS PROFIT	32	42	53	64	191	35
5.5							
6.0	G & A COST	10	12	14	15	51	9
7.0	SELLING EXPENSE	9	10	11	13	43	8
8.0	DEPRECIATION	4	4	4	4	16	3
9.0	PROFIT BEF TAX	9	16	24	32	81	15
10.0	INCOME TAX	5	8	12	17	42	8
11.0	PFT AFTER TAX	4	8	11	15	39	7

FIG. 133   *Profit Statement*

a computer are shown in Figures 132 and 133. The example shown
is of a simplified profit and loss statement covering four quarters
with both an annual total column and a column of percentages
of sales.

PROGRESS TEST 26

1. The use of computers is not only for basic data processing but
also the production of management reports. Discuss.   (**1, 2**)

2. A computer has been installed in your company. You were involved in the design of the cost control information that will be provided by the computer. List the shop floor control information that you have specified. **(2(c))** [I.C.M.A. Dec. 1971, Q6]

3. It has been said that computer-based systems are ideally suited to the application of management by exception techniques. State briefly when you think this statement is true and give an example of a specific application of management by exception using a computer. **(2,** *see also* **III, 21, 22)** [I.C.M.A. June, 1971, Q4]

4. Much publicity has been given to the impact of computers in business, yet, "it is still true that management's real functions remain unchanged". Discuss this question. **(3, 4)** [I.C.M.A. May 1972, Q1]

5. Simulation is often employed in the design of computerised inventory control systems. Explain in detail what is meant by the above statement. What other areas of systems design employ simulation? **(5, 6)** [I.C.M.A. Nov. 1974, Q4]

6. An increasing number of companies are using models to simulate corporate activities and a number of computer packages have been developed to provide assistance in this area.

(*a*) Explain what is meant by "models" in this context; and

(*b*) Give details of the facilities you would expect a comprehensive modelling package to provide. **(5–7)** [I.C.M.A. May 1977, Q1]

Examination Technique

Examination questions in respect of data processing and management information systems are usually descriptive and aim to test the candidates' knowledge of how well-defined principles are applied to business situations or problems.

The subject is very wide and practical, candidates should always take care to demonstrate fully the wider implications of what may appear to be very narrow questions.

The examination candidate is recommended to observe the following points.

1. Read each question thoroughly before attempting an answer, in order to avoid any initial misunderstanding of the requirements of the question. A good answer to the wrong question does not score marks.

2. Allocate sufficient time to answering each question. It is fatal to omit an answer to a question through spending too much time on other questions. It is much better to have a fairly complete answer on all the questions rather than no answer at all on some of them.

3. Having determined the requirements of each question, the first one to be attempted should be selected. It is good practice before committing yourself to the answer paper to jot down main headings or topics to be covered on a scrap pad. By this means, initial thoughts may be clarified and the full scope of the question appreciated.

4. The answer may then be written on the answer paper, observing the following points.

(*a*) Write legibly to enable the examiner to interpret your answer easily.

(*b*) Show a good command of English, sentence structure and grammar.

(*c*) Outline the answer on the basis of topic or subject headings sub-analysed as appropriate as follows:

(*a*)
   (*i*)
   (*ii*)
(*b*)
(*c*)
   (*i*)
   (*ii*)
   (*iii*)

By this means the examiner can easily assess the points being made and can more readily appreciate their relevance and award marks accordingly.

(*d*) Keep to the subject and be as concise as possible without unnecessary padding—you either know the subject or you do not. Make sure you do before sitting the examination, even if only to save examination fees.

5. Allow sufficient time to read the answers before handing in the paper so that corrections can be effected.

6. Answer questions from your own experience whenever possible, as this shows the examiner that you are conversant with the subject in question.

7. Some answers require the presentation of a flowchart or other recording technique, and it is important to use drawing aids in their construction, i.e. charting symbol templates, coins (for circles), and a rule (for straight lines). Neatness of presentation is very important if maximum marks are to be gained.

Data Representation in the Computer

NUMBER SYSTEMS

It is necessary to represent data for processing in a computer by pulse sequences, which create signals to allow data to be stored magnetically. As the pulse sequences are represented by "on" and "off" electrical states, the basis of representing data is combinations of pulses and no pulses. A pulse represents 1 and no pulse represents 0. Therefore the basis of representing data in the computer is in combinations of 0s and 1s in the form of a code. This is the foundation of the binary number system, which is a *base-two system*.

Our common decimal number system uses ten digits, 0–9, and is therefore a base-ten system. It is not possible to use this number system for computer operations as it is not feasible to have ten states of electricity—electrical current is either on or off.

1. Decimal number system. The position of each digit determines its value, and each position to the left increases it by a power of 10: Table XIX shows this clearly.

TABLE XIX   DECIMAL NUMBER SYSTEM

Base number	Coefficient	Position	Value
10	0 (10^0)	1	Units
10	1 (10^1)	2	Tens
10	2 (10^2)	3	Hundreds
10	3 (10^3)	4	Thousands, and so on.

As an example, the year 1974 can be represented in the following way:

$$(1 \times 10^3) + (9 \times 10^2) + (7 \times 10^1) + (4 \times 10^0)$$
$$= (1 \times 1000) + (9 \times 100) + (7 \times 10) + (4 \times 1)$$
$$= 1000 \quad + 900 \quad + 70 \quad + 4 \quad = 1974$$

2. Binary number system. In this system also, the position of each digit determines its value, but with the binary system each position to the left increases it by a power of 2, as can be seen from Table XX.

TABLE XX   BINARY NUMBER SYSTEM

Base number	Coefficient	Position	Value
2	0 (2^0)	1	1
2	1 (2^1)	2	2
2	2 (2^2)	3	4
2	3 (2^3)	4	8
2	4 (2^4)	5	16
2	5 (2^5)	6	32
2	6 (2^6)	7	64
2	7 (2^7)	8	128
2	8 (2^8)	9	256
2	9 (2^9)	10	512
2	10 (2^{10})	11	1024
2	11 (2^{11})	12	2048
2	12 (2^{12})	13	4096
2	13 (2^{13})	14	8192
2	14 (2^{14})	15	16 384

To express a number in binary, it is necessary to record the presence of a bit (*bi*nary digi*t*) in appropriate positions which add up to the number required. In respect of the year 1974, the binary equivalent is:

$$(1 \times 2^{10}) + (1 \times 2^9) + (1 \times 2^8) + (1 \times 2^7) + (0 \times 2^6)$$
$$1024 \quad + \quad 512 \quad + \quad 256 \quad + 128 \quad + 0$$
$$(1 \times 2^5) \quad + (1 \times 2^4) + (0 \times 2^3) + (1 \times 2^2) + (1 \times 2^1)$$
$$+ \quad 32 \quad + \quad 16 \quad + \quad 0 \quad + \quad 4 \quad + \quad 2$$
$$+ (0 \times 2^0)$$
$$+ \quad 0 \quad = 1974$$

The binary equivalent of 1974 is 11110110110 (indicating the position values required to obtain the desired number).

It is readily apparent that only four decimal number positions are necessary to represent 1974, whereas no less than eleven binary number positions are required.

3. Octal number system. The octal system is related to the binary system, but each position to the left increases by a power of 8, hence the term "octal".

The system is used to provide a more compact method of recording data than is possible with the basic binary system. There are only eight numbers in this system: 0, 1, 2, 3, 4, 5, 6, 7, and three binary positions are equivalent to one octal position.

Octal position values are shown in Table XXI.

TABLE XXI   OCTAL NUMBER SYSTEM

Base number	Coefficient	Position	Value
	0 (8^0)	1	1
8	1 (8^1)	2	8
8	2 (8^2)	3	64
8	3 (8^3)	4	512
8	4 (8^4)	5	4096

The way in which the eight numbers of the octal system are represented in the computer is shown in Table XXII.

TABLE XXII   REPRESENTATION OF OCTAL NUMBERS IN THE COMPUTER

Decimal number	Octal number	Binary representation
0	0	000
1	1	001
2	2	010
3	3	011
4	4	100
5	5	101
6	6	110
7	7	111

The eight numbers fully utilise the bits of the first position (8^0), and it is therefore necessary to proceed to the next higher position (8^1) for recording octal numbers (*see* Table XXIII).

TABLE XXIII   RECORDING OCTAL NUMBERS

Decimal number	Octal number	Binary representation
8	10	001 000
9	11	001 001
10	12	001 010

In respect of the year 1974, the octal equivalent may be determined by continuously dividing the decimal number by 8, the remainders of each division determining the octal number.

$$
\begin{array}{rll}
8 & 1974 & \text{remainder } 6 \\
8 & 246 & \text{,,} \quad 6 \\
8 & 30 & \text{,,} \quad 6 \\
8 & 3 & \text{,,} \quad 3 \\
  & 0 &
\end{array}
$$

The octal equivalent of the decimal number 1974 is therefore 3666 which signifies the separate numbers to be used for multiplying the individual octal position values, as follows

$$
\begin{aligned}
&(3 \times 8^3) + (6 \times 8^2) + (6 \times 8^1) + (6 \times 8^0) \\
=\ &(3 \times 512) + (6 \times 64) + (6 \times 8) + (6 \times 1) \\
=\ &\quad 1536 \ | + \quad 384 \quad + \quad 48 \quad + \quad 6 = 1974
\end{aligned}
$$

Computers can process data in this form, but more usually various codes are used to represent various types of character.

COMPUTER CODES

4. Six-bit alphameric code (Binary Coded Decimal—B.C.D.). With this code, numeric, alphabetical and special characters are represented in coded form using the first six binary positions, i.e. 32, 16, 8, 4, 2, 1 (*see* Tables XXIV and XXV). In addition, a seventh binary position is used for a parity bit position.

Binary coded decimal is structured in the manner outlined in Table XXIV.

TABLE XXIV   BINARY CODED DECIMAL

	Check bit	Zone bits		Numeric bits			
Binary position	2^6 C	2^5 B	2^4 A	2^3 8	2^2 4	2^1 2	2^0 1

The numeric bits are used to represent decimal digits in binary form, each digit utilising the four bit positions. By this means, the four bits in various combinations represent the decimal numbers 0–9. It is possible to obtain sixteen combinations from the four bits on the basis of

$$2^4 = 2 \times 2 \times 2 \times 2 = 16$$

and this is important for extending the character repertoire to the 64 combinations necessary for most data processing requirements. To obtain the 64 characters, it is necessary to utilise the zone bits in conjunction with the numeric bits, but first of all let us consider the sixteen combinations from the four numeric bits shown in Table XXV.

TABLE XXV   FOUR NUMERIC BITS

Decimal number	Place number			
	8	4	2	1
0	0	0	0	0
1	0	0	0	1
2	0	0	1	0
3	0	0	1	1
4	0	1	0	0
5	0	1	0	1
6	0	1	1	0
7	0	1	1	1
8	1	0	0	0
9	1	0	0	1
10	1	0	1	0
11	1	0	1	1
12	1	1	0	0
13	1	1	0	1
14	1	1	1	0
15	1	1	1	1

Sixty-four combinations are obtained in the following way:

Bit combinations	Number of combinations
Four numeric only (as above)	16
A zone bit plus four numeric bits	16
B zone bit plus four numeric bits	16
A plus B zones plus four numeric bits	16
Total combinations	64

The sixty-four combinations may be assigned to represent:

> 10 decimal digits (0–9).
> 26 alphabetic characters (A–Z).
> 28 special characters (e.g. @, %, (,), &, £).

The C position (2^6) is used for checking that each character has the correct number of bits, which must have an even number of 1 bits. If the 1 bits do not produce an even number, a 1 bit is added to conform to this requirement. If the number of 1 bits in a character is even without the check bit, then the check bit is 0.

B.C.D. coding may be on the following basis:

> Numeric characters, 0–9, are coded as indicated above.
> Alphabetic and special characters may be coded as shown in Table XXVI.

TABLE XXVI   CODING NUMERIC, ALPHABETIC AND SPECIAL
CHARACTERS

Character	Check bit	Zone bits		Numeric bits			
	C	B	A	8	4	2	1
A	1	1	1	0	0	0	1
B	1	1	1	0	0	1	0
C	0	1	1	0	0	1	1
X	0	0	1	0	1	1	1
Y	0	0	1	1	0	0	0
Z	1	0	1	1	0	0	1
@	0	0	0	1	1	0	0
%	1	0	1	1	1	0	0

Each character is separately coded and the year 1974 is represented in the following way:

	2^3				2^2				2^1				2^0		
8	4	2	1	8	4	2	1	8	4	2	1	8	4	2	1
0	0	0	1	1	0	0	1	0	1	1	1	0	1	0	0
	1				9				7				4		

5. Six (seven)-bit character code. This code is similar to B.C.D., consisting of the same basic structure of a check bit, two zone bits and four numeric bits. The code is designed for use with character machines, and uses different bit combinations to B.C.D.

6. Eight-bit alphameric code (Extended Binary Coded Decimal Interchange Code—EBCDIC). This code uses eight binary positions for each character format and forms the basis of the eight-bit byte for IBM System/360 computers.

Such a code enables a character repertoire of 256 characters to be used, embracing upper case and lower case alphabetic characters and an extended range of special and control characters. The basis of the 256 characters is

$$2^8 = 2 \times 2 \times 2 \times 2 \times 2 \times 2 \times 2 \times 2$$

This number of characters is possible since four zone positions are used not two, as with six-bit B.C.D. The code also provides for a parity bit.

The structure of the code is as follows:

Check bit	Zone bits	Numeric bits
Bit positions	0 1 2 3	4 5 6 7

Examples of code combinations are shown in Table XXVII.

TABLE XXVII   EXAMPLES OF CODE COMBINATIONS

Character	Zone bits	Numeric bits
A	1100	0001
B	1100	0010
C	1100	0011
X	1110	0111
Y	1110	1000
Z	1110	1001
a	1000	0001
b	1000	0010
c	1000	0011

7. Hexadecimal code. This coding system has a base of sixteen; each position to the left increases by a power of sixteen, hence the term hexadecimal (six + ten). There are sixteen numbers in this system, 0–15, and in order to represent the sixteen values by a single symbol the numbers 0–9 are defined accordingly, while the numbers 10–15 are assigned letters to represent them.

10	11	12	13	14	15
A	B	C	D	E	F

Each decimal number is therefore allocated an hexadecimal equivalent, which in turn is expressed in terms of the first four positions of the binary system, as shown in Table XXVIII.

It is possible to represent all kinds of information, data and instructions, etc. in hexadecimal code, regardless of the code used in the computer internally. The coding used internally may be EBCDIC characters, zoned decimal numbers, and so on. All are coded in some form of binary and in respect of IBM System/360, as the basic unit of data is the eight-bit byte based on EBCDIC

TABLE XXVII   HEXADECIMAL CODE AND EQUIVALENT EBCDIC CODING

Decimal number	Hexadecimal symbol	Coding					
		Binary				EBCDIC	
		8	4	2	1	0123	4567
0	0	0	0	0	0	1111	0000
1	1	0	0	0	1	1111	0001
2	2	0	0	1	0	1111	0010
3	3	0	0	1	1	1111	0011
4	4	0	1	0	0	1111	0100
5	5	0	1	0	1	1111	0101
6	6	0	1	1	0	1111	0110
7	7	0	1	1	1	1111	0111
8	8	1	0	0	0	1111	1000
9	9	1	0	0	1	1111	1001
10	A	1	0	1	0		
11	B	1	0	1	1		
12	C	1	1	0	0		
13	D	1	1	0	1		
14	E	1	1	1	0		
15	F	1	1	1	1		

two hexadecimal symbols may be used per byte. The equivalent EBCDIC coding for the decimal and hexadecimal numbers 0–9 is shown in Table XXVIII. Note that the zone portion for 0–9 utilises the hexadecimal equivalent for 15, that is 1111 (F).

Each hexadecimal position has the basic sixteen symbols, but their value is determined by the respective position of each.

The hexadecimal position values are shown in Table XXIX.

TABLE XXIX   HEXADECIMAL POSITION VALUES

Base number	Coefficient	Position	Value
16	0 (16^0)	1	1
16	1 (16^1)	2	16
16	2 (16^2)	3	256
16	3 (16^3)	4	4096
16	4 (16^4)	5	65 536

By way of an example, if we wished to code Year 1974, it would be represented as follows (reference would require to be made to the appropriate code):

Characters							
Internal	Y		E		A		R
code—	1110	1000	1100	0101	1100	0001	1101	1001
EBCDIC							
Hexadecimal							
code	E	8	C	5	C	1	D	9
Decimal		1		9		7		4
Internal							
code—	1111	0001	1111	1001	1111	0111	1111	0100
EBCDIC							
Hexadecimal							
code	F	1	F	9	F	7	F	4

Hexadecimal provides a compact means of recording, and is used for listing the contents of storage during program assembly, amongst other things.

If it is required to express the year 1974 in hexadecimal directly, then this may be done by means of a conversion table or by inspection. The hexadecimal equivalent of 1974 is 7B6, which may be interpreted as follows:

Position	Coefficient	Hexadecimal value		Decimal value
1	16^0	1	$6 \times 1 =$	6
2	16^1	16	$11 \times 16 =$	176
3	16^2	256	$7 \times 256 =$	1792
			Total	1974

It is readily apparent that only three digits are required to express in hexadecimal the decimal number 1974, which consists of four digits. The pure binary equivalent of 1974 requires eleven digit positions.

Word Processing

Word processing is primarily concerned with the normal typing requirements of a business as distinct from the reports produced by data processing systems. Whereas data processing is concerned with processing data in the most efficient manner, word processing is concerned with processing words in the most efficient manner.

The term word processing is currently used as a more fashionable or sophisticated name for automatic typing which was first used by IBM to describe the integration of dictating, automatic typing and copying processes in the typing department. Word processors may be called jet-age typewriters, but that is only part of the story as word processing equipment has electronic intelligence which generally consists of a processing unit supported by a separate memory. It is this intelligence which is the main distinction to the older automatic typewriter.

The technique is meant to provide increased cost effectiveness in respect of the typing requirements of a business. Technological developments are such that it is difficult for the prospective user of word processing equipment to keep pace with the changes taking place. It is this factor which makes the choice of suitable equipment very difficult especially when this is linked to the need to learn how to use it in the most effective manner. There are many different makes and models on the market which have different characteristics and capabilities.

Word processing equipment should not be implemented without first conducting a feasibility study as it involves a change of method and necessitates the use of capital intensive equipment instead of typists. The method or technique of word processing is primarily for accomplishing the following office functions:

(*a*) transcription;
(*b*) editing;
(*c*) final typing;
(*d*) error correction;
(*e*) copying;
(*f*) storage and retrieval.

The equipment is designed to speed up such processes by making them more automatic.

Word processors are of significant value where the typing requirements of a business consist of high volume routine correspondence such as personalised standard letters whereby standard paragraphs are stored on magnetic media such as cards, cassettes, diskettes or mini-diskettes, etc. The standard paragraphs and personalised details are indicated on a form by the author. The machine then prints the standard letter reducing the detail entered by the operator to the personalised details only. It is this factor which achieves the main objectives of economy and efficiency because standard paragraphs are not constantly retyped at the speed of the typist but at the automatic speed of the machine which can be in the region of 920 words a minute. With conventional typing the speed of a typist is greatly reduced by the need to make corrections, completely retype text, paper handling, interruptions and fatigue. A possible speed in the region of fifty to seventy words a minute is reduced to ten to fifteen words a minute due to these factors. Extensive retyping also increases stationery costs, additional wear on typewriter ribbons and the typewriter.

Lengthy reports or high quality text which usually require extensive editing and revision can be processed to advantage on word processing equipment as the correction of errors is simplified because it is only necessary to backspace and re-type the character to erase the error as characters are stored magnetically in the same way as in a computer system. This feature also enables words to be added to, or inserted on, any line on the magnetic media without having to repeat the remainder of the line. Word processing equipment offers no advantage in respect of short one-off letters or memos.

The main benefits of word processing systems may be summarised as follows:

(a) increased volume of output;
(b) higher level of quality;
(c) increased speed of output;
(d) higher level of productivity;
(e) reduced level of fatigue;
(f) lower level of costs.

Index

Accessing the computer, 118, 119
Access time, 230
Accounting computer, *see* Visible record computer
Accounting machine, 22, 26–8
Accounting treatment, initial costs, 344, 345
Accuracy of information, 347
Adaptive system, 371, 372
Addressing data, 230
Address register, 47
Add-to-storage concepts, 301, 308
Advantages and disadvantages of a computer, 52, 53
application packages, 339
direct access storage, 234
electronic accounting machine, 78, 79
magnetic tape, 226, 227
paper tape, 185, 186
ALGOL, 300
Alphabetic characters, 178, 179
Alphanumeric keyboard, 68
Amplification, 390
Annual operating cost, 343, 344
Application packages, 336–40
Application philosophy, 140, 141
Applications, 273
Applications, interactive, 126, 128
Areas for improvement, choice of, 238
Arithmetic/logic unit, 47–9
Arithmetic operations, 48, 294
Assembler, 333, 334
Assembly code, 299, 300
Asynchronous transmission, 169
Auditing, 100–102
Automatic closed-loop system, 387–389
Automatic data processor, 31
Automatic decision-making, 48
Automatic punch, 194

Backing storage, 75, 218–35
BASIC, 123, 124, 300
Basic elements of control, 380
Batches, 82
Batch processing, 80
Batch processing configuration, 36
Batch/real-time, comparison, 115, 116
Benchmark tests, 285, 286
Benefits of a computer, 239
Benefits of on-line systems, 112, 113
Benefits of producing information, 422, 423
Binary chop, 231
Binary coded decimal, 450–3
Binary number system, 448
Block coding, 289, 290
Block diagram, 258, 259
Blocking of records, 223
Block size, 223, 225
Bottom-up approach, 418
Branch, 294
Bubble memory, 235
Budget preparation, 439, 440
Buffeting, 393
Bureau, *see* Computer bureau
Business models, 440, 441
Business systems, 360
Byte, 50, 51

Capacity of storage, 50, 51
Capital budgeting, 438, 439
Card fields, 179–81
Card punching, 192
Card reader, 59
Card verifying, 192, 193
Centralised data processing, 15
Central processing unit, 43, 46–52, 57
Chaining, 232
Check digit verification, 98–100
Checks and controls, 101

Chief programmer, principal duties, 105

Chief systems analyst, principal duties, 104

Clerical procedure chart, 259

Closed-loop system, 387–90

Closed systems, 363

C.M.C.7 (Caractére Magnétique Code), 175, 176

COBOL, 300, 319–27

Coding systems, 287–90

Communication, elements, 395

Communications, 241
  processor, 164, 165
  software, 110, 112
  terminals, 165, 166
  theory, 394–8

Comparative balance sheet, 145, 147, 150

Comparative income/expense, 145, 149

Comparator, 383

Comparison of data processing methods, see Methods of data processing

Compatibility of package programs, 337–9

Compatibility of processors, 43, 46

Compile, 334–6

Compiling, 61

Computer
  advantages and disadvantages, 52, 53
  bureau, 153–9
  codes, 450–6
  configuration, 34–8, 40–3, 76
  definitions, see Definitions of a computer
  instructions, 294
  output on microfilm (COM), 187–90
  procedure flowchart, 259, 260
  program, 12, 294–328
  run, 12, 272, 273
  run chart, 259, 274–84

Computer Service and Bureaux Association (COSBA), 155

Conditional branch, 294

Confidentiality of information, 94

Configuration, definition, 34

Conflict of system goals, 378, 379

Construction of a punched card, 177

Control, 26, 27, 29, 143
  basic elements, 380
  interface, 381
  relationships, 364
  unit, 46, 47

Control system, definition, 380

Core storage, 51

Corporate objectives, 374, 375

Cost considerations of using a computer, 239

Cost effectiveness, 346

Counter, 294, 295, 296

Coupling, 368

Criteria for assessing economic viability of computers, see Economic viability of computers

C.R.T. display, 57, 68

Cybernetic control process, 383–5

Cybernetics, definition, 383

Cylinder concept, 229, 230

Daily menu, 143

Damping, 390

Data, 8, 403

Data
  collection systems, 211–16
  control, 94, 95
  division, 325–7
  elements, 432
  input, 82
  module, 39, 234
  pen, 214
  preparation, 11
  representation in punched cards, 178
  transfer instruction, 294
  transfer speed, 230
  transmission, 160–9
  validation, 95–100

Data processing, 84, 85, 436
  costs, control of, 421, 422
  manager, principal duties, 102, 104
  methods, see Methods
  standards, 286, 287

Data processing—*cont.*
  steering committee, 242, 243
Database
  administrator, 434
  approach, 418
  defined, 427
  essential considerations, 428–30
  management system (D.B.M.S.),
    431, 432
  problems of setting up, 430, 431
Dataplex system 2 service, 167
Datel services:
  100 service, 166
  200 service, 166
  400 service, 166
  600 service, 166, 167
  2400 service, 167
  2400 dial up service, 167
  4800 service, 167
  international service, 167, 168
Decimal number system, 447
Decision tables, 262–9
Decoder, 47
Decoupling, 368
Definitions of a computer, 31
Delay factor, 390–4
Demand forecasting, 439
Deterministic system, 370, 371
Diagnostic routines, 333
Digital computer, 31
Direct access, 109, 110, 228
Direct data display, 141
Direct input, 171, 172
Disadvantages of using a bureau,
    155
Disc packs, 228
Disc units, 58
Discounted cash flow, 352–4
Diskette, 233
Distributed processing, 16–19
Document analysis form,
  input, 254, 255
  output, 252–4
Documentation of procedures, 101
Dumping technique, 92
Duplex transmission, 169

E.13B, 175
EBCDIC code, 453
Economic aspects of computers, *see*
  Financial and economic aspects
Economic viability of a computer,
    346–8
Education and training programme,
    241
Effector, 383, 385
Eight-bit alphameric code, *see*
  EBCDIC
Electronic accounting machine, 75,
    78, 79
Electronic computer, 31
Emulation, 328
Enquiries, 144
Environment division, 325
Error signal, 383
Exception principle, 381, 382
Exception reporting, 383
Exchangeable magnetic discs, *see*
  Magnetic discs
Execution phase, 308

Faceted code, 288
Feasibility study, 237–40
Feedback, 383, 385, 386
F.E.T., 51
Fields, 179–81
File
  activity (hit rate), 11, 86
  amendment, 9, 82–4
  analysis form, 255
  conversion, 80–2
  organisation, discs, 231, 232
  record specification, 261, 262
  reference, 11
  safety, 92, 94
  security, 12, 91–4
  updating, 9, 85, 86
Financial and economic aspects of
  computers, 342–9
Financing computers
  leasing, 356–8
  purchasing, 350–2
  renting, 354–6
Firmware, 40
First generation computers, 32
Fixed-length fields, 184
Fixed-length records, 225, 226
Fixed-variable-length fields, 184
Flexible disc unit, 58
Floppy discs, *see* Diskette

Flowcharting, 269, 272
Flowcharts, 88, 89, 93, 244–7, 265, 268, 270, 274–84, 295, 297, 306, 310–12, 314, 315, 317, 318, 335
Flowchart symbols, 271, 272
FORTRAN, 300
Fourth generation computers, 33, 34
Frequency division multiplexing, 168
Front-end processor, 164, 165
Functional information systems, 410
Functional systems approach, 416, 417
Futuristic information, 406

General ledger master file, 150, 151
Generation technique, 91, 92
Grandfather—father—son, *see above*: Generation technique
Graphical output, 190
Graph plotter, 190
Grid or X chart, 252
Gross-to-net, 132, 135

Half-duplex transmission, 169
Hand punch, 194
Hard discs, *see* Magnetic discs
Hardware, 11, 67, 76
Hexadecimal code, 454–6
High-level language, 300
Historical outline of data processing, 12–14
Hit rate, *see* File activity
Holographic memory, 235
Homeostasis, 394
Human element, 376–8
Hunting, 392

Identification division, 325
Implementation, *see* Systems implementation
Importance of information, 405
Improving flow of information, 419–21
Income/expense report, 145, 148
Incomplete information, 404, 405
Indexed sequential, 231

Indirect input, 172
Informal information, 414
Information, 9, 403–6
    adviser, 419
    benefits of producing, 422, 423
    control, 409, 410
    desirable properties of, 405, 406
    external environment, 406, 407
    for responding to change, 406
    from time sharing systems, 404
    futuristic, 406
    importance of, 405
    incomplete, 404, 405
    internal environment, 407
    operating management, 424
    operational planning, 408, 409
    output element, 404
    programmable, 409
    purpose of, 403, 404
    strategic planning, 407, 408
    systems, 401–12
    tactical control, 409, 410
    top management, 423, 424
Initial costs, 342, 343
Input, 25, 26, 28, 76
Input/output relationships, 363
Input/output terminals, 165
Input specification and layout, 260, 261
Input to output approach, 417
Instruction counter, 47
Instruction phase, 308
Instruction register, 47
Integrated discs, 233, 234
Integrated file structure, 430
Integrated flexible disc, 68, 69
Integrated system, 73–5, 87–91
Intelligent terminals, 166
Interactive
    distribution control system, 128–130
    general ledger system, 140–51, 273, 284, 285
    payroll accounting system, 130–140
    processing, 126–51
Interconnecting activities and elements, 368
Interface, control, 381
Intermediate document, 8

Internal environment information, 407
Internal working storage, 49–52
International Datel services, 167, 168
Interrogation, 401, 403

Jump instruction, *see* Branch instruction

Keyboard encoding, 196, 197
Key-to-cassette, 200, 201
Key-to-disc, 197–9
Key-to-diskette, 198, 200
Kimball tags, 213, 214

Large scale integration (LSI), 62
Laser memory, 235
Laser printer, 186, 187
Leasing a computer, 356–8
Light pen, 187
Line printer, 186
Logging in and out procedure, 120–2
Logic operations, 48, 49
Loop, 294
Low-level language, 298–300

Machine code, 298, 299, 302–4
Magnetic
  discs, 228–233
  encoded output, 190
  ink characters, 174–6
  ink character encoding, 205
  ink character verification, 205, 210
  stripe ledger card, 71, 72
  tape (cassette), 227, 228
  tape codes, 219
  tape encoding, 196–201
  tape handler, 58
  tape (reels), 218–27
  tape uses, 222
Mainframe computer configuration, 23–5, 34–40
Maintenance contracts, 347, 348
Management control and financial reports, 144, 145
Management information systems (M.I.S.), 401–12
  desirable properties of, 405, 406

Manual closed-loop system, 389, 390
Manual method, 22, 25, 26
Mark
  encoding, 201, 204
  verification, 204
Marketing, 348
Master file, 7, 113
  general ledger, 150, 151
Master menu, 141, 143
Matrix printer, 57, 58, 68, 186
Mechanistic system, 370
Menu, 141, 143
Methods of data processing
  comparison of, 25–9
  keyboard accounting machine, 22
  mainframe computer, 23–5
  manual, 22
  microcomputer, 23
  minicomputer, 22
  selection and review of, 22
  visible record computer, 23
Microcomputer, 23, 62–9
Microminiaturisation, 33
Microprocessor applications, 63, 64, 66
Minicomputer, 22, 55–61
Mini-diskette, 233
Mini-floppy discs, *see* Mini-diskette
Modelling package, 442, 443
Models, *see* Business models
Modem, 164, 165
Modular, 34
Monitoring performance, 243
M.O.S., 51, 62
M.O.S.F.E.T., 51, 62
Multiplexor, 164
Multiprogramming, 114, 116, 117

Negative feedback, 386
Network structure, 433
Noise, 395, 397
Number systems, 447–56
Numeric characters, 178

Objectives of a feasibility study, 237
Objectives of systems, 374
Object program, 334
O.C.R. character
  encoding, 201
  verification, 201

Octal number system, 449, 450
Off-line data transmission, 163, 164
Off-lining, 117
On-line
  applications, 109, 110
  benefits, 112–13
  data transmission, 160–2, 164
  definition. 109
  interrogation facilities, 401, 403
  processing, 109–13
  tape punch, 194
Open-loop system, 386, 387
Open systems, 363
Operating system, 59, 60, 69, 114, 116, 117, 332, 333
Operational planning information, 408, 409
Operations manager, principal duties, 105
Optical character encoding, 201–3, 206, 207
Optical characters and marks, 173, 174
Optical mark encoding, 201, 204, 206, 207
Organic systems, 370
Organisation of a batch processing installation, 102–5
Original documents, 102
Oscillating, see Hunting
Output, 25, 27, 29, 77, 86, 87, 113, 114, 186–90
  analysis chart, 255, 256
  specification and layout, 260
Output to input approach, 417, 418
Overflow area, 231, 232
Overlay, 231

Paper tape, 181–6, 193–5
  codes, 182, 183
  reader, 181
  verifying, 194, 195
Parallel transmission, 168
Pareto law, 380, 381
Parity checking, 182, 183, 222, 223
Payroll application, 156, 157
Payroll master file, 135, 138–40
Piecemeal approach, see Functional systems approach
Planning systems, 368, 370

Polling, 169
Positive feedback, 386
Printed output, 186, 187
Printers, 57, 58, 68, 186
Probabilistic system, 371
Problem solving, 438–40
Procedure division, 327
Procedure narrative, 259
Processing, 76, 77
  activities, 1
  methods, see Methods of data processing
  operations, 4–6, 73–5
  routine, 273
  steps, 114
Processing techniques
  batch, 80–105
  interactive, 126–51
  multiprogramming, 114, 116, 117
  on-line, 109–13
  real-time, 113, 114
  time sharing, 117–24
Processor, see Central processing unit
Processor memory, 75
Program, see Computer programs
Program flowcharts, see Flowcharts
Program input, 82
Programmable information, 409
Programming, 78, 123
Program preparation, stages, 296, 298
Program switches, 312, 313
Punched card, 176–81, 192, 193
Purchase accounting, 157, 158
Purchasing a computer, 350–2
Purpose of information, 403, 404

R.A.M., 51, 52, 65
Random enquiries, 87
Random file, 232
Read/write heads, 228, 229
Real-time computer configuration, 40–3
Real-time concept, 113
Real-time processing, 40, 113, 114
Record, 7
Recruitment of data processing staff, 241, 242
Redundancy, 397, 398

Reference input, 383
Remote job entry, 110
Remote batch terminals, 165
Remote controller, 161, 162
Renting computers, 354–6
Reports, 130
Requisite variety, 382
Response time, 394
Retail terminal system, 211–13
R.O.M., 51, 52, 65
Run chart, *see* Computer run charts

Sales accounting, 158
Sales invoices, 158
Second generation computers, 32, 33
Self-organising system, *see* Adaptive system
Semi-conductor memory, 51, 52
Sensor, 383
Sequential list structure, 433
Serial code, 289
Serial transmission, 168
Services available, computer bureaus, 153, 154
Sets, 433
Silicon chip, 62, 63
Simplex transmission, 169
Simulation, 441, 442
Single-address instructions, 308, 309
Six-bit alphameric code, 450–3
Six (seven)-bit character code, 453
Software, 40, 64, 65, 69, 331–40
Source document, 6, 7
Source program, 296, 333, 334
Sources of application packages, 337
Special characters, 179
Speed and volume factors, 346, 347
Steering committee, 242, 243
Stock accounting, 158, 159
Stock control, 129, 130
Stocking and replacement strategies, 130
Storage, 25, 27, 28, 77
Strategic planning information, 407, 408
Structural data relationships, 432, 433
Sub-objectives

production department, 376
sales department, 377
Sub-optimality, 378, 379
Sub-routines, 331, 332
Sub-system objectives, 375, 376
Supermarket ordering system, 215, 216
Switches, *see* Program switches
Synchronous transmission, 169
System
definition, 359
elements, 360–3
operation, 131, 132
relationships, 363–8
resources, 360
status, 129
tuning, 393, 394
updating, 243
Systems analysis
and O. & M., 249, 252
definition, 248
team, 248, 249
Systems design, 256, 257
Systems flowchart, 259
Systems implementation, 243
Systems objective, 73, 130, 375
Systems specification, 257, 258
Systems theory, 359

Tactical control information, 409
Tangible benefits, 347, 348
Tape punch attachment, 194
Terminals, 118
Testing of transactions, 101
Third generation computers, 33
Threshold of control system, 381
Time division multiplexing, 168, 169
Time lag, 390
Timeliness of information, 392
Time sharing, 117–24
Top-down approach, 418
Top management support, 240
Total information system, 410–12
Total systems approach, 415, 416
Transaction data, 9
Transaction driven processing, 9, 11, 126–51
Tree structure, 433
Trial balance, 145, 146
Turnaround document, 205, 209

Turnkey operations, 340
Two-address instructions, 300, 301
Two-tape method, 195
Types of
  application package, 337
  computer bureaux, 153
  software, 331

Unconditional branch, 294
Unit record, 181
Units of storage, 50
Unity of direction, 374
Universal processing unit, 67
Utility programs, 69, 332
Utility routines, 60

Validation checks, 96–8
Variable input, 132
Variable length fields, 184
Variable length records, 226
V.A.T., 74
Verification, check digit, 98–100
Verifying, cards, 192, 193
Virtual storage, 232, 233
Visible record computer, 23, 70–9
Visual display, 187
Visual record printer, 68

Word processing, 457, 458

X chart, 252